D0078099

RESEARCHING
SOCIAL LIFE

RESEARCHING SOCIAL LIFE

edited by

Nigel Gilbert

SAGE Publications
London • Newbury Park • New Delhi

WARNER MEMORIAL LIBRARY
EASTERN UNIVERSITY
ST. DAVIDS, PA 19087-3696

10/1/09

Introduction, editorial arrangement, Chapter 2 and Chapter 16
© Nigel Gilbert, 1993
Chapter 1 © Martin O'Brien, 1993
Chapters 3 and 5 © Sara Arber, 1993
Chapter 4 © Michael Hornsby-Smith, 1993
Chapter 6 © Rosemarie Newell, 1993
Chapters 7, 12 and 13 © Michael Procter, 1993
Chapters 8 and 9 © Nigel Fielding, 1993
Chapter 10 © Keith Macdonald and Colin Tipton, 1993
Chapter 11 © Jane Fielding, 1993
Chapter 14 © Robin Wooffitt, 1993
Chapter 15 © Christian Heath and Paul Luff, 1993
Exemplar A © Patricia Taraborrelli, 1993
Exemplar B © Keith Macdonald, 1993
Exemplar C © Jay Ginn, 1993

First published 1993

All rights reserved. No part of this publication may be
reproduced, stored in a retrieval system, transmitted or utilized
in any form or by any means, electronic, mechanical,
photocopying, recording or otherwise, without permission in
writing from the Publishers.

SAGE Publications Ltd
6 Bonhill Street
London EC2A 4PU

SAGE Publications Inc
2455 Teller Road
Newbury Park, California 91320

SAGE Publications India Pvt Ltd
32, M-Block Market
Greater Kailash – I
New Delhi 110 048

British Library Cataloguing in Publication data

Researching Social Life
  I. Gilbert, Nigel
  301.072

  ISBN 0–8039–8681–5
  ISBN 0–8039–8682–3 (pbk)

Library of Congress catalog card number 92–056768

Typeset in Linotron Times by Photoprint, Torquay, Devon
Printed in Great Britain by Butler and Tanner Ltd, Frome and London

HM 48 .R48 1993

Researching social life

Contents

III Back home

IV Endings

Acknowledgements

We are very grateful to Karen Phillips and Stephen Barr of Sage for their encouragement during the preparation of this book, and to Agnes McGill, Jon Gubbay, Geoff Payne and several anonymous reviewers who read and commented on it while it was in draft.

The research described in chapter 3 was a joint enterprise, involving Sara Arber and Mike Savage as Project Directors, Miranda Cormell (Research Officer), and Megan Dale (Administrative Assistant). Paul Watt contributed to the research and academic publications. We are grateful to Mike Savage for helpful comments on a draft of this chapter.

Grateful thanks are due to Mary Corcoran, Roger Homan and Ray Lee for generous help in the preparation of chapter 4.

The research on which Exemplar C is based forms part of the Older Women's Working Lives Project, funded by the Economic and Social Research Council (Grant R000233240). For access to the General Household Survey data for 1987 we are indebted to the ESRC Data Archive, University of Essex, and to the University of London Computer Centre. We are grateful to the Office of Population Censuses and Surveys for permission to use GHS data.

The work reported in chapter 15 was partly supported by Rank Xerox Cambridge EuroPARC and by the MRC/SERC/ESRC Joint Cognitive Science and HCI Initiative.

The authors and publishers wish to thank the American Sociological Association for permission to use copyright material from J.M. McPherson and L. Smith-Lovin (1986) 'Sex segregation in voluntary associations', *American Sociological Review*, 51: 61–79.

Contributors

Sara Arber is Senior Lecturer in Sociology at the University of Surrey. She teaches social research methods, the sociology of health and the sociology of gender. She is co-author of *Secondary Analysis* (Sage, 1988), with Michael Procter and Angela Dale, and *Gender and Later Life* (Sage, 1991), with Jay Ginn. Her main research interests are women and ageing, women's employment, occupational pensions and inequalities in women's health. She is currently working with Jay Ginn on a project on 'Older Women's Working Lives'.

Jane Fielding is a Research Fellow in the Department of Sociology at the University of Surrey. She has been teaching computing courses in the social sciences since 1985, and now teaches the use of the statistical package, SPSS, to undergraduates and postgraduates. Her main research interest is stress and the police role, with particular attention to gender differences.

Nigel Fielding is Reader in Sociology at the University of Surrey and editor of the *Howard Journal of Criminal Justice*. He has been teaching field methods and the sociology of deviance and control at Surrey since 1978. He has research interests in police studies, criminal justice and qualitative methodology. His current research is on software for the analysis of qualitative data. With Ray Lee, he is editor of *Using Computers in Qualitative Research* (Sage, 1991) and is author of several books, most recently, C. Kemp, C. Norris and N.G. Fielding *Negotiating Nothing: Police Decision Making in Disputes* (Avebury, 1992).

Nigel Gilbert is Professor of Sociology at the University of Surrey. He has been teaching research methods, social statistics and courses on the sociology of economic life at Surrey since 1976. His main research interests are in the social aspects of computing, cognitive science and social simulation. Previously he has worked on issues in social stratification and the sociology of scientific knowledge. With Paul Luff and David Frohlich, he edited *Computers and Conversation* (Academic, 1990), has edited several other collections, and is author of *Opening Pandora's Box: A Sociological Analysis of Scientists' Discourse* (Cambridge University Press, 1984), with Michael Mulkay, and *Modelling Society* (Allen and Unwin, 1981).

Jay Ginn has been a Research Fellow in the Department of Sociology at the University of Surrey since 1989. She used secondary analysis of the General Household Survey to study elderly people's health, income and access to informal care, reported in *Gender and Later Life* (Sage, 1991), co-authored with Sara Arber. She is currently working on a project with Sara Arber analysing older women's labour force participation and pension entitlements.

Christian Heath is Senior Lecturer at the University of Surrey and Visiting Scientist at Rank Xerox Cambridge EuroPARC. His teaching includes courses on the analysis of language use and social interaction, sociological theory and organizational behaviour. His current research includes a series of interrelated studies of work, interaction and technology, a study of metaphor, and a project on interpersonal communication in medicine.

Michael Hornsby-Smith is Reader in Sociology at the University of Surrey. He currently teaches courses in the sociology of religion, industrial sociology and industrial relations. His main research interests since 1974 have been the social and religious transformations of English Catholicism. More recently he has undertaken analysis of the European Values Surveys. He is author of several books including *The Changing Parish: A Study of Parishes, Priests and Parishioners After Vatican II* (Routledge, 1989) and *Roman Catholic Beliefs in England: Customary Catholicism and Transformations of Religious Authority* (Cambridge University Press, 1991).

Paul Luff is a Research Fellow at the University of Surrey and a Visiting Researcher at Rank Xerox EuroPARC Cambridge. His research interests include examining the relationship between recent developments in the social sciences and the design of new technologies. In particular, he is investigating the use of computer systems in naturalistic settings and the development of systems to support collaborative work.

Keith Macdonald is Senior Lecturer in Sociology at the University of Surrey. In the past he has worked on large scale research projects at Aston and Edinburgh Universities, but recent work has been documentary and historical studies of professions, especially accountancy and the military.

Rosemarie Newell has been a Lecturer at the University of Surrey since 1982. She has a wide range of experience in social, psychological and market research. Her main research interests are in parenting styles and skills, housing for the elderly, and the effect of disability on life chances. She is currently investigating the effects of middle class unemployment.

Martin O'Brien is a Lecturer in Sociology at the University of Surrey. He teaches social and cultural theory and the theory and politics of social welfare. His main research interests are social and political theory, the sociology of the environment, and the sociology of the media and culture. Previously he has worked on the sociology of nursing and health and on the sociology of the community.

Michael Procter teaches in the Sociology department at the University of Surrey. He helped to set up the MSc in Social Research in 1973 and has taught mainly in the areas of quantitative research methods. His current research is focused on cross-national comparisons of attitudes; in the past he has worked on studies of poverty and on the social psychology of adolescence.

Patricia Taraborrelli obtained an MSc in Social Research Methods (with Distinction) from the University of Surrey in 1990, where she later lectured on the Sociology of Health and Illness and on Research Methods. Her interest in informal care and the carers of dementia sufferers is reflected in her current doctoral research. She is at present a Tutorial Fellow in the School of Social and Administrative Studies at the University of Wales, Cardiff.

Colin Tipton, Lecturer in Sociology at the University of Surrey, teaches Politics, Social History and Research Methods. His main research interest is politics and society in Southeast Asia.

Robin Wooffitt is a Research Fellow in the Social and Computer Sciences research group in the Department of Sociology at the University of Surrey. His research interests concern language and social interaction, particularly conversation analysis, the organization of factual discourse, and language and social identity. He is author of *Telling Tales of the Unexpected: the Organisation of Factual Discourse* (Harvester Wheatsheaf, 1992).

Introduction

Nigel Gilbert

Researching social life is partly about having the right knowledge: for instance, how to design samples, when to take fieldnotes and how to analyse interview data; and partly about practical skills: how to lay out questionnaires, how to get access to historical archives and how to get the cooperation of an interviewee. It is because research is such a mixture that this book includes chapters which touch on philosophy and theory as well as more down-to-earth 'exemplars' which recount the problems and false starts of real research projects.

The book is organised around the idea of the research process – roughly, deciding what you want to find out, finding a setting or a sample, collecting some data, analysing the data and writing up the results. Thus, the book is subdivided into parts, on 'Beginnings', 'Into the field', 'Back home' and 'Endings' . But as the story of an actual research project in chapter 3 makes clear, the process can be a lot messier than is implied by this image of a steady progression through clear stages.

As a first step, however, it is important to clarify what counts as social research, and, in particular, how it differs from 'fact gathering' . In the first chapter, it is argued that social research has to be concerned with **understanding**, not just with description. Moreover, social research has to be located within an academic discipline – sociology, education, management, social work or whatever – which offers perspectives, methods and a 'tradition' . The final chapter, chapter 16, returns to these concerns.

Chapter 2 introduces some of the **conceptual tools** which a researcher will need. It is concerned with the link between theory and data – a link which continues to trouble philosophers as well as sociologists. Do data exist 'out there', waiting to be collected by the researcher? Or is what we find influenced or even determined by the theories and the methods we employ to understand the social world?

Chapter 2 and most of the following chapters conclude with a project which can be carried out by yourself or with others with minimal resources and in a reasonably short time. These projects are important because it is difficult to become a good researcher simply by reading about research; you need to have a go yourself. Every chapter also includes a list of 'Further reading' which suggests where to look for a deeper or more extended treatment of the issues it covers.

Practical experience of research skills is emphasised in chapter 3, which illustrates the **life history of research** through a detailed account of one research project. This project aimed to find out more about 'housing mobility', that is, the pattern of moves between different forms of housing tenure. The project was based on a social survey of 1,000 council tenants in one local authority and exemplifies the practical, political and managerial issues which are frequently encountered in research projects.

These first three chapters offer an overview of the research process. The next two chapters are concerned with issues which have to be considered before one starts collecting data: how to get access to data sources and how to select whom to interview or observe. Social research is not always welcomed in all quarters and this means that researchers have to make decisions about whether they conceal what they are doing from some or all of their respondents ('covert' research) or whether they will be open about their objectives but risk being repulsed. And some groups are much more capable of resisting enquiries than others. These questions of **access**, which also involve difficult problems of research **ethics**, are addressed in chapter 4.

Once access has been gained, it is usually neither practicable nor wise to interview everyone and observe everything. Some kind of sampling of data is needed, regardless of whether the research is survey based or involves observational or documentary methods. Chapter 5 discusses the standard ways of obtaining **representative samples**, and considers whether representativeness is always necessary and appropriate.

Once decisions about access and sampling have been made, it is time to go 'into the field'. Chapters 6 to 10 examine various ways of collecting data. During the 1950s and 1960s, there were great advances in the 'technology' of asking standardised questions to representative samples of respondents. This had the result that the interview survey became the data collection technique most closely associated with social research. Chapter 6 discusses the current state of the art, offering advice about how to construct, not just **interview schedules**, but also questions for interviewing over the telephone, and questionnaires for surveys sent through the mail. Chapter 7 deals in more detail with one of the trickiest aspects of this style of research: how to measure people's **attitudes**.

Although using structured interviews is a common method of data collection, especially in commercial and policy related research, less formalised and more qualitative methods are also very important. Chapter 8 is about the kind of **focused interview** which is more like a guided conversation and deals with how to construct an interview guide, how to conduct an interview and how to transcribe a recording. Focused interviewing is often combined with observation of people in their 'natural' settings, a style of research called ethnography. **Ethnography**, as a research technique, emerged from anthropology and chapter 9 traces this history, considering also the practicalities of ethnographic research and, in particular, some methods of analysis of ethnographic data, since it is at the analysis stage that this style of research presents the most difficulties.

Chapter 9 is followed by the first of three 'Exemplar' chapters, each of which show how the advice presented elsewhere in the book turns out in practice, in actual research projects. Exemplar A describes the course of an ethnographic research project concerned with the carers of sufferers from Alzheimer's disease. This project lasted only a few months, was carried out without any funding, yet yielded findings of considerable significance for social policy and illustrates that worthwhile research does not have to be large scale nor have ambitious objectives.

Not all social research involves asking people questions. Many of the classics of sociology were based solely on **documentary evidence**, the topic of chapter 10. The documents of interest to social researchers include not only public documents such as official reports and newspapers, but also personal records such as diaries and letters, and some objects which, although they document social life, were never intended as records, for example, statutes, novels, photographs and even buildings. The second Exemplar (B) shows how documents, including minutes of meetings, financial accounts, and the style and architecture of the headquarters of professional bodies in England, were all used as evidence for a study of the institutionalisation of professional associations.

The result of collecting data in any of these ways is likely to be a mass of material, too great in quantity to be analysed unless one is prepared and able to be systematic. The management of quantitative data has been revolutionised by the computer, and computers are now also beginning to be used to assist in handling qualitative data, such as interview transcripts. Chapter 11 discusses the **management** and **coding** of both types, explaining the technology and the options available. Once you have got quantitative data sets onto a computer, programs can be used to prepare tables and frequency distributions. This is illustrated in chapter 12, which uses an example to illustrate the steps you need to go through to do simple **analyses of survey data** using the most widely used computer package, SPSS/PC.

You do not necessarily have to collect survey data yourself to do quantitative research. Government departments, research companies and academic social researchers often deposit their data sets as computer files in national archives, from which copies can be obtained for further analysis. This is 'secondary analysis', which is fast becoming one of the most important forms of social research. It opens up quantitative research to those who do not have the considerable resources needed to carry out a large scale survey. As chapter 13 notes, **secondary analysis** demands some skills not needed for other forms of social research, including being able to devise ways of testing hypotheses against data originally collected for other purposes. The kind of difficulties which this raises and the ways that they can be overcome are illustrated in the next chapter, Exemplar C. This describes a project based on secondary analysis which examined how differences in occupational pension provisions lead to major inequalities among elderly people, particularly according to gender.

The next two chapters illustrate approaches to analysing qualitative data such as interview transcripts and audio and video recordings. Both chapters focus on the analysis of the **interactional organisation** of these materials. Chapter 14 uses as example an extract from a taped interview with a 'punk', in which the punk provides an account of a violent incident. The analysis shows how the account is organised to indicate the innocence of the punks and the provocative nature of police action. Chapter 15, which draws on the tradition of **conversation analysis**, shows how one can analyse fragments of dialogue recorded on audio or video tape to provide insights into the organisation of social interaction.

Research only becomes effective when it is written down and published for researchers, policy makers and others to use and to criticise. The final chapter of the book is about **writing** about one's research. It examines the format of a typical research article and explains some of the historical background to publication conventions in the social sciences.

The coverage and treatment of topics in this book is based on the course taught in the Department of Sociology at the University of Surrey for first and second year undergraduates. The contributors are all lecturers and researchers in the Department and have not only had experience in carrying out research in the ways they describe, but also of teaching it, both to undergraduates and to graduate students. The book has been much influenced by feedback from many generations of students, a surprising number of whom have gone on to become social researchers themselves. We hope that you, like our students, will find that the skills of social research can be used both to help in understanding our society better and to support work in many professions and careers.

1 Social research and sociology

Martin O'Brien

Contents

This book is about exploration and discovery in the social world, the world that each of us helps to create, the world that we all inhabit. It is the purpose of this book to help you to make your own discoveries, to help you find out why the social world is as it is: why the societies we live in are structured as they are; why there are differences between groups within societies; why not everyone holds the same beliefs and commitments and why people act differently in different circumstances. Each of us makes discoveries of this kind throughout our lives. We find out new things about the social world simply by living in it, by growing up in it and by the experiences we have of it. We are all aware of the different dimensions of our social life to some degree. We experience the different expectations that are placed upon us as children or parents, in churches or in schools, at home or at work. Yet, most of the time, this awareness exists only in fragments: we know how to deal with each situation as it arises but we are rarely aware of how these situations connect together to build up our total social life.

By studying this book, by completing the projects it contains and by following up on the further readings listed at the end of each chapter it is our intention to help you to build up such a picture. Whether you work in academic sociology, in a caring profession, in urban planning or community work or whether you are simply interested in finding out more about our collective social life, the chapters in this book are designed to guide you towards a more complete assessment of the nature of the society around you.

At the start of this guide you must be aware that researching social life is a process with many components. It requires skills in collecting and analysing data, in developing and applying concepts, in assessing evidence and in presenting coherent and consistent arguments to demonstrate the significance of empirical observations. It is important to develop all of these skills in order to put research to good use. Yet, before one can begin to develop these skills, it is necessary to gain some insight into the discipline from which they derive. The authors of this book are all sociologists, connected with the University of Surrey in England and each of us uses a sociological imagination (cf., Mills, 1959) when we conduct research. Consequently, readers of the book need to know something of the 'mission' that the discipline of sociology represents. This chapter will outline some of the key features of sociology as an approach to understanding social life: this will be done, first, by making some general remarks on sociology, on its assumptions and its language; second, by discussing what is unique about sociology as a way of understanding and interpreting the social world; third, by discussing the role of theory in social research; fourth and finally, by discussing two exemplary pieces of research which show how adopting a sociological imagination makes visible aspects of the social world which were previously obscured from our perception.

1.1   The discipline of sociology

There is an old adage, first coined by the American economist Duesenberry, that economics is the study of the choices that people make while sociology is the study of why people have no choices (cited in Boudon, 1981: 6). In other words economics is the study of freedom whilst sociology is the study of constraint. Now, if things were as easy as this there would be no reason for sociologists to reflect on their own discipline but, fortunately or unfortunately, things are not quite so simple. Because whilst sociology does indeed investigate the constraints that people face – the things that limit our choices and our actions – it also investigates a whole range of other things, including how societies change and develop, how people interact, how professions and prestigious groups develop rituals, how architecture and design influence our behaviour and perception, how human–machine interaction influences working patterns and much, much more. Sociology is, characteristically, a very nosey discipline indeed, with its fingers in very many pies all at once. In consequence of this, it is too limiting to think of sociology as being only one thing. Like any other discipline that is alive and flourishing there are numerous ways that we can characterise sociology.

For example, we can think of sociology as a profession comprising a hierarchy of paid members who fulfil specialised roles – such as teachers, tutors, researchers and administrators, and so on.

Or we can characterise sociology as a collection of methods for studying empirical questions. These methods, as in other analytical disciplines, range from the observational (watching what happens), through the interactional (asking about what happens), to the mathematical (predicting and modelling what happens).

We can also characterise sociology as an array of theories for assessing the significance of what happens and what its methods bring to light. Again, like any other analytical discipline, sociology is alive with debate and controversy over the meaning and significance of what it uncovers.

We can see sociology as a set of – sometimes discrete, sometimes overlapping – areas of interest: such as the sociology of work, of the family, of the media, of development, and so on.

We can say that sociology is a branch of learning: a particular way of developing skills of reading, writing, analysis and argumentation. The implication of this is not that there is only a single way of reasoning and argumentation in sociology; rather, the discipline is characterised by a variety of logics and assumptions. Yet, these differ from the logics and assumptions of other disciplines – such as economics or psychology, for example. This chapter will address some of these specifically sociological assumptions and logics.

Finally, from the reader's point of view . . . well, perhaps it is best to leave it to you to decide what you think sociology is.

The point is that all these ways of describing sociology are correct: sociology is many things to many people. It fulfils a wide variety of functions and is used for a wide variety of purposes.

On top of this variety in characterising the discipline itself is the fact that sociologists also seem to have their own special language for talking to each other, like a secret code, replete with masonic mental handshakes, that has to be cracked before you can understand any of their messages. Sometimes this secret code appears to follow the rule, 'don't use one syllable when twenty will do'. Sociological language is filled with 'ologies', 'ations' and 'isms': for example, ethnomethodology, rationalisation, interactionism, and the like, some of which, very confusingly, actually refer to very simple things: the study of how real, actual people go about making sense of the world around them; the process of applying logic and means–ends reasoning to social organisation and behaviour; and the study of how people relate to each other in different situations, respectively. Of course, these concepts refer to much more than this in the conduct of sociological enquiry. The point is that it is rarely difficult to gain a basic understanding of sociological terms.

Yet what can sometimes seem worse than even the language problem is that sociology has its own structure of ideas – a sort of scaffolding of concepts, terms and theories that at first sight can look as if they have all been heaped up in a big messy pile with no discernible design. As you read sociology books you can find yourself stumbling across concepts that initially appear to have no relationship to each other at all – in a single text you might be confronted by concepts of gender, class, race, institutions, epistemology, function, structure, and many more – that come tumbling down onto your head when you are not watching.

Perhaps the best analogy might be to say that first encountering sociology is a bit like landing in the middle of a strange new town without a map. You know there is a way around the sprawling mess; you know there is a logic to it somewhere; you know that all these streets and roads connect up somehow and that it is not really an alien city on another planet. The problem is that without the map it is not possible to work out what the logic is: try as you might, every street you take seems to take you further away from where you are intending to go.

Well, at first, sociology can look like that; it can be maddeningly confusing and complicated and even I, after serving ten years hard sociology for my sins, still find myself lost sometimes in the labyrinth bequeathed to me by my sociological forebears.

But sociology is not that messy really. It just looks that way when you first meet it. In fact, there is a great deal of sense and order in the discipline if you have the right map to find your way around. The purpose of this chapter is to try and bring some order to the subject; to define some fundamental characteristics of sociology that give it an identity and that can be used to begin the process of making connections between the parts of the conceptual scaffolding that represents sociological practice.

1.2   Sociological understanding

It is important to make these connections between the different dimensions of sociology because the discipline should, and when carried out properly does, speak to people's experiences in society. Sociology deals not only with the grand, abstract categories of our world – like 'capitalism', 'the state', 'social class', 'modernity', and so on – but also with how these institutions and relationships affect people and how we, as members of society, actually experience them. I would say that this insight – this focus on systematically addressing the connections between the macro, large-scale phenomena of our social world and the different experiences of people in society – is one of the key characteristics of sociological enquiry.

This type of understanding can be observed in the introduction to sociology by Norbert Elias (1979). Elias points out that, by and large, people build their interpretations of the world and construct explanations and accounts of what is going on around them, based very largely on the experiences they have only within their own groups (1979: 55). But, to understand what sociology is all about, Elias tells us, you have to begin to look at yourself from a distance, 'as one human being among others' (1979:

13). Other human beings have different experiences from our own, different interpretations from our own, different beliefs from our own.

Of course, one could argue that such an observation is little more than plain common sense: everyone knows that different people think differently, act, interpret and believe differently. Therefore, what gives such a common sense observation the status of sociological insight? Sociology tells us that, not only do people think, believe and act in different ways but also that this thinking, believing and acting has two other features to it that we need to come to terms with if we are truly to understand our social world. First, people do not just think, believe and act randomly: they think, believe and act in regular ways. Systems of belief, thought and action vary – over time and across space – in patterns that are associated with different groups of people, with different cultural characteristics and different social positions. This patterning is as true within a society as it is between societies. For the sociologist, statements, like 'Muslims think one thing and Christians another' are no more than common sense. What the sociologist wants to find out is why some Christians and Muslims think and act differently from other Christians and Muslims. The sociologist wants to discover what accounts for the variation, what explains the patterned diversity within and between the societies that we inhabit.

The second feature that sociology urges us to come to terms with is that these patterns of thought and action are not immaterial. That is, they do not just simply exist without having some effect on the society in which they are found. Sociology directs our attention to the ways that the interactions between these thoughts, beliefs and actions create and recreate the characteristics of a particular society. How, for example, are gender differences organised in societies?; how are rewards and punishments organised?; what are the rules of interaction governing different situations?; what are the patterns of settlement and why did they develop as they did?; what effects do cities have on their inhabitants?; and so on.

Sociology addresses questions such as these precisely because common sense often confuses us and clouds our understanding of the opportunities and inequalities in, and the causes and experiences of, social change – both in the past and in the present.

To put the same thing differently, we can follow a statement by Zygmunt Bauman (1990: 15–16) in his book *Thinking Sociologically*. For Bauman, sociology 'defamiliarizes' things. That is, it takes us away from our comfortable, limited, commonly accepted and often unconsidered opinions about what everybody and everything is like and makes us more sensitive to the way that those opinions are formed and maintained. It alerts us to the ways that things which at first sight appear obvious and 'natural' are actually the result of social action, social power or social tradition. This characteristic of sociology used to go by another name. Sociology, it used to be said, 'demythologises' the world. That is, it disturbs and disrupts all the myths and the apparently fixed and immutable characteristics of the world we live in.

Of course, it could be argued that sociology, far from disturbing our myths simply adds to the total number of myths through which we understand society. Sociology may be as mythical as common sense and far from 'demythologising' may in fact 'remythologise' society, translating ordinary understandings into sociological analyses that are of no greater value.

However, uniquely among the array of disciplines which study human behaviour and organisation, sociology also enables reflection on the conditions of its own knowledge production. Sociology is the study of both the societies in which sociology emerged and the study of the development of that knowledge. It relates what we know – or think we know – about the social world we inhabit to our actions within it. Sociology traces the development of its own concepts in the social world that the discipline seeks to describe and understand. Giddens describes this process as a continuing spiral: 'Sociological knowledge spirals in and out of the universe of social life, reconstructing both itself and that universe as an integral part of that process' (italics omitted) (1990a: 15–16).

Furthermore, when investigating social life, it is important to emphasise that we do not live in a world of abstract and disconnected individuals. Both Bauman (1990) and Elias (1979) observe that we live in a world where individuals and groups are interdependent and interconnected; a world where events generated by one group of persons have effects on many other groups. Viewing these interconnections, observing and understanding their consequences is the essential business of sociological analysis.

If this focus on interconnections is sociology's primary 'business', what is the framework for its transactions: how does sociology go about examining these interconnections?

Again, we can compare Elias and Bauman on this point. Elias, in particular, proposes that sociology is – or, if it is not yet, it should be – a 'science' somewhat similar in outlook to other scientific disciplines: biology, chemistry and physics, for example (1979: 18, 33). Bauman, on the other hand, is more reticent in his judgement. For Bauman, the question of sociology's scientific status depends upon how one understands what sciences are and what they do. If the goal of science is to close down ambiguity and to restrict the range of possible explanations of the world, then sociology is ill-suited to the label. If, on the other hand, the goal of science is to open up mutual understanding and foster tolerance and sensitivity to other ways of describing and explaining events in the world, then sociology can claim scientific status along with other mature disciplines whose aims are to share knowledge and experience. Bauman writes:

> If anything, thinking sociologically undermines the trust in the exclusivity and completeness of any interpretation. It brings into focus the plurality of experiences and forms of life; it shows each as an entity in its own right, a world with a

logic of its own, while at the same time exposing the sham of its ostensible self-containment and self-sufficiency. Sociological thinking does not stem, but facilitates the flow and exchange of experiences. (Bauman, 1990: 231–2)

Yet what Bauman also draws our attention to is a major split in sociological analysis. A split between what we might want to call, on the one hand, a 'positive' tradition, begun at the very inception of sociology by Auguste Comte, and, on the other, an 'interpretive' tradition, largely associated with the work of Max Weber. The word 'positive' is used here to connote a view of sociology as a progressive, cumulative, explanatory, 'scientific' project. Sociology's 'positive' tradition can be said to include those thinkers who tried, with the aid of sociology, to explain, predict and in some cases ultimately control the social world. Within this tradition we can include sociologists like Comte, Durkheim, Spencer and Parsons (see the work of Aron, 1967/1968) together with more recent advocates such as Stinchcombe (1968). This positive tradition posits that society can be explained 'scientifically', according to laws and rational logics – whether these be based on social stages (as with Comte), social facts (as with Durkheim) or on social systems (as with Parsons) is not the point here. However much they differed in their outlook, for each sociology offered a positive, scientific tool for explaining social events.

The second tradition, the 'interpretive' tradition, seeks not so much explanations and predictions of social events as understanding what meaning and what significance the social world has for the people who live in it. Within this tradition are sociologists like Weber, Goffman and Garfinkel (see Cuff et al., 1990).

The point is that these two traditions are associated with two different versions of the sociological enterprise. Within the first, 'positive', tradition are situated schools of sociology such as functionalism, structuralism and political economy. Within the second tradition are situated schools of sociology such as symbolic interactionism and ethnomethodology.

I do not wish to give the impression that sociology is an 'either/or' enterprise; sociology is not a coin with two faces which shows either heads or tails. In fact there are incessant and interminable – and potentially unsolvable – disputes about where the boundaries of these versions of sociology lie: about which bits of sociology can be called 'scientific' in some sense, and which bits are more properly 'interpretive'. Many of these debates revolve around seemingly tangential issues such as the role of social institutions in society, around the description of social structure, around the nature of cause and effect, and so on, and if you decide to pursue sociology further you will encounter many of these debates in your journey through different sociological perspectives. Thus sociologists are not looking for the one ultimate answer that solves all questions. Sociology, properly conducted, involves the continual generation of new questions about social life so that our ability to explain and understand what is happening in society improves.

Once again, it may seem somewhat facile to claim that sociology tries to understand what is happening in society: so does everyone else. What has sociology got to offer that is so different and so special as to make it worthwhile pursuing a complex branch of study?

To try and answer that think, for a moment, about our history. Five thousand years ago we were just emerging from the Stone Age. Two thousand years ago marks the birth of Christ. In the Stone Age, technology and social organisation, population and global trade were at vastly lower levels than they are now. Even two thousand years ago the levels of technology and communications, the levels of trade and the systems of production were nowhere near our contemporary national grids for electricity, our high speed trains, aeroplanes and automobiles, our computers and telephones. Things have changed dramatically in this period of time.

But historians and historical sociologists urge us to think of time in different ways: if you say '5,000 years' or '2,000 years', it sounds like a long time. But if you think about it in terms of the human life-span it is no time at all. Taking 20 to 25 years as a 'generation', it is only just over 200 generations since we were using stone tools. In 200 generations we have gone from examining the rocks of the earth to examining the rocks of the moon. We have gone from using the open fire to cook meat to the thermonuclear explosion to cook the earth itself. Since the year 0 AD there have been, approximately, only 80 or so generations. In 80 generations a substantial number of human beings have traded the donkey for the Ferrari as the apex of personal transport; the cart for the supersonic jet as the apex of goods and passenger movement about the globe. It means that only 80 sets of parents had the chance to teach the next generation how to design, build and power these fantastic instruments. Not only cars and aeroplanes but also computers and microwaves and all the other 'wonders' of our present technology that many of us take for granted have developed within the life-span of only 80 sets of parent–children relationships.

But, in fact, we need to take an even more limited historical view. Because the fundamental changes that are affecting our lives, the amazing leaps forward in technology that have just been mentioned all occurred, roughly, within the last 350 years. Only 14 generations of humans, approximately, have really been needed to move from the cart to the aeroplane. That is a fantastic and mind-boggling rate of change.

The relevance of this discussion becomes clear when we realise that it is within that period that sociology emerged and developed. It is within that period that the foundations for understanding society were laid and it is this rapid, seemingly uncontrollable rate of change that explains why sociology emerged when it did; why people needed to formulate a programme of study of social life. That tiny speck of our collective history going back only a mere 14 generations or less is what sociological analysis is largely about. Sociology studies, by and large, our era, our sciences and technologies, or 'modern society' (Giddens, 1990a, ch. 1 includes a similar discussion of sociology and modern society).

The sociologist wants to know how all this change in our modern society happened: who did the changing, what sorts of organisations were needed to carry these changes forward. On this issue we can understand that one of the main forms of sociological understanding is historical understanding (Giddens, 1990b: 19). This type of understanding urges us to recognise that the societies we inhabit today did not just come into being the day before we were born. They were built, manufactured and fought for, by people who lived before us; people just like you and me having the same genetic make-up, the same biology, physiology, anatomy and, as far as we are able to judge, the same intelligence and emotional problems as we have today. What they did led, partly, to our history, just as what we do, in our present, will comprise the history of our successors. Our children will inherit our present – what we do in and with the world today – as their history.

In this dimension, sociology is the study of how 'history' is made, how it is fabricated – both in the past and in the present – by people doing, believing, and thinking things. The sociologist does not ask historical questions simply out of a curiosity for what happened in the past, for such an enterprise may be left to the historian. The sociologist studies the past precisely in order to throw light on the present, on the ways that our own actions and commitments can be understood.

A second type of understanding mentioned by Giddens (1990b: 19–21) is anthropological. Some of the major dimensions of this form of understanding were mentioned earlier in this section. People think, believe and act differently. There are different ways of life, different cultures both between societies and within them. People follow different codes and conventions in different times and places. The sociologist wants to know how understanding these things helps us to understand our own situation, our own codes and conventions. The sociologist also wants to know how these different ways of life emerged, how they are maintained in modern society, how they interact and how they affect one another. The sociologist wants to know this because he or she wants to know how knowledge, conventions, codes and rules develop and become fixed in institutions. Or, alternatively, how and why they change over time.

And finally, Giddens points us to another, closely related, type of sociological understanding. This is 'critical' understanding. For Giddens, critical understanding involves only critique, an almost negative type of understanding that attends to what is wrong with society, what problems and fault lines society has. Such an interpretation is only one side of being critical. Critical understanding also involves investigating points of social crisis. That is, understanding where and how one thing gives way to another, in the sense of a critical temperature or a critical mass. In these latter uses 'critical' means 'at the point of change'. Sociologists want to know at what points and in which events social change is imminent. They want to know this because they want to see beyond or outside of our present social arrangements; to take different standpoints on the social world, to see how things might be otherwise, if different conditions held. And to do this they must be prepared to have their own beliefs and their own opinions shaken to their very foundations.

Once you begin to grasp these forms of understanding then, and only then, do you begin to understand what sociology is all about and why it is worth bothering with.

1.3   Sociological theory

If sociological understanding is about making connections – connections between action, experience and change – then the major vehicle for realising those connections, for coming to an understanding of their significance, is sociological research. But in order to grasp what is unique about sociological research we must first consider the place of theory in sociology.

Many people and organisations engage in research on society. For example, marketing firms wanting to get information on the population so they can sell video recorders, cars or cigarettes spend large sums of money and spend a great deal of time researching consumer preferences; the police also conduct research into crime rates and offender and/or victim characteristics in order to build up more effective policing strategies; health authorities, wishing to discover the distribution of diseases or the take-up rates of their services, conduct research studies in order to target services where they are needed; opinion pollsters who want to know which way the political wind is blowing regularly conduct opinion surveys to predict the outcome of local and national elections. There are many other examples of organisations that have an intrinsic interest in conducting research into different dimensions of our collective social life. But, strictly speaking, these are not forms of sociological research. They are not sociological in so far as they proceed most often without the conscious assistance of a theoretical framework. The word 'conscious' is used here because all research is underpinned by theory at some level and we will return to this below. Whether this underpinning is acknowledged or not, research cannot proceed without at least a minimum of theoretical scaffolding. Sociology's ability to make connections between action, experience and change is based on the explicit use of theory.

1.3.1   What is 'theory'?

A simple way of understanding 'what is theory' is to compare theory with a kaleidoscope, the child's toy consisting of a tube, a number of lenses and fragments of translucent, coloured glass or plastic. When you turn the tube and look down the lens of the kaleidoscope the shapes and colours, visible at the bottom, change. As the tube is turned, different lenses come into play and the combinations of colour and shape shift from one pattern to another. In a similar way we can see social theory as a sort of kaleidoscope – by shifting theoretical perspective the world under investigation also changes shape. The components of the world being investigated combine and recombine into new patterns as they are viewed through different theoretical perspectives. Different theories bring different aspects of the world into view: theories are like the lenses of the kaleidoscope; when you slot different ones into place things you could not see before suddenly become visible; patterns that were indistinct become sharper.

Of course, there is much more to sociological theory than this – as chapter 2 makes clear. The purpose in making this comparison between theory and the kaleidoscope is simply to provide an image of why theory is important in sociological research. The role of theory is precisely to make things that were hidden visible, to define some patterns and give some meanings to the sorts of observations that social researchers continually make when investigating society. But it is important to remember that the world contains many different patterns depending upon how you look at it. For, just as sociology is not one thing and one thing only, so the world is not just one big undifferentiated 'thing', existing out there waiting for the researcher to discover. Seeing the world in different ways is the essential and fundamental role of social research and the ability to see these differences and to make sense of the different points of view that a researcher can take is the basic contribution that theory makes to the research process.

1.3.2 Research is 'theory dependent'

Again, it is important to make this connection between theory and research because all research is 'theory dependent' (Clegg, 1990; Fox Keller, 1990; Harvey, 1990). Whether the theory is acknowledged or not, pure 'empirical' research is impossible. At the simplest level theory may simply involve assumptions about how we know the world. That is, we may believe that knowledge about the world is given to us by divine inspiration, or we may believe that knowledge is given to us through our perception (through our 'senses' of sight, touch, taste and so on), or we may believe that knowledge is already present in our heads and is 'triggered' by stimuli from the outside world. In each of these cases these assumptions or beliefs are theoretical because we cannot know for sure exactly which is right or even whether we get our knowledge from a combination of all three. At a different level, research may be underpinned by a mathematical theory which we use on a computer to predict the outcome of an election or a recession, for example.

These very basic theories – what we might call 'first-level' theories – invariably will be embedded in other, more complex, theories about the way the world works and about how people will behave and respond in given situations. For example, our theory may tell us that people are more likely to respond truthfully in an interview if we question them politely than if we threaten them with blackmail on the basis of their responses. Such a theory is testable but few researchers would incorporate the test into their research because it would be taken as a reasonable supposition which does not need verification. None the less, without putting it to the test on each and every occasion in which we conduct interviews, the supposition remains theoretical – we might possibly, on some occasions, be wrong to suppose that diplomacy gives better results than the threat of blackmail.

Going one stage further, it is possible to identify theory which is designed explicitly for something. For example, we may have a theory about how people learn to behave in certain ways and consciously use that theory to change behaviour for the better. This type of theory is often visible in health education and social policy programmes, one example being recent policies on 'health promotion' such as the 'Heartbeat Wales' programme (see Catford and Parish, 1989). The Heartbeat Wales programme is one of many British health promotion programmes that have parallels in other national contexts: in Europe and America, in Africa and Asia (see, for example, the collection edited by Morley et al., 1987; or the collection of articles in *Health Promotion*, 1986). These programmes attempt to change both people's health behaviour and, sometimes, also the social conditions in which those behaviours occur. Heartbeat Wales uses the mass media, 'healthy industry' award schemes, new roles for health service workers, and much more, to try and improve the health of the people of Wales. Much of the emphasis on behaviour change in this programme is based on 'social learning theory' (after Bandura, 1977).

Social learning theory proposes that health programmes aimed at stopping people smoking, encouraging them to take exercise and so on, must take into account the ways that people learn and unlearn the behaviours and habits of a lifetime. Because this type of theory is about how people *should* behave (in order to be healthier, for example) we can call it **normative theory**: at its simplest, theory that is directed towards establishing norms of behaviour or belief. A great deal of theory in sociology has a 'normative' dimension; a dimension which posits how social relations might operate in a more egalitarian or more 'open' way.

The preceding discussion is intended to show that all research – and much social policy – is based on 'theory' at some level or another. But such theories are not properly sociological in the sense that I have defined sociology above. They do not display, let alone combine, the historical, the anthropological and the critical forms of understanding that are characteristic of the discipline of sociology. In order to clarify the ways that theory inheres in the practice of sociology the next section presents two examples of research that clearly demonstrate the conscious use of these different types of understanding in accounting for patterns of action, experience and change in the social world.

1.4   Sociological investigation

A very clear example of sociological research which combines the histori-cal, experiential and critical dimensions of sociological understanding is that conducted by Liddle and Joshi (1986) on the changing experiences of Indian women caught between the demands of the caste system and the labour market. For the time being, this section will simply describe the conduct of Liddle's and Joshi's work. You will have the opportunity to find out more about this kind of research in chapter 9 and about using documents in historical research in chapter 10. The following discussion is based on Harvey's (1990) excellent account of Liddle's and Joshi's work.

Liddle's and Joshi's research was a study of the impact of class and caste on women's subordination in India. They began with the question, why are women subordinated in the relations between the sexes? Such a question cannot be researched directly because it admits of too many possible solutions. Instead, Liddle and Joshi addressed a series of related questions designed to bring out the complex interplay between gender, class, caste and the experience of British imperialism in India. These included, among other things, issues relating to Indian history and especially India's relationship to Britain across the nineteenth and twentieth centuries. This information helped them to chart changing relationships between the indigenous system of caste and the imported system of class that developed in India as a result of the imposition of a capitalist economic structure on to the Indian caste-based economy.

As a result of this work Liddle and Joshi decided to focus their attention on instances where Indian people had managed to change their economic position through the acquisition of new statuses and social identities made available through participation in the capitalist economy imposed under British imperialism. By doing this the researchers hoped to show how the interactions between gender, class and caste affected women's experiences of employment.

Liddle's and Joshi's historical research indicated that the transition to independent employment was a critical point in the conflict between the genders. The reason for this was because women's subordination in India resulted from a combination of male control over economic resources within the caste system and cultural conventions controlling women's behaviour and movements. Their study of professional women's experi-ences focused on this dual control system. Being middle class professional women themselves they could also draw on their own experience of the tensions and struggles that breaking away from the caste system involves. Hence, their research was focused on both a critical change in social relations and how that change is experienced by particular groups in society.

Liddle and Joshi noted that some members of lower castes were able to rise in social and economic prestige and power through the economic

wealth they had made in capitalist production. Such a rise in prestige and
power was previously very difficult in India's rigid caste structure so that,
for some, capitalism represented an 'escape route' out of low social status.

For Indian women, however, the impact of the imported class system
was ambiguous. While it meant that some were able to use the capitalist
economy to change their status, the majority were subjected to the
contradictory demands of the caste hierarchy and the impact of western-
ised cultural expectations of men's and women's behaviour. Even for those
women who were able to gain independent employment – and thus a
degree of economic autonomy from the caste hierarchy – the experience
was double-edged and dependent on traditional authority patterns.

The research techniques they used for their research were fairly
conventional social science tools: a structured questionnaire, a semi-
structured interview and an unstructured interview, each designed to focus
the research on to the respondents' experiences of the transition (see
chapter 9). They found that the women's experiences, to a certain extent,
repeated the more global pattern that their historical research had
uncovered. For example, women entering employment independently had
only a limited range of career options at their disposal – jobs which
included travelling were extremely difficult for women to take because of
cultural taboos against women journeying alone; professional jobs where a
woman's expertise was greater than that of male colleagues generated
unease and discomfort in working relations. Similarly, the option to gain
independence and status was almost entirely restricted to educated women
from higher caste backgrounds because the transition required the support
of families as well as economic backing for training and education. For the
majority of women who had neither of these the imported capitalist
economy created a double system of exploitation based on both class and
caste.

By combining their historical analysis with ethnographic research Liddle
and Joshi showed that the experiences of particular women in particular
places and at particular times are inextricably tied to the social and political
structures that surround them. As a corollary, this research about women
then becomes useful for women by showing how their own personal
experiences are shaped and constrained by social and political forces and
by bringing to light dimensions of Indian women's history and experience
that were previously invisible.

The second example of research which combines the dimensions of
historical, experiential and critical understanding is David Armstrong's
(1983) work on the development of community-centred health services in
Britain. Armstrong's book is called *Political Anatomy of the Body*. In it he
uses the work of the French philosopher Michel Foucault to shed new light
on that apparently stable and fundamental characteristic of human experience – our bodies. The purpose of his work is, initially, to show how the
very nature of our bodies – how we experience them, how we talk about
them and how we treat their health and illness – underwent a fundamental

transformation during the first half of the twentieth century. By examining medical history and by investigating how the architecture of medical space (that is, the design of buildings for treating health and illness and the social relations they contain) changed over time, Armstrong argues that, to put it rather simply, our bodies 'grew'. That is, they changed from simply the physical anatomy – liver, lungs, head, legs, etc. – to a social entity. Previously, 'the body' in medical diagnosis and treatment began and ended with the limits of physical anatomy and the structure of our internal organs. However, across the course of the early twentieth century, medicine began to take into account social factors in health and illness: in particular it began to consider the emergence, spread and control of illness as a function of the relationship between bodies. Our bodies became extended to include the 'community' where they were sited. It was the structure and characteristics of this 'community' as much as the physical body itself that was used by medicine to explain the distribution of health and illness and it was by interfering in this community that medicine believed it could control illness.

Armstrong argues that such a reinterpretation of health and illness together with a redefinition of what comprised and influenced the body enabled medical professionals to gain power over aspects of life that were previously self-regulated or controlled within the patterns of our everyday lives – in the family, the locality, the workplace and so on. In redefining their object – the sick/well body – as a social entity medical professionals came to intervene in a wide range of our behaviours and habits that were previously outside of their control, such as child-rearing, physical activity and social conditions. In the controlling of this space of everyday life, medical professionals, along with a number of other professional groups, succeeded in acquiring greater power while the members of the communities themselves were 'disempowered'. Today, the medical profession acts as gatekeeper to a whole range of community resources and services which are not strictly medical but more properly social, such as the provision of short- and long-stay accommodation, home-helps, voluntary services, housing aids and many more. The point is not that this is a bad thing – it is not the intention here to pass judgement on this historical development. Rather, what Armstrong's analysis shows us is that it is not the members of communities themselves who decide what their needs are and how best they can be met. Instead, these decisions are taken by 'experts' and resources and services are distributed by them on the basis of their ability to define what their object is and how best to provide for its requirements. In turn, this ability depends as much on the power of the professional groups to retain control over these tasks as it does on a 'correct' analysis of what makes bodies ill or healthy.

By redefining the body as a social rather than simply a physical entity, according to Armstrong, medical professionals were able to translate their power over physical bodies into power over community resources. The development of community-centred health services in Britain, accordingly, represented an increasingly sophisticated medical technology for controlling health by intervening in people's behaviour, habits, living conditions, the responsibilities of parents, families and other community institutions.

The point about Armstrong's research – what makes it sociological in the sense that sociology has been defined above – is that, first, it shows how, at a certain point in time, a critical change occurred that gave medicine a new health object, namely the community; and second, it forces us to reflect on new health programmes in a new way. Instead of thinking about health projects as somehow naturally better or obviously common sense ways of going about the business of health care, Armstrong's work shows us that what exists now in the field of health care is as much a result of a political as a medical history. It shows us that our current understandings of health and illness and our current experiences of health care services are rooted in an unfolding historical programme. Once you scratch the surface of medicine and health in this way all that seemed previously obvious suddenly appears as strange: it appears not as what is obviously the best scientific method for treating health and illness but, instead, as the most successful historical project, backed by the most powerful professional groups.

1.5 Conclusions

This first chapter has tried to show that sociological understanding, sociological theory and sociological research are intrinsically interconnected: they comprise a 'triad' of characteristics that mark out sociology as a distinct approach to investigating society. Sociology is not market research, nor is it policy research, nor is it opinion polling. This is not to say that these forms of investigation are not valuable in their own right, nor is it to say that sociologists cannot use the same methods to ask questions about social structure and social change. The point is that sociology distinctively relies upon and often combines an historical, an experiential and a critical dimension in its consciously theoretical approach to researching social life.

1.6 Further reading

Giddens (1990b) is a readable introduction to sociology as is Bauman (1990). Giddens's book, especially the introductory chapter, provides a summary of many sociological positions in an easily digestible way. For the beginner, Bauman's text has the advantage of highlighting key concepts and terms so that some of the language of sociology is brought into sharper relief.

Harvey (1990) is a well-crafted exploration of critical themes in socio-logical research covering studies of class, race and gender.

For those who wish to find out more about feminist sociology Abbott and Wallace (1990) write clearly and comprehensively.

2   Research, theory and method

Nigel Gilbert

Contents

In the previous chapter, it was suggested that social research and sociology are linked, so that good social research depends on sociological understanding and sociological discovery requires good social research. In this chapter, we shall look more closely at what counts as good social research and how the methodological tools which are described in the rest of the book fit into the research process.

2.1   Three ingredients of social research

There are three major ingredients in social research: the construction of theory, the collection of data and, no less important, the design of methods for gathering data. All of them have to be right if the research is to yield interesting results.

We can see these three ingredients in most accounts of good research. Goffman (1959, 1961), for example, spent much of his career exploring the social world of organisations. He writes about hotels, schools, prisons and hospitals. But what is interesting *theoretically* about such places? As a sociologist, Goffman's concern is with one of the fundamental problems of sociology, that is, how social relationships are coordinated and regulated. He notes that in many 'establishments', there are commonalities in the ways employees present themselves to the 'customers' and that this presentation is not just an issue for the individual employee; it is a collective effort. He uses an analogy based on the theatre. In a theatre, a performance is given on stage, but the activity out front is only possible because of the efforts of those who work backstage. In the same way, Goffman argues, the performance of hotel porters, prison officers, mental hospital orderlies and so on relies on the support of other members of the staff:

> For example, in a medical hospital the two staff internists may require the intern, as part of his training, to run through a patient's chart, giving an opinion about each recorded item. He may not appreciate that his show of relative ignorance comes in part from the staff studying up on the chart the night before; he is quite unlikely to appreciate that this impression is doubly ensured by the local team's tacit agreement allotting the work-up of half the chart to one staff person, the other half to the second staff person. (Goffman, 1959: 83)

Goffman's theories about the presentation of self in organisations are intended to be applied across many social settings, indeed, to all 'establishments'. That is, his work is not just about the behaviour of people at the Ritz hotel or in Nether Poppleton Mental Hospital, but about these places and all similar ones. Of course, he could be wrong, but, like a good theorist, he sticks his neck out and asserts that he has found something which is to be found in all 'establishments'. There will be more to say about testing such generalisations later, but for the moment it is important to notice that it is a sign of good research that it concerns itself with 'regularities' which transcend the specifics of time or place.

The second ingredient of social research is the collection of data. Theories ought to be based firmly on data if they are to be useful in understanding the social world. What does Goffman do? As the quotation above illustrates, Goffman does provide data to test his theory, much of it splendidly unexpected. He uses data from his own meticulous observations obtained during periods of study of life in institutions, and he uses data from other people's observations, including from novels and even etiquette books.

Which brings us to the third ingredient: the design of methods of data collection which accurately report on the social world. One of the problems with Goffman's work is that, although the data are vividly described, the methods he used to gather his data and to select his examples are not very clearly or explicitly explained. As a consequence it is hard to be sure that his observations are typical. A second example, concerning crime statistics, will show the importance of understanding what a method of data collection involves.

Crime statistics seem to show that working class youth commit more crime than middle class youth (e.g., see the review in Braithwaite, 1981).

A generation of sociologists tried to devise and test theories to explain this observation (e.g. Cloward and Ohlin, 1960; Schur, 1971; Quinney and Wilderman, 1977). Some suggested that working class youth had more opportunity to commit crime and therefore succumbed more often. Others proposed they had fewer opportunities to pursue success and riches through legitimate channels and so were forced to turn to crime. Yet others argued that working class and middle class youth were located in different subcultures with different norms and that the working class subculture permitted or even encouraged law breaking.

These different explanations assumed that the official crime statistics were correct. Increasingly, however, criticisms of these statistics accumulated. For example, the basis of the statistics is 'crimes known to the police'. And the police only know about crimes which they themselves have spotted or which are reported to them by the victims. If the police patrol working class areas more than middle class areas (a reasonable strategy if the statistics show more crimes among working class youth), they will tend to notice more crime in working class areas. They will also find it easier to apprehend working class youth for criminal acts. It was thought that one way around these biases in criminal statistics is to interview a sample of young people and ask them, in confidence, whether they have themselves been involved in any crimes. Interestingly, the rate of self-reported crime shows little difference between middle and working class young people (e.g. Short and Nye, 1958). Chapter 8 discusses the collection of such self-report data and their validity.

These criticisms of official statistics and the results of self-report surveys presented sociologists with a new set of data and suggested a quite different sociological problem: why working class youth are *convicted* of crime more often than middle class youth. Theories began to be proposed which focused not so much on 'criminal' activities, but on the activities of the police and their role in apprehending youth (e.g. Pearson, 1983). Thus new methods of data collection produced new data and new theories.

There are two alternative conclusions which we could draw from this example. One is that there is one right way of looking at the social world and that social research strives to find this way. If we find that crime statistics offer a biased view, other, more valid methods of data collection must be found to get us closer to the truth. Empirical reality is treated as the privileged source of our theoretical understanding of the social world. In its starkest form, this is the position known as **empiricism**. The alternative position denies that one can ever read off theories from observations of the social world. What we as social researchers see as 'empirical reality' is a consequence of the theories which we bring to bear in organising our understanding of it. In short, theories are treated as the privileged source of our understanding of empirical reality. For example, we might conclude that attempts to discover the 'real' or 'true' crime rates among working and middle class youth will never be finally successful: different theories suggest different definitions of 'crime rate'.

2.2   Constructing theories

But what exactly is a theory?

As chapter 1 noted, a theory highlights and explains something which one would otherwise not see, or would find puzzling. Often, it is an answer to a 'Why?' question. For example, why does the sun shine?; why are some people poor and others rich?; why are so many people unemployed in western capitalist societies?; and so on. Thus one characteristic of a theory is that it can be used as an explanation.

Suppose that someone proposed a theory of unemployment – that the rate of unemployment depends on current interest rates, for example. Then the theory could be offered as a reasonable (if partial) answer to a question about why there are now so many people unemployed: interest rates are high. Of course, we might want to know quite a lot more than this in answer to the 'Why?' question. It would be interesting to know just what the mechanism connecting interest rates and unemployment rates is supposed to be, what counts as a 'high' interest rate, and whether there is anything that could be done to reduce interest rates and thus rates of unemployment. Nevertheless, the theory that interest rates and unemployment are connected does offer a solution to what would otherwise be a puzzle and is not obvious from straightforward commonsense, both characteristics of good theory.

As well as providing explanations, theories often provide predictions. For example, if the interest rate is falling, and the theory is correct, it would be possible to predict that the unemployment rate would also fall.

One of the most famous sociological theories is Durkheim's theory of suicide. Individual acts of suicide are almost always puzzling. Often the first thing families and friends ask after a suicide is, why did he or she do it? But as Durkheim (1897) observed, suicide is also puzzling on a wider, societal level. Overall suicide rates in different communities and countries vary widely, yet within any one community they tend to be fairly constant from one year to the next. Why is there such variation between the rates in different communities?

Statistics about the suicide rates in particular countries are available from the World Health Organisation (WHO, 1990) (see Figure 2.1). There has been a considerable amount of research on how such suicide rate statistics are constructed and what they mean (e.g. Atkinson, 1978). This work indicates that there is no simple relationship between official statistics on suicide and a 'real' rate of suicide; indeed, just like crime statistics, the research raises deep questions about the process of labelling certain deaths as 'suicides'. However, again just like crime statistics, the statistics themselves, however they may be constructed, are social facts which warrant sociological investigation. Hungary, for example, has a very high suicide rate compared with other European countries. Hungary has also been experiencing rapid economic growth and a major change in cultural

Bahamas	2.2
Greece	3.1
Italy	5.5
Spain	5.7
UK	6.3
United States	10.2
Sweden	14.4
France	15.9
USSR	17.4
Austria	18.9
Denmark	20.1
Finland	23.7
Hungary	32.0
Sri Lanka	35.8

Age-sex standardised mortality rates per 100,000 population for suicide and self-inflicted injury (standardised against the overall world age-sex distribution) for 1989 (or latest year for which statistics are available). An 'age-sex standardised mortality rate' is the national rate adjusted to allow for differences between countries in the age and sex distributions of their populations. *Source*: WHO (1990), Table 10.

Figure 2.1   *Suicide rates in selected countries*

and political values since the break up of the communist bloc. We might guess that Hungary's high official suicide rate is caused in some way by these rapid social, cultural and economic changes. This statement certainly answers a 'Why?' question. But as a theory, it is still lacking.

One problem is that, as it stands, it refers only to Hungary. A statement relating to a single case, such as Hungary, would not normally be considered to be a theory. A theory needs to be able to cover a range of settings. But we could look for other countries also experiencing rapid socioeconomic changes and see whether they too have high suicide rates. If we found several such countries, we would have a more impressive theory and one which represents a general pattern or 'regularity'.

For example, Sri Lanka has also been subject to major disturbances in the last few years and its suicide rate is also very high (see Figure 2.1). Indeed, after some thought and some delving into suicide statistics, one might suppose that 'the rate of suicide increases in times of economic collapse or boom, or generally when there is rapid social and economic change', a conclusion which Durkheim also proposed and which he explained using the concept of **anomie**. Anomic suicide, according to Durkheim, results when society's regulation of the individual through normative controls breaks down and this is likely to happen where there is social and economic instability.

2.2.1   Induction and deduction

The process which we have just worked through, of finding a single case and observing a relationship, then observing the same relationship in

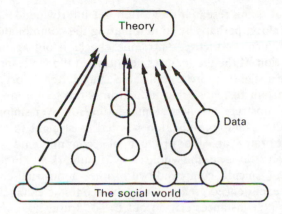

Figure 2.2   *Theory construction by induction*

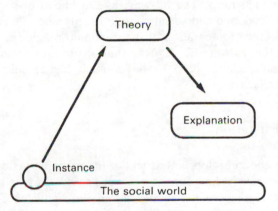

Figure 2.3   *Theory use by deduction*

several more cases and finally constructing a general theory to cover all the cases, is known as **induction**. It is the basic technique for moving from a set of observations to a theory and is at the heart of sociological theory construction and is illustrated in Figure 2.2.

Once a theory has been formulated, it can be used to explain. For example, the theory about suicide rates being high in countries with high rates of social and economic change can be used to explain why the former Soviet Union has a high suicide rate (it, too, had been undergoing marked change at around the time when the statistics in Figure 2.1 were compiled). This process, starting with a theory and using it to explain particular observations, is known as **deduction** (see Figure 2.3). Deduction takes the data about a particular case and applies the general theory in order to deduce an explanation for the data. Thus induction is the technique for generating theories and deduction is the technique for applying them.

For the sake of defining the terms, we have discussed induction and deduction as though they are quite distinct. Logically, that is true. But in the course of doing research they often get intertwined. First one has an idea for a theory, perhaps by contemplating the commonalities of a set of cases and inducing a theory. Then one checks it out against some data, using deduction. If the theory does not quite fit the facts, induction is used to construct a slightly more complicated, but better theory. And so on.

It is important to realise that induction is not foolproof. It is certainly possible to construct erroneous, misleading or over-simple theories by induction. For example, induction has led us straight to the theory that high suicide rates are the product of economic and social change. Unfortunately, this is not the whole story. Denmark and Finland both have high rates of suicide compared with other industrialised nations, yet neither has experienced great political or economic changes recently.

These counter instances can be put to good use, however. The theory can be extended in scope and deepened in its explanatory power if we look to see what characteristics Denmark and Finland share which might explain their high rates. The answer, as Durkheim discovered from his data, is that economic and social change is only one influence on suicide rates. The degree of integration of the dominant religion is also important and this is the reason, he argues, that Protestant countries, such as Denmark and Finland, tend to have much higher suicide rates than otherwise similar countries.

2.2.2 Falsification

This leads to another important aspect of theory construction, the strategy of **falsification**: always look for the awkward cases. If we had stuck with the cases that fitted the original theory about the significance of social and economic change, that is, if we had looked no further than Hungary and Sri Lanka, we would not have formulated the wider theory which brought in the religious dimension.

Falsification as a strategy is important for two reasons. First, by directing attention to 'awkward cases' it helps to improve theories. Second, it has been argued that it is a useful criterion for what should count as a theory. The criterion is that it must be possible in principle to falsify a theory. That is, it must be possible to imagine some data which if found would demolish the theory.

The preceding theory about suicide rates being linked to economic and political change may not be a good theory, but by the criterion of falsification it is at least a theory. It is possible to imagine some data which would destroy the theory: a single case of a country experiencing great changes but having a low suicide rate would do. But consider the statement, 'People who kill themselves are suicides.' This is *not* a theory. First, the statement is not an answer to a 'Why?' question and, second, it is impossible to think of data which would falsify it. In fact, this statement is a **definition** of suicide, not a theory.

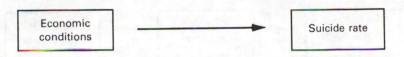

Figure 2.4 *A theory about a cause of high suicide rates*

One of the problems of research is that the search for falsifying observations is in principle never-ending. No matter how much data one collects that fits the theory, it is always possible that a falsifying instance might turn up next. The consequence is that there is an asymmetry about a researcher's confidence in theory: one can be quite sure that a theory is wrong if there are any data which falsify it, but one cannot be sure that a theory is right, because there may yet be some data which will disconfirm it. Scepticism is therefore the right attitude to assertions that this or that theory is correct.

2.3 Concepts and relationships

Durkheim writes, in *Suicide*:

> The fact that economic crises have an aggravating effect on the suicide tendency is well-known. . . . Even fortunate crises, which have the effect of raising a country's prosperity, have an effect on suicide like economic disasters. . . . Every disturbance of equilibrium, even though it may involve greater comfort and a raising of the general pace of life, provides an impulse to voluntary death. (Thompson, 1985: 108–9)

Durkheim is arguing that there is a causal link between economic crises and suicide rates. Crises cause ('have an effect on') suicide. Such causal statements are often shown graphically, with arrows to mean 'cause'. Figure 2.4 illustrates Durkheim's theory in this way.

Figure 2.4 can be read as saying that there is a causal relationship between economic conditions (the occurrence or absence of economic crisis) and high or low 'suicide rates'. We call the elements in boxes **concepts** and the lines between the boxes **relationships**. Theories are composed of concepts linked by relationships.

In this example about suicide, there are only two concepts and one relationship. But most theories are a lot more complex. Let us turn from suicide to a rather different example – 'gentrification'. Poor housing areas become 'gentrified' when run down homes occupied by poor people are taken over by the relatively rich. The process of gentrification has been studied in a number of urban research programmes in the United States and the United Kingdom (e.g. Smith and Williams, 1986) and is interesting because it is an example of the unintended consequences of apparently beneficial social policies.

The theory goes like this. Social planners and politicians attempt to

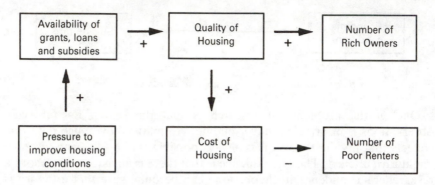

Figure 2.5   *A theory of gentrification*

improve a poor locality for its residents by providing favourable loans, redevelopment grants, and so on. The effect is that the overall quality of the area improves. This raises the value of the housing and makes properties not yet improved particularly attractive to developers. The price of housing goes up and with it the rents charged by private landlords. If rents are controlled, landlords take advantage of rising market prices to sell their property. The rise in housing costs pushes the original, poorer residents out and they are replaced by richer owners. The poor neighbour-hood has been gentrified, displacing the established residents, often to even poorer housing stock.

Figure 2.5 summarises the theory as a diagram. Each box represents a concept and each line a causal relationship. The causal effect can either be positive (meaning that the cause and effect both vary in the same direction) or negative (meaning that as the cause increases, the effect decreases, or vice versa). For example, as the quality of the neighbourhood rises, the price of housing rises also – a positive effect. As the price of housing rises, the number of poorer residents falls – a negative effect.

If you wanted to test a theory like this, it would be difficult to do it all at once. It is too complicated; there are too many relationships to consider (although some of the most recent statistical techniques, such as those mentioned at the end of chapter 12, can help). Instead, it is best to break the theory down into parts, each covering just one relationship. So, one might test the causal relationship between the Quality of Housing and the Cost of Housing and then, separately, the relationship between the Cost of Housing and the Number of Poor Renters. Each such part is known as a **hypothesis** and it is hypotheses that researchers generally test and try to falsify.

2.3.1   Indicators

So far, this chapter has been concentrating almost entirely on theories. It has been argued that theories are things which aim to explain puzzling observations. They are composed of one or more hypotheses, each of which consists of concepts linked by relationships. Theories must be capable of being tested, or falsified. Now we must move on to examine in more detail what is involved in testing a theory.

In order to test a theory, we need to compare the predictions it makes with measurements made of the social world. For example, we need to see whether, as the Quality of Housing increases, so does the Number of Rich Owners, which is what the theory of Figure 2.4 predicts. However, this is more complicated than it seems because concepts cannot be measured directly. Before Quality of Housing can be assessed, one has to have some definition of 'quality' and some means of applying that definition to actual neighbourhoods.

In general, in order to test theories, there must be a way of measuring each concept, that is, for each, there must be an **indicator**. An indicator is a method of measurement which aims to measure the concept accurately. If we want to test the hypothesis that the Quality of Housing was related to the Value of Housing, we would need independent indicators for both these concepts. The value of housing could be measured by averaging the asking price for houses for sale (but there would still be some issues to settle, such as: what is to be counted as a 'house'?; what about a property which has tenants?; what if the price actually paid for property is less than the asking price?; and so on). An indicator for Quality of Housing is more difficult to devise. One indicator which would not be suitable is the value of the housing, for this would then be getting measurement of the two concepts confused. One approach might be to consult a panel of experts, such as estate agents, surveyors or lawyers and ask them to assess the quality of the housing. Another way would be to conduct an attitude survey of the general public. A third way would be to rely on some more direct measure, such as the average number of months since the exterior woodwork was repainted. Obviously, there is room for debate and for careful thought about the right choice, and factors such as the cost of the research and the speed with which data can be obtained will need to be considered as well.

2.3.2   Validity and reliability

Naturally, researchers want their indicators to be as good as possible. This means that the measurements which they make should be **valid** (accurately measuring the concept) and **reliable** (consistent from one measurement to the next). For instance, suppose that you want to measure people's consumption of alcohol (a concept). You choose to do this using a questionnaire in which you will ask respondents to tell you how much they drank during the previous month. In fact, this is not a good indicator of alcohol consumption. People tend to under-report consumption – they say that they drink less than they actually drink – casting doubts on the validity of the indicator. Also, people have difficulty remembering in detail what they were doing as long as a month ago. This means that if you were to ask someone repeatedly over the course of a few days what they had drunk during the previous month, it is quite likely that they would give you different answers, just because they were not remembering consistently. The indicator is not reliable.

In order to know whether an indicator is valid and reliable, we need to understand how it works, that is, the way the indicator measures its concept. Consider a couple of the indicators mentioned in the previous section. Official statistics measure suicide rates in as much as they record the decisions of coroners' courts, bodies which apply procedures laid down in legal statute for assigning causes of death. Coroners, of course, do not have direct access to the cause of death; they themselves use a set of indicators and a body of 'theory' – common sense and legal knowledge – to decide whether a particular death is the result of suicide or some other reason (Kitsuse and Cicourel, 1963; Atkinson, 1978) and this needs to be recognised when we use the indicator. The quality of housing in a neighbourhood may be measured by an indicator consisting of the average time since house exteriors were painted because houses in poor condition are rarely repainted, while houses which are in good condition and are being looked after by their owners tend to be repainted regularly, as soon as the paintwork begins to show signs of age.

2.3.3   Measurement theories

As these examples show, the validity and reliability of an indicator will depend on the adequacy of the way in which it measures its concept. One way of thinking about an indicator is that it links a concept (e.g. Quality of Housing) with observable facts (e.g. average time since repainting). The adequacy of this link depends on a theoretical proposition, known as the indicator's **measurement theory**. The measurement theory for the indicator of housing quality is the proposition that 'houses in poor condition are rarely repainted, while houses which are in good condition and are being looked after by their owners tend to be repainted regularly, as soon as the paintwork begins to show signs of age'.

Like any other theory, a measurement theory can, and should be tested. The more it is tested against data, the more confident one can be in the adequacy of the indicator which relies on that theory. But like all theories, measurement theories can still eventually turn out to be wrong or incomplete. What are the consequences of using an incorrect measurement theory?

One consequence could be that we are led to draw the wrong conclusions when inducing theories from observations. This is what happened in the case mentioned at the beginning of this chapter, that working class youth seemed to be committing more crime than middle class youth. The measurement theory implicit in using official crime statistics to measure crime rates (that official statistics validly measure the number of criminal acts committed) turned out to be false. The effect of using the wrong measurement theory was that incorrect theories which attempted to account for a spurious differential crime rate were constructed.

Another consequence of using incorrect measurement theories is that one may falsify correct theories, or fail to falsify incorrect theories, because the indicators are not measuring the concepts properly. This has the unfortunate implication that if a theory is apparently not corroborated by the data, we do not know whether this is because the theory is in fact wrong, or whether it is because the measurement theories on which the indicators rely are incorrect. Of course, the solution to this dilemma is to test the measurement theories.

However, this can lead to trouble. As a good researcher, I want to test my hypothesis. I therefore devise some indicators for the concepts in my hypothesis. But before using the indicators, I need to satisfy myself about the adequacy of the indicators. To do this, I need to investigate the measurement theories on which they are based. This will involve devising indicators to test the measurement theories. These indicators will themselves rely on measurement theories . . . We seem to have embarked on an endless task!

2.4   Social research as a social process

The answer to this conundrum comes from the fact that research is never conducted without reference to other studies. It can always rely on previous knowledge and previous experience. This means that rather than having to justify every measurement theory and thus every indicator, researchers can call on other people's work.

Social research, like other scientific work, is situated within a 'paradigm' (Kuhn, 1962), a scientific tradition. The paradigm influences research in several ways. The problems researchers tackle are derived from sociological perspectives which, although in constant flux, have been fashioned through a hundred years of sociological thought. The indicators we use and the measurement theories on which they are based have been honed by many previous researchers through thousands of projects. Instead of having personally to test every measurement theory you use and having to justify every theory you mention, you can rely on standard indicators, standard concepts and standard theories.

Linking new research to the existing paradigm is one of the functions of the 'references' that are sprinkled throughout journal articles. These references not only acknowledge previous work (saying, in effect, 'the idea I am mentioning is not my own invention, but was previously proposed by someone else'), but also and more importantly, borrow the authority of earlier research (saying, 'it is not just me who thinks this research method, this hypothesis, etc. is correct, but also the person I am citing'). Chapter 16 discusses the techniques of writing and referencing in more detail.

This is just one example of the way in which we, as sociologists, can examine the social processes which contribute to the construction of sociological knowledge. There is no reason to exempt sociology or science in general from investigation by sociologists (Yearley, 1984).

Learning about how to do social research is thus not just a matter of becoming proficient at some technical skills, although knowledge of technique is very important. It is also about learning the culture of social science so that you can become a proficient member of the social scientific community.

2.5 Conclusion

In this chapter we have seen that what makes social research different from mere data collection is that it is an activity conducted within a research community. This community provides a body of theory in which the research needs to be located. Sociological theory, like all theory, aims to be explanatory, answering 'Why?' questions. It also aims to be general, offering explanations which transcend the particularities of time, space, or personal circumstance.

Theories are generally constructed through induction, extracting the common elements of many specific instances, and are applied to explain other instances by means of the logic of deduction. Theories are made up of hypotheses, individual statements which relate together theoretical concepts.

Theories must be susceptible to falsification, that is, they must be framed in such a way that they could be proved wrong. Testing a theory involves choosing indicators for each of its concepts, using the indicators to collect data, and comparing the data with predictions made from the theory. An indicator should be valid and reliable. This can be determined by examining the measurement theory on which it is based. However, in practice, most researchers most of the time use standard indicators which have been developed and used by other sociologists before them and whose validity is largely unquestioned.

2.6 Project

This chapter has suggested a particular model of social enquiry, one which proposes that social research involves theories, data, indicators and theory testing. In some ways this model can be regarded as itself a theory – a theory about social research. Like any theory, it ought to be capable of being compared with data.

For this project, you should locate in the library a recent issue of one of the major journals in your field. In sociology, this might be one of *Sociology*, *Sociological Review*, the *British Journal of Sociology*, the *American Sociological Review* or the *American Journal of Sociology*. Find an article in your chosen issue which looks interesting.

Read the article closely to see the way in which the author puts forward his or her argument. Write down, in as few words as you can, the theory being advanced in the article. List the concepts which are used in the theory. For each concept, identify the indicators which the author uses. For each concept and indicator, briefly suggest what the implied measurement theory is.

For some articles, these steps are easy to carry out. In other cases, you may find the theory, the concepts or the indicators hard to pin down. Is this because there is something amiss with the research being reported in the article, or because the model of social enquiry proposed in this chapter does not fit the research in the article you have been examining?

2.7 Further reading

Hughes (1976: chs 1 and 2) addresses many of the issues touched on in this chapter in more detail.

Stinchcombe (1968) is very good on forms of social theory and how theories are constructed. Blalock (1969) is also good on this, although rather more formal and mathematical.

3 The research process

Sara Arber

Contents

The process of research can be broken down into a series of stages. In order to make sensible plans before starting a project, you will need an overview of these stages and the likely time each will take to complete. Ethnographic, documentary and survey research differ in the nature of the research stages and the extent to which any particular stage can be clearly planned in advance. Of these three types of research, survey research fits most neatly into predictable stages and is therefore the easiest to plan. This chapter will describe a survey research project, outlining its development from initial inception to final reporting of results. It will also provide an example (others can be found in the three Exemplar chapters later in the book) of the 'reality' of actual research which is not always in accord with the ideals set out in manuals on social research methods.

3.1 The role of planning in social research

You need to adopt a systematic and logical approach to research, the key to which is the planning and management of your time (Howard and Sharp, 1983). Having a plan will enable you to realise when you are getting behind schedule or into difficulties, and when you need help from a supervisor and possibly a reassessment of your plan. Checking progress against the plan is a 'motivational device' which allows you to see that you have achieved intermediate goals on the way to completing the work.

Although the research process can be represented as a series of discrete stages, in practice a number of activities are generally in progress at the same time, for example, you can select a sample while designing the questionnaire and recruiting interviewers. And because sociological research is primarily about discovering new knowledge, we should not be surprised when a project develops in unexpected directions. Indeed, since research involves the continual interaction of ideas and data, you should always be on the look out for serendipitous or unexpected findings (Merton, 1948). These may suggest further fruitful avenues and sometimes dramatically alter the course of the work.

3.1.1 The reality of research

One good way of understanding the complexities of research is to read accounts from experienced researchers about what really happened in the projects they carried out. One source of such accounts is Bell and Newby (1977), who distinguish between **normative** methods texts which present an idealised and standard set of procedures, and their own book which provides descriptive accounts of research as 'a deeply social process' (1977: 11). They argue that normative methodology gives the impression that 'sociological research was "context-free" – i.e. carried out by non-people in non-places' (1977: 10). In reality, research takes place in a political context, including the micropolitics of interpersonal relationships and the politics of research units. A later collection (Bell and Roberts, 1984) emphasises the way in which the financial and political context influences the process of social research. These books and others (e.g. Hammond, 1964; Bell and Encel, 1978; Roberts, 1981) provide insights into the research process, emphasising the difference between the way sociological research was actually carried out and what is found in methods textbooks. Through personal stories they show how mistakes may be creative and highlight the stresses and tensions that all researchers face.

This chapter presents a personal account of one piece of research as an example of planning the research process. This study had very specific policy-related aims, but also examined theoretical issues relating to intergenerational housing mobility. The chapter provides an illustration of

Month 1	Initial discussions with Local Authority
	Presentation of formal proposal
Month 2	Negotiation about Contract
	Documentary research and literature review
	Initial design work
	Taped interviews for developmental and pilot work
	Sample selection
Month 3	Finalise interview schedule
	Recruit 40 interviewers
	Print 1,200 interview schedules (each 44 pages)
	Interviewer training (2 days)
	Preparation of interviewer briefing notes, etc.
Month 4–5	Period of fieldwork
	Interviewing
	'Immediate' checking and editing of interviews
	Coding
	Data Entry
	Typing comments and 'random probes'
Month 6	Finalise all interviewing, coding, data entry.
	Preparation of SPSS-X and SPSS/PC files
	Interim Report to Local Authority
Month 7	Editing checks and data cleaning
	Analysis incorporating feedback from Local Authority in
	response to Interim Report
Month 8	Final Report to Local Authority
Month 16	Submission of first academic journal article
Months 18 and 25	Presentation of academic conference papers
Month 26	Publication of Occasional Paper based on the research

Figure 3.1   *Timetable for Survey of Public Housing Tenants*

the process of survey research from initial conceptualisation through to publication for varied audiences. It is divided into sections which follow the topics of the chapters in this book. In addition, a section is included on financing and managing a research project.

3.1.2   The Survey of Tenants in Public Housing

The genesis of this study was a number of policy questions which were of interest to a Local Authority in South-East England. The funder specified a survey of public housing tenants. The research had to be completed quickly so that the results could be fed into their policy and planning cycle. This single piece of research had several objectives: the policy objectives specified by the Local Authority, and some sociological research questions on the housing mobility of council tenants and their children which resulted in a number of academic publications (Savage, Watt and Arber, 1990a, 1990b, 1991).

Figure 3.1 shows the timetable for the whole project. The Local Authority required an Interim Report within five months of the start date in order to fit into its planning cycle, and the Final Report was required two months later. To keep to this tight time schedule, each stage of the research had to be planned in advance. The planning involved specifying not only the timing of each stage, but also the required resources and costs of each element of the research (see section 3.9). Contract research is competitive. The University of Surrey and several market and social research companies were invited to tender for this Local Authority funded study, which required making an oral presentation, writing a detailed research proposal and preparing costings in advance.

The aim of the survey as specified by the Local Authority was to examine the satisfaction of public housing tenants with a range of services, including the repairs service, a newly introduced scheme to encourage residents' associations and tenant participation, and a new tenants' magazine. The Authority was interested in tenants' preferences about improvements such as central heating and replacement windows, and whether tenants would opt for a private landlord rather than remaining with the Local Authority, a possibility opened up by the 1988 Housing Bill. A representative sample survey was the most appropriate research strategy for these objectives, since it would provide accurate estimates of the views of all tenants in this Local Authority area. In addition, our own sociological goals were adequately met using a survey approach, for example, to test the hypothesis that mobility out of public sector housing was associated with labour market position.

3.2   Conceptualising the issues

Research topics may come from personal interests or experiences, from previous reading in sociology or related disciplines, from musing in the bath, be defined in advance by a sponsor, suggested by a supervisor, or from a combination of sources. Whatever the origin, your first task, prior to writing a research proposal, is to search the literature in the area of interest. This may stimulate ideas which had not occurred to you, assist in the formulation of the specific research questions to be investigated, and help you devise a theoretical or analytical framework (Bell, 1987; Gash, 1989). There is often a temptation to keep reading, rather than progressing to the next stage of research. You will need to consult your planned timetable and be ruthless about curtailing your literature review, at least for the time being.

It is usually worthwhile using volumes of Abstracts, such as *Social Science Abstracts*, which provide summaries of books and articles, and can save weeks of effort. Another way of facilitating a literature review is to conduct a computer-assisted catalogue search using words or combinations of keywords, to identify titles or article abstracts. This is often costly, with the cost being directly proportional to the number of references identified, but costs are decreasing as online bibliographic and social science abstracts are increasingly held on CD-ROM and accessible with a microcomputer.

Research should be cumulative, building on the work of others. A number of studies of housing satisfaction had already been conducted by Local Authorities. An early priority was therefore to find out about comparable work in progress or recently completed, contact the researchers, and obtain copies of their questionnaires. In this way, we learnt from the work of others, their experiences of what went well and what they would have done differently. There is nothing wrong with using questions from another survey where appropriate. In our case it allowed the possibility of comparing findings from different areas of the country, and one Local Authority of a particular political persuasion with Local Authorities of a different political hue.

Relevant papers and memoranda were obtained from the Local Authority, to provide an understanding of how it had interpreted central government policies in recent years, particularly the policy initiated by Mrs Thatcher to encourage tenants to buy their homes. Information was obtained on the sale of Local Authority housing stock, showing that this had occurred disproportionately in certain areas, a matter of concern to the Local Authority.

Government and official publications can provide relevant background information. Bulmer (1980) discusses the under use of official statistics in sociological research and outlines their value. We used data from the 1981 Population Census (OPCS, 1984) to provide information on the socio-economic and housing characteristics of the population in the Local Authority area. We found that the area was the most expensive housing market outside London in 1985 (Owen and Green, 1989), and a rapidly growing local labour market (Champion and Green, 1985). There were skill shortages in the area, especially of clerical and skilled manual labour, groups which traditionally have been housed in Local Authority tenancies.

From our analysis of documentary sources, official statistics and the existing sociological literature, we derived a number of sociological hypotheses which could be explored with data from this policy oriented survey. The main theoretical issue we chose to pursue was the housing mobility of tenants in public housing, that is, the pattern of moves between different sectors of the housing market (owner occupation, public housing and private renting). We wanted to examine whether the adult children of tenants tended to be restricted to public housing because they were unable to break into owner occupation in a high cost housing area. Social mobility is a mainstay of sociology, with numerous studies of the relationship between the occupation of fathers and the occupational achievement of their adult children (e.g. Goldthorpe, 1980; Heath, 1981; Payne, 1987), yet there is no comparable work on intergenerational housing mobility. In addition, housing mobility provides a critical test of consumption sector cleavage theory as proposed by Saunders (1984, 1986, 1990). He argues that divisions arising out of consumption of goods and services, especially housing, are key factors affecting political allegiances and other areas of life. To sustain his argument, it would be necessary to show that housing divisions are not the simple by-product of social class. The relationship between housing mobility and position in the labour market had hitherto not been the subject of survey research.

To examine housing mobility required the introduction of two new sets of questions. First, a set on the housing history of the tenant: when they first entered Local Authority tenure, their previous tenure, and their housing tenure at age 14. These questions were asked about each adult in the household. Second, a set of questions about the housing history of each adult child who had left home.

3.3 Gaining access

Gaining access requires detailed planning and may take several months of preparatory work to achieve, especially if access is required to organisations such as hospitals or to an institutional setting. Gaining access includes a number of discrete issues (see chapter 4). First, access to a group of research subjects or a setting may require extensive negotiation and the permission of 'gatekeepers'. Second, cooperation from individual members of the study sample or the participants in a setting is required in order to maximise response, while ensuring informed consent. Third, access to documentary materials – for example, memoranda and committee minutes – which are not publicly available requires negotiation and permission. In the Public Housing survey, an additional access issue was the need to obtain permission to use the research data for our own sociological publications.

Access to the names and addresses of public housing tenants was provided by our sponsor, the Local Authority. However, it was still essential to prepare the ground to ensure the respondents' informed consent (see section 4.4.2). The Local Authority sent out letters in advance to each tenancy selected for the study, providing information about the research, stressing that it was an independent piece of work being undertaken by the University on behalf of the Local Authority, and reassuring respondents that all information would be treated entirely confidentially. Tenants were assured that they had the right to decline to take part in the research.

The Local Authority was concerned that tenants should not be misled in any way. Interviewers carried an official identity letter from the University that included their photograph and they were instructed to show this letter to respondents. Before beginning the interview, interviewers read an Introduction which reiterated many of the points made previously in the letter and reminded respondents that they did not need to answer any questions if they did not want to.

An issue relating to access was the researchers' rights to data collected in a survey which was financed entirely by the Local Authority for its own purposes. As academic researchers we would not have embarked on this research unless we were sure we could publish our academic findings. This was raised as an essential prerequisite at the initial meeting with the Local Authority and was written into the research contract, signed by the Local Authority and the University, using a form of words which was acceptable to both parties. This stipulation generated extensive discussions and held up the final signing of the contract. The contract required publications to have prior written consent from the Local Authority, but consent could only be withheld for specific reasons. In the event, no changes to publications have been required.

It is essential that researchers consider carefully all issues relating to access prior to embarking on a research study, and if necessary, include the researchers' publication rights in a written contract.

3.4   Designing samples

The purpose of sampling is usually to study a representative subsection of a precisely defined population in order to make inferences about the whole population (see chapter 5). In this research, the 'population' consisted of current tenancies in the Local Authority area. We had to decide how to select a sample from the population of approximately 9,000 tenancies in the Local Authority area and who to interview in the case of joint tenancies.

Where there was a sole tenant, it was clear who should be interviewed, but the decision was more difficult for a joint tenancy or where the tenant was married or living as married. One alternative was to interview both tenants (either separately or at the same time). This would have provided a fuller and more accurate picture of the views and characteristics of tenants, but was ruled out because of the higher interviewing costs and the likelihood that the response rate would have decreased if interviews with both parties were required.

Having decided on one interview per household, we could have interviewed whoever opened the door, but this would probably have biased the sample towards women. Or we could have specified interviews with the Head of Household, or the prime wage earner, but this would have biased the sample towards men. Because women and men are likely to be concerned about different types of issues, the most appropriate sample was one which included equal proportions of 'husbands' and 'wives'. To achieve this, we required interviewers to obtain equal numbers of interviews with 'husbands' and 'wives' in their area. For example, if an interviewer's area covered 25 tenancies, and nine were sole tenants, the interviewer had to divide the remaining 16 between eight 'husbands' and eight 'wives'. This procedure worked as planned and allowed interviewers the maximum discretion in conducting their interviews.

The 'sampling frame' was an up-to-date list of current tenancies in the Local Authority area, listed by house number within street. The sponsors wanted separate results for tenancies in different parts of the area, for example, in rural areas and in some smaller estates which had recently undergone a house modernisation programme. There were also some very big estates which were quite homogeneous in the characteristics of their tenants. Since reliable results were required about the views of tenants living on different estates, and the estates were of varying size, we proposed a 'disproportionate stratified sample' (Moser and Kalton, 1971). The whole area was divided into three sections or strata, which were assigned varying probabilities of selection: tenancies in the rural areas and some estates of particular interest had a one in three chance of selection, those in town estates had a one in six chance of selection, and those in the very big estates had a one in nine chance of selection. This yielded a selected sample of 1,225 tenancies. We assumed that we would achieve interviews with 80 per cent of the selected tenancies, which would thus produce the desired sample size of 1,000.

3.5 Designing questionnaires

Before starting work developing a questionnaire, the researcher should decide on its approximate length and the nature of the questions. Large scale surveys generally require identical question wording for each respondent so that results are reliable and so that comparable information is obtained from each respondent, facilitating data entry and statistical analysis.

Survey questionnaires can include any of three broad types of questions: 'closed' questions, where the respondent selects a response from a set of alternative answers; 'open' questions, which allow the respondents to give whatever answer they like with the response either written down verbatim or tape-recorded; and 'pre-coded' or 'field coded' questions, where the respondents give whatever answer they like and the interviewer codes their answer into one of a number of response categories provided on the interview schedule (see chapter 6).

Open questions in a survey require subsequent coding 'in the office' after the interview is complete, a process known as post-coding. The costs of this coding and the time it takes need to be considered when designing the questionnaire. It was decided that the interview schedule would be mainly pre-coded, with a minimum of questions requiring post-coding.

The first step in designing a structured survey interview is to conduct tape-recorded qualitative interviews. This may include discussions (focus groups) with groups of six to eight people drawn from the population under study (see chapter 8). Such preliminary qualitative research helps to clarify the researcher's conceptual framework, identifies issues which are import-ant to the respondent but which the researcher might not have considered, and indicates the vocabulary respondents use to talk about their situation. These issues are discussed in chapters 6 and 8. The short timescale of the public housing survey meant that this stage of qualitative development work had to be brief.

The process of designing questions to measure the concepts under study was one of gradual development, partly by 'trial and error'. Questions were drafted to cover the issues identified by the Local Authority, for example, a section on the repairs service. Our first version of this section asked about the three most recent repairs undertaken by the Local Authority and, for each repair, about how the repair was reported, the response of the repairs staff, how quickly the work was done, the quality of the workmanship, and so on. Because during development work we realised that asking about three repairs was very time consuming and most respondents had had a similar experience for each repair, we decided only to ask detailed questions about the last repair. The questions also needed to be re-formulated to take into account respondents who had not had any repairs, and the concern expressed by many tenants that they were given very short notice of the date on which a repair would be done.

The interview schedule was then piloted on tenants who were not in the sample. These pilot interviews provided invaluable insights for altering question wording, adding questions about issues which were of particular concern to respondents but which we had not thought of, omitting or changing questions, and altering the order of questions to provide a more logical flow. This gradual process of questionnaire development is made easier by using a word processor to draft the document, since questions can be easily modified and moved about to produce a more coherent order.

It is important that the researchers themselves undertake pilot work because only they fully understand the concepts which the questions are intended to measure. In an ideal world, the interview schedule should be completed and then a pilot study of, say, 50 interviews conducted, but time constraints in this research were such that we considered it more important to use the available time to continue refining the questionnaire.

In this research, the sponsor had to approve the final questionnaire. We were surprised that all the questions were accepted without amendment, but the sponsor wished to add about ten additional questions. These were difficult to accommodate at this late stage, because they added to the length of an already over-long questionnaire, and there was insufficient time to do further piloting or to ascertain their most appropriate position. In the event, these additional questions did not produce data as reliable and valid as those which were fully piloted.

Qu. 23. Could you tell me if you strongly agree, agree, disagree or strongly disagree with the following statements about life on your estate / in your local area.

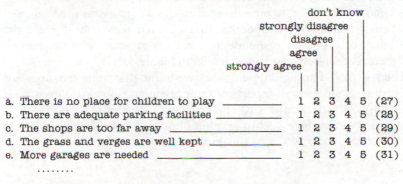

		strongly agree	agree	disagree	strongly disagree	don't know	
a.	There is no place for children to play _____	1	2	3	4	5	(27)
b.	There are adequate parking facilities _____	1	2	3	4	5	(28)
c.	The shops are too far away _____	1	2	3	4	5	(29)
d.	The grass and verges are well kept _____	1	2	3	4	5	(30)
e.	More garages are needed _____	1	2	3	4	5	(31)

....

Qu. 35. What are the 3 best things about your house/flat?
    (probe for up to 3 things)

	(63–4) 1st	(65–6) 2nd	(67–8) 3rd
Nothing at all/nothing else _____	00	00	00
Size or layout of house/flat; number/size of rooms _	01	01	01
Good quality house/flat; structurally sound _____	02	02	02
Good location of property; good lookout _____	03	03	03
Floor level of flat; position in terrace _____	04	04	04
Property looks nice from outside _____	05	05	05
Garden – appropriate size; layout; soil _____	06	06	06
Central heating; warm; good heat insulation _____	07	07	07
Good size kitchen; good layout of kitchen _____	08	08	08
Good living room/big enough to eat in _____	09	09	09
Good bathroom/toilet _____	10	10	10
Nice area/estate; good upkeep of estate _____	11	11	11
Quiet/peaceful area _____	12	12	12
Near to shops/other amenities _____	13	13	13
Familiar; lived here a long time; it's home _____	14	14	14
Good contact with Council; Council good landlord _	15	15	15
Good sound insulation; good partition walls _____	16	16	16
Likes neighbours; friendly neighbours _____	17	17	17
Other (specify)	18	18	18
....			
No Response _____	99	99	99

Figure 3.2   *Examples of questions and coding on Public Housing Tenants Survey*

3.6   Measuring attitudes

Attitudes were measured using a number of different measurement strategies. One was the Likert scale, where the respondents say whether they 'strongly agree, agree, disagree or strongly disagree' with a series of statements, for example about the quality of services and facilities provided on the Local Authority estates. Respondents who said that they did not know were coded into a fifth category (see question 23 in Figure 3.2). In other questions, respondents were asked whether they considered certain aspects of their housing were 'very important, important or not important'. Attitude scaling is discussed in chapter 7.

A second strategy used in measuring attitudes was to assess the 'salience' of particular issues for respondents, that is, what they considered most important. For example, respondents were asked what they most liked about their present home (see question 35 in Figure 3.2). Up to three items could be specified. During the pilot work we found that some tenants were entirely dissatisfied with all aspects of their home and gave responses such as 'It should be knocked down' and 'nothing' – code 00 in Figure 3.2. Likert scales cannot give such a graphic illustration of the priorities and concerns of respondents as can this kind of field coded question.

3.7   Interviewing and managing interviewers

The public housing survey aimed to achieve 1,000 interviews each lasting about an hour and a quarter. Interviews had to be completed within a six week time period (see Figure 3.1), so it was necessary to recruit and train a large number of interviewers. Forty interviewers were recruited on the assumption that the average interviewer would complete 25 interviews, although some might do substantially less and others more.

Interviewers were recruited from various sources, including Masters students, older undergraduate students, interviewers who had worked for other departments in the University, and people responding to advertisements in the local paper. Interviewer briefing notes were prepared which provided detailed information about the survey, specific information about individual questions, and practical information including the amount and method of payment of interviewers and their travelling expenses.

A two-day training programme was held for interviewers. The objectives of the research were described and it was explained that the intention of the Local Authority was to make policy on the basis of the survey results. The interview schedule was discussed in detail, and the trainees then watched a mock interview with a public housing tenant. The method of sampling was explained, including the requirement to interview equal numbers of 'husbands' and 'wives' in each interviewer area. Administrative arrangements and the methods to be used in filling in interview record sheets were outlined. Finally, each interviewer had an opportunity to run through an interview and raise queries.

An aspect of the interview process which required detailed discussion was the use of **random probes** (Schuman, 1966). In each interview, six questions were identified for a random probe, the interviewer writing down exactly what the respondent said and then questioning them further to obtain more detail about their responses. Random probes provide a check on the validity of questions, and yield a representative sample of verbatim comments which can be used as illustrative quotations when writing up the research. Random probes are particularly useful in structured surveys because they provide illustrative material about what underlies respondents' views. Since each interview schedule only had random probes on six questions, the length of interview was only extended by a few minutes. The six questions were chosen to provide a representative sample of verbatim comments from 50 respondents for each question on the interview schedule.

The interviewers then each conducted one or two interviews which were checked by the researchers to ensure that the training had been successful. Completed interviews were returned in batches of six to ten, and were checked thoroughly by one of the researchers within a day or two of receipt. This process of editing was to identify and correct interviewer errors and made sure that 'not applicable' codes were correctly indicated. If queries could not be resolved, the interviewer was contacted by telephone, and if necessary encouraged to check back with the respondent either by telephone or in person to correct the response. Editing is a time consuming process but essential in the production of reliable and valid data. Through a process of thorough editing and providing feedback, interviewers were made aware that high quality work was expected.

Interviewers were provided with a coversheet for each sample address to record the name and address of the tenant and to mark the outcome of each visit. In many cases, the interviewer made an appointment to return at a time which was more convenient for the respondent. If the respondent was not in, the interviewer was encouraged to call back on at least four occasions at different times of the day.

Most of the interviews were completed within the planned six week period. Areas where potential interviews remained were reallocated to more experienced interviewers and completed within the following two weeks. Interviews were achieved in 83 per cent of the selected sample of tenancies; this was a higher response rate than originally anticipated.

3.8   Coding and managing data

In surveys which are mainly pre-coded, decisions about coding and the allocation of numerical codes for computer data entry have to be made prior to finalising the interview schedule. Coding categories are assigned in parallel with the development of closed and pre-coded questions. For pre-coded questions, a full range of possible answers must be obtained during the pilot work. These are listed on the interview schedule and the interviewer field codes the answer given by the respondent into the appropriate category (see question 35 in Figure 3.2).

Once the questions have been finalised and the order agreed, it is necessary to add column numbers to the questionnaire (see in chapter 11). These are so that information from each question is always stored in the corresponding position in the computer data file. Providing column numbers next to the answer categories for each question (these are shown in brackets in Figure 3.2) facilitates accurate data entry.

Some respondents gave answers which did not fit into the categories on the interview schedule. When a number of respondents gave the same additional answer, these were recoded from the 'other' category into new codes. It is desirable not to create too many additional codes at this stage; the ideal is to identify the full range of possible responses during pilot work and include them on the actual survey questionnaire.

In this survey, the occupational data required post-coding. Occupational descriptions of each adult in the household and the adult children who had left home were coded into the Registrar General's 16 Socio-Economic Groups (SEG) using the 1980 Classification of Occupations (OPCS, 1980). Occupational coding was made easier by constructing a shortened coding sheet listing the most common occupations with their SEG codes.

The only other information coded after the interview was details of the most recent repair requested. Two separate coding frames were developed from the replies to the first 50 interviews. The first classified repairs by type and the second coded the urgency of the repair.

Data from the interview schedule were entirely coded as numbers and entered on to the computer. Since over 600 characters of information were keyed in for each interview, the data file for the complete survey contained over 600,000 characters. Data entry is a skilled and time consuming job which is best left to professionals. This aspect of the research may need separate costing – the charge is usually specified per 1,000 key strokes. It is also important to be aware how long data entry is likely to take and to plan for this in the time schedule.

The survey researcher must decide what statistical package to use for analysing the data. The decision will be influenced by the complexity of the data and the nature of the proposed analyses (see chapters 12 and 13). For a relatively straightforward survey, the most popular choice is SPSS (Statistical Package for the Social Sciences). Both the mainframe version and PC version were used for this research. SPSS/PC has the advantage of being able to run on the researcher's own personal computer, which made the later stages of writing up the survey much easier.

The SPSS system file, which names and labels all the variables and assigns missing value codes, should be prepared prior to completion of data entry. This file can be tested in advance on a small subset of the data. Once most of the data have been entered, initial distributions for each variable can be prepared and carefully checked for responses that are out of range. This aspect of the editing process is often referred to as data cleaning. Any errors identified are printed out together with the respondent's Identification Number (see chapter 11), and the original interview schedule rechecked to ascertain the correct response. Editing checks can also be performed by cross-tabulating variables and checking that there are no impossible combinations of values.

The final few interviews were added to the data file once the initial analyses had begun, and so these had to be rerun. Interviewing stopped when we had achieved 1,038 interviews.

3.9   Budgeting and managing a research project

Research of whatever scale needs careful attention to resources and budgeting. Even when working on your own, it is useful to estimate the likely amount of time which will be spent on each stage of the research. For example, if 30 focused interviews are proposed, each lasting approximately an hour, the interviewing alone will take at least 60 hours, or two working weeks, since there will be travelling time to get to the interview and time spent before and afterwards 'chatting' to the respondent. This will be an underestimate if you have to spend time making appointments and perhaps travelling long distances. If you want to prepare transcripts from tape-recorded interviews, a good guide is that it takes eight hours to transcribe a one hour tape in full. This would be 240 hours (30 × 8) devoted to transcribing – six week's work.

You also need to plan how much time to set aside in the early stages for negotiating access, developing a sampling frame, selecting the sample, and initial bibliographic work. Undoubtedly the longest stage of any project will be analysing the data and writing up the research. You should plan for a minimum of one third of the time on analysing data and writing up, and it more usually takes closer to half the time.

It is also necessary to estimate in advance the direct costs of the research as well as the indirect costs in terms of time and other opportunities forgone. There may be direct costs in travelling to consult specific libraries or collections of bibliographic material, costs of travelling to conduct interviews, costs of printing questionnaires, and postage for self-completion questionnaires. The Project Director of larger scale research must carefully cost the salaries of the staff and each element of the budget in order to write a research proposal for funding or to respond to a sponsor's research brief. If an underestimate is made in any element of the proposed costing, it is usually impossible to seek further funds later, and the whole project may be in jeopardy, take longer than planned, or fail to meet the original objectives. Costing a research proposal is therefore an important stage in any research.

Detailed work on budgeting needs to go hand in hand with the development of the timetable. Figure 3.3 provides an illustration of the

Staff costs	£(1988)
Research Officer	6,600
Full-time for six months (including National Insurance and superannuation)	
Administrative Officer	3,400
Full-time for four months (including National Insurance)	
Ad hoc Research Officer support	1,200
200 hours at £6 per hour	
Ad hoc Coding and clerical support	400
100 hours at £4 per hour	
Interviewing	12,000
1,000 interviews at £12 per interview	
Interviewer Training	1,600
40 interviewers at £40 each	
Total staff costs	£25,200

Other Direct Costs	
Interviewers' travelling expenses	2,000
1,000 interviews at an average of 10 miles each at 20p per mile	
Researchers' travelling expenses	100
Printing Interview Schedules	1,200
1,200 schedules, each 44 pages	
Data entry	1,000
1,000 completed interviews, with 600 characters per interview	
Photocopying	500
20,000 sheets at 5p per sheet	
Total other direct costs	£4,800
Contingency for miscellaneous costs	£500
Grand total of costs	£30,500

Costs borne by the University and covered by Overhead Charge
  Use of mainframe and microcomputers and associated software
  Use of Library and other University services, e.g. payroll, cashiers office.
  Use of laser printer
  Stationery, postage and telephones
  Meeting rooms for Interviewer Training
  Large Room dedicated for use as the Survey Office for three months.

Figure 3.3 *Estimated costings for Public Housing Tenants Survey, 1988*

costing of the public housing survey in 1988 prices. At the bottom of the figure there is a list of the resources which were provided by the University as part of the overhead charged as an additional percentage cost on all externally funded research contracts. This overhead levy is likely to be at least 40 per cent of staff costs.

The research involved a substantial commitment of the Project Directors' time. They worked nearly full-time on the study for three months and part-time for several months afterwards. These indirect costs are not included in Figure 3.3. A full-time Research Officer was involved in all stages of the research from initial design work and piloting through to analysis and writing the reports for the Local Authority. An Administrative Officer worked full-time for three months during the main period of the survey. She was based in the survey office and was responsible for liaising with interviewers, organising their payment, checking in interviews, coding, and entering the verbatim comments collected from the random probes into a database. Ideally, the people involved in a large research study should have complementary rather than identical skills.

There are two alternative methods of paying interviewers: either by the hour or by the interview. For casual employment, such as interviewing on a one-off survey, it is generally preferable to pay by the interview, providing the researcher can be assured that the quality of work achieved is of a high standard and interviewers are not cutting corners in their interviews or, worse, making up their interviews. Roth (1966) provides a salutary account of the possible ways in which 'hired hands', such as interviewers, can cheat or make up their data. The use of random probes is a good way of checking on interviewers, since they usually produce very unexpected and 'unique' answers. Thorough checking of each interview on receipt also helps maintain quality. In cases of doubt, the researcher returned to the house where an interview was conducted and re-asked some questions from the interview.

The main advantage of payment by completed interview is that the researcher has complete control over the expenditure on interviewing. In this research, interviewers were paid £12 per interview, which meant that total interview costs were budgeted at £12,000 and the final sum was close to this figure.

Interviewers had to attend a two-day training course for which they were paid £40. However, the payment was not made until they had satisfactorily completed five interviews. For novice interviewers, this was an incentive to complete the first few interviews, which are often a nerve-racking experience. Once some interviews have been successfully accomplished, most interviewers gain confidence and continue without any problem.

In this research, some items of expenditure were not estimated correctly. Travelling expenses were over 50 per cent higher than projected, and less than expected was spent on clerical support. Overall, the project at the end was in balance, but it is always worth including an item in the budget for unforeseen contingencies.

3.10 Writing up the research

The most important part of any research project is not collecting data, but publishing it in a form which will transmit the research results to interested parties. Many student projects, as well as funded research, suffer from setting aside too little time for the final stage of writing up the research. It is relatively easy to write up the factual results of a project. In the public housing study, the sponsors wanted basic distributions for each variable and some two-variable tables, with a minimum of analytic comment. The reports for the sponsor, composed mainly of descriptive 'facts', were therefore written relatively quickly.

A social scientific or academic report, whether for a student thesis or for a journal article, involves a very different kind of writing. In the forefront is not description but conceptually informed analysis. However, such analysis cannot usually be started until you are thoroughly familiar with your data. So an initial stage of exploring the data needs to be undertaken as a means to an end, rather than an end in itself. Students writing their undergraduate and postgraduate theses often produce a first draft which is essentially a description of the data. It is then necessary to stand back and identify the conceptual issues which will be explored more rigorously and in a theoretically informed way in the final report. Only a proportion of the data collected will be included in academic reports or publications. It is important to restrict an academic paper, or a chapter in a thesis, to one essential idea and explore that in depth rather than trying to skate over too many issues without doing justice to any of them. These issues are discussed further in chapter 16.

A social scientific paper or report must engage with academic debates. The first academic paper written on the public housing project addressed the issue of whether consumption sector cleavages manifested by differences in housing tenure represent a clear axis of division in the ways suggested by Saunders (1984, 1986, 1990). The paper demonstrated that this was not the case (Savage, Watt and Arber, 1990a). A more descriptive account of the housing survey data, which included background information about methods, was published as an Occasional Paper (Savage, Watt, Arber, 1990b). Figure 3.1 shows that these academic publications came out some time after the final report to the sponsors.

A good stimulus for writing academic papers (for this author at least) is to offer to give an oral presentation, for example at a conference. Presenting ideas to an audience forces the researcher to clarify the key findings and present them in a clear and logical way. Essentially the same is required for a written paper, except a much fuller theoretical and conceptual grounding for the research and a more detailed discussion of the data and analysis is needed. For example, we offered to give a paper at the 1990 British Sociological Association annual conference, and an extended version was subsequently published in a volume of papers (Savage, Watt and Arber, 1991). This paper specifically addressed the housing mobility of public housing tenants' adult children, showing that it is the adult child's occupational class that is the prime determinant of becoming an owner occupier. There is little evidence of a barrier to ownership resulting from spending childhood years in public housing.

3.11 Conclusion

This research on public housing tenants was undertaken for external sponsors who required a tight timetable to allow the results to be fed into their planning cycle. This forced us to work to a closely defined plan for the various stages of the research. By specifying this timetable in advance, we were able to monitor progress and make adjustments as necessary. Research studies, of whatever scale, benefit from clear planning, a realistic timetable and frequent reassessment of progress against plans.

3.12 Project

Write a proposal for a research project which would take a single researcher a maximum of six months. You may like to defer the completion of this project until you have read up to chapter 10 in this book. In drawing up your proposal the following notes may be helpful.

1. The proposal should begin with a summary of your aims and objectives, stating clearly what you hope to accomplish by undertaking the research. You should locate the problem within existing theoretical and empirical research.
2. Choose whatever methods seem most appropriate for your research problem. You should specify your proposed methods in some detail and indicate their relationship to the objectives stated in (1). If quantitative methods are to be used, you should include details of the design of the research, the size of the sample, and the sampling frame. If any special difficulties or problems are likely to arise, such as selecting the right kind of people for a sample or gaining access to a research setting, you should discuss these problems and say how you hope to approach and resolve them.
3. Provide an outline timetable which indicates the length of time to be devoted to each stage of the research.
4. No details of the desired budget or likely costs of the research are required in the proposal.
5. Provide an alphabetical list of the references to the publications to which you have referred in your proposal.

3.13 Further reading

Bell and Newby (1977) is a sociological classic which provides eight personal accounts of the research process from researchers who look back on their role in major studies.

Bell and Roberts (1984) offers personal accounts of real research and its problems. A number of authors focus on how the political and financial context influences the research process. These accounts are not only often more instructive but also a good deal more readable than many methods texts.

Bell (1987) uses educational research as examples, providing a clear guide about how to do relatively small-scale projects which can be completed in two to three months. It contains useful chapters on literature searching and note taking.

Forcese and Richer (1970) is an early set of readings which contains many of the classics in research methodology. It goes beyond the blithe and often idealised descriptions of the way research should be carried out, illustrating how to proceed and pointing to the pitfalls along the way. It is organised around the various stages of a research project.

Howard and Sharp (1983) provide a very clear account of how to plan a research study, and is particularly helpful for Masters and PhD students. The range of problems faced by students at each stage of their research is outlined and solutions suggested.

Mason (1989) was produced by the Office of Population Censuses and Surveys as a survey manual. It provides clear guidance and many examples of the materials used in each stage of designing and managing a survey.

Roberts (1981) is an antidote to Bell and Newby (1977), which contained no contributions from women and no awareness of feminist sociology. It provides an excellent set of personal accounts of research, mainly by women, and some now classic articles on feminist methodology.

PART I

Beginnings

4   Gaining access

Michael Hornsby-Smith

Contents

This chapter will consider the problems of gaining access to informants and respondents and to other sources of data in the social research process. Two broad types of factors are relevant. The first is the openness of access, which relates to questions of the power of those being studied to exclude intrusive inquiry, and the overtness or covertness of the research methods being employed. For the researcher there are particular problems with the defensive capabilities of powerful elites and institutions when 'studying up' and of negotiating with gatekeepers and sponsors. Different problems arise when 'studying down' and researching weak non-elites or vulnerable minority groups. Second, questions of research ethics arise over the types of research methods to be employed. Chief among these is the debate about overt and covert styles of research and the extent to which researchers should seek informed consent from their subjects. Other issues which must be addressed are assurances of confidentiality and anonymity and the rights of individuals and institutions.

	Nature of access	
Research methods	Closed	Open
Overt	e.g. powerful elites	e.g. vulnerable minorities
Covert	e.g. deviant groups	e.g. religious groups

Figure 4.1 *A framework for the consideration of access in research*

4.1 A framework for analysis

In order to research social life and collect data for subsequent analysis and interpretation, it is first necessary to gain access to sources of data. These may be respondents or informants or material sources such as historical documents. They all vary in their accessibility to the inquisitive researcher. Some may be closely protected by the administration of forms of official secrecy or by gatekeepers who safeguard the privacy of powerful people or institutions. Others may be relatively accessible and entirely open to contact from outsiders. In other words there is a huge variety of research situations, each with its own particular problems of access to the researcher.

In seeking access the researcher has to decide whether or not to inform the subjects of the research about his or her role and about the particular focus of the proposed investigation. In other words, are overt or covert methods of investigation to be used? Of course, in a real research situation this distinction may become blurred but for the purposes of outlining some of the problems which will be faced by the researcher even before sampling and data collection, it is useful to consider problems of access in terms of the two factors: the openness of access and the overtness or covertness of the proposed research methods. These alternatives are summarised in Figure 4.1 which also indicates typical cases in each of the four cells.

4.2 Negotiating closed access

Let us consider first how to make relevant research contacts in the case of 'closed access' groups able to erect discouraging barriers against the intrusive outsider or, in some other way, to achieve invisibility and evade detection. Joan Cassell has described a two-stage process of penetrating a closed access group (1988: 93–5): getting in (achieving physical access), and getting on (achieving social access).

She describes the difficulties she experienced in negotiations lasting well over a year in gaining access for a study of surgeons in the United States. In the end, and seemingly rather fortuitously, a chief surgeon friend of her ex-husband (who was a doctor) allowed her physical access. She then had the difficult task of negotiating social access. Hardened by her struggle, she advises that

> among the characteristics needed to penetrate a closed access group are brute persistence and blind compulsivity. One has to keep pushing, and trying, and hoping, and smiling, and pushing some more. For this, a researcher needs a thick skin and a certain imperviousness to rejection. (Cassell, 1988: 94–5)

Nobody said that social research is easy! Once having penetrated a closed group, the researcher requires considerable social sensitivity and charm:

> One must fit in, if that seems to be called for; not fit in, if it seems inappropriate. One must dress acceptably, speak acceptably . . . The fieldworker . . . should adopt a role or identity that meshes with the values and behaviour of the group being studied, without seriously compromising the researcher's own values and behaviour. (Cassell, 1988: 96–7)

A similar indication of the need for persistence and some good fortune in gaining access in closed situations is given by Stephen Wood in a study of redundancy. In his attempt to explain why three firms allowed him access, although large numbers of others had turned him down, he dismisses a simple exchange theory which assumes that the researcher has something to offer the firm in exchange for the opportunity to undertake research. Whatever validity this model might have, some 'kind of "contingency" approach to the entry problem' (Wood, n.d.) which recognises that a large number of factors may be relevant is necessary.

In a comprehensive overview of 'the politics of distrust', Lee (1992) points out that for some closed groups research may be ideologically anathema. Others see research as a threat because of the repercussions it might have inside the research setting, it disrupts operational routines, there are fears of exploitation or it may result in damaging disclosures (e.g. of illegal activities). One way of countering these fears is by acquiring an appropriate sponsor who acts as a 'bridge', 'guide' and 'patron' with the group to be researched. 'Doc', the leader of the Norton street gang in 'Cornerville' in the late 1930s, is the classic exemplar (Whyte, 1955). Not infrequently access is conditional on a battery of both formal controls (such as surveillance of the researcher and limits on the subsequent publication of the findings) and informal controls (where access is impeded by obfuscation or deception). Lee, therefore, refers to 'access careers', stressing the point that gaining access is a process of continual renegotiation, bargaining, and establishing trustful relations with gatekeepers and those to be studied (Lee and Renzetti, 1990; Lee, 1992). Thus Johnson (1976: 77) stresses the need for a multistage 'progressive entree' strategy which 'attempts to achieve access to the setting while minimizing premature closure of the research project'. Gaining access is a political rather than a normative problem so that 'playing it by ear' is an inevitable component of the negotiations, with the researcher frequently having to make instant decisions and think on his or her feet.

4.2.1 Overt studies in cases of closed access

A large proportion of empirical research has been done on relatively powerless groups: 'sociology is done *on* the relatively powerless *for* the relatively powerful' (Bell, 1978: 25, emphases in original). It is far more difficult to study powerful individuals and bureaucracies because 'people in power have more reason for obscuring the truth than others' (Encel, 1978: 47). However, as Bell notes: 'sociology that "studies up" often won't be seen as scientific – funds will be difficult to obtain, sampling frames nonexistent, access (unlike the working class) well-nigh impossible and so on' (1978: 29). Broadly speaking, elites and powerful people and institutions are frequently able to deny access because they do not wish themselves or their decision-making processes to be studied, it is inconvenient, they are busy and wish to assert their rights to privacy, and so on. Yet the social researcher concerned to understand the politics of everyday life or to enhance the citizen's 'right to know' about, for example, the workings of major military academies (Spencer, 1973), must seek ways of achieving access to powerful groups. Despite the fact that there are well documented cases where access has not been achieved, such as the attempt to study long-term prisoners in a maximum security wing of Durham prison (Cohen and Taylor, 1977), perhaps surprisingly, limited access has been achieved by overt means by a number of researchers.

In their study of Anglican bishops, Medhurst and Moyser (1987) found that achieving access was relatively straightforward because they had previously published in Church journals, had been given personal recommendations by academic theologians and had legitimising funding from the British Social Science Research Council, because they were both active in orthodox Christian communities, and because of the novelty of their project.

Other researchers have not found it so easy. Form (1973) reported a wide variety of experiences in studies of industrial relations in several different countries. In some cases distrust among the different parties (management and several trade unions) was so ubiquitous that bargaining about access took a considerable time. His experiences led him to suggest a bargaining political exchange model for achieving access and to identify a large number of issues over which the researchers had to bargain at different levels of the organisations and with different and sometimes antagonistic factions. In organisations characterised by internal conflict, weaker factions may be more easily approached because they wish to avoid giving stronger factions credibility. Where informant cooperation is necessary, high status researchers and influential sponsors are helpful.

Two British studies of company directors are instructive about the task of negotiating access. Winkler (1987) reports that it took a full year of a three-year project to negotiate access to executive directors in their everyday working lives in 19 companies out of more than 130 with whom the proposed project was discussed. In the 'extended face-to-face negotiations' which were necessary, he found that group discussions arranged under the prestigious umbrella of the Institute of Directors were most successful. Also effective were approaches using the indirect sponsorship of senior businessmen who introduced the researchers to their friends: 'Our discussions with them were always surrounded with conventional alcoholic and gastronomic bribery. Gaining access to elites can be expensive as well as arduous, but not without its diversions' (1987: 136)! In Winkler's judgement, those who participated in the research did so because they found it implicitly flattering, they saw it as a means of paying off their obligations to the sponsors, some managing directors saw it as a means of providing intellectual stimulus to their boards, and because they wished to see 'how they rated alongside the famous' (1987: 137).

In a study of British Steel Corporation directors, Brannen also stresses that 'the management of access is a political process' (1987: 167):

> The observer . . . has to enter the symbolic world of those he is to observe: he must learn their language, their customs, their work patterns, the way they eat and dress and make himself respectable. There is an initial period when he must understand what expectations are held of him and when he is taught how he can behave. But he also has to teach respondents so that he can carry out his observer role effectively. (Brannen, 1987: 169)

Other overt research in situations of relatively closed access have been reported by Wagstaffe and Moyser (1987) on the 'threatened elite', that is local community leaders suspicious of academics, unscrupulous intruders and 'do-gooders'. An example is the black community leaders in inner-city areas who fear the abuse of findings and manipulation. 'Ideally, one should cease to be a stranger.' In other words time must be spent forging links with the community, exploring how the proposed research can be 'mutually and reciprocally advantageous' to both the researcher and the respondents, developing personal contacts with community leaders, and so on, all in a situation of 'total frankness' (1987: 193–5). In his study of farmers and farmworkers in Suffolk, Newby (1977) achieved access through the district organiser of the National Union of Agricultural and Allied Workers who led him to his chief informant, a local branch secretary, 'Jack Hector' with whom he lodged during the course of his fieldwork. Newby refers to this arrangement as serendipitous and, like other researchers, stresses the importance of 'such strokes of fortune' in research (1977: 117).

In the United States, Klatch (1988) successfully carried out fieldwork with women of the American 'new right' although she held quite different political values. She warns of 'the dirtiness of real-life data' and describes how she learned to describe her interest in 'women active in the conservative movement' rather than the more derogatory 'right wing women'. She reports that her graduate student status granted her some legitimacy and she adopted a 'non-argumentative approach'. Finding common threads with respondents helped to build trust and she learned to interpret 'eye contact and non-verbal signals'. Even so, she found it a 'delicate balancing act between building trust and gaining acceptance while not misrepresenting (her) own position' (1988: 77–82).

Finally, a reference to the issue of the gender of the researcher is relevant. Pettigrew (1981), a young female anthropologist married to a Sikh, has described how her gender and its cultural significance in the Punjab constrained the access accorded to her in her study of rural factions and state-level political leaders. This is a timely reminder of the importance of ascriptive characteristics in limiting research possibilities. In another study, Hunt (1984) has described how her field work with police depended on her negotiation of her role as a 'streetwoman-researcher'. Corcoran suggested that being Irish and a woman was a distinct advantage to her in her study of illegal Irish workers in New York. As a woman, she

> could relate to the immigrants in a non-threatening way. A man in this situation would have had to overcome suspicions that he might be an immigration official or some kind of informer. I did not have such difficulties as my gender alone negated any residual doubts about my motives. (Corcoran, 1991: 63)

4.2.2   Covert studies in cases of closed access

One of the most difficult areas to study is that of sexual deviance. In a well-known study, Laud Humphreys has described in detail how he investigated male homosexual activity in public toilets.

> Like any deviant group, those engaging in homosexual activity have developed defences against outsiders: secrecy about their true identity, symbolic gestures and the use of eyes for communication, unwillingness to expose the whereabouts of their meeting places, extraordinary caution with strangers, and admission to certain places only in the company of a recognized person . . . I had to enter the subculture . . . under the guise of being another gay guy . . . [and] of making the contact 'stick'. (Humphreys, 1970: 24)

Humphreys first spent some time learning about the homosexual subculture, frequenting gay bars and attending after-hours parties, and found that it was possible to observe homosexual encounters by taking on the participant role of the 'voyeur-lookout' (1970: 27). By systematically recording the participants' car licence numbers and using archival data made available by friendly policemen, he was able to acquire the names and addresses, marital status and occupational data of most of the sample. A year later, having changed his appearance and car, he interviewed them as part of a wider social health survey of men in the community. Humphreys's work is a classic of its kind. Although he went to extraordinary lengths to safeguard the identities of his sample, the study raised a huge controversy among social scientists because of its covert and potentially damaging nature. These ethical considerations will be considered later in this chapter.

Another well-known example of covert participant observation in the case of relatively closed industrial organisations was that of Melvin Dalton in his study of managers in a range of industrial enterprises. He described his methods as 'a blend of open and covert tactics – open where I was sure of my ground, covert where I was uncertain of the obstacles and the time to act or where I feared defeat' (1964: 69–70). While 'helpful slips of the tongue' were useful spin-offs from his formal interviews, his interest in the interplay between formal and informal behaviour led him to

> seek the aid of experienced, reliable, and, as nearly as possible, representative intimates . . . expand my existing circle of intimates and to develop confidential exchanges with acquaintances. To this end, I gave every legitimate service and possible courtesy and went beyond what was normal in giving personal aid. From this group of personnel I selected, over a period of about three years, as *intimates* those who (1) trusted me; (2) freely gave me information about their problems and fears and frankly tried to explain their own motivations; (3) had shown repeatedly that they could be counted on not to jeopardize the study; (4) accepted what I was able to tell them and refrained from prying into the information I was getting from others; and (5) gave me knowledge and aid (warnings, guidance, 'tips') of a kind that, if known, would have endangered their careers. (Dalton, 1964: 65–6, emphasis in original)

For example, Dalton reported a 'tacit exchange of favors' with a secretary from whom he was able to obtain confidential information about managerial salaries in exchange for counselling about her interest in a specialist (whom she subsequently married) (1964: 66–7).

Covert methods of research have also been employed in studies of relatively closed political and religious organisations. Both Nigel Fielding (1981) and Roy Wallis (1976) pragmatically used combinations of overt and covert research methods. In his study of the political ideology of National Front members, Fielding combined the roles of 'sympathetic researcher' in his approaches to officials in the party headquarters, with that of 'potential convert' in his field work in a local branch and in a public demonstration, arguing that both methods produced 'useful but qualitatively different material' (1982: 84). Similarly Wallis carried out a (not very successful) questionnaire survey of those people on an out-of-date mailing list of a Scientology organisation which he had received from an informant in a chain sample; subsequently he was able to interview some of these respondents. Later, in response to a circular from the headquarters inviting people to take a first basic course in Scientology, he attended as 'an interested outsider'. Wallis reports that while he did not feel covert participant observation to be unethical in this context, he was, 'nevertheless, not prepared to lie about my interest in Scientology. I was only prepared to represent it less than fully'. When he realised that he would at an early stage be required to indicate his agreement with the claims of the founder, he felt this would be dishonest and quietly left the centre and terminated his covert research (1977: 152–5).

4.3 Researching situations of open access

In general, the greater the degree of openness, the easier it is for researchers to 'get in' and make contact with potential respondents. However, Cassell's (1988) distinction between physical and social access is important. Formally open institutions, such as some of the new religious movements, may become decidedly closed and react defensively, erecting barriers against what they perceive as external threats from hostile intruders. This seems to have been the experience of Wallis with the Scientologists, discussed previously.

Furthermore, it might be assumed that it is only the socially powerful elites who are able to maintain situations of closed access while relatively powerless non-elites do not have the resources to prevent open access. Such an assumption would be mistaken. Access to black minority groups would be relatively closed to white researchers (Johnson and Cross, 1984; Walton, 1986). Similarly, access to the street homeless and unemployed working class youths would be relatively closed to armchair academics and elderly researchers, respectively. None of these groups would ordinarily be considered to possess much social power but all of them would be able to resist social access. Many people wishing to evade the 'poll tax' are thought to have successfully avoided completion of the 1991 British census. In the case of radical feminist groups, both physical and social access would be difficult for the male researcher. In practice, therefore, the distinction between closed and open access, useful for analytical purposes, is often blurred and may change during the course of research.

In the following discussion, consideration will be given to cases of relatively open physical access though it must be understood that the achievement of social access still presents considerable problems to the researcher and still has to be negotiated carefully. As in the case of closed physical access, both overt and covert methods have been employed.

4.3.1 Overt studies in cases of open access

The case of overt research where there is relatively open access will be illustrated by reference to a study of Roman Catholics in four English parishes (Hornsby-Smith, 1987). Although there are no formal barriers to investigation, for historical reasons Roman Catholics have been defensive and suspicious of strangers. A first approach was therefore made to the parish priests concerned and the broad aims of a study of social and religious change among English Catholics was explained to them in face-to-face conversations. In each case they agreed to circulate an explanatory handout drafted by the researchers to all Sunday Mass attenders. They also agreed to announce at Mass that the researchers posed no threat to Catholics and that all data collected would be confidential and would not be seen by the priests.

Since Catholics are widely dispersed among the general population and no sampling frame for them exists, a two-stage research design was employed. Letters on university headed notepaper, to signify respectability, were sent to a systematic random sample of people on the electoral register informing them in broad outline of the nature of the study of social mobility and social attitudes, indicating that an interviewer would call shortly, inviting their cooperation, and assuring them of confidentiality. They were invited to telephone the university if they had any queries or worries. Interviewers carried identifying letters to reassure respondents; this was particularly necessary in an inner city area with considerable evidence of urban anomie in high rise flats. Catholics identified at this first stage were approached subsequently for a second and more focused interview specifically to investigate the nature of their religious identity, beliefs and practices. Response rates of 60 per cent at the first stage and 84 per cent at the second stage (Hornsby-Smith, 1987: 10–11) were regarded as good for this type of study.

In another situation of relatively open access, Mary Corcoran (1991: 45–64) worked as a waitress and used contacts cultivated in bars to gain access to Irish immigrants working illegally in New York. An Irish room-mate became a key informant and living in the area enhanced her credibility. She used her broadening circle of acquaintances to establish her role as a researcher and her informants introduced her to illegal workers whom she was later able to interview. Particularly helpful was the emergence of the Irish Immigration Reform Movement, a pressure group formed by immigrant activists. She introduced herself to them and through their regular meetings was brought into contact with a wider range of immigrants. She observed that the perception of her as an Irish person gave her insider status and facilitated unconditional access. In addition, as we noted previously, her gender meant that she was able to relate to immigrants in a non-threatening way.

Both examples illustrate the need to provide appropriate reassurance to defensive groups, even in situations of physically open access, before social access can be achieved.

4.3.2   Covert studies in cases of open access

The final category of studies relates to instances of open access where the researcher has decided, for whatever reason, to use covert methods. There are two well-known and controversial examples of research on religious groups which fall into this category. In *When Prophecy Fails* (1964), Festinger and two colleagues reported on a participant observation study they carried out opportunistically with two small groups who claimed to have received messages from a planet 'Clarion' predicting a catastrophic flood three months later. They and some hired observers joined the group as participants and carried out an intensive investigation both before the predicted disaster and afterwards during the period of disconfirmation.

In their Methodological Appendix they explain why they decided to undertake covert observation without the knowledge or consent of the group members. In their first contact with the key members of the group they found that 'their secrecy and general attitude toward nonbelievers made it clear that a study could not be conducted openly'. They therefore infiltrated the group with a variety of expressions of interest following a press report and 'tried to be nondirective, sympathetic listeners, passive participants who were inquisitive and eager to learn whatever others might want to tell us'. They aimed to establish themselves in the group sufficiently well before the predicted disaster 'so that we could safely proceed to ask relatively intimate questions of the various members'. In this case, it seems that the fact of joining the group convinced the leaders that they were sincere and gave them social access (Festinger et al., 1964: 234–5, 240). The problems faced by the researcher in this type of study, such as 'going native', have been well described in Alison Lurie's novel *Imaginary Friends* (1987).

An interesting English example is to be found in Roger Homan's study of the language which 'old-time' pentecostals used among themselves. Homan notes that 'whenever I presented myself as a stranger, I found, predictably, that I was treated as a subject for evangelism and addressed in the everyday language of the uninitiated' (Homan and Bulmer, 1982: 106). After three years of overt non-participant observation he realised that he would only be able to observe the internal language of pentecostals if he signalled that he understood it himself (Homan and Bulmer, 1982: 108). Like Festinger et al., his choice of covert methods was largely pragmatic though he felt sufficiently uncomfortable about it to defend his methods in detail (1980) and in dialogue with Martin Bulmer (Homan and Bulmer, 1982).

In *Investigative Social Research*, Jack Douglas (1976) gives one of the most robust defences of covert methods. Rejecting the cooperative classical paradigm of research as based unambiguously on truth-telling, openness and trust on the part of respondents, he proposes an investigative conflict paradigm which recognises the problems of misinformation, evasions, lies and fronts (1976: 57). The best way of coping with these problems is by direct experience. 'Building and using cooperative methods, especially friendly and trusting relations, is a major strategy of the general investigative paradigm' (1976: 133). Among the recommended tactics are those of opening up informants by 'phased assertion'. He illustrates his analysis with examples, which are frequently hilarious, taken from studies of massage parlors and nude beaches. Inevitably those who have used covert methods have been strongly crticised for what some see as unacceptable ethical behaviour. Such issues will be considered in the following sections of this chapter.

4.4   Ethical issues in gaining access

It is clear from the preceding discussion that a great deal of social research is controversial and raises ethical issues which need to be addressed seriously. Thus Form (1973: 83) has asked 'why should anyone trust a snooping sociologist?' This is especially the case where research is intrusive of privacy, for example in such areas as sexual or financial behaviour or where 'it deals with things sacred to those being studied which they do not wish to be profaned' (Lee and Renzetti, 1990: 512).

The problem of differential access to groups with differential power to resist intrusion also gives rise to concern. In general, it is the most vulnerable and weak groups in society, without the resources to defend themselves from inquisitive investigators, rather than powerful elites and decision-makers, who are the focus of much research attention. This, it is argued, results in a distorted picture of social reality which can sometimes only be addressed by researchers who are prepared to infiltrate covertly, be 'economical with the truth' and take risks. Thus Howard Newby confessed: 'I was not telling outright lies, but I was engaging in systematic conceal-ment' (1977: 118) in his study of Suffolk farmers and farm workers. Weighing the arguments, Punch suggests that:

> *some* measure of deception is acceptable in *some* areas where the benefits of knowledge outweigh the harms and where the harms have been minimized by following convention on confidentiality and identity. One need not always be brutally honest, direct, and explicit about one's research purpose. One should not normally engage in disguise. One should not steal documents. One should not directly lie to people and, while one may disguise identity to a certain extent, one should not break promises made to people. Academics, in weighing up the balancing-edge between overt and covert, and between openness and less-than-open, should take into account the consequences for the subjects, the profession, and, not least, for themselves. (Punch, 1986: 41, emphases in original)

4.4.1   Codes and guidelines

One way in which social researchers have attempted to control unethical methods of investigation has been the specification of ethical codes of conduct by professional bodies. Such codes can effectively control research norms where membership of such bodies is essential for occupational practice. This form of professionalisation has been taken much further in psychology than it has in sociology, where breeches of earlier codes of ethics (British Sociological Association, 1973) were not effectively sanctioned and where revised codes have largely been restricted to offering 'guidelines' for good practice (British Sociological Association, 1991).

One difficulty has been that a number of classical studies, some of which have been discussed above, have been highly regarded by many social scientists in spite of the ethical controversies which they have raised. A second problem, raised by Douglas (1976), is that social life inevitably involves conflicts of interest which are protected by networks of the lies, evasions, deception and distrust which are pervasive and intrinsic elements of all human relationships. Negotiating research access, therefore, is an exercise in 'the politics of distrust' (Lee, 1992). From this perspective, restrictive codes of ethics are an unrealistic denial of social reality. A third view is that privacy claims might be legitimate for individuals but when applied to powerful elites or institutions they merely serve to underpin existing structures of power and inequality.

The attempt to allow for such considerations has resulted in a move away from more restrictive **codes** of conduct based, for example, on the concept of informed consent, to the search for ethical **guidelines**. These recognise that, in the last analysis, it is the individual researcher who must take responsibility for the methods he or she uses and that rigid codes are too restrictive and cannot be applied to every conceivable research situation. Recent attempts to balance the rights and responsibilities of social researchers are the British Sociological Association's *Statement of Ethical Practice* (1991) and the Social Research Association's 'Ethical Guidelines' (1990/91). The former, for example, stresses that it 'is meant, primarily, to *inform* ethical judgements rather than to *impose* on (members) an external set of standards' (British Sociological Association, 1991, emphasis added). It addresses relationships with research participants, sponsors and funders, covert research, anonymity, privacy and confidentiality and warns that research documents do not enjoy legal privilege and can be subpoenaed. It urges that 'as far as possible sociological research should be based on the freely given informed consent of those studied'.

4.4.2 The question of informed consent

According to the British Sociological Association (1991), informed consent 'implies a responsibility on the sociologist to explain as fully as possible, and in terms meaningful to participants, what the research is about, who is undertaking it and financing it, why it is being undertaken, and how it is to be disseminated'. It recognises that, especially in field research, the obtaining of consent may be regarded 'not as a once-and-for-all prior event, but as a process, subject to renegotiation over time' and it also stresses the principle that informed consent should be obtained 'directly from research participants . . . while at the same time taking account of the gatekeepers' interest'.

In many situations, however, the achievement of informed consent from all participants is impossible. The argument is well put by Maurice Punch (1986: 37):

> My position is that a professional code of ethics is beneficial as a *guideline* that alerts researchers to the ethical dimensions of their work, particularly *prior* to entry. With formal organizations and certain communities, where entry has to be negotiated through hierarchical channels, a statement of purpose is normally essential to satisfy gatekeepers. Thereafter it may be *situationally* inappropriate to repeat continually that purpose and to identify oneself. . . . To negotiate access and consent from everyone would be almost futile, while matters would become absurdly complex if some said 'yes' and some said 'no'. In natural settings involving public behavior, such as watching crowd behavior . . . or studying avoidance rituals . . . , then consent seems superfluous and physically unattainable. Any attempt to achieve it in the latter case would only serve to undermine the behavior one wished to observe. (emphases in original)

4.5   Ethical issues of covert research

Ethical issues are most acute in the case of covert research where informed consent is most clearly not sought. One critic has gone so far as to suggest that the studies of the National Front (Fielding, 1981), pentecostal groups (Homan, 1980), scientologists (Wallis, 1976) and homosexuals (Humphreys, 1970) were instances of 'unscrupulous researchers gaining access to unwary groups' (Shipman, 1988: 39). This judgement seems wildly exaggerated, given that both Fielding and Homan also employed overt forms of data collection and participated in events which were formally open to interested members of the public. The same applies to Festinger's study. In each case the researcher was at pains to disturb the natural environment as little as possible. This was particularly the case in Humphreys's study of male homosexuals (1970) and Homan's study of pentecostals (1980).

All the researchers discussed in this chapter have described their methods in detail and defended their choice of covert means in the research situations in which they found themselves. The latest edition of Humphreys's book contains a postscript on ethics. In this he stresses that a prime commitment of the researcher 'should be to the enhancement of man's self-knowledge' and argues that there are social policy spin-offs from research so that 'the greatest harm a social scientist could do to [a deviant] would be to ignore him' (1970: 168–9). The book also reproduces the claims of a libertarian who protests that 'no information is valuable enough to obtain by nipping away at personal liberty' by using covert methods of research as Humphreys had done (1970: 181). Horowitz and Rainwater robustly respond that this 'really represents a denial of the ability of people to understand themselves' and claim that 'sociologists uphold the right to know in a context of the surest protection for the integrity of the subject matter and the private rights of the people studied' (1970: 183, 185).

In Britain, Homan (1980) initiated an extended debate about the methods he had employed in his study of pentecostals. Later he responded convincingly to criticisms of his methods in a dialogue with Bulmer (Homan and Bulmer, 1982). He concludes by reporting that 'consideration for my subjects, in which I was counselled by two pentecostal ministers whom I used as informal collaborators, argued for the adoption of covert methods' (1982: 121).

In the concluding chapter of *Social Research Ethics*, Bulmer (1982b: 217–51) summarises what he regards are the chief demerits of covert participant research: it is a violation of the principle of informed consent, it involves an unwarranted invasion of personal privacy and 'out-and-out deception', it involves risks to research participants (an example would be Humphreys's follow-up survey), it harms the observer (a charge which Homan admitted) and public trust in sociology (queering the pitch for future research), and finally, alternative overt forms of research could have been employed. However, and perhaps unexpectedly, Bulmer's position 'is not that secret participant observation is never justified, but that its use requires the most careful consideration in the light of ethical and practical considerations' (1982b: 217). In the final analysis, therefore, Bulmer provides a loophole similar to that implied in the British Sociological Association (BSA) statement on research ethics.

This review has introduced a range of controversial but defensible researches. It has not been the intention to suggest a simple solution to the ethical dilemmas of social research. Rather, the reader is invited to read the accounts of research which have been referred to in this chapter. Those of Humphreys (1970) and Homan (1980; Homan and Bulmer, 1982) in particular provide important debates. My conclusion is that there are no absolute answers to ethical questions of access for they frequently depend on unanticipated contingent factors. Rather, there is the 'situation ethics of the field' (Punch, 1986: 71) in which the researcher is obligated to act responsibly and make up his or her own mind in the light of professional codes of ethics or guidelines, and given the specific circumstances of his or her own research problem and field. In the last analysis, the buck stops with the researcher and there are no easy solutions.

4.6 The multiple responsibilities of the researcher

The BSA statement which has been referred to draws attention to the multiple responsibilities of the researcher in his or her attempts to advance knowledge: to the sponsor and funder as well as 'society at large, research participants and professional colleagues and sociological community'. In practice the interests of these various groups are often in conflict so that some sort of balance or compromise, 'the result of deliberation and not ignorance' (British Sociological Association, 1991), must be sought.

It has been noted that two alternative responses have been suggested. On the one hand there are the professional codes which aim to establish a normative framework for legitimate research and require the conformity of practitioners to specific rules, such as the informed consent of participants. On the other hand, others from a conflict perspective have argued the pervasiveness of distrust and the necessity of deception to investigation. The normative approach, taken literally, would exclude a great deal of covert fieldwork. Arguably our knowledge and understanding of everyday social life would be much poorer, the pursuit of societal rationality hindered, and the interests of the powerful protected as a consequence (Punch, 1986: 34). In contrast, unrestricted conflict approaches seem lacking in respect for the dignity and rights of individuals in manipulating participants for their own research ends.

The position taken here is similar to that of Punch who is 'skeptical both of codes and of conflict methodology'. Some form of compromise solution seems inevitable (1986: 29–30) as the researcher endeavours to balance his or her obligations to extend certified knowledge while at the same time respecting the rights of others. In seeking this balance the researcher has the ultimate responsibility of judging between the competing claims. He or she will have significant resources, not only the accounts of earlier researchers and the debates about their methods in the professional literature, but also a number of ethical codes or guidelines which are the product of decades of reflection by the research community.

4.7 Project

This chapter has drawn attention to the variability of research situations and the problems associated with gaining access to sources of data, in particular, to respondents and informants. It has also suggested that there are serious ethical issues which must be faced by any potential researcher in gaining access (and indeed, throughout the whole research process). These include the choice of methods, and the extent to which they are open with any sponsors, gatekeepers or respondents about the main purposes of the investigation and any use to which the findings might be put.

Let us suppose that a large research foundation invites researchers to apply for funding in four areas: (1) industrial relations strategies employed by middle management in multinational corporations; (2) the meaning of tourist experiences on package holidays; (3) the sexual behaviour of cohabiting students; and (4) the religious beliefs of adherents to the 'new age' movement.

In each case write a one page outline of how you would propose to achieve the necessary access to the relevant respondents, indicate how informative you would be about your research aims, and justify your choice of research methods.

4.8   Further reading

Hammond (1964), Vidich et al. (1971), Bell and Newby (1977) and Bell and Encel (1978) all provide fascinating collections of research accounts, warts and all.

Douglas (1976) offers an aggressive conflict perspective for social investigations while Bulmer's collection (1982c) and Homan (1991) debate ethical aspects of social research.

5 Designing samples

Sara Arber

Contents

The way in which one designs a sample will depend on one's research goals. Some researchers select samples in order to provide the maximum theoretical understanding, while others are primarily concerned to obtain a representative sample so that they can make inferences about the whole population. In the latter case, one studies a sample in order to learn something about the larger grouping of which it is a part; this larger grouping is called the **population** or **universe of enquiry**.

If we had sufficient time and resources we might study the whole of a population, rather than just a sample taken from that population. Indeed the British population census which is conducted every 10 years covers everyone in Britain. However, researching a sample can yield more accurate results than using the complete population. For instance, in survey research, if fewer people are studied, more resources can be spent on each interview, permitting better quality interviewers, more supervision and better coders. Decisions about the sample design for a research study must always take into consideration the trade off between using a larger sample or studying a smaller one more intensively.

While this chapter emphasises sampling where the 'unit' being studied is the individual, the procedures and theory underlying sampling are equally applicable for other units such as hospitals, small businesses, towns, households or visits to a museum. Although the chapter focuses mainly on sampling for surveys, sampling is equally relevant for a researcher undertaking an observational study and a media analyst wishing to obtain a sample of newspapers or television programmes. Whatever the method of enquiry researchers should address the question of whether they can generalise their findings to a wider group and the degree of confidence with which they can make such generalisations.

5.1 An introduction to sampling concepts

This section provides a brief introduction to some of the key concepts in sampling, before the range of sampling methods used in social research are outlined.

Defining the population

The first step in most research studies is to define the 'population' to be covered. For example, a study of the sexual behaviour of young people might define the universe of enquiry as people aged 14 to 19 living in Manchester. Here, it would be necessary to consider whether the population of interest includes young people living away from home as students, or in institutions, such as the armed forces, in prison or in mental hospitals. Thus, the 'population' is any well-defined set of elements. The researcher then selects a sample from this population.

Sample statistics and population parameters

The term 'statistics' is used when referring to summaries about the sample, and 'parameters' for summaries of the population. The average (or **mean**) income of a sample of 300 recent university graduates is a **statistic**. It may be used to estimate the mean income of all recent university graduates, which is a population **parameter**.

Representativeness

The aim of most researchers is to make the sample representative of the population from which it was selected. For example, there should be the same proportion of men and women in both the sample and the population, and the same distributions of all other variables. If the population characteristics are known, the degree of representativeness of a sample can be checked. We could check the representativeness of a sample of university students against university records, to see whether the sample contains the correct proportions of students in each department and students in each year of their studies.

Sampling error and non-sampling error

Sample design is concerned with two different sources of potential error. The first is sampling error, consisting of random errors associated with the fact that only one out of many possible samples has been drawn from the population. Sampling error is estimated by the standard error (see section 5.5).

In social research there are always sources of error other than sampling error, and these are liable to bias estimates of population parameters. Some of these non-sampling errors are connected with the sampling process, such as incomplete sampling frames, non-response error and selection error (see sections 5.7 and 5.8). Other sources of non-sampling error are associated with each stage of the research process, and include poor questionnaire design, interviewing and coding errors. Of course, you should try to minimise all these sources of error (see chapters 6, 8 and 11).

Sampling frames

A sampling frame is a list of the members of the population under investigation and is used to select the sample. This list should be as complete as possible. The researcher needs to be aware of possible shortcomings, such as omissions and duplications, and should attempt to correct for them. The sampling frames available for the adult population will be discussed in section 5.7.

There is often no ready made sampling frame available for the population of interest, so the researcher has to piece together a sample from more than one source. Sometimes it is necessary to negotiate access to specialised lists. You may need to be creative in thinking about whether any lists exist which cover the population you wish to study, and use skill and diplomacy to obtain access to them.

A good example of constructing a sampling frame from several sources is a study of women who returned to full-time work within nine months of childbirth. Brannen and Moss (1988) defined the population of interest as women born in Britain, living in Greater London, who were having a first birth and who were living with their partner. There were no available sampling frames which covered this population, so the authors pieced together the sample from three main sources: maternity hospitals, employers and private nurseries. Women were visited on the maternity wards of seven large hospitals and asked if they would mind being contacted again, 47 large employers were asked to pass on the names of women on maternity leave, and the 33 nurseries in the Greater London area which were found to take children aged 9 months or under were contacted. From these sources, over 4,000 mothers having first births were obtained, but of these only 295 intended to return to full-time work, and 255 took part in the first interviews.

Non-response

The ability to make inferences from a sample to a population is based on the assumption that the achieved sample is not biased by non-response. To the extent that non-responders differ in significant ways from responders, the researcher has a biased sample.

The aim should be to maximise the response rate, since the lower the non-response rate, the greater the likelihood that the achieved sample will be biased. Interview surveys should aim to achieve at least an 80 per cent response rate, although in many cases 70 per cent may be a more realistic figure, and 60 per cent may be acceptable for self-completion questionnaire surveys.

5.2 Types of sampling methods

There are two broad types of sampling method: **probability** sampling and **purposive** (or non-probability) sampling. Probability sampling is where each element in a population is chosen at random and has a known, non-zero chance of selection. In purposive sampling the chance of selection for each element in a population is unknown and for some elements is zero. Probability and purposive sampling are appropriate for different types of research and so the first issue is to consider the aims of the research (see Figure 5.1).

Probability methods of sample selection are best if the researcher wishes to describe accurately the characteristics of a sample in order to estimate population parameters, for example a survey of the needs of elderly people or the attitudes of tenants in public housing. Probability samples are also most appropriate for analytic studies which involve testing empirical hypotheses, such as the research on housing mobility described in chapter 3.

Where the researcher's aim is to generate theory and a wider understanding of social processes or social actions, the representativeness of the sample may be of less importance and the best sampling strategy may be focused or judgemental sampling (see section 5.3).

Purposive samples are ideal when developing interview schedules and

---

Probability samples are best if the purpose is:
  (a) Description – estimation of population characteristics.
  (b) Explanation – testing of empirical hypotheses.

Purposive samples are best if the purpose is:
  (a) Exploration and theory development.
  (b) Developing and testing survey research instruments – pilot work.
  (c) Selection of a small number of first-stage units, e.g. selection of four schools to
      conduct a survey of pupils' aspirations.

Definitions

Probability sampling is where each element in a population (well-defined universe of
    elements) has a known and non-zero chance of selection.

Purposive (non-probability) sampling is where the chance of selection for each
    element in a population is unknown and for some elements is zero.

Figure 5.1   *Purposes of probability and purposive samples*

other research instruments. Development and pilot work should be
conducted on as wide a range of respondents as possible so that the
research instruments are adequately tested. For example, a survey of
attitudes to general practitioners should include pilot work on patients with
private general practitioners to make sure that the interview is appropriate
for this section of the population. Since private general practitioners are
used by only a small proportion of the population, if the interview schedule
were to be tested on a random sample, it is quite likely that it would not be
tried on anyone with a private general practitioner.

A sample may involve a mixture of both probability and purposive
sampling. For example, in a study of the occupational aspirations of
secondary school children, the researcher may only have sufficient
resources to study a small number of schools. These should be selected
using purposive sampling to represent the range of types of schools which
are expected to influence their pupils' aspirations in different ways. Within
each school the sample of students to be surveyed should be selected by
probability sampling.

5.3   Sampling in small scale and qualitative research

Although researchers usually seek a representative sample of the subgroup
they wish to study, they often have only sufficient resources to study a
small number of people. This is particularly likely if repeated interviews
are used to increase understanding of social processes. Oakley's (1974)
influential study of housework was based on a sample of 40 married women

with at least one child aged under five. She designed the sample to obtain an equal number of middle class and working class women because she hypothesised that class was particularly salient for the lives of these women. The sample was selected from the practice lists of two general practitioners in London, one in a predominantly working class and the other in a predominantly middle class area.

Important sociological work is often based on relatively small samples drawn from one local area. Although these samples may attempt to be representative of a specific category of people, they are not probability samples from which precise inferences can be made about the characteristics of the population from which the sample was drawn. Using a probability sample is often unrealistic for small scale or qualitative research.

Many sociological research studies focus on very specific subgroups of the population, for whom sampling frames are not readily available. For example, Mansfield and Collard (1988) aimed to understand 'normal' marriages and the processes of adjustment and development within such marriages. It would have been prohibitively expensive to examine a large representative sample of newly married couples. Instead, they studied 65 couples who had married in church, interviewing husbands and wives separately and then together. These couples were then reinterviewed five years after their marriage.

The researchers' primary goal was an understanding of social processes rather than obtaining a representative sample. This was achieved by interviewing in detail and at length, and conducting interviews on more than one occasion with both partners.

On some occasions researchers redefine their study population to conform to the available lists. For instance, Mansfield and Collard's (1988) research became a study of first marriages solemnised in church because they were unable to obtain a list of civil ceremony marriages. It is essential to consider how such a sample may influence the conclusions. For example, the processes of negotiation between partners in the early months of marriage may differ for couples who had a church rather than a civil ceremony. This difference may arise because couples with civil marriages are more likely to have previously cohabited and are more sexually experienced than those who had a church marriage. There may also be age and class differences. Thus, the researcher should recognise the constraints on interpretation which arise from their method of sampling, and honestly and clearly note them for their readers.

5.3.1 Snowball sampling

Snowball sampling is often used to obtain a sample when there is no adequate list which could be used as a sampling frame. It is a method for obtaining samples of numerically small groups, such as members of ethnic minorities and drug takers. The approach involves contacting a member of the population of interest and asking whether they know anyone else with the required characteristics (for example, people born in England whose parents came from Poland). These individuals are interviewed in turn and the same question asked. This continues in subsequent interviews until no further sample members are obtained. Then another member of the population of interest is identified, preferably from a different area or social class, and the process of asking for friends or relatives with the required characteristics begins again.

Because the snowballing technique involves the personal recommendation of a contact and thus vouches for the legitimacy of the researcher, it may be the only feasible method of finding a sample of people engaged in illegal activities, such as drug taking (Plant, 1975). It is therefore useful when the potential subjects of the research are likely to be sceptical of the intentions of the researcher (Hedges, 1979). Snowball sampling can only be used when the target sample members are involved in some kind of network with others who share the characteristic of interest. This is both a strength and a potential weakness of the method. An advantage of snowball sampling is that it reveals a network of contacts which can itself be studied. A potential problem is that it only includes those within a connected network of individuals. For example, it would fail to find anyone who had no contact with other second generation Polish people. This would be a serious source of bias if the research problem was the continued maintenance of Polish cultural traditions. In snowball sampling, as in any other method of obtaining a sample, it is essential to assess and report the representativeness of the sample and any likely sources of bias.

5.3.2   Theoretical sampling

Another sampling strategy used in qualitative research is **theoretical sampling** (Glaser and Strauss, 1967). This approach eschews attempting to obtain a representative sample, arguing that sampling should be entirely governed by the selection of those respondents who will maximise theoretical development. The sampling should aim to locate strategic data which may refute emerging hypotheses. Sampling stops when 'theoretical saturation' is reached, that is, when no new analytical insights are forthcoming from a given situation. Theoretical sampling directs the researcher to collect, code, analyse and test hypotheses during the sampling process.

This goal is quite different from that of a researcher seeking a representative sample. There is a similar reliance on theoretical, rather than statistical, sampling in the procedure known as analytic induction described in chapter 11. In analytic induction, a basic assumption is that

(a) Independent controls

Age	%	Social class	%	Work status	%
21–35	40	Class I & II	25	Not in employment	40
36–50	35	Class III	60	In paid employment	60
51–65	25	Class IV and V	15		
Total	100		100		100

(b) Interrelated controls

Social class:	I & II		III		IV & V		
Work status:	N	W	N	W	N	W	**Total**
21–35	3	4	7	20	2	4	40
36–50	5	7	10	8	3	2	35
51–65	4	2	4	11	2	2	25
Total	12	13	21	39	7	8	100
	25		60		15		

N = Not in paid employment   W = In paid employment

Figure 5.2 *Quota controls for a survey of women*

propositions should apply to all cases, thus, the researcher searches for and studies 'negative cases' (Denzin, 1970).

5.4 Quota sampling

Quota sampling is a non-probability method which aims to make the sample representative of the population by setting quota controls.

Interviewers have to find sample members to fill pre-specified quota controls, which are linked to the topic being researched. For example, a study of women's purchasing behaviour suggests a control on employment status, since the shopping behaviour of full-time housewives differs from that of women in paid employment. The researcher must know the proportion of people with each characteristic in the population in order to specify the quota controls. These proportions can generally be obtained from the Population Census or from large government surveys, such as the General Household Survey (see chapter 13). Figure 5.2 illustrates the use of three quota controls (age, social class and employment status) for a survey of 100 women aged 21–65.

The independent controls shown in Figure 5.2(a) will ensure that the sample contains the correct representation on each of the three quota control variables separately. However, the resulting sample may have an unrepresentative combination of characteristics. For example, all the class IV and V women may be housewives over age 50. To ensure that the sample has the correct combination of characteristics, interrelated (or interlaced) controls can be used (see Figure 5.2(b)). As quota controls become more complex and the number of variables and categories to be interrelated increases, it becomes more difficult for interviewers to find people to fill each quota cell, and the costs of the research escalate. Thus, there is a trade off between the higher costs and the increased representativeness of using more detailed independent or interrelated quota controls.

Quota samples are widely used in market research, opinion polling and audience research for three main reasons. First, interviewing costs are much lower than for probability samples because there is no need for call-backs, and travelling distances and times are much reduced. Second, administrative costs prior to fieldwork are lower. There are no costs of obtaining a sampling frame and drawing the sample, although there may be costs in setting the quota controls. Third, the period of interviewing can be very short. For some research topics it is essential that interviews are completed on the same day and results produced and published within a day or two, for example, opinion polls about political events and audience views about television programmes. A probability sample could not be used for a survey of attitudes to a politician's speech, because by the time all sample members had been contacted they would probably have forgotten the speech and the sample results would no longer be news-worthy.

The archetypical quota sample is one where interviewers stand in the High Street to fill their quota cells. The resulting sample may be biased because it over-represents frequent shoppers and under-represents people who work outside town centres. Secondly, there may be a danger of unconscious bias from interviewers who only stop people they think will be friendly and accommodating. Thirdly, interviewers may only stop people who they think will fit into one of their quota categories, with the result that the boundaries of quota categories tend to be under-represented. For example, a quota category of women aged 51–65 may contain few aged 63–5 because interviewers perceive such women as older than they actually are or hesitate to ask in case of causing offence.

To overcome biases inherent in High Street quota samples, quotas may be obtained by household interviewing in specific geographical areas, such as constituencies. These geographical areas are chosen using probability sampling to provide a set of nationally representative areas. The non-probability element is restricted to the final stage of selecting individuals. Within each sample constituency, interviewers are instructed to start at a specified house in a certain street, then call at every nth (e.g. third) house, following a specified route called a 'random route'. When someone answers the door, initial screening questions identify whether anyone present in the household fulfils the quota categories, and, if so, they are asked for an interview. Because there are no call-backs, such a 'random route' approach will under-represent those who work long hours or are frequently not at home, and over-represent people who spend a lot of time at home.

A major drawback of quota sampling is that, since it is not a probability sample, it is impossible to estimate the standard error and so the researcher

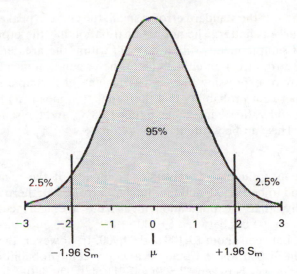

95%

2.5%

2.5%

−3   −2   −1   0   1   2   3

−1.96 S_m   μ   +1.96 S_m

Figure 5.3   *Sampling distribution of sample means*

cannot calculate confidence intervals or use inferential statistics (see section 5.5). As with any sample, it is possible to assess the representative-ness of a quota sample by comparing the sample with known population characteristics, using characteristics other than those specified in the quota controls.

5.5   Probability sampling

This section provides an overview of the statistical underpinning of sampling theory. A fuller discussion can be found in Moser and Kalton (1971) and in most introductory statistics books. If you have previously had little contact with statistics, you may prefer to skim this section and go on to section 5.6.

The aim of probability sampling is to make inferences from the value of a sample statistic to the value of a parameter of a previously defined population with known margins of error. For instance, one might use the mean income of a sample of 300 university graduates ($\bar{x}$) to estimate the mean income of the population of all university graduates (μ).

Any number of samples of 300 university graduates can be drawn from the population, and each sample will have its own mean income ($\bar{x}$). If the means of a very large number of samples are plotted on a graph, the graph is called the sampling distribution of sample means, and will always form a **normal distribution** (a bell-shaped curve). The normal distribution has certain fixed properties and is illustrated in Figure 5.3.

The spread of the curve depends on a quantity called the **standard error** of the mean (S_m). If the standard error is small, the curve is peaked and if it is large, the curve is flatter. The normal distribution has the property that 95 per cent of sample means will always fall within the area enclosed by 1.96 standard errors (S_m) on either side of the population mean (μ).

Another way of expressing this is that, for any one sample mean ($\bar{x}$), there is a 95 per cent probability that the population mean (μ) lies within the band defined by the sample mean minus 1.96 S_m and the sample mean plus 1.96 S_m. This can be written:

$$\bar{x} - 1.96 \, S_m < \mu < \bar{x} + 1.96 \, S_m$$

For example, in a sample of university graduates, if the mean annual income is found to be £9,500, and the standard error £200, there is a 95 per cent probability that the population mean (the average income of all university graduates) lies between £9,500 − 1.96 × 200 and £9,500 + 1.96 × 200, that is, between about £9,100 and £9,900. If, however, the standard error had been £1,000, there would be a 95 per cent probability that the population mean was between £7,500 and £11,500. The latter would be a much less precise and therefore less useful finding.

The standard error indicates the **precision** of estimates of population parameters. One of the aims of sample designers is to achieve a sample with as high a precision as possible, in other words, with a low standard error. Crucial to this is the size of the sample: the larger it is, the smaller the standard error (see section 5.9). The *proportion* of the population sampled has little impact on the standard error, at least for fairly large populations. It is only the *size* of the sample that matters.

5.6   Selecting a simple random sample

The most straightforward way of obtaining a probability sample is to select a simple random sample (SRS) for which each element in the population has an equal (and non-zero) chance of selection. There are three main methods of selecting an SRS from a sampling frame: the lottery method, selection with random numbers and, the most widely used, systematic selection.

Whatever the method of selection, it is first necessary to obtain a sampling frame which identifies uniquely every member of the population. Suppose a sample of 50 small businesses is to be selected from a population of 400. The **Sampling Fraction** (SF) is the chance of selection of each element in the population. It is calculated from the sample size (n) divided by the population size (N), that is, SF = n/N. In the lottery method, names of the 400 small businesses could be put into a hat or drum, thoroughly mixed and a sample of 50 taken out. This is feasible when the population is not very large, but would be unrealistic with a population numbering more than a few thousand.

Random numbers are more frequently used than the lottery method. A unique identification number is assigned to each member of the population, in the case of the small businesses, from 001 to 400. Random number tables (in the back of most statistics books) or computer generated random numbers can be used. Using random number tables, the researcher starts at a randomly selected column in the tables, and examines 3-digit numbers in that column. When the 3-digit number lies between 001 and 400, that small business enters the sample. This continues until a sample of 50 has been obtained. Using this method, the same random number could be selected more than once. There is little to be gained from interviewing the same person twice! So it is usual to sample **without replacement**. Sampling **with replacement** (or unrestricted random sampling) is where each element in the population has the possibility of entering the sample more than once. In the lottery method, this would mean that once a sample member had been drawn their number would be returned to the drum to have the same chance of selection as all the others in the population.

5.6.1   Systematic selection

Both the lottery and the random number methods of selection are cumbersome and time consuming when a large population is to be sampled. In such cases, systematic selection is more usual. Using systematic selection, all elements of the population are listed and a fixed **sampling interval** is used to select sample members. The sampling interval is the reciprocal of the sampling fraction. For example, if 50 small businesses are to be selected from a population of 400, the sampling fraction would be 1/8 and the sampling interval would be 8. Every eighth small business on the list is selected after a random start between 1 and 8 (the sampling interval). For instance, if business number 5 is selected first, then business number 13 would be selected, then number 21 and so on.

Systematic selection is always without replacement. It is not exactly equivalent to simple random sampling, because once one element has been selected into the sample, the selection of all other elements is determined by the order of the list. It is impossible for neighbouring elements on the list to enter the sample. This is generally an advantage, because sample members will be more evenly spread across the population than in a true SRS.

Providing that there is no periodicity in the list which relates to the sampling interval, for example, so long as every eighth business does not share a particular characteristic, systematic selection will result in an unbiased sample. Systematic selection from a list such as the Electoral Register (discussed in section 5.7.1) improves the precision of the sample compared with using an SRS because it spreads the sample more evenly throughout the area. It will yield a more representative sample with a lower standard error than an equivalent SRS, which could by chance result in a sample where all sample members lived in the same street. In effect, the systematic selection is stratifying the population by streets (see section 5.9.1).

Before discussing probability samples which are more complex than simple random samples, the next two sections will examine the use of sampling frames and discuss how to minimise survey non-response.

5.7   Using sampling frames

It is essential to evaluate the adequacy of sampling frames in terms of their completeness of coverage and whether there are any omissions or duplicate entries. Consider, for example, a self-completion questionnaire study of employees in a multinational corporation. It would be relatively easy to obtain names and addresses of employees from the company. However, by the time the questionnaires are sent out, some employees may have left and new employees joined. Those who had died or left would be 'out of scope', and their inclusion in the sampling frame would not bias the sample. They would simply be left out of the calculation of the response rate. However, the omission of new employees is more serious because the resulting sample would under-represent recent recruits. To overcome this potential bias, one might seek to update the sampling frame by obtaining lists of new employees and selecting from these as well.

Another potential problem is that employees may have moved between different plants or offices within the company. If the lists for each plant were compiled at different times, the same individual might be on more than one list – a duplicate element – or might be omitted from the sampling frame entirely. Duplicate listings could be checked and one entry deleted, but if the population is large, this might be very time-consuming. The danger of leaving duplicate elements in the sampling frame is that including a lot of duplicates would bias the sample to over-represent occupationally mobile employees.

5.7.1   The Electoral Register

The most widely used sampling frame of the adult population in Britain is the Electoral Register. It is usually used as a sampling frame of the non-institutional population, that is, omitting people in prisons, long-stay hospitals and residential homes. The Electoral Register excludes those ineligible to vote, such as aliens and Peers. But more serious is the exclusion of those who for various reasons have not registered to vote. Because the Electoral Register is compiled annually in October and published each February, it is always between 5 and 17 months out of date.

The Electoral Register is particularly well-suited to using systematic selection. Each elector has a unique identification number and is listed within their dwelling, dwellings are listed in number order within each street, streets are listed alphabetically within each polling district, and polling districts can be easily amalgamated to form wards and constituencies. The identification number of the last elector in a polling district corresponds to the total number of electors (that is, the population) in that polling district. It is therefore easy to work out a sampling interval for the systematic selection of a fixed number of individuals from a polling district (or ward).

Electoral registers are widely available in public libraries and main Post Offices, and can be purchased from the local Council. Registers for the whole country are available in various central locations, such as the Office of Population Censuses and Surveys in London and the British Library. However, because the Registers are not always available in magnetic form, drawing samples is expensive in clerical time (Wilson and Elliot, 1987).

The Electoral Register is a more accurate sampling frame for addresses (or dwelling units) than it is for individuals, because individuals may be geographically mobile or not registered to vote. The Register can be used for selecting a sample of addresses using a process called **firsting** (Moser and Kalton, 1971). An address is selected into the sample only if the sampling interval falls on the first elector at that address. If this procedure is not used, the probability of selection of an address varies with the number of electors at that address.

Several studies have estimated the accuracy of the coverage of the Electoral Register (Gray and Gee, 1972; Smith, 1981; Butcher and Dodd, 1983). Comparisons between the Electoral Register compiled in late 1980 and the April 1981 population census showed that 6.7 per cent of adults were not on the Register at the time it was compiled, and it was estimated that 16 per cent would be incorrectly registered by the time it expired in February 1982 (Butcher and Dodd, 1983). Under-registration of addresses was lower, 3.6 per cent in April 1981, confirming that the Register is a more accurate sampling frame of addresses than of individuals. There were systematic biases in the Electoral Register, with greater non-registration of younger adults, 14 per cent aged 18–19 and 17 per cent aged 21–4, than of older people, 2 per cent aged 50 and above. This is partly because of the greater geographical mobility of young adults. Over a quarter of people who had moved in the year preceding the census were not on the Register, a third of those aged 20–4 compared with a tenth of people over 50.

There was also variation in the adequacy of coverage according to nationality (Butcher and Dodd, 1983). Nearly a third of New Commonwealth citizens were not on the Electoral Register. Additional coverage checks in London showed higher under-registration of individuals in inner London (14 per cent), particularly among people living in privately rented accommodation. Indeed, nearly half of unemployed people under 30 were not on the Register.

These findings mean that using the Electoral Register as a sampling frame may bias results for some groups, particularly young adults, those in privately rented accommodation, New Commonwealth citizens and unemployed people. Following the publication of these findings, Electoral Registration Officers in Local Authorities have taken steps to improve coverage. The present situation may be better than that portrayed by Butcher and Dodd (1983), but on the other hand, the assumption by many that the Electoral Register would be used for checking Community Charge (the 'poll tax') registration may have been a stimulus to non-registration in the late 1980s and early 1990s.

5.7.2   The Postcode Address File

Since the mid-1980s, the Postcode Address File (PAF) has been increasingly used as a sampling frame for government and other national surveys of households and individuals. It has advantages over the Electoral Register in being more up-to-date (it is updated quarterly by the Post Office), having a more complete coverage and in being available as a computer file (Dodd, 1987; Wilson and Elliot, 1987). It is therefore more easily accessible, more convenient and cheaper to use. The final sampling units are 'delivery points' which are similar to addresses. A disadvantage is that names are not recorded in the Postcode Address File and there are no data about the number of households or adults resident at an address.

The sampling frame used by researchers is the 'Small User File' which lists delivery points normally receiving under 25 items of mail per day. Thus, those few private households which receive larger quantities of mail are excluded. About 10 per cent of delivery points in the file are non-residential addresses and therefore 'out of scope'. It is likely that in future the PAF will become the sampling frame of choice for the majority of national or large-scale probability samples in the United Kingdom.

5.7.3   Two phase sampling

Many social research questions focus on specific subgroups of the population for whom adequate sampling frames are not available. If a probability sample is required and the subgroup includes more than about 3 per cent of the population, a two phase sampling procedure can be used. This involves an initial screening phase (or sift) of a larger population in order to identify the subgroup. The procedure can only be used for subgroups whose identifying characteristic can be easily ascertained. For example, it would be inappropriate as a method of identifying drug users (Hedges, 1979) or groups with a particular sexual orientation, but feasible for identifying a specific ethnic group, disabled people or a particular age group.

In the first phase, all addresses in a large probability sample are contacted with a short screening questionnaire to discover whether anyone in the household has the required characteristic. This screening phase may be carried out by the interviewers if a high proportion of sample addresses contain someone with the relevant characteristic. For example, the

Women and Employment Survey used an interview screen to identify a sample of women aged 16–59 (Martin and Roberts, 1984). The OPCS Survey of Disability (Martin et al., 1988), which aimed to obtain a national probability sample of disabled people in private households, used a postal screen to identify households containing anyone with specific disabilities. To achieve this 80,000 addresses drawn from the Postcode Address File were sent a short self-completion questionnaire, asking if any household member could not do, or had difficulty doing a number of tasks, such as climbing stairs, or reading. The screening phase should obtain a high response rate and, in the disability study, an 80 per cent response was achieved. Personal interviews may be used to follow up those who did not reply in order to increase the response rate or to estimate if there is any non-response bias.

The second phase selects a sample from the people identified during the screening phase. In the Martin and Roberts (1984) study, all women aged 16–59 identified in the screening phase were included in the final sample. Alternatively, a subset of previously identified cases can be selected using a probability sampling method.

A telephone sift may be appropriate for some research topics. An interesting example is a study of the wives of men employed in the offshore oil industry in Aberdeen (McCann et al., 1984). The researchers were refused access to employee names and addresses by the oil companies in Aberdeen and had to think of an alternative way of obtaining their sample. They assumed a very high level of telephone ownership among oil workers. Random-digit dialling was used to telephone over 10,000 numbers in the Aberdeen area. They asked some simple screening questions: 'Does anyone in the household work in the oil industry?' If Yes, 'Do they work off-shore?' When a potential sample member was identified, the name and address was requested. From over 8,000 households with obtainable numbers, 421 men working in offshore oil were identified. Less than 5 per cent of numbers were unanswered after three calls, and only 4 per cent of those identified as in 'oil households' refused to answer further questions.

5.8   Components of survey non-response

One of the researcher's tasks is to consider each potential source of non-response and try to minimise it. The sources of non-response are shown in Figure 5.4, together with the achieved response in a survey of patients' attitudes towards changes in the general practitioner service (Arber and Sawyer, 1979). Each source of non-response will be considered in turn.

Refusals

The largest component of non-response is usually made up of people who refuse to be interviewed. The level of refusals is influenced by a number of factors:

		Overall response (%)	Inner London response (%)
Completed interviews		82	72
Refusals		9	13
Non-contacts	out at time of call	4	7
	temporarily away from home	1	1
Movers		3	6
Uninterviewable	(e.g. ill, deaf, can't speak English)	1	1
Total		100	100

Source: Arber and Sawyer, 1979, Table A.1

Figure 5.4   *Sources of non-response*

1. How interesting respondents find the subject matter. For example, a survey of attitudes to the health service will obtain a higher response rate than one about financial service organisations. If the target population is very specialised and finds the research topic particularly salient, there may be no refusals, for example, there were no refusals in Oakley's (1974) research on housework.
2. The perceived importance of the study. If the research is thought to be worthwhile or to contribute to improving services or facilities, the response will be higher.
3. The greater the perceived 'legitimacy' of the research, in terms of the conduct of the study, the survey organisation and the research sponsor. For this reason, government surveys often achieve higher response rates than those run by commercial organisations.
4. The skill and persistence of the interviewer in providing appropriate and reassuring replies to respondents' queries, and in encouraging hesitant respondents. Interviewer training plays an important role here.
5. There may also be area and cultural differences in willingness to respond.

Information on the first three of these factors should be provided to the respondent through a preliminary letter or a letter left by the interviewer and in an introduction read out before the interview (see chapter 6).

   The survey illustrated in Figure 5.4 had an overall refusal rate of 9 per cent and a rate of 13 per cent in Inner London. Each of the other components of non-response was also higher in Inner London. Government surveys have been found to achieve about an 8 per cent lower response rate in London than in the rest of Britain (Barnes, 1991).

Non-contacts

Non-contacts are minimised by increasing the number of call-backs at the sample address, calling at different times of day and on different days of the week. Often the interviewer can arrange an appointment through another household member and make themselves available at whatever time is convenient for the respondent. At least three call-backs are usually recommended. Nevertheless, some people may not be contactable because they are away for long periods of time, for example, for the summer holidays, temporarily working away from home or in prison.

Movers

People who have moved will only form a component of non-response when the sample includes specific named individuals rather than a random individual living at a particular address. An example of the former is a study of family planning clinic attenders in Trinidad, where the sample came from names and addresses held by clinics (Cross and Arber, 1977). Many of these were out-of-date, so interviewers had to find where the woman had moved to by enquiring from the current residents or from neighbours. If the new address was within five miles of the old, the woman was interviewed at her new address. Similarly, Oakley's (1974) research on housework (referred to in section 5.3) was based on a sample of 65 names of women drawn from two general practitioners' lists. Of these, 16 (25 per cent) had moved or could not be traced, seven were not contactable and two could not be interviewed within the timescale of the research.

Uninterviewable

In any survey, some respondents cannot be interviewed because they are too ill, deaf or unable to speak sufficient English. Whether special measures are taken to reduce this potential source of bias will depend on the aims of the study. A study of very elderly people (e.g. Bury and Holmes, 1991) would have to arrange for proxy interviews, in which another person responds on behalf of the sample member, otherwise the needs of the most frail would be under-represented. A study of the employment of Asian women would need to employ either interviewers who spoke appropriate languages or interpreters, otherwise the sample would be biased against those with least fluency in speaking English.

5.8.1 Assessing the representativeness of samples

Whatever the magnitude of non-response, all surveys should assess the representativeness of the achieved sample and identify the nature and extent of any bias. This can be done by direct or indirect methods (Moser and Kalton, 1971). Direct methods involve further follow-ups and attempts to 'retrieve' non-respondents, for example, by using more experienced interviewers to try to 'convert' refusals into respondents. Very brief self-completion questionnaires can be sent to non-respondents to obtain basic socio-demographic information or telephone follow-ups can be attempted. Extrapolations of the characteristics of 'hard core' non-respondents can be made from the characteristics of the retrieved segment, although it is questionable whether these two groups are comparable.

Indirect methods of assessing the representativeness of a sample involve comparing the sample against known population characteristics, such as age, sex and social class, obtained from the census or large government surveys. If significant under-representation is found for a particular subgroup, the data from those in the subgroup who did respond can be replicated an appropriate number of times to simulate the results of missing sample members. This procedure is called **weighting**. For example, if there were 25 per cent fewer men aged 20–9 in the sample than would be expected from the population distribution, the researcher can consider weighting this subgroup by 1.33. However, weighting assumes that respondents are in all respects comparable to non-respondents, which may not be the case.

5.9   More complex sample designs

In practice, most surveys use a more complex sample design than the simple random samples discussed in section 5.6. When planning large surveys, a compromise usually has to be reached between the desire for high precision and the constraints of time and money. Time and cost savings must be balanced against any likely losses in precision. As we noted in section 5.5, precision is measured by the standard error; the lower the standard error, the more precise the estimates of population parameters from the sample.

The three aspects of sampling which affect precision are illustrated in Figure 5.5. The first is associated with the degree of variation in the population under study, for example, the variation in income in a sample of the general population is likely to be larger than in a homogeneous sample of comparable size, such as recent university graduates. This variation is usually measured by the **standard deviation** or **variance**.

The second aspect is the sample size. The standard error is inversely proportional to the square root of the sample size. For instance, to halve the standard error it is necessary to quadruple the size of the sample.

The third aspect affecting the standard error is the sample design. We will next outline how building stratification into the selection of a sample can produce a substantial gain in precision, while only increasing the cost by a small amount. After this we discuss the use of clustering to reduce the costs of field work, especially interviewing, although clustering has the

1. *Variation in the population*
   A more varied population will have a larger standard error
2. *Sample size*
   A larger sample size gives a smaller standard error
3. *Sample design*
   a. More stratification results in a lower standard error
   b. More clustering results in a higher standard error

The standard error of the mean is estimated using the formula:

$$\text{Standard error} = \frac{\text{standard deviation}}{\text{square root of the sample size}}$$

$$\text{or } S_m = \frac{s}{\sqrt{n}}$$

Figure 5.5 *Factors affecting the Standard Error*

disadvantage of increasing the standard error of the sample, thereby decreasing the precision of population estimates.

5.9.1 Stratification

Stratification involves dividing the population into separate strata on a characteristic assumed to be closely associated with the variables under study. A separate probability sample is selected from within each stratum. Building stratification into a sample design is recommended because it increases precision for very little additional cost. Stratification ensures that the sample is representative on the characteristic(s) used to form the strata.

A simple random sample will *on average* be representative of the population. However, any one sample may be quite unrepresentative on key characteristics. Suppose we want to study the career aspirations of university students and have sufficient resources to interview a sample of 125 students. Using simple random sampling, it would be possible to draw a sample which under-represents students from some departments, and over-represents others. Since career aspirations are likely to be closely linked to the subject studied at university, it is desirable that the sample should have the correct representation of the students' departments. This can be achieved by stratifying the sample using departments as separate strata.

Prior to sample selection, the sampling frame is divided into departments (strata). This is straightforward because lists of students by department are easily available. Suppose the population consists of 5,000 university students and a sample of 125 is to be drawn. This would represent a 1/40 sampling fraction and a sampling interval of 40. The 5,000 students are listed by department and then systematic selection is used with a sampling interval of 40. A random start between 1 and 40 is selected, say

Sample size (*n*) = 125 Population size (*N*) = 5000 Sampling fraction = 1/40
Sampling interval = 40 Random start for selection = 13

Stratification by Department

		Population Number in department	Sample Number in department
Physics		320	8
Chemistry		120	3
Biochemistry		160	4
•		•	•
•		•	•
Sociology		200	5
Total		5000	125

Stratification by Department and Year

Physics	Year 1	120	3
	Year 2	100	3
	Year 3	100	2
Chemistry	Year 1	40	1
	Year 2	40	1
•		•	•
•		•	•
Sociology	Year 3	70	2
Total		5000	125

Figure 5.6 *Selecting a Stratified Sample of University Students*

13. The 13th person in the first listed department is chosen, followed by the 53rd, 93rd, and so on (see Figure 5.6).

Systematic selection from a list ordered by one or more stratification factors automatically forces the sample to be representative on these factors. In this example, the sample contains exactly the same proportion of students in the physics department as in the whole university, and similarly for each department.

Another variable which is likely to affect career aspirations is students' year of study. The researcher could stratify both by department and by year within department, as illustrated in the bottom half of Figure 5.6. This would yield a sample which was representative of students by department, by year of study, and by both variables in combination.

Stratification produces a lower standard error because the 'total variation' for any particular variable (such as career aspirations) in a population may be regarded as composed of variation 'between strata' and variation 'within strata'. In stratified random sampling, variation 'between strata' does not enter into the standard error because, by definition, this component of the variation in the population will be automatically reflected in the sample. The greater the proportion of a variable's 'total variation' that is accounted for by 'between strata' variation, the greater the gain in precision from stratification. For this reason, each stratum

Aim: to select a sample of 2,000 hospital nurses.
First stage: Select hospitals
Second stage: Select nurses from within sample hospitals

Options available:

Number of hospitals selected	Number of nurses selected	
5	400	Lower cost, lower
10	200	precision
20	100	
40	50	
50	40	Optimum
80	25	
100	20	
200	10	Higher cost, higher
400	5	precision

Costs include:
  (1) Interviewing costs, subsistence and travel
  (2) Administrative costs of negotiating access to obtain the lists of hospital nurses from each sample hospital and drawing the sample.

Figure 5.7   *Variation in degree of clustering in a national sample of hospital nurses*

should be made as different as possible while maximising the similarity of elements within strata.

5.9.2   Clustering and multi-stage samples

A clustered design is one where more than one stage of selection is used. **Clustering** is used to reduce the time and costs of the research, but it increases the standard error.

Clusters are often geographical areas (such as local government wards) or institutions (such as schools, hospitals or employers). Suppose you want to interview a national sample of 2,000 hospital nurses to find their views about current changes in health care. A simple random sample is rarely used for a national interview survey because of the prohibitively high costs of travelling throughout the country to carry out the interviews. Instead, a cluster sample in which the first stage units are hospitals would be preferred. Within such a two-stage design, the key question is the degree of clustering. The range of choices is illustrated in Figure 5.7.

At one extreme, it would be possible to take a highly clustered sample of only five hospitals and interview 400 nurses in each. At the other extreme, a very widely dispersed sample could be selected, selecting five nurses from each of 400 hospitals. Because costs arise mainly from paying interviewers for their time, travel and subsistence, the latter design would cost a great deal more than the former.

A clustered sample may also yield substantial savings in administrative costs and sample selection costs as compared with an equivalent simple random sample. A complete sampling frame is only required for the primary sampling units, in this case, the sample hospitals. Negotiating access to obtain lists of nurses from a hospital and the time spent in drawing the sample from each list can be costly, and it is much cheaper to do this only in the selected hospitals.

A clustered sample reduces precision and increases the standard error because elements within a cluster tend to be alike. Nurses within the same hospital are likely to have similar characteristics. For example, there is likely to be less variability in nurses' attitudes within hospitals than between hospitals. A highly clustered sample of nurses, selected from only 10 hospitals, would have a much higher standard error than a sample of the same size selected from 200 hospitals. The latter would have a standard error comparable to that of a simple random sample.

To maximise precision, it is advisable to build in as much stratification as possible within each stage of selection. For a national sample of hospital nurses, all the hospitals in the country should be stratified by characteristics such as region and type (teaching, acute general, psychiatric, geriatric, etc.). This would ensure that the sample hospitals are a correct representation according to region and type of hospital. Within each selected hospital, the nurses should be stratified, for example according to Grade, prior to systematic selection of the sample of nurses. The resulting sample would then have the correct proportions of nurses at each level from senior management through ward sisters and staff nurses to nursing auxiliaries.

Samples with two or more stages of selection are called multi-stage samples. A three-stage sample has three separate stages of selection, for example, selection from constituencies, then wards, and finally adults within selected wards. A three-stage sample will generally result in a larger standard error than a two-stage sample. The majority of the probability samples used for national surveys are multi-stage samples which include stratification at each stage of selection. These usually use a method of sample selection called probability proportional to size (PPS) sampling. Details of the PPS sampling method can be found in Moser and Kalton (1971: ch. 8).

5.9.3   Design effects

The estimation of sampling errors for stratified and multi-stage samples is more complex than for simple random samples. A stratified random sample will result in a standard error which is smaller than for a simple random sample of the same size, while the standard error for a clustered sample will be greater than for a comparable simple random sample. The relationship between the standard error of a complex sample design and that of a simple random sample of the same size is called the design effect or Deff (see Moser and Kalton, 1971: ch. 5).

5.10 Project

1. You are interested in the attitudes of Catholics to recent changes in the Catholic church. A Catholic magazine included a self-completion questionnaire on this topic and received over 10,000 replies from their readers. What would these data tell you about the attitudes of Catholics?
2. The government wishes to understand more about the reasons why juveniles commit offences. For this study, they decide to select a probability sample of 300 offenders from boys attending 10 detention centres. What could you learn about juvenile delinquency from this sample?
3. How would you obtain a sample of the following groups?
   (a) Drug addicts: to study the process of becoming a drug addict.
   (b) Adults who are diabetic: to study the effect of diabetes on family and social relationships.
   (c) Second generation Italians (i.e. people who were born in England and whose parents were born in Italy): for a study of the maintenance of Italian cultural practices.
   In each case, first define more precisely the population to be studied, then suggest alternative sampling strategies. How well does your proposed sampling strategy represent the population you initially defined?
4. Outline how you would select a national probability sample of:
   (a) 5,000 women aged 16–59. (This is the sample selected in Martin and Roberts (1984)).
   (b) 400 elderly people from a medium sized town.

5.11 Further reading

De Vaus (1990: ch. 5 and pp. 140–2) is a survey methods text which provides a good but brief introduction to sampling.

Hedges (1979) provides an excellent discussion and evaluation of the range of techniques which can be used to obtain samples of numerically small populations.

Hoinville and Jowell (1977) is a practical guide to sampling, written by authors with considerable experience of running large surveys.

Despite being 20 years old, Moser and Kalton (1971, chs 3–7) still provides the most comprehensive discussion of survey sampling. Parts are quite advanced in its treatment of the statistical underpinnings of sampling theory.

Williams (1978) is an excellent text for the beginner, illustrated with many examples.

Kalton (1983) is a statistically sophisticated discussion of sampling concepts and sample designs in survey sampling. It requires a reasonable grasp of elementary statistics.

Kish (1965) is a more advanced text, but one which provides the standard technical reference on sampling.

Patton (1987) has an excellent chapter on sampling in qualitative research.

Lynn and Lievesley (1991) provides an up-to-date practical guide to drawing national samples.

PART II

Into the field

6 Questionnaires

Rosemarie Newell

Contents

Most people have encountered survey research, in one form or another, as either participants in surveys or recipients of information from surveys. The most familiar are those carried out by market researchers with clipboards who stop passers-by in the High Street to ask about anything from what they drink to how they will vote. Magazines and newspapers often carry out surveys, and most of us have received questionnaires through the post asking what we have purchased and what we might purchase in the future. All sorts of organizations from airlines to the Gas

Board want to ask us questions. Commercial organisations use the results of surveys to make decisions about the development of products, their pricing, their market penetration and the profiles of their customers.

Sociologists also regard surveys as an invaluable source of data about attitudes, values, personal experiences and behaviour. Researchers use face-to-face or telephone interviews, or postal questionnaires. One of the most important parts of any research survey is the development of the questions. The success of a survey will depend on the questions that are asked, the ways in which they are phrased and the order in which they are placed.

The challenge for the researcher is how to select questions that will obtain the most valuable information. This a skill to be learnt like any other in social research, and this chapter provides guidelines to help you with devising such questions. The chapter will also make the distinction between questionnaires and interview schedules; discuss the use of open-ended and closed questions; show how to avoid ambiguous, leading, double-barrelled and hypothetical questions; describe the types of questions that can be asked and the order in which they should be placed; and finally, discuss the varieties of format for questionnaires and interview schedules.

6.1 Choosing a method of questioning

Social research involves detective work. You begin with a problem and then ask a number of questions about it, such as, 'what?', 'who?', 'where?', 'when?', 'how?' and 'why?'. In some research, the most important question may be 'What are the consequences?'. Consider addiction to gambling:

- *What* is gambling addiction? It is necessary to determine what counts as gambling and what counts as addiction to gambling.
- *Who* becomes addicted to gambling? It would be wise to limit your study to a particular group, say, teenagers who become hooked on slot machine gambling. What types of people are they? Are they still at school, employed or unemployed?
- *Where* does the gambling take place? If you choose slot machine addiction, the location will be arcades, recreational and amusement centres and pubs.
- *When* does the gambling occur? How regularly? For what length of time?
- *How* does it occur? This question may cover several aspects of gambling behaviour, from investigating the physical act of gambling to how the addiction is funded.
- *Why*? The key question for the researcher: the main purpose of the study will be to seek an **explanation** for the gambling addiction.

Most research studies will include questions within these categories.

Once you have decided upon a research topic, the next important step is to choose an appropriate method. You may decide on a qualitative study, collecting data by interview, or you may choose a quantitative method, carrying out a survey by means of a self-completion questionnaire. You could also conduct a telephone survey, which although it involves interviews, can be carried out on a larger scale than face-to-face interviews.

For some studies, it may be sufficient to question a small sample; for instance, a small-scale study involving in-depth interviewing may provide ample data on what it is like to be married to an alcoholic. However, a study wishing to examine British attitudes towards European Monetary Union is likely to benefit from a larger-scale study to ensure that the views obtained are representative of the general population. In this case, a postal or telephone survey may be the best means of obtaining data. Which method you choose will be determined by the topic and the time and financial resources available.

6.1.1 Postal surveys

Researchers are not in complete agreement about what should properly be called a questionnaire. Sometimes it is used to mean a document containing a set of questions for respondents to complete themselves ('a self-completion' questionnaire) and sometimes to mean the list of questions which an interviewer reads out to respondents. To avoid confusion, throughout this chapter it is the former that is meant: a questionnaire is given to respondents for them to fill in.

Questionnaires are generally used for postal surveys, although they can also be distributed by hand, for example, in a school or workplace. The questionnaires follow a standardised format in which most questions are pre-coded to provide a list of responses for selection by the respondent (coding is discussed in chapter 11). The questions must be phrased so that they are immediately comprehensible because respondents will not be able to obtain help with anything they do not understand.

The main advantage of self-completion questionnaires is that a large population can be surveyed, relatively cheaply. Costs are lower because interviewers are not used, and pre-coding and computerisation speeds up analysis. It is also possible for respondents to fill in questionnaires at a time convenient to them. The main arguments against using postal questionnaires have generally been that the response rate is low (many postal surveys do not achieve more than a 50 per cent rate of return) and that even when respondents do complete questionnaires, their answers may be incomplete, illegible or incomprehensible. The researcher must also have information about the target population in advance of the study, as well as a very clear idea of what questions will elicit answers to the research problem. As many of the questions will list pre-coded answers, exploration to obtain these categories will have to be done before developing the self-completion questionnaire.

6.1.2   Face-to-face interviews

Interviewers need to be provided with some form of document to guide questioning; this may consist of both pre-coded and open-ended questions (see section 6.4). It is important here to note the distinction between an **interview schedule** and an **interview guide**. A schedule contains set questions in a predetermined order adhered to in each interview. An interview guide, on the other hand, is used for a focused interview and will list areas to be covered while leaving the exact wording and order of the questions to the interviewer. In some cases, the interview guide will be quite sketchy to allow for the possibility of non-directive interviewing in which the interviewee's replies determine the course of the interview.

Interviewers may record responses directly onto an interview schedule by pen or use a tape-recorder to record the interview for later transcription. Portable computers, programmed with interview schedules, are becoming increasingly popular.

Interviewing can have both advantages and disadvantages. Interviews can be more flexible and, in the hands of a skilled interviewer, extract more information from the individual than a postal survey. The disadvantage is that it is expensive to carry out interviews because of the cost of paying interviewers, travel, and analysis of the data. It is also possible for interviewer bias to occur (see chapter 8).

Often, interviews are used in preliminary research before a postal survey is carried out in order to develop ideas for questions and to determine what pre-coded answers should be offered in the postal questionnaire.

6.1.3   Telephone surveys

Interview schedules are also used for interviews conducted via the telephone. Telephone surveys have similar merits to those involving face-to-face interviews, but have the added benefit that it is possible to reach a wider population at less cost.

Although telephone surveys are less popular with social scientists than they are with market research companies, they can be an effective way of conducting social research. Developments in computer technology have now made telephone interviewing easier. A computer-assisted telephone interviewing (CATI) system is able to sample the specified population, provide guidance for the interviewer's introduction, display the interview schedule item by item with appropriate filter questions (see section 6.5), and record the interviewees' responses.

Telephone surveys do have disadvantages. The main problem is that certain groups such as the poor, the young, the sick and disabled, and those who are frequently away from a telephone (perhaps in the course of their work) may be under-represented. Sensitive questions are difficult to ask at a distance, and it is less easy to supply stimulus material, such as prompt cards (see sections 6.3.1 and 6.7) to the interviewee.

Furthermore, telephone interviewing is very different from face-to-face interviewing and the training of interviewers in telephone technique must be thorough. Interviewers cannot interpret the reactions of the interviewee by observation so they must learn to present questions clearly and listen carefully for any signals that might indicate lack of understanding. A further problem concerns concentration; if the interview is not pre-arranged, the interviewer may not get the full attention of the interviewee.

It might well be assumed that since all three of the above methods have significant deficiencies, the chances of obtaining valid and reliable data are very small. This is not so, argues Dillman (1978), who claims that many difficulties can be overcome by using a 'total design method'. By giving minute attention to every aspect of the survey process, from the training of interviewers to the devising of questions, from the letters asking for participation to the paper on which questionnaires are printed, the quality of response for all types of surveys can be improved. This approach is to be thoroughly recommended: giving careful attention to the planning and execution of the research project will enhance the likelihood of producing useful results.

6.2 How to begin

Before embarking upon any research exercise, it is important to explore the previous work that has been carried out on the subject. This will not only provide a framework for developing questions for the new research, but will also ensure that the project can build upon previous studies. Start, therefore, by obtaining academic papers, books and reports based on related research. Questionnaires and interview schedules that have been used in a study are sometimes included in published work and can prove a useful foundation for one's own research.

Begin with a research hypothesis, for instance, 'the most popular leisure activity is television viewing', and use this hypothesis to choose which questions need to be asked.

A first draft of a questionnaire will be based largely on questions derived from previous studies and on **brain-storming**, that is, writing down all questions which may be useful for the study. It is not enough that questions should reveal interesting information; the data obtained *must* relate directly to the study. Often, it is quite difficult to decide which are the important issues, but preliminary background reading will usually help to elaborate a set of hypotheses that will help to sort the relevant from the irrelevant (see chapter 2).

If you were to investigate whether television viewing was the most popular leisure activity you would need to begin by defining 'popular'. Does this mean 'most liked' or 'most often carried out', or both? You would probably want to know whether different sections of the population had different patterns of leisure. A number of variables would therefore have to be considered, such as age, sex, marital status, employment status, educational level, social class, degree of physical fitness, and so on. You may be able to think of several areas which have a bearing on the research topic, but each question must have a direct relevance to one of the variables of the hypothesis – be ruthless in weeding out questions that do not. It is advisable to keep the hypothesis and the objectives of the research very firmly in mind when developing questions.

When drafting questions, you also need to consider **reliability** and **validity** (see chapter 2 and section 7.4). A study can be said to be reliable if similar results would be obtained by others using the same questions and the same sampling criteria. In order to make it possible for repeat studies to be carried out, first, questions should be worded clearly and unambiguously so that they can be asked in the same way in follow-up studies. Second, instructions for both administration and completion should be the same for all questionnaires or interview schedules. Third, the sample of the population under study should be well defined and the details provided in the research report.

A study can be said to have validity if it actually measures what it sets out to measure. This is more difficult than it sounds. For example, what set of criteria could be used to measure happiness? Some researchers might use variables such as health, marital relationships or employment status, while others might choose spiritual or psychological factors (see the discussion of measurement theories in chapter 2).

6.3   Types of information

There are four main categories of information which can be obtained from a survey. They are listed below with examples of how questions might be phrased.

Attributes

Attributes include personal or socioeconomic characteristics, such as sex, age, marital status, religion, and occupation.

Obtaining valid and reliable information about occupation is more difficult than it might seem at first. You could ask some simple questions, as in Figure 6.1. However, what constitutes paid employment? Would, for

Are you in paid employment?	Yes
	No
If *yes*:	
What is your occupation?	....

Figure 6.1

Have you ever belonged to a political organisation?	Yes
	No
Are you a member of a political organisation at the moment?	Yes
	No
Do you intend joining a political organisation in the future?	Most likely
	Likely
	Unlikely
	Most unlikely
	Don't know

Figure 6.2

example, two hours' work per week in a bar put the respondent into the 'employed' or 'unemployed' category? A good example of the kind of careful and thorough questioning needed to get over these kinds of difficulties can be found in the interview schedule used in the General Household Survey (e.g. OPCS, 1990: 226).

Behaviour

Behaviour constitutes what the individual has done, is doing, and may possibly do in the future. For example, questions to gain information relating to behaviour are shown in Figure 6.2. There may, of course, be difficulties in defining what is meant by a political organisation and it may be necessary for the researcher to make it clear to the respondent what is meant by the term. For example, should Greenpeace, the ecological pressure group, and the Institute for Economic Affairs, a politically committed research institute, be counted as political parties?

Attitudes

Attitudes imply evaluation and are concerned with how people feel about an issue (see chapter 7). Questions about attitudes usually employ scales: a

I think all cars should be made to drive on unleaded petrol.	Strongly in favour
	In favour
	Neither in favour nor against
	Against
	Strongly against

Figure 6.3

The number of heterosexual people diagnosed as HIV positive has grown rapidly during the last year.	True
	False

Figure 6.4

statement is made and individuals are asked to indicate their level of agreement in a positive or negative direction. For example, see Figure 6.3.

Beliefs

Beliefs can usually be assessed by asking whether something is seen as true or false. For example, see Figure 6.4.

6.4 Forms of question

In both interview schedules and questionnaires, there are two forms of question which can be asked: **closed questions** and **open questions**.

6.4.1 Closed questions

Closed questions are drafted in advance, complete with all the possible answers which could be given. Each respondent is asked to choose from one of the answers. For example, a closed question asking about highest level of educational attainment would ask respondents to choose from a list of categories such as basic education, degree, and professional qualifications. Other questions, such as 'Are you married?' have the appearance of open questions, but are only answerable by 'yes' or 'no'.

Closed questions have advantages because they can be pre-coded and the responses can easily be put on a computer, saving time and money (see chapter 11). They also have particular advantages in studies using questionnaires as they are less time consuming for the respondent to complete.

However, such structured questions also have the disadvantage that they

> Under £5,000 per annum
> £5,000–£9,999 per annum
> £10,000–£14,999 per annum
> £15,000–£19,999 per annum
> £20,000–£24,999 per annum
> £25,000–£29,999 per annum
> £30,000–£34,999 per annum
> Over £35,000

Figure 6.5

force the respondent to choose between the answers provided. When faced with a question such as: 'Do you have a good relationship with your mother?' the respondent may wish to say 'yes and no', 'it all depends', or 'it has improved since I lived away from home'. This difficulty can be overcome to a certain extent by asking for more information. When the respondent is asked to indicate either 'yes' or 'no', this can be followed by a 'why?' or 'please provide further details' allowing for more elaboration. Where lists are given, a category of 'other' should always be provided for those who cannot find an appropriate pre-coded response.

Ranges can be given which make completion and coding easier. For example, when asking about income, the responses shown in Figure 6.5 could be offered. In face-to-face interviewing, such ranges of answers can be printed on a card (a 'prompt card') and given to the respondent.

6.4.2   Ranking scales

A ranking scale is a form of closed question which can be valuable when trying to ascertain the level of importance of a number of items. A list of choices is provided and the respondent or interviewee is asked to rank them. See, for example Figure 6.6. It is advisable to limit the range of alternatives as it may be difficult for the individual to rank a large number. This is particularly important when carrying out face-to-face and telephone interviews, where more than four or five items can be unmanageable. It is helpful in face-to-face interviews to allow the respondent to look at a prompt card showing the choices.

6.4.3   Open questions

Open questions are those that allow individuals to respond in any way they wish. For example, asking the open question 'What do you enjoy doing in your leisure time?' will allow the respondent or interviewee to state any activity from abseiling to zither-playing.

Which do you feel are the most important factors in choosing a University?
Please rank the following in order of importance to you. Number them from
1=most important, to 7=least important.

Closeness to a town or city.
Good academic reputation.
Good chance of getting a job after graduation.
Attractive campus.
Good social facilities.
Good accommodation.
Availability of real ale.

Figure 6.6

Open-ended questions can be most usefully employed by skilled interviewers, who can allow interviewees to develop answers much more fully
than they could if they were completing questionnaires.

It is also very useful to use open questions when beginning a new
research project. If investigating the reasons why elderly people choose to
move into purpose-built, warden-assisted housing, the researcher would do
well to begin by asking open-ended questions of a small sample of people
living in such accommodation. From this small-scale study, it would be
likely that the most fundamental reasons would emerge; for example,
previous house too large to maintain, financial advantages in moving to
smaller accommodation, the desire to be near others of similar age group,
the security of having a warden nearby, and so on. If a larger study were to
be carried out, answers to these open questions could then be used to
devise pre-coded categories for closed questions.

Open questions do have their drawbacks. In questionnaires, it is
relatively simple for respondents to tick pre-coded categories, whereas
answers which are unrestricted require more thought and consideration. A
further disadvantage of using open questions is that they produce responses which may be ambiguous, wide-ranging and difficult to categorise.
Answers can be time-consuming to code and analyse and therefore
expensive to deal with when conducting large-scale studies.

The type of study will determine whether open or closed questions are
best. But it is worth bearing in mind that

closed questions should be used where alternative replies are known, are limited
in number, and are clear cut. Open-ended questions are used where the issue is
complex, where relevant dimensions are not known, and where a process is
being explored. (Stacey 1969: 80)

In most questionnaires and interview schedules, both open and closed
questions will be included. However, when large numbers of individuals
are to be studied by self-completion questionnaire, it is best to use mainly
closed questions.

6.5   Developing questions

Your choice of questions will obviously depend on the subject matter of your study. However, a number of important guidelines need to be considered.

Relevance to participants

Moser and Kalton (1971) argue that it is important to consider the ability and willingness of individuals to answer questions. By this, they mean that it is essential to assess whether those to be studied will have the knowledge to answer the questions, whether the questions are relevant to them and whether they wish to reveal the information.

Clarity

A fundamental point is to ensure that questions can be clearly understood and are not subject to any ambiguity. Although this applies both to interview schedules and questionnaires, it is particularly important when producing a document for self-completion. If someone is interviewed and does not understand a question, he or she can at least ask for some elaboration, but when the questionnaire is the only means of communication, confusion will discourage the respondent.

Getting the wording right may present a problem, particularly if a wide-ranging population is under study. Smith (1975: 171) argues that question wording is a significant problem in survey research and suggests that there must be a shared vocabulary between researcher and respondent. The wording should not appear too simplistic for some, seeming to insult their intelligence; on the other hand, it must not be too sophisticated for others. If words or phrases are complicated, then misunderstanding may result. It is preferable to avoid jargon: words like 'social interaction', 'alienation' or 'socialisation' may be everyday terminology to sociologists, but their meanings may not be fully understood by others. It is worth remembering that it has been estimated that about 5 per cent of the population are functionally illiterate and the majority do not have a reading vocabulary beyond that used by the tabloid press. Of course, if the sample comes from a particular group, for example, pharmacists, medical practitioners, or lawyers, it would be appropriate to use the vocabulary common to these groups.

It is important to have the same frame of reference as those under study and this is one of the most difficult aspects of producing questions. Certain words may be interpreted in differing ways, depending on individual perspectives. For example, common words like 'equality' or 'independence' may mean different things to different people. Other more technical words such as 'fault' or 'fracture' will be understood differently by tennis players, horse riders and geologists. Therefore, questions need to be developed carefully to match the sample to be used. For example, a study on patients' views of doctors included the question, 'Do you feel in awe of your doctor?', but it was found that the question was not understood by a large number of respondents.

The important principle is to use simple words and uncomplicated sentences.

Leading questions

Television or radio interviewers' questions are sometimes preceded by 'Wouldn't you agree that . . . ?', or 'Isn't it the case that . . . ?'. The object is to **lead** the individual into agreeing with a particular statement. Researchers, however, need to take a more objective stance and avoid leading questions. For example, if you are carrying out a study of employees' attitudes to the organisation in which they are employed, you should not ask: 'Don't you agree that Eco Oil Incorporated is an excellent Company in which to work?' or 'Isn't it the case that Eco Oil offer a good range of benefits to employees?' Rather, an open-ended question such as: 'What benefits are there in working at Eco Oil?' or a closed question listing various company benefits, such as pensions, medical cover and canteen facilities, or asking the respondent to rate which benefit is regarded as most valuable, would yield more objective and helpful results. It is important to establish what the respondent thinks is important, without being directed by the researcher. It can be argued, however, that this desire for objectivity can sometimes be unproductive. For example, the question, 'Don't you think that the recent redundancies show that the company is not interested in its employees' welfare?' is clearly leading, but it may evoke a deeper and more thoughtful response than a bland question which receives only a conventional and unreflecting answer.

Double-barrelled questions

Double-barrelled questions are those which ask two questions in one. For example, if the question 'Do you travel abroad in the course of your work and do you enjoy it?' is asked, it may be that the answer to the first part is yes, while the second is no, so that the respondent is not sure how to answer. The questions should be separated: 'Do you travel abroad in the course of your work?' ; if yes, 'Do you enjoy travelling abroad in the course of your work?' Two questions in one will lead to confusion. Another example is a question in which a person is asked, in one sentence, whether they know about something and what they think of it: 'Do you know anything about the government's new council tax, and what is your opinion of it?'

It is also advisable to avoid double negatives. If you were to ask someone whether he or she agrees that, 'Those not over 18 should not be allowed to drink alcohol in pubs, restaurants or at home', it is not clear what an answer 'no' is intended to mean.

Hypothetical questions

For most studies, hypothetical questions are best avoided. These questions usually begin with 'What would you do if . . . .?' or 'Would you like to . . . ?' What the respondent or interviewee says he or she might do when faced with a given situation may not be a good guide to their actual future behaviour. There are some questions which inevitably produce favourable replies: 'Would you like to have a higher income?' is unlikely to be met with a negative response.

There are, of course, instances where it may be useful to ask people to imagine what they would do in a certain situation: 'If you saw a serious traffic accident would you offer your name and address to the police as a witness?' Whether such hypothetical questioning is useful will be dictated by the subject matter of the study.

Secondary information

In most instances, it is inadvisable to ask respondents or interviewees about someone else's views, that is, request secondary information. An individual may not know a relative's opinions on say, capital punishment, abortion, or sexual equality. Neither will respondents necessarily be able to describe the experiences of another person. However, if the other person is not easily available for interview, it is common practice to ask a member of their household for *factual* information about them (for example, their age, sex, occupation and so on). This is called using a 'proxy' for the intended interviewee.

Periodicity

When investigating behaviour which requires the individual to specify a time or a number, supply specific categories. Thus, when asking how often the respondent attends the theatre or reads a newspaper, offer the alternatives: daily, 2–3 times a week, once a week, twice a month and so on. Terms such as 'often', 'frequently', or 'regularly' are too vague and should be avoided.

Sensitivity

Even seemingly straightforward questions can be sensitive for respondents and therefore give rise to invalid data. For example, Sudman and Bradburn (1983) suggest that library membership is viewed by some as a 'socially desirable' activity, and library card ownership may consequently be over-reported. Sudman and Bradburn note that there are three main areas where over-reporting may occur:

1. 'Being a good citizen', that is, voting behaviour, relationships with government officials and community activities.
2. 'Being a well-informed and cultured person', for example, newspaper

and book readership, and attendance at concerts and plays, involvement in educational activities.

3. 'Fulfilling moral and social responsibilities', that is, contributions to charity, helping family and friends, and being in employment.

Conversely, there may be under-reporting of certain aspects of individuals' lives, such as illness and disability, criminal behaviour, sexual activities, smoking, drinking and financial status.

Because of the dangers of either over-reporting or under-reporting, questions need to be phrased so that they do not intimidate those taking part in the study. Careful preparation of questions, using foresight and experience to predict those which may prove to be sensitive, will ensure that you get the best response from participants.

6.6   The format of a questionnaire

A questionnaire should be designed with the respondent in mind. To reiterate, ensure that the right questions are asked, that the order of questions is logical, and that the pre-coding is effective. The questionnaire also has to be simple to process in terms of post-coding and computerisation. However, the primary aims are to make it an attractive document for the respondent to complete, to ensure that accurate answers are given and that misunderstandings are eliminated.

An introductory letter should be included as part of the questionnaire so that it does not go adrift. For a postal questionnaire, the date by which the questionnaire needs to be returned should also be given; generally two weeks from the distribution date. Either a stamped addressed envelope or a 'Freepost' envelope must be included.

The questionnaire should provide clear instructions. Explain at the beginning what is needed, if necessary providing illustrations. It is particularly important to ensure that participants understand whether a single response to a question is wanted, or whether several responses to one question would be appropriate.

Here is a checklist of key points to remember.

1. All closed questions must be pre-coded, allowing for as many alternatives as possible. Always include an 'other' category.
2. For some open-ended questions, prompts may be needed.
3. Ensure that you have appropriate columns for computerisation of the data (see chapter 11).
4. Remember to include filter questions and provide clear directions so that the respondent need only read questions which are appropriate to his or her circumstances.
5. Each question must be numbered. If appropriate, section headings and subsections are useful as guidance for both respondent and

researcher. When the topic changes, an introductory sentence should
be provided.

6. Neither split questions between pages, nor ask a question on one page
    and ask for a response on the other.

7. An identification number must be put on every questionnaire to enable
    checking and reminders to be sent if questionnaires are not returned.

The questionnaire should not appear to be too lengthy. Anyone
receiving a 20 page unsolicited document through the mail is unlikely to say
'Wonderful, I'm looking forward to spending a couple of hours on this!'
and may well feel that the rewards are outweighed by the costs of carrying
out the exercise. For most studies, a questionnaire should take less than
half-an-hour to complete. So, list the questions you require, edit as much
as possible, and try to limit the layout to no more than six sides of paper. It
is more likely that there will be a good response rate if a concise
questionnaire is provided.

The order in which questions are asked is important; the questions
should not jump from subject to subject. A question about marital
relationships, followed by one about work experience, then one on home
ownership before a return to the subject of marital relationships, would be
an example of poor ordering. When positioning the questions, try to follow
the same sequence one would in normal conversation, with each question
arising logically out of the one before.

Questions should not only fit together but also be grouped together
according to subject. If the ordering of questions is unpredictable, it will
frustrate respondents and make the study appear ill-considered and
amateurish.

It is also essential to provide clear linking sentences, particularly when
moving on to a different topic. Phrases such as: 'Moving on to . . .', 'The
next set of questions concern . . .', or 'I'd now like to ask you about . . .'
can be used.

The interest of the respondent needs to be engaged and maintained. It is
best to begin with simple and easy questions which are non-threatening.
Once the individual begins to complete the questionnaire, or take part in
the interview, the chances of successfully obtaining the more sensitive
items of information improve. Even if the later questions are left
unanswered, it may still be the case that earlier responses will be valuable
for the study.

Questions concerning socioeconomic data are normally best asked at the
end of questioning. However, there are exceptions. For example, if you
are examining experiences of child-rearing, you would need to ask early on
whether the respondent had children, so that those who were childless
could be redirected or excluded.

Postal questionnaires should begin with closed questions, where responses can simply be ticked, rather than open questions which may

Q.1 Is this your first job?	Yes	if yes, go to question 3
	No	if no, go to question 2
Q.2 Where did you work before joining the Company?	. . . .	
Q.3 When did you join the Company?	. . . .	

Figure 6.7

require the respondent to give considerable thought to an answer. It is preferable to ask open questions at a point when the respondent has become committed to the questionnaire.

Both questionnaires and interview schedules usually need to include filter (or skip) questions to guide both respondent and interviewer through the questions, avoiding those which are irrelevant to the respondent. Interviewees answering the questions shown in Figure 6.7 who have not had a job before should not be asked the question about their previous employment. This is the purpose of the instructions to the interviewer on the right hand side. Filter questions are essential to avoid confusion and wasting the time of those interviewing or those completing questionnaires.

Producing the questionnaire in a booklet form looks professional and makes the document easier to handle. Generally an A4 paper size allows for questions to be well-spaced and clearly printed.

Choose an attractive typeface for the document. In these days of sophisticated word-processing programs, people are used to receiving good quality paperwork. So, choose a typeface which is easy to read, using a range of sizes to make instructions and questions clear to the respondent. If the budget will allow, use good quality paper. One colleague always produces documents on thick, beige paper because she believes that (1) it stands out from the mass of other paper which might be received, (2) it is pleasant to handle, and (3) people will not have the heart to throw away such an attractive document. She says it works. In reality, finances may be limited, so you will have to do your best with whatever you have available. However, remember that its appearance will have a significant influence on whether the questionnaire is completed or not.

A note of thanks expressing appreciation for the assistance given should be placed at the end of the questionnaire.

When each questionnaire is returned, it needs to be checked for missing information.

It will certainly be necessary to send reminders to those who have not

Good morning/afternoon/evening. I am from the University of Surrey. We are conducting a survey on behalf of the Borough Council, to find out what tenants think about their housing and various aspects of the service provided by the Council. A representative sample of Council tenants have been selected for interview in this survey. It is important that you take part, so that an accurate picture of the views of tenants is obtained.

Everything you say will be treated confidentially. It is important that you answer all questions honestly. The Council will not be able to identify any actual comments made by specific tenants.

The interview will take about 45 minutes. Would it be convenient now, or if preferred I could come back at another time? When would be most convenient?

If anyone else is present, ask if there is anywhere you could go for the interview which is quiet.

Figure 6.8   *The interviewer's introduction from the Public Housing Survey*

returned questionnaires. Decide on a timescale; plot the rate of return on graph paper and send reminders when the response rate begins to fall. Usually, reminders include another copy of the questionnaire and are sent within two weeks of the date given for the return of the questionnaire. Telephone calls may be necessary to encourage completion and return.

6.7   The format of an interview schedule

The interview schedule, or interview guide, will be handled by a trained interviewer; these documents may be used for face-to-face or telephone interviews. It is important that the same guidelines are followed by each interviewer and, therefore, instructions must be explicit.

Even if the interviewee has received prior notification of the interview by letter or telephone, the interview schedule must begin with a brief introduction, stating who the interviewer is, which organisation he or she represents and the purpose of the interview. Confidentiality and anonymity should be stressed. The introduction in Figure 6.8 was used in the public housing survey described in chapter 3.

Interview schedules, like questionnaires, must provide filter questions to ensure that the interviewer can move smoothly from section to section. This is particularly important in telephone interviewing when silences over the telephone while the interviewer sifts through the questions may confuse or annoy interviewees. Several filter questions, and examples of other features of interview schedules, are shown in Figure 6.9, an extract from the housing survey.

For some closed questions, it can be more convenient to offer grouped answers on a prompt card (see Figure 6.10). For example, in most

IF HOUSEHOLD TOOK UP TENANCY IN 1983 OR LATER (IN LAST 5 YEARS)

ASK SECTION 1, if not, GO TO SECTION 2.

SECTION 1. INITIAL TAKE UP OF TENANCY

1. When you moved into your present house/flat did you move:

From Council Waiting List	1 (1)
From temporary Hostel (Homeless) accommodation	2
Moved because of modernisation programme	3
Transfer or exchange of Council property	4
Other (Specify)	7
NA/NR	9

(a) Is your present house/flat temporary (short-term) accommodation?

Yes – temporary accommodation	1 (2)
No – permanent home	2
Don't know	8
NA/NR	9

2. When you first took up the tenancy what was the internal decoration like?

Very good	1 (3)
Good	2
Acceptable	3
Poor	4
Very poor	5
Don't know	8
NA/NR	9

If Poor or 'Very Poor'

(a) How did you feel about this?

Extremely upset/very disturbed/desperate	1 (4)
Very unhappy	2
Unhappy	3
Did not mind/not concerned	4
Quite happy	5
NA/NR	9

(b) Did you receive a decoration allowance (because of the poor decorative order of the property)?

Yes	1 (5)
No	2
Don't know	8
NA/NR	9

Figure 6.9 *An extract from the Public Housing Survey*

instances the exact date of birth of respondents is not of interest, but just their age group. Participants also find it more convenient (and, in terms of age, sometimes less embarrassing) to indicate a range, as shown in Figure 6.10(a). Cards can also be used to list various alternatives from which the

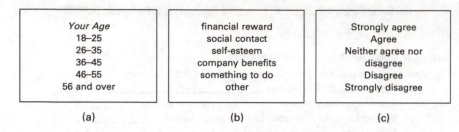

(a)　　　　　　　　　　(b)　　　　　　　　　　(c)

Figure 6.10

interviewee can choose. For example, when asking the question: 'What are the most important aspects of being employed?', the card can list the responses shown in Figure 6.10(b). Cards can be used for attitude questions. For example, the responses offered for the proposition, 'The government should provide housewives with an income' might be as shown in Figure 6.10(c). Supplying prompts will also help respondents remember events which they might otherwise have forgotten.

If there is a long list of statements to be read or shown to interviewees, it is possible that items at the top of the list are attended to more closely than those in the middle or at the bottom. To reduce this potential bias, the items in the lists can be rearranged with some interviewers using one order and others using an alternative.

An interviewee cannot look at a card when being interviewed by telephone so an alternative technique is to read all the items and obtain a yes/no answer to each one separately. The number of items will need to be limited to three or four for this to work.

6.8   Preparing for fieldwork

When developing a questionnaire or interview schedule, there are two preliminary steps you should take. First, try your draft out on a few friends. Second, 'pilot' the questionnaire or schedule on a small sample drawn from the same population as the main study.

It is very useful to try a questionnaire or schedule on friends and colleagues who will cast a critical eye over the questions and the order in which they are placed. This will also help to ensure that instructions and guidelines are clear. It is surprising how often a question which seems perfectly satisfactory to the author proves to be ambiguous to others. It is better to discover this before it is too late. The questions can then be revised and a working document produced.

The next stage is to conduct a pilot study. The number of people to be included in this initial study will depend on the ultimate size of the main sample, but as a guide, providing that there is sufficient time and money, a 10 per cent pilot sample would be helpful. It is vital that this initial group has similar characteristics to those of the population to be studied. From the pilot, the researcher will be able to assess whether the line of questioning is appropriate and whether the document is understandable and simple to use.

In most cases, potential respondents are not obliged to take part in a study and must therefore be persuaded to do so. As Sudman and Bradburn suggest:

> Their only reward is some measure of psychic gratification: the opportunity to state their opinions or relate their experiences to a sympathetic and nonjudgmental listener, the chance to contribute to public or scientific knowledge, or even the positive feeling that they have helped the interviewer. (Sudman and Bradburn, 1983: 5)

The theory of social exchange propounded by Blau (1964), among others, argues that individuals' actions are motivated by the 'rewards' they are likely to receive from others. Although there may be certain 'costs' in performing any particular action, most individuals try to ensure that these are outweighed by the benefits they receive. In general, the material rewards offered by researchers to participants taking part in a study are likely to be low. However, if individuals feel that they have been specially selected and that their participation is highly valued, this may be sufficient reward. The costs are the time taken to provide answers and the mental effort required; furthermore, the questions may make the individual feel anxious or embarrassed and these costs may in the end outweigh any rewards.

An effective introductory letter is especially important when carrying out postal studies because it helps secure the cooperation of potential participants. When an individual receives an unsolicited questionnaire through the post, his or her immediate reaction may be to ask any or all of the following questions: 'What is the study about?' 'Who is carrying it out?' 'How long will it take to complete?' 'What are they trying to sell to me?' An introductory letter may allay some of these doubts and anxieties.

Begin by introducing yourself and your organisation, and briefly state the aims and objectives of the research. In most instances, the individual has nothing to gain by taking part and it is therefore necessary to emphasise why the study is important and to make the individual feel that he or she will be making a valuable contribution to research by participating. You will also need to state why the individual was chosen for the study so a brief outline of the sample is useful.

It is also vital to stress that confidentiality will be maintained and that information provided will only be used by those involved in the research. State that the report derived from the study will only include statistical information and unattributable quotations.

Letters should be personalised by a signature. Attention can be drawn to a telephone number so that individuals approached can seek more information.

6.9 Conclusion

This chapter has provided some guidelines and offered some practical assistance so that most of the difficulties of preparing questions can be foreseen and avoided. The fundamental idea underpinning the approach outlined here is that attention must be given to all aspects of the questioning process if a satisfactory response rate and valuable data are to be obtained.

The researcher must give thought to what is to be investigated, what form and types of questions are relevant and whether the questions ask for information which is available to the participants. Questions should be clear, composed of everyday words and simple sentences, and the order in which they are presented should be logical. Questionnaires and interview schedules should be drafted, tested, edited and tested again, before being used for the survey.

6.10 Project

Now you have been given some guidelines, try to put these into practice by developing a self-completion questionnaire. Imagine that you have been asked by the Health Education Council to carry out an investigation into leisure activities. You have been asked to select a representative sample of the population (see chapter 5) and ask questions about *all* leisure activities in which the respondents have been involved during the past month. You will need to devise a working definition of 'leisure activity' to guide the design of the questions. The Health Education Council is particularly interested in distinguishing between active and passive activities. Therefore, you will need to ask questions about sport (e.g. horse riding, athletics, weight-training, fishing), creative pursuits (e.g. gardening, painting, DIY, playing musical instruments) as well as television and radio.

As this will be a self-completion questionnaire, try to include as many closed questions as possible, with pre-coded categories.

So that correlations can be made when you analyse the data, choose a number of variables which may be relevant, for example: age, sex, employment status, income, marital status, physical health, and so on.

Prepare a draft, test it with a friend, and then try the final questionnaire out on a small sample of about five people.

6.11 Further reading

A very useful book which comprehensively covers all aspects of questioning is Sudman and Bradburn (1983). It is particularly helpful on the subject of designing questions on 'sensitive' issues and also addresses the problem of ensuring that the answers gained accurately represent the views of the respondent.

Stacey (1969) has two brief, but valuable chapters on asking questions and carrying out a survey; they are succinct and to the point.

Moser and Kalton (1971) can be recommended for its comprehensive discussion of several aspects of survey research. It is particularly helpful in discussing some examples of social surveys. It includes a typical question-naire produced by the market research company Gallup.

Dillman (1978) provides a good review of postal and telephone methods, and describes the ways in which survey methods can be enhanced to increase response rates and obtain the most valuable data.

7 Measuring attitudes

Michael Procter

Contents

The content of many surveys can conveniently be divided into two components: 'objective' and 'subjective'. The first of these certainly needs to be printed in quotation marks, since there is a point of view according to which all social facts are social constructs.

For instance, gender looks like a clear example of an objectively ascertainable variable: if you have a Y chromosome you are male; if not, you are female. But of course it is only relatively recently that the chromosomal determination of sex has been understood, and yet gender has been regarded as an important characteristic at least throughout recorded history. Also, it is not uncommon for a person's social gender to be different from their biological sex. But the problematic nature of gender can be taken further. There is no necessary reason why the most fundamental classification of human beings should be dictated by this dichotomy. Of course, it is a very useful classification, and it is related to the need for reproduction, which is indeed essential to the survival of the species, but this justification does not apply to people who are out of the reproduction game, such as many gay men. Still less does it apply appropriately to transsexuals: people of either sex who identify with the other gender. So it is not difficult to imagine a society developing a classification quite different from the simple dichotomy that is virtually universal at present.

However, this is mentioned here in order in future to ignore it: from a naive point of view, which will be adopted from this point on, there is a radical difference between the two components. There are the approximately objective, factual variables such as age, gender, and even social class, since this is typically classified on the basis of ostensibly factual information about the respondent's occupation. Then there are the variables that result from asking the respondent for a frankly subjective reaction: an opinion on a social issue, or something of the sort. This latter component is often referred to as attitudinal. ('Opinion' and 'value' are examples of terms used as near-synonyms to attitude: for present purposes there is little point in trying to differentiate them.)

7.1 What is an attitude?

The first point to be made is that an attitude is a hypothetical construct: no one has ever seen or touched one, and its existence and properties must be inferred indirectly. This is in itself not an embarrassment: there are plenty of other perfectly respectable examples of unobserved constructs, including not only most of social science but also large chunks of physics. What is important is that the particular construct should be linked in well understood theoretical terms to other constructs, and that it should be possible at least in principle to make empirical observations that could produce evidence either consistent or inconsistent with those theoretical links. It has to be admitted that in practice there is not as much theory or evidence as one would like. However, the idea of an attitude is so natural that despite these failings it remains central to much research in sociology and social psychology.

There is little point in reviewing the different definitions of attitude that have appeared over the years. What does seem to be common to most of these definitions is that an attitude is a predisposition to behave in a particular way. If a friend eats no meat, attends hunt saboteur meetings and demonstrates outside the pharmacology department's animal laboratories then you might explain all of this in terms of a particular attitude to animal welfare.

There is a long-standing debate, sometimes called the 'attitude–behaviour problem' which refers to the common (indeed, almost universal) finding that there is no simple relationship between verbal and non-verbal indicators of an attitude. In the classic study by LaPiere (1934), it was found that restaurants which declined to accept reservations for Black guests in response to a telephone enquiry, almost without exception admitted such customers when they arrived without a booking and gave 'exemplary service'. The general point to be made is that if there is an underlying attitude it will not be the sole determinant of either the verbal or the non-verbal behaviour, and high correlations can be expected only if the entire situation is very carefully analysed. In particular, it seems likely that LaPiere's restaurateurs, motivated chiefly by commercial consider-ations, believed that they would be less likely to lose custom by discreetly admitting a Black customer who was actually in the foyer than by risking a scene. The latter problem did not exist for the telephone booking, so that in that setting the balance of advantage was in favour of refusing the reservation.

In short, a verbal statement is only a **behavioural indicator** of an attitude and the attitude–behaviour problem is really just one aspect of the more general one of imperfect relationships between different behaviours.

7.2   A preliminary example

Before getting more deeply into the theoretical and methodological problems of attitude measurement, let us consider the problem of measur-ing political radicalism through a questionnaire, either self-completed or administered in the course of a survey interview. A number of points will emerge to be dealt with in more detail in later sections.

You might begin by thinking of a simple question to ask: for instance, 'Do you consider yourself to be politically radical?' Respondents could be invited to simply answer 'yes' or 'no', or to choose one of, say, five answers from 'yes, very' to 'no, on the contrary'. (In principle they could be allowed to make an open response, but in practice this would be too complicated to analyse in a typical survey sample of 1,000 or more.)

There are several objections to such an approach. The one emphasised here is that the researcher is asking the lay respondent to make a social-scientific judgement: the question assumes that the respondent uses the term 'politically radical' in essentially the same way as the researcher, even when applying it to him- or herself. Even if there were agreement on the beliefs that tended to be part of radicalism, a person's judgement is likely to be situation-dependent: when I am with some of my colleagues (ageing 1960s revolutionaries) I might think myself a conservative; in the company of some students, imbued with the New Realism, I might think myself a dangerous radical. Only an 'objective' observer, such as a researcher aspires to be, may be expected to apply the same criteria in a roughly consistent way across a range of individuals and settings.

It would perhaps be more reasonable to ask the respondent to answer a question that did not demand as much prior analysis on their part. For instance, we could ask which political party he or she belongs to or identifies most closely with, and then use our knowledge of the parties to classify people into radicals and non-radicals, or to locate them on a radical–conservative scale. A different problem here is that people sometimes identify with parties for non-ideological reasons – because of class identification, or family tradition, perhaps – so that you measure the wrong construct.

Alternatively, we could try to formulate a question that would encapsulate our concept of radicalism more directly. Suppose we saw it in terms of the Labour Party's celebrated Clause Four, which calls for the common ownership of the means of production, distribution and exchange. Then we would ask our respondent to indicate an opinion of that view, either by a simple agreement or disagreement, or on a scale from complete endorsement to complete rejection.

What are the problems now? The first is that a single item is a very unsatisfactory way of measuring an underlying attitude.

Here is an analogy that may help. Suppose that you want to get a brief message from one mountain top to another by using teams of shouters, who are recruited in pairs. The big difficulty is that, for religious reasons about which there is no room to go into in detail, every 'signal shouter', who will obediently shout the same message in unison with the other signal shouters (the words 'Party tonight!', say) is accompanied by a 'noise shouter'. All the noise shouters will shout different words. If you have just one pair of shouters the noise is just as audible as the signal, which may well not be received. But if you use 10 pairs, the message will be shouted 10 times as loud, whereas the different noises will tend to cancel each other out, so that the signal has a much greater chance of being correctly received. Something rather like this can be observed at the last night of the Proms, London's summer classical music festival, where, during an interval in the music, a small, carefully rehearsed section of the Promenaders shouts a humorous message in unison, which is quite audible over the random chatter of thousands.

The same analysis can be applied to measurement problems.

It is convenient to see any behaviour as being determined by an equation of the following form:

$$B = A + R$$

Here B means an item of behaviour (in the case of attitude measurement it will be verbal behaviour), A means attitude, and R means randomness. In words, a particular item of verbal behaviour (a statement of opinion, say) is determined partly by a relevant attitude and partly by a large number of other influences, which can be regarded as essentially random.

If we consider two related statements (related in the sense that they may be regarded as manifestations of the same underlying attitude), called B_1

and B_2, then their two equations will be identical in form, though slightly different in detail:

$$B_1 = A_1 + R_1$$
$$B_2 = A_2 + R_2$$

It is often reasonable to assume that A_1 and A_2 are essentially the same thing (because both statements are, as already specified, to do with the same attitude), but that R_1 and R_2 are different random influences.

Suppose, now, that we consider both B_1 and B_2 (for the same individual). This **compound behaviour** now contains a double dose of both the attitudinal determinant and the random influences. The difference between these is that the attitude is duplicated (like the shouted signal), and therefore reinforced, whereas the random influences (like the shouted noise) are not duplicated, and thus become diluted. So the share of the compound behaviour that is due to the attitude is greater than is the case for either of the individual statements.

To put this in more concrete terms, any single statement, intended as an indicator of an underlying attitude, will always be heavily contaminated with other influences, and thus measure the attitude rather poorly; several statements, all chosen so as to reflect the same underlying attitude, will do so collectively far more effectively.

Some technical details will be added to this observation below, under the heading of reliability and validity.

The second problem is that it is certainly unrealistic to see political radicalism solely in terms of an attitude to Clause Four. To put it in more technical terms, most attitudes are multidimensional. In the present context this means that we would almost certainly want to include in our conception of radicalism other issues that are logically unconnected with the question of common ownership. Examples that occur to me (though one would usually use less subjective sources, as will be outlined later) include nuclear disarmament and pacifism, redistribution of resources within a nation and between nations, racial and gender divisions, sexuality, freedom of information and other civil liberties, and so on. Each of these is a very broad heading, and might be represented by a range of specific statements. For instance, the redistribution area might include statements about levels of income tax and inheritance tax, and about direct confiscation of wealth; and about terms of trade and financial relations between developed and 'third world' countries.

Appropriate analysis would probably show that, rather than a single dimension of radicalism, there are several, and that, although there may be some tendency for a respondent who is in favour of reducing expenditure on armaments also to be in favour of increasing overseas aid, there will be many individual exceptions, so that, in brief, the two views may be seen as belonging to two distinct dimensions of radicalism.

All of this implies that it is always desirable, and often essential, to adopt a multiple-indicator approach. This means putting together a collection of statements thought to be relevant to the concept to be measured. First, of course, the concept itself must be defined as closely as possible, with what help one can get from a search of the literature. The statements are then assembled from a variety of sources, including written materials of various kinds (e.g. the press, pamphlets, polemical books) and oral statements taken from group discussions and unstructured interviews. They are edited to try to avoid the pitfalls discussed in chapter 6. The final versions of the items are then put to a sample from the appropriate population and the responses analysed so as to determine how best to use them to represent the attitude. In practice one usually starts with too many statements, so as to be able to select a subset of the best.

A number of approaches have been proposed within this general framework and these are described in the next section. However, in order to understand them, it is necessary to know about a key statistical concept: correlation.

7.2.1 Correlation

The correlation coefficient is a number between 0 and 1 (calculated from a rather complicated formula – or by giving the appropriate command to a computer program) that indexes the strength of the relationship between two variables. If the correlation is zero then the two variables are completely unrelated: for instance, if there is no tendency whatsoever for agreement with one of two statements of opinion to imply agreement with the other. On the other hand, a correlation of 1 means perfect association: here it would mean that agreement with one statement would unerringly imply agreement with the other. Correlations can also be negative: a value of −1 would mean that everyone who agreed with one statement disagreed with the other. (One might get something approaching this situation because the wordings of the two statements were in some sense 'opposite ways around' : one that favoured first-strike use of nuclear weapons and another that favoured immediate unilateral disarmament, perhaps.)

Of course, in practice we always find correlations of intermediate value. You can either interpret these essentially qualitatively – 'a higher correlation means a closer relationship' – or you can try something slightly more technical. In brief, if you square a correlation coefficient, the resulting value (which must necessarily be positive, of course) can be interpreted as the proportion of the variance in one variable that is shared with the other.

7.3 Techniques of attitude scale construction

There are a large number of methods of constructing attitude scales, which will be described rather briefly in this section. Many of them are of importance more because of their frequent mention especially in the older literature than because they are still recommended.

7.3.1 Thurstone scaling

Leo Thurstone (1928) was the first important pioneer in this field. He suggested a method that involved the following steps:

1. Collect statements of relevant opinion, chosen in such a way as to range along the presumed scale of attitude, from most favourable to most unfavourable. Edit them for clarity, etc. End with about 100 statements.
2. Recruit a panel of about 300 judges, and ask them to sort the statements into 11 numbered piles, from most to least favourable, with a middle, neutral category. Each statement thus receives 300 scores. The average of these is that statement's scale value.
3. Twenty statements or so are selected for further use, in such a way that they cover the range of the scale and avoid statements on which the judges disagree too widely.
4. In use with a study sample (as opposed to the panel of judges), the final set of statements is offered to the respondents, who are asked to indicate the ones they agree with. Their scale scores are then the averages of the endorsed items' scale values.

However, this method is extremely expensive in time and other resources and is rarely used today.

7.3.2 Likert scaling

Rensis Likert (1932) developed a method that, as well as making different statistical assumptions, had the great advantage over Thurstone scaling of dispensing with the initial large panel of judges. (An example of a set of items based on this approach is described in section 3.6.)

1. The initial collecting of opinion statements proceeds as before.
2. The statements are administered to the study sample (without a preliminary panel of judges).
3. Respondents are asked to respond to each item by placing their response on (typically) a five point scale, most often

    strongly agree . . . agree . . . can't decide . . . disagree . . . strongly disagree

    These are usually coded 5 . . . 1.
4. For each item the 'item-whole' correlation is calculated between that item and the sum of the remaining items. Items with excessively low correlations are eliminated from further analysis, on the grounds that

they must be failing to tap the attitude that is measured by the other items. The computer program SPSS/PC (see chapter 12) includes a procedure called RELIABILITY which carries out all of these calculations.
5. Scale scores for individuals are determined by summing the retained item scores.

An important difference between Thurstone and Likert scale items should be explained. A typical Thurstone item is worded in such a way that some respondents will agree with it, some will disagree because it is too favourable to the issue in question, and some will disagree because it is too unfavourable. For instance, a statement designed to measure attitudes to the present government might say 'about half their policies have been successful'. Strong supporters and opponents would both reject this statement (and would be catered for by parallel statements attributing higher and lower success rates). On the other hand, a Likert item would say 'the present government has been successful'. This would be rejected by all opponents of the government, but could be accepted by all their supporters, however enthusiastic.

Likert items are called **monotonic** and Thurstone **non-monotonic**. To understand these terms, think of each person as occupying a position on a vertical line extending from most 'con' (at the bottom) to most 'pro' (at the top) with respect to the government (or other social object). Statements of opinion are arranged on the same line, in increasing favourableness from bottom to top. A moderate Likert item will be rejected (for simplicity suppose we only permit two responses, agree or disagree) by all respondents positioned well below it and accepted by all those well above it. There will be individuals in the immediate vicinity of the item who hesitate: the more favourable they are, the greater the probability that they will accept. On the other hand, a Thurstone item will be rejected by respondents too far above it or below it. As we consider individuals who are close to the item, going from bottom to top, the probability of acceptance will first rise and then fall again.

In essence, monotonic means 'order-maintaining': as we go up the attitude continuum the probability of accepting a Likert item at first remains steady at 0, then rises over its immediate vicinity, then remains steady at 1; having risen it never falls again. A non-monotonic Thurstone item, on the other hand, first rises in probability and then falls again.

Nowadays most attitude items are constructed so as to be monotonic (and are often referred to as 'Likert items', especially if the responses form a five-point scale), although the analysis usually follows the factor model described below in section 7.5.

7.3.3 Guttman scaling

Louis Guttman (1944) was one of a team of eminent social scientists recruited to the US Army during the Second World War. The method that bears his name has been extremely influential (even though it is not often used in its original form) because Guttman continued for many years to develop his methods into more general forms.

The essential idea behind his original formulation is that of a cumulative scale. One problem with, say, a Likert scale is that though a particular set of responses will always add up to the same total score, the same total score may arise from many combinations of responses. For instance, a score of 10 on a five-item scale could come from 'disagree' (scored 2) on each item, or from one 'strongly agree', one 'disagree' and three 'strongly disagrees'. In practice one would seldom get quite such different combinations, but clearly it would be preferable if the same score always meant the same thing.

It is easiest to give an example of such a desirable property from achievement testing. Suppose your class is given a maths test consisting of three questions which require respectively addition, multiplication and differentiation. Each answer is scored 'pass' or 'fail'. In principle there could be eight different patterns of pass/fail ($2 \times 2 \times 2$), but in practice there would only be four: some would pass all three items, some would pass the first two but fail the third, some would pass only the first, and some would fail all three. To put it slightly differently, a score of 2, say, would in practice identify someone who can add and multiply but not differentiate: we would not expect to find someone who can differentiate but not add.

One attitude item can also be regarded as more difficult than another, in the sense that it will be endorsed only by a respondent with a stronger positive attitude. For instance, a respondent with a moderately negative attitude to smoking might agree that television advertising of cigarettes should be banned. Someone with a stronger negative attitude, who agreed with a ban on smoking in all public places, would almost certainly also agree with the first item. There would probably be rather few individuals who would reverse this: who agreed with the public smoking ban but thought television advertising should continue. Of course, since there is no logical connection between the two items, whether this neat relationship actually holds is an empirical question, and the development of a multi-item cumulative scale of this kind (often simply called a Guttman scale) involves a complicated statistical analysis.

In more recent years, Guttman, Lingoes and others have developed multidimensional extensions to this method, called generically Smallest Space Analysis. In parallel with this, other groups of researchers have developed very similar analyses called Multidimensional Scaling. At one level these may be regarded as alternatives to Factor Analysis (see section 7.5) that make more realistic assumptions about the measurement properties of the data. Specifically, many of these methods assume only ordinal measure, whereas Factor Analysis is usually regarded as requiring interval measure: the difference between 'agree' and 'strongly agree' should be quantitatively the same as that between 'strongly disagree' and 'disagree'.

7.3.4 Magnitude estimation

Magnitude estimation has its origins in the attempts of psychologists to measure the relationship between the strength of a physical stimulus (the intensity of a light, the pressure level of a sound, a weight resting on the hand, an electric current) on the one hand, and the strength of the corresponding experience on the other. The same stimulus is offered at a range of different objective intensities, and the subject is asked to give a subjective numerical rating to each one. The results, averaged over a dozen subjects, are plotted. It turns out that people can handle this task in a quite consistent way, though the details differ between sense modalities.

Sellin and Wolfgang (1964) found that their respondents could give similarly consistent ratings on a social perception task. They constructed brief narratives focusing on the theft of goods worth a varying amount, other details of the offence being held constant. Ratings of the perceived seriousness of each offence were plotted on the vertical axis, with the actual amount on the horizontal. As with physical stimuli, respondents (judges, police officers and students) spontaneously gave ratings that followed a consistent curve. Emboldened by this success, Sellin and Wolfgang asked for seriousness ratings on other offences not involving a quantifiable loss, such as smoking marijuana, assault and sex abuse. It seemed reasonable to assume that seriousness was being rated in the same way as when a money amount was mentioned; if this is so, one can assign a seriousness score to any offence and estimate the aggregate seriousness of a year's offences in a way that makes far more sense than merely counting 'crimes known to the police' : for instance, there is a basis for assessing the effect of a decrease in crimes against the person and an increase in property offences.

Since Sellin and Wolfgang (1964), magnitude estimation has been used much more widely, to obtain, for instance, quantitative measures of a candidate's political popularity. Respondents have been asked, instead of giving an oral numerical response, to draw a line whose length reflects their strength of feeling. Originally this was done on paper, with obvious inconvenience from the researcher's point of view, but respondents can now use a joy-stick (meant originally for playing Space Invaders) to draw the line on a computer screen, which automatically measures the length and 'acquires' the data for instant statistical analysis.

7.3.5 Expectancy-value scaling

Fishbein and Ajzen (1975) propose a method of not just measuring but also analysing attitudes, the expectancy-value (E-V) approach. This is based on the assumption that we consider a number of dimensions in evaluating any social object, and refers back to early theoretical formulations that refer to affective and cognitive components in attitudes. Respondents are asked to what extent they approve of each of a set of dimensions (the affective, or 'value' component), and then to what extent they believe each dimension applies to the issue being considered (cognitive, or 'expectancy'). Each expectancy is combined with its value to get an overall E-V score. For instance, overall preferences between energy technologies (nuclear, fossil fuel, tidal power, etc.) were evaluated by asking to what extent (in probability terms) each was characterised by low cost, risk of catastrophe, long- and short-term pollution and favourable technological spin-offs. Before this, the liking or disliking for each dimension was elicited. The contribution of each dimension to the overall evaluation was estimated by multiplying the probability score by the liking score. A technology would tend to be favoured overall if liked dimensions were seen as having high probability, and disliked dimensions had low probability. For instance, catastrophe was highly disliked, but seen as very unlikely for tidal power.

The advantages of the E-V approach are, first, a convenient format and, second, the possibility of analysing the reasons for an overall score. In the example just given, it was found that overall attitudes measured separately seemed to be far more highly correlated with negative than with positive dimensions: respondents tended to approve of a technology because of the absence of bad points rather than because of the presence of good ones. This in turn would tell policy makers that if they wanted to gain public acceptance for nuclear power, say, it would do little good to emphasise low costs and favourable spin-offs; what was needed instead was a changing perception of the dangers of catastrophe and long-term pollution.

7.4   Reliability and validity

A pair of key methodological concepts that have been touched on elsewhere in this text are reliability and validity. The distinction between them may be seen in these terms: **reliability** is about whether a measure works in a consistent way; **validity** is about whether the right concept is measured. It is very easy to produce a highly reliable measure of political radicalism in the following way. The person to be measured is asked to stand bare-foot with their heels against a wall. A hard-bound book is held horizontally just touching the top of the person's head and a pencil mark is made on the wall at the level of the book. The distance of the mark above the floor in centimetres is measured with a steel tape measure. This quantity is then subtracted from 300 to give a final score. Such a measure will be highly reliable in that essentially the same score will always be obtained for the same respondent, at least in the short term.

What about validity? Without going into the concrete procedures that might be applied here, the question is essentially about whether a person with a high score is 'really' more politically radical than someone with a low score. Because of the curious subtraction involved in the scaling procedure, a higher score will be obtained by a shorter person. It is possible to surmise, without going and looking up the evidence, that, other things being equal, people from higher social strata will tend to be better nourished and therefore taller. There is repeated, if variable, evidence of an association between lower social position and left wing political tendency. So there may be a slight tendency for shorter people, who score higher on our 'instrument', actually to be more radical. Thus the procedure may not be totally invalid. But it is very clear that it is entirely possible for a measure to have essentially perfect reliability yet no useful validity. Of course, the converse is not true: if a measure is unreliable it works inconsistently, so it cannot provide a consistent measure of anything.

Reliability and validity are most often described in terms of correlation or some closely related concept. Validity is conceptualised as correlation between the measure (any measure, not only attitudinal) and a relevant independent criterion. The crudest version of this is called face validity, and here no formal correlational analysis is attempted, though the underlying ideas remain. For instance, an end-of-term test may consist of multiple-choice items based on statements taken from the course lecture notes or textbook. Usually no evidence for the validity of these items is offered other than that they 'obviously' measure knowledge of what the course is about. When we are trying to measure something as slippery as an attitude this should never be regarded as sufficient justification: it is not difficult to find examples of obvious errors based on such a glib approach to the problem.

The simplest case of a proper correlational analysis is called predictive validity. For instance, the validity of an aptitude test, to be used for selecting candidates for a course of training, may be defined as the correlation between the test score and some subsequent measure of success, such as a passing-out exam or an on-the-job performance measure. The criterion measure must be assumed to be a perfect indicator of success, obviously questionable in itself.

Clearly the problem is far more severe when there is no objective external criterion – as when, for instance, we try to devise a measure of an attitude. A conceptually convincing solution (that is, however, difficult to apply) is offered by the idea of construct validity (Cronbach and Meehl, 1955). This requires that the measure being evaluated should represent a hypothetical concept that is well embedded in theory, so that the nature of the relationships between it and other concepts is well understood. Then by analysis of the statistical relationships between the various measures, and comparison of these relationships with the corresponding theoretical relationships, the appropriateness of the measures can be assessed. To give a more concrete example, if theory requires that the correlation be 1, but the correlation between measures is 0.5, then the validity of each measure (assuming them to be equally good) is 0.71. The details of the reasoning will be skipped, but notice that 0.5 equals 0.71 times 0.71. Having established the validity of a measure in this way, it can be used to help in calculating true correlations with other variables, and so on. The difficulty, of course, is in getting a sufficiently precise theoretical baseline from which to begin. In reality a lengthy process ensues, in which an initially insecure baseline is gradually reinforced by adding more and more similarly wobbly buttresses. It is a perfectly sound engineering principle that the same strength can be achieved by a single strong component or several weaker ones, and this seems a plausible analogy to follow.

Reliability is measured without reference to external criteria. It includes two slightly different concepts: stability and consistency. **Stability** is usually measured by administering the same instrument twice to the same respondents, the time interval being chosen so as to minimise the effects of memory while avoiding the likelihood that 'real' change may have taken place. A stable measure will be indicated by a high test–retest correlation. A low correlation may mean an unstable measure, prone to be affected by short-term irrelevancies such as mood, distraction, or differences in the circumstances of completing the instrument; or it may mean an attribute that is genuinely very changeable, such as, apparently, voting intentions. Because of this ambiguity the concept is seldom accorded much import- ance nowadays. **Consistency** is generally considered more significant. An early form of assessment entailed splitting the constituent scale items into two subscales, computing total scores separately for the two halves, and finding the correlation between the two subscales. A high correlation would mean consistency between the halves. Of course, the exact value of the correlation would depend on just how the split was made: first half versus second half, odd versus even, etc. Almost universally used instead is **Cronbach's alpha** coefficient (Cronbach, 1951), which is approximately the average of all the possible split-half correlations, and thus measures the consistency of all items, globally and individually.

A conceptually very powerful approach to the problem of establishing validity is offered by Campbell and Fiske (1955). They point out that reliable variance in an item will come partly from a consistent dependence on the concept it is designed to measure, and partly from irrelevant characteristics of the method. For instance, some respondents show a consistent (hence, reliable) preference for one end of a Likert-type scale – usually the 'strongly agree' end, the so-called 'acquiescent response set'. Or the very fact that we are relying on a verbal response may mean that a respondent with literacy problems will lack confidence and thus consis- tently avoid the extreme categories. To avoid such problems we should use several different methods. We can very simply include essentially the same item twice, but with reversed meaning, and compare people's responses. Then the pattern of correlations between items, using the same and different methods and tapping the same and different attitudes, can yield important insights into the true validity of our measures.

In conclusion, it may be noted that it is very simple to calculate a quantitative measure of the reliability of an instrument, because it is based entirely on internal criteria, but almost impossible to do the same for

Please tell me whether or not you think it should be possible for a pregnant woman to obtain a legal abortion if . . .

A. If there is a strong chance of serious defect in the baby? (ABDEFECT)
B. If she is married and does not want any more children? (ABNOMORE)
C. If the woman's own health is seriously endangered by the pregnancy? (ABHLTH)
D. If the family has a very low income and cannot afford any more children? (ABPOOR)
E. If she became pregnant as a result of rape? (ABRAPE)
F. If she is not married and does not want to marry the man? (ABSINGLE)

Source: Davis (1977)

Figure 7.1 *Attitudes to abortion*

validity. Perhaps the best advice is to bear the problem in mind, and find ways of improving validity, even if it cannot be definitively measured.

7.5 Factor analysis

If a set of attitudes is indeed multidimensional (as was argued in section 7.2), how is it to be analysed? There are several ways to approach this problem, but probably the most commonly used is a statistical method called **factor analysis**. This is generally regarded as an advanced method, but the results are not too difficult to understand, and what follows is an example of such an analysis. (You could duplicate these results using the computer program SPSS/PC+, which is described in a little more detail in chapter 12.) This example is rather simpler than the problem of political radicalism discussed earlier. Respondents to a general purpose survey in the United States (the General Social Survey carried out every year by the National Opinion Research Center) were asked the question shown in Figure 7.1. Respondents were invited to answer 'yes' or 'no' to each reason; 'don't know' was also permitted, but excluded from analysis. These items are monotonic, so, although they have only two possible values rather than the traditional five-point scale, they could in principle be analysed according to the Likert model.

The 'words' in parentheses after each reason for abortion are the names by which the corresponding variables will be referred to in the computer analysis that follows.

You may not like the wording of some of the reasons. For instance, some may find the patriarchal implications of reason F irritating or even offensive. Others might say that, realistically, even today many women (and even more women's parents) would find the idea of having a child without being married pretty horrifying, and therefore an important hypothetical situation to ask respondents to consider. The choice of wording, like most research decisions, is not value-free. On the other hand, these questions came out of the standard process of examining spontaneous statements of opinion in open-ended discussions. In short,

	ABDEFECT	ABNOMORE	ABHLTH	ABPOOR	ABRAPE	ABSINGLE
ABDEFECT	1.00					
ABNOMORE	.35	1.00				
ABHLTH	.58	.26	1.00			
ABPOOR	.39	.70	.33	1.00		
ABRAPE	.58	.37	.54	.43	1.00	
ABSINGLE	.35	.70	.29	.71	.43	1.00

Figure 7.2 *Correlation matrix*

this example is an instance of secondary analysis, where we are dependent on someone else's decisions, with all the potential difficulties (and advantages) which will be discussed in chapter 13.

The items were selected so as to cover the main range of grounds that might be used to justify abortion. By using several statements rather than just one (such as 'Do you think abortions should be legal always, most of the time, sometimes, seldom or never?') the overall reliability of a derived score will be much improved. In addition, the researchers leave open the possibility that people's attitudes in this area may be multidimensional. Of course, in a sense a person's responses to these items will be six-dimensional, since they are making six responses, but the use of factor analysis entails the assumption that the six items are not entirely independent, but can be understood in terms of a smaller number of underlying attitudes; the question is, how many.

The first thing that the factor analysis program does is to calculate the correlation between each pair of variables (see Figure 7.2). You will notice first that every single correlation is positive: a respondent who approves of abortion on any ground tends also to approve on any other ground. However, the coefficients vary quite a lot, from 0.26 up to 0.71: ABPOOR, ABSINGLE and ABNOMORE are closely related, as are ABHLTH, ABRAPE and ABDEFECT, but the correlations between the two subsets are smaller. From this one might suspect that people's views tend to fall into two categories, and indeed factor analysis can be seen as a more systematic way of investigating patterns of correlation.

The factor extraction takes place in a 'black box' that it would be inappropriate to delve into in an introductory discussion. A summary of the results is presented in Figure 7.3.

An **eigenvalue** is a concept in matrix theory, the area of maths that

Factor	Eigenvalue	Percentage of variance	Cumulative percentage
1	2.98	49.6	49.6
2	0.86	14.4	64.0

Figure 7.3 *Factors and the variance they explain*

	Factor 1	Factor 2
ABDEFECT	.01	.78
ABNOMORE	.85	−.03
ABHLTH	−.07	.78
ABPOOR	.81	.05
ABRAPE	.13	.67
ABSINGLE	.84	.00

Figure 7.4 *The relationship between the factors and the attitude items*

underlies all multivariate statistics. For present purposes it can be regarded as the variance of each factor – a measure of its importance in explaining the measured items. Because there are six items the total variance is 6.0 and the percentage of variance explained in each case is the eigenvalue divided by 6. The second figure in the cumulative percentage column is 64.0, that is 49.6 plus 14.4, so altogether these two factors successively summarise almost two thirds of the original variation.

But what are these factors? They are inferred from the correlations among the items, but they are understood as underlying the items. Each entry in the table in Figure 7.4 indicates the extent to which the row item is determined by the column factor. ABDEFECT, for instance, is determined almost exclusively by factor 2, whereas ABNOMORE belongs almost entirely to factor 1. As you look down the columns you can arrive at an interpretation of each factor: factor 1 is to do with attitudes to abortion on social grounds, or with 'elective' termination, whereas factor 2 is to do with medical grounds, or matters outside the woman's control. (Yet again, it is impossible to express this in a value-free way: coping with this is part of the researcher's responsibility.)

Although there are two distinct factors, they are not independent: the factor analysis reports that there is a moderate correlation, 0.54, between the two factors. Approval on one set of grounds tends to go with approval on the other set. Common sense (which can be confirmed by further analysis) suggests that the correlation is less than perfect mainly because many people approve on medical but not on social grounds.

Of course, discovering the structure of people's attitudes is only the beginning. Having identified the two factors, a program like SPSS can assign to each respondent a score on each factor, based on their individual item scores. Then the real analysis begins. Instead of having to tabulate each of the six items by various explanatory variables, we need only tabulate the two factors, thus simplifying both the computer analysis and the subsequent interpretation. As an illustration, Figures 7.5 and 7.6 show the tables that result from examining the relationship between factor 1 and sex, and between factor 2 and occupation.

All the variables in these tables are dichotomous: sex is naturally a two-state variable, and the others have been recast into similar classifications for simplicity of analysis. (In professional research this might be regarded

	Male	Female	
Tend to approve	51.3%	49.8%	50.5%
Tend to disapprove	48.7%	50.2%	49.5%
	(622)	(731)	(1353)

Figure 7.5   *Attitude to abortion on 'social' grounds: percentage approving by sex*

	Non- manual	Manual	
Tend to approve	57.8%	40.6%	48.9%
Tend to disapprove	42.2%	59.4%	51.1%
	(611)	(648)	(1259)

Figure 7.6   *Attitude to abortion on 'medical' grounds: percentage approving by occupational group*

as a rather wasteful way to treat data.) As far as the two factor scores are concerned there is no natural dividing line, so for reasons of statistical efficiency they have been split into roughly equal-sized categories. As explained earlier, it is impossible to say exactly where the neutral point lies. The obvious division for occupation is into manual and non-manual categories, so this is what has been done: as it happens, this is also close to a fifty-fifty split.

The creation and interpretation of tables of this kind is outlined in chapter 12 but for now the focus will be on just a couple of figures in each table. In both tables, each cell contains the number of individuals in that combination of row and column categories, expressed as percentage of the column total (shown in parentheses). Notice that 51.3 per cent of men tend to approve of abortion on social grounds, compared with 49.8 per cent of women. This is really no difference at all. First, such a difference is almost certainly not statistically reliable: simply because of random sampling variability we could easily get precisely the opposite result in another sample; and in any case, 1.5 per cent difference is not enough to get excited about. So the conclusion must be that there is no real difference in men's and women's attitudes in this respect.

But there is a substantial difference in attitudes to abortion on social grounds between manual and non-manual workers: a tendency to approval is expressed by 41 per cent and 58 per cent of the respective groups. To put it slightly differently, a non-manual worker is 17 per cent more likely to be in the more approving group.

To summarise, then, a set of six attitude items can be summarised successfully by two factors, which can then be used as variables in their own right. The advantages are not only in simplification: it will generally be found that, because of the reduced noise in the derived variables, the relationships with explanatory variables are more distinct than is the case for the raw variables. That is, of course, the essence of construct validity.

7.6 Summary

The measurement of attitudes deserves great care and close attention to detail. The general point to recognise is the necessity to improve reliability and validity. At a minimum that means wherever practicable adopting a multiple indicator approach. If you are seriously interested in this area of research design you should look through some of the suggestions for further reading, and build up a repertoire of methods, so as to avoid always forcing your respondents into the same mould.

7.7 Project

To do something worthwhile with your own data probably means a class project. Decide on a researchable area, probably one that other students will be interested in, since you will need willing research subjects. You could, for instance, examine attitudes to participating in higher education. This may well be multidimensional: for instance, some people are more concerned with 'pure' benefits of education such as general intellectual development, self-actualization, and so forth; whereas others will emphasise the practical advantages to the individual and to the nation. Do a bit of reading around, to get an idea of the necessary breadth of coverage. Start collecting items: keep a note of statements made in the press, especially student journals; record group discussions and extract coherent opinions. Edit your collection, bearing in mind the rules discussed in chapter 6. Assemble between 10 and 20 items into a questionnaire, adding a few factual questions concerning gender, age, course of study, parents' occupations, etc. Ideally, design and attempt to achieve a proper sample – though that is a project in itself. Set everyone in the class a quota: you will need at least 200 completed questionnaires. Put the data onto a computer and (if you know enough about factor analysis, or can get more detailed advice) use this chapter's example as a model. For a relatively small data set you may be able to manage without a specialised package like SPSS if you can get advice on a good spreadsheet program like Excel or Lotus 1-2-3. You will not be able to do factor analysis, but you can weed out items that do not seem to correlate with anything else, and then add together the remaining scores. Finally, look at the relationship between your scales and students' background characteristics. Which disciplines seem to be related to which justifications for education? Are there class background differences?

If you cannot collect your own data, you will find that many data sets available for secondary analysis (see chapter 13) are particularly suitable for attitude research: as well as the NORC GSS from which this chapter's illustration was taken (see Davis and Smith, 1992), there are the annual British Social Attitudes Survey and the Eurobarometer series sponsored by the European Commission. If you have access to suitable computing facilities you can learn a lot by obtaining one of these data sets from your national Data Archive and hunting through it for groups of connected attitude items. The British Social Attitudes Survey, in particular, is the subject of an annual report (e.g. Jowell et al., 1992) that might give you some ideas on where to start.

7.8   Further reading

Many of the classic papers are brought together in Summers (1970). Though outdated, Oppenheim (1966) gives a useful guide to many of the practical details of scaling. The expectancy value approach is best described in Fishbein and Ajzen (1975). Lodge (1981) has written an excellent practical guide to magnitude scaling. To learn about factor analysis you should start from a foundation in basic statistics including correlation and regression; then Norusis (1991) gives a very clear account directly related to SPSS output.

8 Qualitative Interviewing

Nigel Fielding

Contents

As the previous chapter shows, sociologists have always been interested in the attitudes and beliefs of social groups, and a good deal of methodological refinement has come about by engaging with the problems posed by trying to get at other people's feelings. A key method of attitude research is the interview, and, as we will see, it has a central role in a diversity of research designs.

8.1 Varieties of research interviews

Interviewing has a strong claim to being the most widely used method of research. Whenever we are getting our bearings, whether it is as a researcher or a new arrival in a foreign land, the quickest, most instinctive method is to ask a question. It is therefore no surprise that interviewing takes many forms. The normal way of differentiating types of interview is by the degree of structure imposed on its format.

In the **standardised** or **structured** interview the wording of questions and the order in which they are asked is the same from one interview to another (see Macfarlane Smith, 1972; and chapter 6). The name for the piece of paper the interviewer holds is the 'interview schedule', and that word 'schedule' seems to convey the formality of this type of interview. It is most familiar from market research; most of us have been stopped in the street or visited at home by an interviewer bearing a schedule to be completed by ticks in the answer boxes corresponding to our answers.

The next type of interview is **semi-standardised**; here the interviewer asks certain, major questions the same way each time, but is free to alter their sequence and to probe for more information. The interviewer is thus able to adapt the research instrument to the level of comprehension and articulacy of the respondent, and to handle the fact that in responding to a question, people often also provide answers to questions we were going to ask later.

The endpoint of this typology is the **non-standardised** interview. This is also called an **unstructured** or **focused** interview. Here interviewers simply have a list of topics which they want the respondent to talk about, but are free to phrase the questions as they wish, ask them in any order that seems sensible at the time, and even to join in the conversation by discussing what they think of the topic themselves. The bit of paper the interviewer holds is called an 'interview guide', and once again the second word, 'guide', conveys a sense of the style of this approach, where interviewers take their own path within certain guidelines.

This chapter is mainly about this latter type of interview. This is both because the standardised types are discussed in chapters 3, 6 and 7, and because the non-standardised interview best fulfils Lofland's (1971) case that the essence of the research interview is the 'guided conversation'. Also, because of its simplicity of design and correspondence to the conversational procedures that are routine in social life, it is very often the type of interview students conduct in their own research projects. Where necessary, comparisons are made with the more standardised types.

After examining the uses of interview data, the chapter considers the conduct of interviews, the design of an interview guide and the practicalities of transcription. The second part of the chapter covers some of the problems of interview methods and the ways these can be overcome, with an emphasis on promoting and assessing validity and on the different perspectives on validity found in different theoretical traditions.

8.1.1   Characteristic uses of interview data

Like other qualitative methods, non-standardised interviews are valuable as strategies for discovery. Standardised interviews are suitable when you already have some idea of what is happening with your sample in relation to the research topic, and where there is no danger of loss of meaning as a result of imposing a standard way of asking questions. However, if you are on new ground – for social research or yourself – a more flexible approach is best. Lofland summarised the objective of the non-standardised format as being 'to elicit rich, detailed materials that can be used in qualitative analysis. Its object is to find out what kinds of things are happening rather than to determine the frequency of predetermined kinds of things that the researcher already believes can happen' (1971: 76).

As well as the typology based on the degree of standardisation there is one other preliminary distinction to make. These types of interview can be administered either one-to-one or to a group. In the former, respondents are seen individually, while in the latter the interviewer, or a group leader, guides the discussion among a small group of respondents. Recently, market research has embraced what Merton called 'focus groups' (Merton and Kendall, 1946) as a way of studying consumer preference. To social scientists, the strength of group discussions is the insight they offer into the dynamic effects of interaction on expressed opinion, which is discussed further below.

Many studies begin with 'pilot interviews', to gather basic information about the field before imposing more precise, and inflexible methods; this is why interviews have their claim to be the most often used research method. Such interviews use a very broad topic guide with as few direct questions as possible. But the flexibility of non-standardised methods is a major attraction and many influential and sophisticated analyses have been based entirely on interview data.

This versatility is apparent in the list of normal uses to which interview data can be put. Interviews can be used to identify the main behavioural groups to be sampled, and to lend insight into how they should be defined. Interviews can be used to get acquainted with the phraseology and concepts used by a population of respondents. Interviews have often been used to establish the variety of opinion concerning a particular topic. They have been used to establish relevant dimensions of attitudes. Interviews are often used to form tentative hypotheses about the motivation under-lying behaviour and attitudes, although this use is much debated, as we will see when we consider the analysis of interview data.

These are the major applications of interview data, but non-standardised interviews have some important subsidiary uses. For those who accept that motivations can be studied this way, interviews can also be used to examine non-motivations, why people do not do certain things. For instance, some years ago when London had its own local government, postal surveys were conducted on why people failed to apply for the welfare benefits for which they were eligible. The surveys had poor response rates, perhaps for reasons similar to the low take-up of benefit itself. An independent research organisation was commissioned to pursue the matter, and dis-covered that individual interviews were the best way to guarantee a response from the semi-literate, the frail, the elderly and the plain suspicious – the main target groups for the campaign to maximise take-up of benefit.

Another subsidiary application is when we need very detailed and extensive data, such as case histories of patients, or detailed records of behaviour, such as criminal careers. In recent years the 'life history' interview has come into vogue, particularly in feminist research and women's studies (Devault, 1990).

The non-standardised approach is also valuable where the subject matter is sensitive or complicated. For instance, a research agency was asked to establish attitudes to nuclear waste as part of a social impact study. The problem was that reaching an informed view on this requires technical information of considerable complexity. No survey questionnaire nor standardised interview could provide the information in sufficient depth or attune it to the varying levels of comprehension likely to be present in the population. Non-standardised interviews allowed the researchers to fine tune the explanation and to satisfy themselves that the respondent had sufficient grasp to reach a considered view. Of course, care must be taken that the technical explanations are not themselves biased.

In similar vein, the flexibility of this approach is a boon where topics have varying salience to the sample population but where it is difficult to anticipate which will register with particular respondents using knowledge only of broad indicators such as age. When the applicability of research instruments cannot be predetermined by sampling assumptions, non-standardised interviews can help. This is how Robb (1954) compiled his sample of East Enders who were anti-Semitic; aware that East Enders were reputed to be anti-Semitic he used interviews to identify such views and select his sample.

8.2   Communication in interviews

Two principles inform research interviews. First, the questioning should be as open-ended as possible, in order to gain spontaneous information about attitudes and actions, rather than a rehearsed position. Second, the questioning techniques should encourage respondents to communicate their underlying attitudes, beliefs and values, rather than a glib or easy answer. The objective is that the discussion be as frank as possible.

Frank discussion can be impeded in several ways. There may be attempts at *rationalisation*. Respondents may offer only logical reasons for their actions, withholding evaluative or emotional reasons which may give a truer insight. We have already noticed the problem of a *lack of awareness*; as well as a lack of information, many people are not used to putting their feelings into words. Respondents may fear *being shown up*. People often avoid describing aspects of behaviour or attitude that are inconsistent with their preferred self-image; questions about such things as personal hygiene or involvement in deviant behaviour are oft-cited examples. Respondents may tend to *overpoliteness* to the interviewer. Being shy or overanxious to impress can distort response. A common problem here is where respondents give those answers they anticipate the interviewer wants to hear. This is a good reason to be very careful about your initial explanation of the focus of the interview.

There are several solutions to these obstacles to frank communication. The manner of the interviewer is important. A relaxed and unselfconscious interviewer puts respondents at ease. Research on interviewer effects suggests that interviewers should not be drawn from either extreme of the social scale, that their demeanour should be neither condescending nor deferential, that they should display interest without appearing intrusive. There is more on interviewer effects below. Another broad tactic is to personalise the discussion to get at underlying attitudes. For example, do not simply talk about 'police policy' in the abstract, ask respondents to tell you about their experiences with the police.

However, this advice is rather broad. There are special questioning techniques to deal with particular communication problems.

When attitudes to a number of items need to be investigated and compared the **repertory grid** is useful. It is particularly helpful in measuring attitude change over time, such as during a course of treatment or a period of socialisation into, say, a new job. Initially dimensions of attitude – **constructs** – are identified. The researcher presents three stimuli to the respondent (a **triad**), and asks them to say which two are most alike and how they differ from the third. The procedure is repeated with a number of triads. Let us say we are studying attitudes to noise. Presented with traffic noise, aircraft noise and noisy children, the respondent may say aircraft and children noise is intermittent, whereas where they live traffic noise is continuous. Thus 'continuity of noise' emerges as a salient dimension of opinion. The virtue of this is that one elicits constructs (such as continuity of noise) direct from the respondent rather than supplying a construct which may be meaningful to the researcher but less so to the subjects. Respondents then relate the set of constructs to each other to form a grid, and, if the procedure is repeated over time, changes can be identified. For example, a constable's degree of identification with the triad of detective, patrol officer and police sergeant can be measured at different stages of training (Norris, 1983).

There are also a number of projective questioning techniques that are designed to encourage respondents to give views indirectly. There is **sentence completion,** for example, 'The noise from the motorway ———'. Another is **indirect questioning**, which works on the basis that people are more prepared to reveal negative feelings if they can attribute them to other people. You might ask 'How do you think other young people feel about noise?' The respondent will have no idea, and not knowing others' views they will offer their own. Another technique is **personalisation of objects,** in which emotion or some other affective quality is attributed to an inanimate object. For example, 'If your house were a person how would it feel about redevelopment?' The technique is normally thought most appropriate for child respondents, but it is surprisingly effective with adults. Finally, there are **picture techniques**, the famous Rorsach blots which prompt people to interpret an ambiguous image. The method is really for clinical psychologists and is very time-consuming, as the researcher has to interpret the respondent's interpretations!

8.2.1 Probing and prompting

Prompting involves encouraging the respondent to produce an answer. In standardised interviews great care is taken to get a response without having to put words in the respondent's mouth. The mildest technique is merely to repeat the question. If this fails, the interviewer may be permitted to do a slight rephrase of the question; if so, the interview schedule will often list acceptable rephrases. It is thought more important that the stimulus (question) be delivered in precisely the same way to each respondent than to allow the interviewer to improvise to get an answer. In standardised interviews failure to elicit a response after a couple of attempts will result in missing data. In non-standardised interviewing the interviewer has more latitude, as we will see below.

Probing involves follow-up questioning to get a fuller response; it may be non-verbal or verbal. An expectant glance can function as a probe as much as a direct request like 'please tell me about that'. Probes are acceptable in standardised interviews, but are likely to be pre-specified. Their use is entirely acceptable in non-standardised interviews, because we probe all the time in normal conversation and our objective is to have a 'guided conversation'. However, the probe should be as neutral as possible. It should not incline the respondent to a particular response.

The less standardised the format the more flexible these injunctions. Indeed, life history and other discursive interview formats may contain prompting of a kind which is heresy in standardised interviews. It is likely to take the form of the interviewer's comment that they have heard others express some view or other, and what does the respondent think of that. Sometimes the interviewer will even say what they think or have experienced. The fact that non-standardised interviewers, especially in feminist methods, talk about 'sharing' their view with the respondent gives an idea of the opposition between those who prefer stimulus–response conventions and those who believe interviewing should be an 'open' method involving a genuine interplay between researcher and respondent. As in all research methods, what is permissible ultimately depends on the analytic task to which the data will be applied.

Probing is a key interviewing skill. It is all about encouraging the respondent to give an answer and as full a response as the format allows. Frequently it involves getting respondents to choose from available alternatives. For example, if, in a standardised format, a respondent answers the question 'Are you very satisfied, not very satisfied or not at all satisfied with your present home?' with the statement 'I couldn't really say' this implies hesitation rather than an absence of opinion. Here the interviewer can say 'Which comes closest to your views?' and repeat the question. If the answer still does not fit, the interviewer is usually instructed to repeat the pre-codes.

Probing is especially important in open-ended questions, and even the most standardised format will usually include a few of these. To get respondents to expand their answers the following probes may be used, in increasing order of imperativeness:

- an expectant glance
- um hm, mm, or yes, followed by an expectant silence
- what else?
- what other reasons?
- please tell me more about that
- I'm interested in *all* your reasons.

That last one would probably make most respondents uncomfortable and is best kept for the truly evasive! Following Dohrenwend and Richardson (1956), Burgess offers a scale which enables one to evaluate the interviewer's degree of directiveness, allowing interviewing styles to be calibrated to the interview situation (Burgess 1982: 111–12). The rule of thumb for when to probe is whenever you judge that the respondent's statement is ambiguous. Generally, anything that would make you wonder what the respondent meant in a normal conversation would be worth probing in an interview (in normal conversation we tend to be more tolerant of the unexplained or unclear, perhaps because we know we can check later with people we will see again). So responses like 'This is important' should always be probed, perhaps by asking 'What do you mean by "important"?' The interviewer's task is to draw out all relevant responses, to encourage the inarticulate or shy, to be neutral towards the topic under discussion while displaying interest. Probing needs skill, because it can so easily lead to bias. That is why effort is put into measuring directiveness. The best way to acquire this skill is to practise interviewing, initially with someone who is prepared to help you review your perform-ance and later in a short series of pilot interviews with people like those who form your sample. A video camera can be very helpful in reviewing and honing your interviewing skills.

8.2.2 The value of group discussions

At the beginning of this chapter it was mentioned that group discussions have a special value for those who want to assess how several people work out a common view, or the range of views, about some topic. The great majority of research interviews are one-to-one, but researchers interested in consensus formation, interactional processes and group dynamics may find the group discussion useful. They allow you to see how people interact in considering a topic, and how they react to disagreement. They can help in identifying attitudes and behaviours which are considered socially unacceptable.

Apart from this use, which is tailored to a particular set of analytic interests, group discussions are quicker and cheaper to conduct than individual interviews with the same number of respondents. However, they have their own distinct disadvantages, too. Not everyone who has been invited will attend, but if some of them have shown up you will have to run the session regardless. The elderly, disabled and members of elites are particularly unlikely to attend a group discussion. If these are important in your sample you may need to target them individually.

Another problem is that group discussions are rather unwieldy; it will help a lot if you share the running of the session, or split the roles so that one person maintains the discussion while the other looks ahead to new topics and introduces them, or so that you take the lead for one topic and a colleague takes it for another. Finally, its hard to get a clear recording in a group discussion; you will probably need more than one microphone, and you should check that your equipment can handle people speaking at different volumes and at different distances from the microphones before conducting the actual session.

This may make it seem that discussions are too difficult to bother with. However, I was rapidly converted to their value several years ago when helping some students convene a group discussion on domestic violence. A group of women from a local refuge were invited and eight of them came. There were both male and female discussion leaders, and several students shared the running of the session, with one mainly concentrating on the equipment. We found that the women were prepared to share information of remarkable emotional intensity, about harrowing experiences we regarded as deeply private and which we had not thought we would be able to address in the interviews. It seemed that, because they all shared the experience of having been abused by their partners, once one respondent launched a line of discussion the others were more than willing to join in. We were certain that we would not have got the amount and depth of data using one-to-one interviews, particularly as we would not have been able to match genders without denying some of the students the experience of interviewing. It was difficult to end the session. The women wanted to continue, and were generating their own topics, which led us on to new and relevant ground. The session finally ended when the building was locked up for the night.

8.3   How to design an interview guide

The best way to learn the ins and outs of a research procedure is to try it out for yourself, provided you recognise that your first efforts must be taken as practice rather than as finished product. To get you started on refining your interview technique we will borrow from John Lofland's excellent discussion of the basics of designing a guide to conducting a non-standardised interview (1971: 75–84; see also Lofland and Lofland, 1984, which contains further relevant material). Having identified a topic which is appropriate to study by interviewing, the first step is thinking over what you find problematic or interesting about it; Lofland calls these things 'puzzlements'. Jot down questions which express each puzzlement. Try to spread the range of the inquiry by asking friends what they find puzzling about the topic, too. What you are doing here is teasing out what is puzzling about the phenomenon in the context of your particular 'cultural endowment'. We are located in a particular social context, with a particular biographical background, and we must recognise that our point of departure is always what is puzzling relative to our particular cultural perspective.

The next step is to write each puzzlement, or research question, on a separate sheet of paper. Now sort the pieces of paper into separate piles which seem to be topically related. These clusters of topics may have to be arranged several times to obtain an order that seems to express the social phenomenon. In the process, some of the puzzlements will be discarded; growing knowledge means you can see they are irrelevant to the phenomenon in which you are interested. Others will emerge as being related, so you can amalgamate them. The puzzlements, expressed as questions, can then be decanted from the sheets of paper onto one list. It should display a logical, orderly sequence, taking the form of an outline.

The last step before you pilot your interview guide is to design probes. Remember, this is a non-standardised interview, so probes may be couched in informal terms or be written flexibly so that the exact words you use to the respondent can be fine tuned to your estimation of their comprehension and ease of response. Devising the probes is at least as important as generating the main questions on the guide.

Let's take the example of a study by Lyn Lofland of urban careers, how people get on when they first move to a new city (discussed in J. Lofland, 1971: 78–82). The outline of the interview guide looked like this:

  I.   Pre-residence images
 II.   Initial contact
III.   Subsequent career
 IV.   Experience of the city

As you can see, the guide is pretty minimal. Nearly all the work goes on in the detailed probes. We can see this when we take a look at the main question featuring in II, initial contact. The question, whose informal wording you should note as it is typical of the non-standardised style, was:

> Can you tell me exactly how you went about finding a place to live, how you got your first place, and so forth?

Such a question would fail to measure up to standardised requirements. It asks more than one question at once, and has a non-specific clause to end with. But if the interviewer has gained rapport that kind of question is fine in a non-standardised format. So here are the probes:

> Probe for: Conception of city areas; Areas would not consider; Contacts with landlords, real estate people (estate agents); Financial constraints; Any need to find place quickly; Internal or external conflicts and compromises; Network involvement (e.g., friend found place, relatives etc).

Clearly the probes are in 'sociologese' and would confuse the respondent if spoken in the words on the guide. They are instructions to look at particular subtopics, reminders to the interviewer to be sure to check on each. They don't have to be put into the exact words which you will ask, because the non-standardised format is discursive, letting the respondent develop their answers in their own terms and at their own length and depth. So the interviewer has to keep all the probe subtopics in mind as the respondent talks, mentally ticking off the ones the respondent mentions and remembering to ask about the ones the respondent does not mention. The idea is to have a list of things to be sure to ask about. One may know so little about the phenomenon that probes cannot be devised in advance. Many times the probes are likely to emerge spontaneously, as in any conversation. Remember, the non-standardised interview tries to be a guided conversation, and the bit of paper you hold is only a guide.

8.4   Interviewer effects

As we have already noticed, the standardised and non-standardised approaches vary greatly in the role they permit the interviewer to play in the interaction with the respondent. A long tradition of methodological research warns of the many effects the interviewer has on the respondent's statements. While advocates of non-standardised interviewing value and analyse the part played in the discussion by the interviewer, proponents of standardised approaches regard these effects as undesirable and seek to maintain forms of quality control which reduce the impact of the interviewer on what the respondent feels able to say. Whatever approach is preferred, it is sensible to take note of some key findings of this tradition of research on interviewer effects.

The classic study dates from 1954 (Hyman), but in 1974 Sudman and Bradburn published a definitive review of what had by then become a considerable body of literature. There was an early concern with whether the demographic characteristics of the interviewer and respondent should be matched; this literature, being largely American, displayed an early preoccupation with race. Hyman found that white interviewers received more socially acceptable responses from black respondents than from white respondents. Similarly, black and Oriental interviewers obtained more socially acceptable answers than did white interviewers, with the differences predictably being greatest on questions of race. Such findings were borne out by many subsequent researches. In fact, as well as race, characteristics such as age, sex, social class, and religion have proven to have an impact which has to be allowed for. Socially acceptable responses are particularly likely to represent convenient ways of dealing with interviewers rather than expressing the respondent's actual view. For these reasons, standardised interviews try to match interviewers to the characteristics of the research population wherever possible.

Another major body of findings concerns the effects of the interviewer's behaviour and conduct of the interview on the responses made. One study showed that variations in respondent 'verbosity' resulted from the willingness of the interviewer to probe (Shapiro and Eberhart, 1947). Aggressive interviewers elicited more information. It has also been shown that response rates and extensiveness of response are different between experienced and inexperienced interviewers, which suggests that, as well as matching, it is important to practise your techniques and to include a full programme of pilot interviews in your research design. These are vital in helping you to get acquainted both with your interview schedule or guide and with respondents of the sort you will encounter in your main data-gathering. If you have a limited number of respondents it may be wise to interview those least likely to provide crucial data first.

While interviewer effects must be acknowledged and controlled if they endanger the validity or reliability of response, there are limits to the extent of matching which can be achieved. There are also limits to the efforts that can be made to conduct the interview the same way every time, and differences in respondents and the context of interviews may make it less meaningful to think in terms of similarity. It could be argued that it may be easier to confide in a stranger, that female interviewers may be less threatening to both female and male respondents and that deference may encourage rather than inhibit response. Such doubts about matching suggest why it is crucial to have as full and accurate a record of the interview as possible, for scrutiny during analysis. This is not only the foundation of our analysis but the best index of the effects we may have had on the things the respondent says. This brings us to the business of transcription.

8.5 Transcription

There are now some sophisticated technologies for the transcription of certain types of interview. For instance, there is CATI (computer assisted telephone interviewing) which is used by pollsters and market researchers when interviewing very large samples (see chapter 6). However, here we are only concerned with the straightforward transcription of one-to-one non-standardised interviews.

The first choice is whether to write down everything the respondent says. This is the choice between verbatim and selective transcription. Verbatim transcription offers the advantage that all possible analytic uses are allowed for. You may not know what will be the most significant points of analysis when you are doing the transcription; doing it verbatim means you have not lost any data that may later become significant. But the disadvantage of verbatim transcription is that it is laborious and time-consuming. The advice is that even if you plan to be selective with most of the interviews you should still transcribe the first few verbatim. These will help guide your analysis and quite possibly reveal lines of analysis you had not thought of. You may even be able to adjust your guide for subsequent interviews to pick up on things your transcription reveals as unexpectedly important. Whether to transcribe all your interviews verbatim may also depend on how many you are doing. If your sample is small, say 20 or less, you should probably transcribe the lot verbatim.

The next choice is whether to tape-record the interview or write notes. If you are doing a standardised interview using a highly pre-specified schedule, you will probably not need to tape record but develop the skill of completing what is in effect a questionnaire as the respondent talks. But if you are conducting non-standardised interviews you will be joining in the conversation too, and without recording you will inevitably lose data as well as have to engage in a very stilted and peculiar interaction as you pause every few utterances to write down what the person says. The advice is to tape-record whenever possible.

Experience with students conducting non-standardised interviews has shown me that most worry about negotiating with respondents to tape record the interview. But recording does put over the idea that their responses are being taken seriously. It is worth pushing hard to tape. Notes are not only very slow but open to doubts about validity. When in Britain police interviews went from contemporaneous note-taking to tape-recording, detectives found that average interview times fell dramatically. An interview that took four hours with note-taking now took half an hour. The quality of the responses also became more factual, and accusations of 'verballing' – putting words in the respondent's mouth – fell to virtually nil (Irving and McKenzie, 1988). Nevertheless, the researcher should ensure that the request to tape is explicit, that confidentiality is offered, and that the respondent knows he or she can switch off the machine in giving a particular answer.

It is also worth remembering that many people now use tape-recordings in their work. Businesspeople record notes to themselves and memos for audiotyping, social workers and probation officers tape discussions with their clients or notes to themselves after client interviews. You can make taping more palatable by offering to supply the respondent with a transcript so its accuracy can be checked (of course, this commits you to full transcription). This is a useful 'foot-in-the-door' device too, because you will then have a further contact with the respondent to discuss the transcript, which often yields more data, including comments by the respondent on what he or she thought of the interview. This can be useful both analytically and in gauging the validity and reliability of responses. If the respondent is worried about the uses to be made of the interview data you can also offer to anonymise the quotes you use in the final write-up and destroy the recording once it is transcribed.

If the respondent is really reluctant you may be able to get recording accepted by starting to write notes. This will be unbelievably slow. After a few minutes you can ask whether they still object to the tape recorder! Finally, because so many people now use tapes in their work, and because many occupational groups are now more accountable, it may be that your respondent not only assents to you recording but pulls out their own recorder to make an independent record of the session. Don't be shy.

A final point concerns audiotyping transcription services. These are available in many towns, and some people have secretaries who can transcribe for them. Even so it is worth transcribing at least some, and preferably all, of the interviews yourself. This is because you have ideas as you transcribe. Transcription is undoubtedly tedious – it can take a day's typing by a competent typist to transcribe a one hour interview. But transcribing makes you very familiar with the data. It helps you to start making connections and identifying themes for analysis. In fact, you should keep a pad handy when you transcribe to write down these thoughts as they occur to you.

Nothing has been said here about the special case of transcription for conversation analysis, a technique for studying the structure of interaction, but this is dealt with in chapter 15.

8.6   Some problems of interview analysis

As we have already seen, researchers worry about the effects interviewers may have on the validity and reliability of the data. The charge of interviewer bias has been levelled particularly at non-standardised interviews. Active commitment to a particular perspective during the interview certainly affects the results. On the other hand, it is easy to overstate the problem of interviewer bias. Selltiz and Jahoda suggest that 'much of what we call interviewer bias can more correctly be described as interviewer differences, which are inherent in the fact that interviewers are human beings and not machines' (1962: 41). They point out that social scientists are universally dependent on data collected by oral or written reports and these are 'invariably subject to the same sources of error and bias as those collected by interviewers'. In dealing with bias, the advice of eminent sociologist Robert Merton still holds true (Merton and Kendall, 1946: 555). He maintains that:

1.   Guidance and direction from the interviewer should be at a minimum.

2. The subject's definition of the situation should find full and specific expression.
3. The interview should bring out the value-laden implications of response.

As Merton's carefully-balanced advice suggests, we cannot simply ignore the matter of interviewer bias. So far we have identified several sources of error or bias arising from carrying out the method badly: misdirected probing and prompting, ignoring the effects of interviewer characteristics and behaviour, neglecting the cultural context in which the researcher is located, and problems with question wording. These are mostly susceptible to quality control measures. But, more profoundly, the logic in analysing interviews is based on several assumptions which can be challenged, and we need to be conscious of these possible criticisms.

The first problem is the assumption that language is generally a good indicator of thought and action. Attitudes and thoughts are assumed to be a direct influence on behaviour and, in turn, language is presumed to be an accurate reflection of both. Nowadays such assumptions would make a social psychologist cringe (Ashworth, 1979). A legion of studies show that expressed attitude is a problematic indicator of what people have done, or will do. The relationship between attitude and action has to be empirically tested in all cases, so that collecting information about people's attitudes is only one part of any study concerned with explaining or predicting behaviour. Of course, there is some value in documenting people's attitudes, provided we do not claim that by doing so we have proven what they do, nor offer predictions about what they will do. These problems are one of the reasons that multiple method studies are desirable – you can combine attitude measures with, say, direct observation, to confirm whether people actually do what they have told you they do. A key reference for those interested in social scientists' efforts to tighten the fit between expressed attitude and actual behaviour is Deutscher's *What we say/what we do* (1973), and there is a discussion of ways of measuring attitudes in chapter 7.

It certainly is not hard to compile reasons to doubt what people say to us in interviews (and, for the logical extreme of the suspicious perspective see the remarks on Douglas's investigative social research in chapter 9). It is hardly a revelation to note that people sometimes lie or elaborate on the 'true' situation to enhance their esteem, cover up discreditable actions or for any of a whole gamut of motives.

A good case is that of 'self-report studies' in the sociology of deviance, as we have already seen in chapter 2. Social scientists have long been aware of the many deficiencies of crime statistics. Ambiguities abound. For example, would you consider the theft of a chequebook with 30 cheques left in it to be one theft or 30? If all 30 cheques are fraudulently 'passed' it counts as 31 – the theft of the chequebook plus each fraudulent encashment. The government has to issue 'counting rules' to help the police and courts figure out how to report for the statistics, but it is easy to get it wrong. As to crimes cleared up, for many years it was standard practice to count a crime as cleared even if the defendants were found innocent in court, and to clear a crime known to have been committed by several people if only one of them was caught. For these and many other reasons criminologists have long worried about the so-called dark figure of crime.

In the 1950s and 1960s many American social scientists thought they had solved the problem with a new technique called self-report. It was based on interviews, usually with young people, in which they were shown lists of offences and asked if they had committed any of them in the last year. The results were staggering. Typically these studies showed that up to 99 per cent of crime was going unreported. The difference between known and admitted crime was especially acute in the case of middle class youths (Empey and Erickson, 1966). Because theories of crime are largely based on official statistics, which show that crime is overwhelmingly a lower and working class phenomenon, the results were very important. But then doubt set in. Most of the studies were done on juveniles, for reasons of easier access (often through schools). Could one generalise to adults? Most of the studies were in the mid-Western United States, because this is where most of those using the technique worked. Were the results valid for city kids? But, most important, sceptics pointed out that there were no checks on the validity of the responses. It was possible that respondents might exaggerate their offending to impress the interviewer as being 'hard'. It was equally likely that they would minimise their involvement, fearing the interviewer would give the information to the police. There was a flurry of further tests, with some using polygraphs to try to see if the respondents were lying, others checking what they said against school records and with parents to see if what the children reported was plausible, and others offering the respondent the chance to change their answers prior to such validity checks to see if they retracted their admitted involvement, and in what direction. The best conclusion of all this work is that self-report is not an adequate substitute for official statistics. And in the 1970s another new technique largely supplanted it, victim studies. While these are subject to other methodological problems they are not as undermining as those that afflict self-reporting. This is not to say that self-reporting is straight-forwardly wrong, and in conjunction with other methods the technique is still used. What it does say, however, is that anyone using the technique must be aware of the methodological problems arising from the question of the fit between accounts and action, and devise means to allow for it in the analysis.

We have already encountered some of the problems with 'social desirability' as an influence on the validity of response. Admitting to involvement in some socially disapproved behaviour can be subject to cultural factors and therefore provide false data. A good case is studies of rates of mental illness in different cultural groups. In New York it was found that, holding class constant, Puerto Ricans had a higher apparent rate of mental illness than did Jews, the Irish or Blacks. However, on subjecting the mental health inventory to a social desirability rating it was found that Puerto Ricans regarded the items as less undesirable than did the other ethnic groups and were probably more willing to admit to them (Dohrenwend, 1964).

Cross-cultural research is especially susceptible to problems in interpreting interview response. It is often difficult to establish equivalence of meaning in work involving translation, especially if the material is attitudinal (is my repudiation of public drunkenness as fervent as a teetotal Muslim's?). Faced with the Marathi language group in India, who have no concept corresponding to the generalised other ('people', 'they', etc.), most researchers would despair. Of course, there are different cultures in every society. The classic culture-based term is 'democracy', which varies tremendously in meaning according to cultural nuances.

There are some even more straightforward problems to wrestle with. It has been found that some people have a consistent tendency to answer 'yes' or 'no' independently of the content of the question. Survey researchers have to check whether people have worked down the page just ticking the same column regardless of content. Also, people are woefully inaccurate. One study found 30 per cent inaccuracy in whether the respondent had voted in an election held a few weeks previously, and similar problems have been found in studies of birth control, social welfare and health information (Gorden, 1980).

It seems, then, that the least tractable problem is the assumption of correspondence between verbal response and behaviour. We can overcome most technical problems, by interviewer training, careful question design and probing, and comparison with results using other methods. But it seems that we need a better theory of why people do and do not act as they say they do. This brings us to our final topic.

8.7   Analytic stances towards interview data

Sociologists differ greatly in their assessment of the status of interview data. This section will review three of the principal perspectives, but this is not exhaustive. The discussion here draws heavily on Silverman (1985).

The first approach is that of positivism, the longest-established, and still dominant, perspective on social science methods. This school of thought is geared to a statistical logic mainly based on survey research. Interview data are regarded as giving access to 'facts' of the social world. They are treated as accounts whose sense derives from their correspondence to a factual reality. Where the account imperfectly represents that reality, checks and remedies must be applied.

For positivists, the idea that responses might be an artefact of the interview setting or its conduct would challenge their validity. The aim is to generate data which hold independently of the setting and the interviewer. They are keen on standardised interviews and suspicious of non-standardised approaches. Each interview must follow a standard protocol, asking each question precisely the same way each time and in the same order. Interviewers should not show surprise or disapproval, offer impromptu explanations of questions, suggest possible replies or skip questions. If care is taken the 'facts' will be established, affording a reliable and valid basis for inference.

The second approach is that of symbolic interactionism. For interactionists, the interview is a social event based on mutual participant observation. The context of the production of interview data is intrinsic in understanding the data. No clear-cut distinction between research interviews and other forms of social interaction is recognised.

For interactionists, the data are valid when a deep mutual understanding has been achieved between interviewer and respondent. The practical consequence is that most interactionists reject prescheduled standardised interviews in favour of open-ended interviews. The latter allow respondents to use their own particular way of defining the world, assume that no fixed sequence of questions is suitable to all respondents, and allow respondents to raise considerations that the interviewer has not thought of.

While interactionism has a strong relativist tinge (believing that the meaning of social action is relative to the researcher's perspective) it retains an orientation to those threats to validity which also worry positivists. For example, a leading text (Denzin 1970: 133–8) lists the following problems to which non-standardised interviews are a solution: the problem of 'self-presentation', especially early in interviews; the problem of fleeting encounters to which respondents are uncommitted, leading to possibilities of fabrication; the relative status of interviewer and respondent; the context of the interview. Clearly these can only be seen as problems if it is assumed that there is a truth or fact which lies behind them. It is a kind of positivism-plus, where the plus is a full attention to the context of the interview as a form of interaction.

But there are some who are so doubtful about the status of interview data that they abandon any concern with the content of response in favour of examining its form. For ethnomethodologists, interview data do not report on an external reality displayed in respondents' utterances but on the internal reality constructed as both parties contrive to produce the appearance of a recognisable interview. In short, they treat interview data as a topic and not as a resource. One consequence is that when standardised, multi-interviewer studies produce invariant data this does not establish the credibility of the data but the remarkable practical accomplishment by which intrinsically variable stimuli were made to produce the same results. As Cicourel put it,

> [i]n spite of the problem of interviewer error, somehow different interviewers with different approaches produced similar responses from different subjects. The question then becomes one of determining what was invariant or, more

precisely, how were invariant meanings communicated despite such variations. (Cicourel, 1964: 75)

There is more about this approach in chapters 14 and 15 on accounts and on analysing interaction. It derives from a perspective on social order which is preoccupied with the everyday production of orderly interaction. Some argue that the approach is indifferent to disparities of power between interviewers and respondents, preferring to see them as cooperatively engaged in producing the interview. However, the problem of 'facts' is solved, since the issue of truth does not arise, except in so far as a community version of reality and truth is assumed. Everyday knowledge is not identified with truth. Indeed, questions of truth are marginalised, since they relate to content, not form.

While these three are important positions on the analysis of interview data, they are not the only ones. Nor can it be said that they do not overlap; it is possible to find research which is informed by more than one perspective. We cannot authoritatively conclude that one is 'better' than the other, but what we must acknowledge is that, in pure form, they are tied to very different theories of the social world. Your choice of which approach to take will reflect not only your theoretical orientation but, hopefully, your thoughts on which provides the fairest reflection of your data.

8.8 Project

All of us have been to school. In this exercise you will need to pair with a partner and conduct a brief interview. Each of you will act as interviewer and respondent in turn. The exercise takes about an hour. Begin by thinking over your experiences at school and choose some aspect of school life about which to ask questions.

Choose an aspect of school about which you are curious. It could be relations with teachers, or how people prepare for exams, or the value of religious education, or many other things. Since you will only be interviewing for about 5–10 minutes you only need to prepare for the beginning stage of the interview. You should write down several questions addressing the research issue, and you should also write down a standard 'project explanation', a general statement of the research issue which you can say to your respondent to get the interview going.

Take 10 minutes to design your questions.

Now choose which of you wants to act as interviewer first. Carry out your interview. The time allowed is 10 minutes. There is no need to take notes on the respondent's replies.

The next stage is debriefing. The interviewer should identify in writing the skills they managed well and those that need improvement. To do this you should discuss it with your respondent. This should take 5 minutes.

Now swap roles with your partner, carry out another 10 minute interview and another 5 minute debriefing.

When you have finished both rounds you should discuss with your partner your experiences of interviewing and the accuracy of your debriefing notes about what was good and what needed more work. This should take 15 minutes.

8.9 Further reading

Gorden (1980) is a comprehensive book with good attention to problems of communication.

Mishler (1986), a social psychologist, emphasises the need to take account of reflexivity and the interaction between interviewer and respondent in analysing interview data.

Norris (1983) offers a beginner's guide on carrying out studies using repertory grid.

Chapter 8 of Silverman (1985) is devoted to interviewing and is particularly good on the different theoretical approaches to interview analysis.

9 Ethnography

Nigel Fielding

Contents

This chapter concerns ethnography, a form of qualitative research which combines several methods, including interviewing and observation. The chapter examines the emergence of ethnography before discussing the practicalities of conducting ethnographic research, including the maintenance of relations in the field, fieldwork roles and methods for recording field data. Considerable attention is paid to matters of analysis, since the eclecticism of ethnographic methods means that ethnographers often confront problems in converting reams of data into a coherent analysis. The intimacy of field relations also prompts a discussion of fieldwork ethics.

The origin of ethnography lies in the classical tradition of anthropology which evolved during the colonial period of the British Empire, although elements of the method date back to antiquity. Thucydides, in his 'History of the Peloponnesian War' (Grene, 1959), subjected his materials to the most searching scrutiny. The ruling principle of his work was strict adherence to carefully verified facts, so that the work would be 'a possession for ever, not the rhetorical triumph of an hour'. But it was not only a matter of chronicle, for the speeches which constitute a quarter of the History shed a most vivid light on the workings of the Greek political mind, on the motives of the actors and the arguments which they used. The concern to balance detailed documentation of events with insights into the meaning of those events is the enduring hallmark of ethnography. We can already discern ethnography's customary mix of observation, documentation and speech (interviews, nowadays). But for these concerns to be separated from the discipline of history and to become a distinctive method for the study of unfamiliar cultures we must wait for the time of the British Empire.

While early anthropologists sometimes accompanied scientific expeditions, the armchair approach was more popular. The system of colonial administration developed by the British relied on district commissioners, local representatives of the colonial power who dealt with all matters affecting the British interest. Such men were ideally located to document the way of life of the indigeneous peoples. Yet, however thoughtful, they were men of action and hardly 'intellectuals' by training or inclination. A system grew up whereby scholars in Britain used district commissioners essentially as fieldworkers, collecting data to be sent for analysis at home. The material was produced to a standard format which enabled similar questions to be explored in any colonial society. It was called the 'notes and queries' approach after a guidebook first published in 1874 which provided the so-called 'man on the spot' with a set of questions to ask native informants (Van Maanen, 1988: 15); it is worth noting the important role that informants were already playing in ethnography.

There is great continuity in the practice of ethnography, despite the dwindling number of cultures which can truly claim isolation from the outside world. Bearing in mind the historical examples, consider this summary of Caroline Humphrey's study, 'Karl Marx Collective: economy, society and religion in a Siberian collective farm' (1983):

> This book, the first ethnography based on fieldwork in a Soviet community by a Western anthropologist, describes the contemporary life of the Buryats, a Mongolian-speaking people in Siberia, through a detailed analysis of two collective farms. After describing Buryat historical traditions and ethnic relations, Dr Humphrey sets out the official theoretical model of the Soviet collective farm, its statutes and forms of social control. She then analyses how far the reality conforms to the model; in what respects it does not; and how the Buryats respond to the inconsistencies between theory and reality. (Humphrey, 1983: Publisher's catalogue, CUP, 1983: 60)

The first thing to notice is that this study is pathbreaking, as ethnography so often is. It explores some hitherto obscure niche of social life. It is not a rule that ethnography must study the unknown, but, as we shall see, some of the constraints on it as a method can be excused by its value as a 'method of discovery'. As a means of gaining a first insight into a culture or social process, as a source of hypotheses for detailed investigation using other methods, it is unparalleled.

The second thing to notice about Humphrey's study is that it involves a small sample, in this case, two collective farms. Ethnography does not have to be limited in sample size, but because of the great emphasis put on 'depth', 'intensity', 'richness' and so on, it usually is. Gathering very detailed material is demanding and few ethnographers are able to devote such effort to more than one or two settings. But notice also that, by focusing on two farms, Humphrey is able to employ a key element of social scientific analysis: the ability to compare and contrast between settings in which similar activities occur.

The third characteristic emphasis in Humphrey comes in the mention of 'the official theoretical model'. That word 'official' is very revealing. We cannot utter it without acknowledging that things could well be otherwise than they appear on paper; there must be an 'unofficial' model, too. Social scientists make an important distinction between 'formal' and 'informal' organisation; for instance, there is the law in the books and the law as it is practised on the street. Thus, Humphrey explores the fit between the official model and the reality of the collective farm. Finding the fit to be less than perfect, she shows how the Buryats handle the breakdown between theory and reality. Ethnography is often a debunking exercise, especially when, as in sociology rather more than in anthropology, it is used to shed new light on the darker corners of our own society.

9.1 The meaning of ethnographic research

Modern ethnography also has an important progenitor we have not yet mentioned, the social reformers of the early twentieth-century US cities. The sociologists associated with the 'Chicago School' came from backgrounds in journalism and social work, and were abundantly aware of the failings of their own society. They brought to ethnography a campaigning, critical edge, and a great sympathy for the underclass who were the principal subject of their studies. The idea of 'appreciation' became a key part of their 'naturalistic' stance (studying people in their 'natural' settings) towards ethnography, a stance which emphasised seeing things from the perspective of those studied before stepping back to make a more detached assessment. These early sociologists were mindful of the Native American adage that one should 'never criticise a man until you have walked a mile in his moccasins'.

Another way of rendering the spirit of the adage is to argue that the researcher must be involved in the ongoing, daily world of the people being studied. As Goffman put it,

> any group of persons – prisoners, primitives, pilots or patients – develop a life of their own that becomes meaningful, reasonable and normal once you get close to it, and . . . a good way to learn about any of these worlds is to submit oneself in the company of the members to the daily round of petty contingencies to which they are subject. (Goffman, 1961: ix–x)

So Goffman thought that every social group had something distinctive about it and the best way to understand it, to see how it was 'normal' no matter how zany it may seem to outsiders, was to get close. He was just following Hughes and the other Chicagoan mentors who taught generations of students to 'get the seats of their pants dirty' in 'real' research which, naturally, had to take place in the 'real' world, not the library.

The principles we can derive from this include the idea that ethnography always involves the study of behaviour in 'natural settings', as opposed to the experimental settings of psychology. Further, it is committed to the idea that an adequate knowledge of social behaviour cannot be fully grasped until the researcher has understood the 'symbolic world' in which people live. By 'symbolic world' we refer to the meanings people apply to their own experiences, meanings developed through patterns of behaviour which are in some way distinctive by comparison to the outside world. To get a full and adequate knowledge of these special meanings the researcher must adopt the perspective of the members, in an effort to see things as they do.

Ethnography has been referred to as 'a curious blending of methodological techniques' (Denzin, 1970). According to McCall and Simmons, it includes

> some amount of genuinely social interaction in the field with the subjects of the study, some direct observation of relevant events, some formal and a great deal of informal interviewing, some systematic counting, some collection of documents and artefacts; and open-endedness in the direction the study takes. (McCall and Simmons, 1969: 1)

That last point is important because it takes us away from techniques and towards analysis, suggesting a preference for 'rolling with the punches' and adapting the research focus to what proves available and interesting rather than imposing an outsider's sense of what is going on. But whether the ethnographer is a Brit in Borneo or a professor on an assembly line the techniques to record and make sense of the experience are likely to include interviews (usually more like a conversation than a standardised interview, and often involving key informants; see chapter 8), the analysis of documents, direct observation of events, and some effort to 'think' oneself into the perspective of the members, the introspective, empathetic process Weber called '*verstehen*'.

Thus, my ethnographic study of the National Front, an extreme Right racist organisation, combined participant observation at marches, demonstrations and meetings, where I passed as a member, plus interviews with party officials and opponents of the party, plus content analysis of party documents, and a good deal of reflection on the differences between my beliefs and those espoused by members (Fielding, 1981).

The ethnographer's encounter therefore involves becoming a part of the 'natural setting'. To do this he or she has first to learn the language in use; in sociological ethnography this not only means jargon and dialect, but special meanings and unfamiliar usages of familiar words. This modicum of understanding gives sufficient purchase on action in the setting to allow the compilation of fieldnotes. From inspection of these, and reflection in the field, the researcher can begin to identify the rules which govern relationships in the setting and discern patterns in members' behaviour.

9.2   Front management and finding a role

The process of participation involves the presentation to members of the ethnographer's 'self', so that the researcher engages in impression (or 'front') management. It involves a vital decision, because the role always has an element of deception and this can present ethical dilemmas. Like many others, Lofland argues that, before choosing ethnographic methods, we should ask ourselves 'am I reasonably able to get along with these people? Do I truly like a reasonable number of them, even though I disagree with their view of the world?' (1971: 94). If we cannot answer 'yes' then field observation becomes too much a matter of masking one's feelings. In special circumstances detailed further below, covert observation may be acceptable; this will obviously entail considerable front management, particularly where covert work is chosen because the group is hostile to research. It is best left to those who are comfortable with deception; several ethnographers who have used this technique have an acting background. A useful observational tactic is the cultivation of an impression of naivete and humility, so that members feel obliged to explain things that seem obvious to them; the literature even speaks of taking on the role of the 'acceptable incompetent' (Daniels, 1967). Would-be ethnographers could well consider adopting a role allowing them to ask naive questions, such as the apprentice or new convert.

The most important problem ethnographers face in the field is that of 'going native', a term with an obvious origin in anthropology. It has to be remembered that adopting the perspective of members is a methodological tactic. One is participating in order to get detailed data, not to provide the group with a new member. One must maintain a certain detachment in order to take that data and interpret it. But it is also important to note that another problem is much less remarked in the literature, though it may be more common. This is the problem of 'not getting close enough', of adopting an approach which is too superficial and which merely provides a veneer of plausibility for an analysis to which the researcher is already committed.

In deciding how close to get, ethnographers must choose a role somewhere between the 'Martian' and the 'convert' (Lofland, 1971). The most basic choice is whether to tell members of the setting what you are up to. This is the choice between overt and covert roles. Covert observation is a contentious procedure which some sociologists repudiate on ethical grounds (see chapter 4). Those that accept the occasional need for it usually justify it on the basis that some groups, especially powerful elites, would otherwise be closed to research (Fielding, 1982). I justified my limited use of covert observation in my study of the National Front (Fielding, 1981) on the basis that this racist group was particularly hostile to sociology. A covert approach is controversial, but may be acceptable in sociology. However, it is almost always inappropriate in anthropology, where the deceptive role is frowned upon and may represent a breach of professional ethical codes. Whatever their discipline, researchers should remember that deception is not required in most circumstances.

There are many problems in covert ethnography. The first is that you must play the role which warrants your presence in the setting; if you are masquerading as an industrial worker you will have to spend most of your time actually working on the assembly line. Your freedom to wander and observe is limited to what is appropriate for the role which has gained you entry. Further, your range of inquiry is limited to what is appropriate for that role; you may be fascinated by the management canteen, but as a shopfloor worker that is not open to you. Also, unless your role includes writing, it will be difficult to take notes in the setting.

Why, then, choose covert observation? Apart from the justifications mentioned above, actually occupying the role you are studying offers an intimate acquaintance with it. There is probably no better way to understand the experiences of members and the meaning they derive from their experiences (e.g. Ditton, 1977). Further, provided you are proficient in the role, you are much less likely to disturb the setting, avoiding the risk of studying an artefact of your presence rather than normal behaviour. But it must be emphasised that covert observation is an intensely demanding method and that you must be able to satisfy yourself that breaking the ethical objections to it is warranted by your research problem.

Choosing an overt approach does not solve all the problems, either. It is increasingly accepted that the most faithfully negotiated overt approach inescapably contains some covertness, in that, short of wearing a sign, ethnographers cannot signal when they are or are not collecting data. Nor is even the most scrupulous researcher entirely able to anticipate the purposes to which the data will be put. In reality, overt and covert approaches shade into each other, so that most observational research involves a 'delicate combination of overt and covert roles' (Adler, 1985: 27).

In overt observation, access is accomplished through an explicit negotiation with a 'gatekeeper'. The gatekeeper will be interested in what your research can do to help – or harm – the organisation. Be prepared to have to sketch in some likely findings, and to offer feedback. If access is promised, remember that the organisation may have an interest in letting you in. This needs to be taken into account in deciding what information to provide. You should avoid promising too much through gratitude. In particular, if you are preparing a dissertation or report, think carefully before committing yourself to providing a separate report for the organisation. You should also allow for the possibility that the gatekeeper's permission may be given without the knowledge or consent of the others being studied.

It is normal to accomplish access through some established contact; my study of police training (Fielding, 1988) came about because the training establishment director had been a student of my former thesis supervisor.

In gaining access this way one also gains a 'sponsor' in the organisation, to whom one is accountable. After all, if things go badly you can leave but the 'sponsor' will remain. Access-givers often serve as initial informants about the organisation. Informants are the unsung heroes of ethnography; it is usual to develop several key informants with whom you discuss your research. While they can help you avoid analytic errors you should remember that they may have ulterior motives in cooperating, such as influencing your account. It should also be remembered that their cooperation may endanger their own position in the organisation (Fielding, 1982, 1990).

All this may make access sound a fearsome business. But we should not be too demure. Many settings are public despite the observer's trepidation; for instance, even the most bizarre political and interest groups hold public meetings, because they wish to gain converts.

Overt observers are able to move about the setting more freely, to ask questions which are clearly research-related and to withdraw when they like to write notes. The role still presents problems. Most organisations contain factions and when people know research is taking place they will be keen to discover whether the researcher is affiliated to one or other faction. It is recommended to maintain neutrality relative to internal divisions.

The researcher may become the scapegoat for things that go wrong; in evaluation research, where budgets stand or fall on the findings, this may be a realistic perception! Where a stance of neutrality proves impossible to sustain it is typical for the observer to align with the single largest grouping in the setting while trying to remain aloof from internal disputes. In evaluation research this often involves a separation of roles, with the observer compiling material which is then analysed by a colleague not bound by relations developed in the field.

Another problem is that of personal involvement. Observers often feel bound to help members in exchange for their tolerating the research; services range from giving lifts and stuffing envelopes to illegal activities. The problem is acute in studies of crime and deviance; in one case, the observer agreed to hide a gun in his house for a criminal expecting a visit from the police (Polsky, 1971).

These problems all relate to the issue of marginality, the idea that the ethnographer is in this social world, but not of it. It leads to fears about whether one has been accepted, and to feelings of loneliness. In covert research there are also worries about whether the deception has been discovered. It is possible to deal with these by observing on a team, so there are others to share the experience. If this is not possible, there should at least be regular meetings with other researchers who know what it is like. But it can be argued that this sense of marginality is actually crucial for the success of the work. This is because it is out of this experience of being simultaneously an insider and an outsider that creative insight is generated. When we construct our analysis we reflect on the self that we had to become in order to pass in the setting, and how that temporary, setting-specific self differs from the person that we are normally. We can begin to identify the things that are distinctive about the people who inhabit the setting, and these are an important basis of our analytic categories. Mention of analysis brings us to fieldnotes.

9.3 Recording the action: fieldnotes

The production of fieldnotes is the observer's raison d' etre: if you do not record what happens you might as well not be in the setting. In order to take full fieldnotes it is sensible to develop your powers of observation gradually. We will discuss mental notes, jotted notes and full fieldnotes. Before doing so it is worth pointing out an observation on the functioning of human memory. Erosion of memory is not related to time so strongly as it is to new input; that is, the more stimuli to which you are subjected during a day the more detail is forced out. It is a good idea, then, to write up fieldnotes before engaging in further interaction after a round of observation. It may be possible to sleep before writing fieldnotes but it would not be sensible to end the day by going to a party!

The 'taking' of mental notes is a skill journalists develop; they do so by practice, sometimes quizzing each other about what they can recall. Good reportage and observation is marked by accurate description of how many people were present; who in particular was present; the physical character of the setting; who said what to whom; who moved in what way; a general characterisation of the order of events (Lofland and Lofland, 1984).

Reporters have one obvious aid, the notepad. In sensitive settings it may not be feasible to scribble notes, which partly accounts for journalists developing the capacity to take mental notes. But as soon as possible these will be transferred to writing. In taking jotted notes you do not record everything that took place, as in full fieldnotes. Rather, you note key words, phrases or quotations which represent more extensive chunks of verbal and non-verbal behaviour, and which will stimulate the memory when you are at leisure to reconstruct the events as comprehensively as such notes and your memory permit.

The jotted note may be most useful when covert observation is taking place but even when subjects are well aware they are being observed it can be disruptive for one member of the setting to be busily note-taking. It is sensible to jot notes at inconspicuous moments. A stock ploy is to develop the reputation of having a weak bladder, enabling frequent retirements to scribble notes. The object of jotted notes is to jog the memory when writing full fieldnotes. It is worth including items from observation on previous occasions which one forgot to record at the time. It is an interesting fact that the process of observation stimulates one's mind in such a way that events thought significant but forgotten are frequently returned to conscious awareness.

In taking full fieldnotes it is possible to move beyond the homilies above and to be quite systematic in suggesting a standard procedure. First, it is essential to write up observations promptly. It should be delayed no later than the morning after observation. Most people lose good recall of even quite simple chains of events after 24 hours; detailed recall of conversation sufficient to enable quotation is lost within a couple of hours. Second, writing fieldnotes requires discipline; you should expect to spend as much time writing fieldnotes as in the observation.

A third matter is the question of tape recording versus writing. While recording speeds things up, it has the disadvantage of leading to a less reflective approach. Being slower, writing often leads to a better yield of analytic themes. Most researchers find the process of writing fieldnotes productive not just of description but of first reflections on connections between processes, sequences and elements of interaction. It is commonly the case that innovation occurs when the mind is not directly exploring the problem at hand. Routine writing up is fruitful in these terms.

A fourth routine matter is that it is essential to produce at least three copies of the full fieldnotes. One set forms a complete running commentary. The others will be cut up (sometimes literally, when employing the 'cut and paste' approach to analysis) or marked by outline codes during analysis.

The contents of fieldnotes are the subject of remarkable consensus among methodologists. Since different analytic uses may be made of them it makes sense to maximise the elements of description and to gather such data systematically. The several rules applying to content are based on the idea that fieldnotes need to provide a running description of events, people and conversation. Consequently each new setting observed and each new member of the setting merits description. Similarly, changes in the human or other constituents of a setting should be recorded. Fieldnotes should stay at the lowest level of inference. Some put it that the notes should be 'behaviouristic' rather than seeking to summarise (see Figure 9.1). Fieldnotes should be directed to the concrete, and resist the urge to use abstractions. Such abstractions and analytic ideas that occur – and it frequently happens in the field – should be recorded separately or in a distinct column in the margin of the page.

Any verbal behaviour which is included should be identified as verbatim or otherwise. A system of notation should be adopted; one convention is that full quotemarks ('') denote verbatim quotation, while single quotemarks (') indicate a precis of what was said.

Finally, it is essential to record your personal impressions and feelings. Doing fieldwork does have emotional costs, and one needs data on one's own attitude in order to document one's evolving relationship to others in the setting. Among other things such information helps compensate for shifts in perspective due, for example, to 'going native'. Covert observation poses special problems in recording, leading to various ploys – the use of hidden tape recorders, note-taking in toilets, hasty exits when

Summarized or over-generalised note
The new client was uneasy waiting for her intake interview.

Behaviouristic or detailed note
At first the client sat very stiffly on the chair next to the receptionist's desk. She picked up a magazine and let the pages flutter through her fingers very quickly without really looking at any of the pages. She set the magazine down, looked at her watch, pulled her skirt down, and picked up the magazine again. This time she didn't look at the magazine. She set it back down, took out a cigarette and began smoking. She would watch the receptionist out of the corner of her eye, and then look down at the magazine, and back up at the two or three other people waiting in the room. Her eyes moved from people to the magazine to the cigarette to the people to the magazine in rapid succession. She avoided eye contact. When her name was finally called she jumped like she was startled.

Based on Patton (1987: 93)

Figure 9.1   *Fieldnotes*

something important has to be written up precisely. These problems may lead to researcher-effects on the setting. Note should therefore be taken of memory distortion, confusion of issues and speakers, and general field fatigue (Bruyn, 1966: 106).

9.4   Comes the crunch: analysis

While there are several approaches to the analysis of ethnographic data, the mechanical procedures researchers use are straightforward and readily summarised, as in Figure 9.2.

Appreciation of the meaning of action and events to members is not gained by simply 'telling it like it is' for them. Mere mirroring is insufficient. One gains insight from a comparison of the participant observer's normal and setting-specific self, appreciating the difference in such a way as to understand on what separate assumptions about reality both are founded. Meaning emerges, then, from experience of the tension between distinct selves. As Spiegelberg puts it, the investigator must not attempt to 'go native' but to move back and forth between his or her own place and understanding and that of the other (1980: 42).

Leaving the setting begins when one is sufficiently confident to feel that

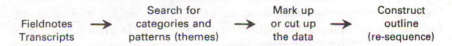

Figure 9.2   *Analysis procedure*

one has identified the chief assumptions on which this particular world-view is based. This enables an increasingly selective focus in observations, with description of matters now seen as peripheral being skipped. The themes which best represent the setting have been identified.

9.5   Validation

Making critical assessments of the reality of some unknown area of social life places a heavy responsibility on ethnographers. They must make sense of something which will remain unknown to most of their readers; precisely because the method is one of discovery it is unlikely that their audience will have any direct way of validating what the ethnographer claims. The ethnographer is never a detached observer. 'Objective' observation is hopeless to achieve.

Given that 'objective' observation is impossible, what grounds might there be for the credibility of the ethnographer's account? The participating observer is involved, not detached. Understanding is derived from experience. Beginning to share in the member's world enables one to gain access to one's own personal experience. Clearly such knowledge is introspective. While one's description and conclusions may be public, the introspective knowledge is not. Followers of the method have therefore pursued a test of **congruence** or principle of verifiability. The idea is that in any natural setting there are norms or rules of action in which members are competent. Understanding on the part of the observer is achieved when the observer learns the rules. The adept observer is able to provide others with instructions on how to pass in the same setting. Following such a recipe one should ideally be able to have similar experiences and hence personally appreciate the truth of the description. In Hughes's description of the principle of verifiability, 'understanding' is achieved when the researcher knows the rules and can communicate them to both members and colleagues in such a way that if a colleague were to follow them he or she could also become a member of the group (1976: 134).

A more sophisticated approach is that of the 'grounded theory' of Glaser and Strauss (1967). It requires

> the development of a systematic understanding which is clearly recognizable and understandable to the members of the setting and which is done as much as possible in their own terms; yet it is more systematic, and necessarily more verbal, than they would generally be capable of expressing. It uses their words, ideas and methods of expression wherever possible, but cautiously goes beyond these. (1967: 124–5)

This is necessary because members are immersed in a setting natural to them, and are seldom concerned to express its essence in a symbolic fashion for outsiders. Yet without such symbolic interpretation one's ethnographic description is hollow, a mere catalogue of events and constituents.

Douglas (1976) takes the matter of verification to what some regard as its illogical conclusion. Ethnography's general orientation to 'naturalism' in sociology means that most observation is informed by a stance of 'appreciation', of trying to see things from the member's perspective. This approach tends to celebrate the knowledge of members on the basis that they, not outsiders, are the experts about their natural setting. But this is not enough for Douglas, who is preoccupied with all the ways members can deceive outsiders. He suggests procedures such as 'testing out' and 'checking out' as antidote. The former involves comparing members' accounts with 'the most reliable ideas and generally patterned facts the researcher has from his prior experience' (1976: 146), while the latter involves 'comparing what one is told by others against what can be experienced or observed more directly'. Among his many examples is the case of massage parlour proprietors. Ethnographic interviews with them suggested that their popularly-supposed sideline offering illicit sex (often called 'relief massage') was false. Douglas just could not believe this; their huge cars and houses did not seem consistent with the volume of legitimate trade. Among Douglas's checks was to send graduate students in search of a massage, a device which soon undermined what the proprietors had been telling him. For Douglas the proper 'investigative' research attitude is 'tough-minded suspicion', a position that contrasts utterly with that of naturalism.

The problem is that Douglas's hard-bitten scepticism obstructs the attempt to construe the world as members do with a view to gaining an understanding of its distinctive characteristics (Fielding, 1982). Yet Douglas's concentration on the delicate balance between appreciation and being conned, between the participant persona and the observer role, does alert us to the fact that the effects of the researcher's presence on the setting is as inevitable as it is hard to gauge.

A case in point is Van Maanen's study of urban policing (1982). Van Maanen had trained as a police officer as part of his observational research and, while some officers knew what he was doing, his esteem in their eyes had been dramatically improved when, after witnessing the beating of a Black man in the back of a police van, he refused to comply with a subpoena of his fieldnotes on the incident. Luckily for him, the case brought by the victim was settled out of court, because there are no legal grounds for refusing to surrender fieldnotes. Nevertheless his stand was known and appreciated by the police. Two years later he returned for more observations. He initially did not appreciate that some of what they did on his return was for his benefit; they were, if you will, 'playing to camera'. He suddenly realised this when they did something that broke with his previous knowledge of their demeanour:

> I once witnessed a bizarre encounter in which a young boy, perhaps 10 or 11 years old, was verbally assaulted and thrown to the pavement because he had aimed a ceremonial upright third finger in the direction of a passing patrol car – a

gesture from a child that would have been routinely ignored or returned in my previous experience. (Van Maanen, 1982: 137)

When he had been with them every day he felt he could maintain a role that did not disturb their routines. But when he came back the action did not flow from the logic of the situation at hand but from what the police thought he might appreciate, as a published 'expert' on police, and one apparently sympathetic to street justice. As he put it,

> in the abstract, relations in the field are such that the researcher is provided with trusted information of the sort necessary to both understand and empathize with the observed, but the researcher's presence itself creates little change or disturbance . . . concretely, however, such relations wax and wane over the course of a study, approach or exceed the upper and lower limits with different individuals on the scene, and vary according to the practical situation. (Van Maanen, 1982: 138)

All this challenges our established canons of verification. The test of congruence may comprise the ideal check on the validity of observations, but it has to be recognised that many consumers of research do not have time to perform it. In fairness to them, and to satisfy ourselves, observers still need to be self-critical. Lofland and Lofland (1984) identify seven ways of evaluating the quality of observation in terms of possible error and bias. First is the directness of the report; direct observation is more reliable than secondhand observation. Second is the spatial location of the observer. Proximity may be social as well as spatial. Third, problems arise from skewing of reported views by the informants' social location. Informants may not have said the same to other members of the setting. Fourth, one needs to guard against self-serving error in describing events by asking whether the observations fit rather too neatly into one's analytic schema. Fifth are plain errors in description of events; one may not be an accurate observer. Sixth and seventh are problems of internal and external consistency. One's analysis needs to cohere around the themes identified, while external consistency is evaluated by checking agreement of key aspects against independent studies.

The Loflands' concerns are ably dealt with in the criteria of subjective adequacy suggested by Bruyn's (1966) 'humanistic' approach. It is worth keeping a notebook evaluating one's observations, using Bruyn's six criteria after writing each set of fieldnotes. Bruyn's first index of subjective adequacy is time; the more time the ethnographer spends with the group the greater the likelihood of adequacy. Second is place; the closer the observer works to the group the greater is the likelihood of adequacy. Third, Bruyn takes account of social circumstances, on the grounds that the more varied the status opportunities within which the observer can relate to the members and the more varied the activities witnessed the more likely the interpretations will be true. Fourth is a sensitivity to language, on the argument that the more familiar the observer is with it the greater is the accuracy of observation. The observer notes, but also becomes adept in, the argot, slang or jargon in use, and is alert to ordinary phrases which bear a setting-specific meaning.

The fifth index is intimacy. Here Bruyn suggests the observer record how he or she experienced and encountered social openings and barriers in seeking accurate interpretation of setting-specific meanings. Intimacy, or how close one is allowed to get, can be constrained by one's own reserve as well as by members. In the sixth index, 'social consensus', the criterion of adequacy is fulfilled by maximising confirmation of the group's expressive meanings, either directly – by checking interpretations with members – or indirectly – by observing what members say about an interpretation. Bruyn also offers a set of objective criteria, and his careful approach is worth examining in its full formulation.

9.6   Sequential analysis

It is commonly recognised that the analysis of ethnographic data is demanding, not least because ethnography produces a mass of data. One of Miles and Huberman's studies of a school system produced over 3,000 pages of fieldnotes (1984). You must remember that not all the detail you have arduously gathered can be regarded as equally precious. If your procedure fulfils the various criteria of adequacy you should have faith in your ability to select the most significant data. These items of description must then be compressed so they adhere around several manageable themes or, formally, analytic schema (Agar, 1986). The essence of the procedure is that one works up from the data, rather than selecting some theory by convenience, whim or prejudice and then dipping into the data for fragments that support it.

Howard Becker has suggested a procedure termed 'sequential analysis' (1971). This has affinity with Simmel's (1950) *zirkel im verstehen*, in which one continually checks data against interpretation until satisfied one has grasped meaning. In Becker's approach the analysis of ethnographic data is carried out sequentially in the sense that analysis begins while one is still gathering data. In the periods between observation one may 'step back' from the data, so as to reflect on their possible meaning. Further data gathering is then directed to particular matters to which the observer has become sensitive by provisional analysis. Further observation may oblige the researcher to abandon the original hypothesis about that part of the process and check out one more consistent with the setting. Thus, hypotheses, or, if you prefer, hunches, are gradually refined. This is a distinct advantage over methods like surveys, where, once the instrument is designed, analytic interests cannot affect the data collected.

The evaluation of hypotheses hinges, then, on indices of the adequacy of data such as those suggested by Bruyn, plus consideration of the fit of one's observations to theory. Regarding the latter, the point is that such theory must be grounded rather than 'grand' theory. Ethnography generates hypotheses for further testing through the researcher's ability to apply a theoretical perspective to observations and pick up uniformities and irregularities in the data. As McCall and Simmons note,

> these uniformities and departures, which provide theoretical richness, are seldom manifest in the data themselves but are obtained only through carefully designed theoretical sampling and analysis based upon the researcher's frame of reference . . . data are not rich in and of themselves but may be *enriched* by proper use of discovery techniques. (McCall and Simmons, 1969: 142, emphasis in original)

Three kinds of conclusions emerge from ethnographic studies. First, and most demanding, the observer may be able to produce complex statements of necessary and sufficient conditions for a particular pattern of action or setting (see Fielding and Fielding, 1986, for examples). Second, the observer should be able to typify some of the observed phenomena as 'basic' to the studied activity, on the grounds that they exercise a persistent influence on diverse events. Third, the observer ought to be able to identify a situation as an example of an event or phenomenon described in abstract terms in a theory. This latter is the least demanding application.

Turning to the mechanics of analysis, towards the end of fieldwork the observer draws up an outline comprising his or her current idea of the principal themes to emerge from the data, along with any analytic ideas he or she has accumulated during fieldwork (this is where keeping an analytic theme notebook is useful). The data, such as fieldnotes or transcriptions of interviews or documents collected in the setting, are then indexed to the points on the outline. Though tedious, all the data should be indexed in this way. When the time comes to compile a first draft of the report one may then discard the less strong or simply repetitive data relating to particular points on the outline.

A somewhat more rigorous procedure is to compile the outline itself from ideas emerging only from the data. The data are read for analytic themes, which are listed. This list is then ordered by placing related items together in compounded items and, when condensed as much as possible, put in order according to an overall theme which seems to relate all the individual items. Because the selection of data pertinent to one of several analytic themes requires its separation from the rest of the field data, so that it may be collated with the other data on the theme, this procedure is sometimes called 'cut and paste'. Nowadays this operation can be performed using computer software. Conventional word processors allow you to retrieve selected segments to facilitate sorting into themes. But there is also software specifically for this, such as 'The Ethnograph', which permits more sophisticated manipulation of the data. Section 11.4 discusses the use of this software in more detail.

Good qualitative analysis is able to document its claim to reflect some of the truth of a phenomenon by reference to systematically gathered data.

Poor qualitative analysis is anecdotal, unreflective, descriptive without being focused on a coherent line of inquiry.

It is important not to misrepresent the generalisability of findings from one setting. Ethnography's demanding nature means you are seldom in a position to claim that findings generalise to all such settings. The compensation for this is the depth of understanding gained of that one setting, which can be a rich source of ideas for further work using methods such as surveys which can claim generalisability.

But the decision to use ethnographic methods must be ethical as well as practical. Some consider it unethical to conduct any research not giving the subjects the right to refuse to be studied, while at the other extreme are those who maintain that 'any investigation that does not deliberately damage the reputation of those studied is ethically justified' (Denzin, 1970: 33). Many professional bodies use the criterion of informed consent; in agreeing to research, subjects must be told its likely consequences, among other things. Yet it may not be feasible to predict the use to which research can be put; a detailed ethnography of a group of mountain villagers may seem innocuous until, years later, the region is engaged in revolt and the agents of a foreign power develop a keen interest in the group's beliefs so they can be won to its side. Are we to desist from our study when harm *might* result at some unknown future time?

What goes in the balance against potential harms is the value to social scientific knowledge of the study. This value may be obvious, as when a group is powerful and little is known about it. But it can be hard to guess. It is doubtful that Rosenhan (Bulmer, 1982c) could have predicted the enormous impact of his team's research on mental hospital diagnoses, for the simple reason that no one would have guessed they were so abjectly unreliable. The study involved placing 'pseudo-patients' in mental hospitals. On arrival they feigned hearing voices, but once admitted and diagnosed they ceased simulating any symptoms. All but one was admitted with a diagnosis of schizophrenia. Not one was caught out, providing crucial evidence about the reliability of psychiatric diagnosis and the labelling of patients. Nor were their diagnoses changed when they switched to normal behaviour, despite many of their fellow patients guessing, as one of them put it, that ' "you're a journalist or a professor, you're checking up on the hospital" '. One case file contained perhaps the ultimate description of compiling fieldnotes – ' "patient engages in writing behaviour" '! But he was never questioned about what he was doing. The staff of a hospital Rosenhan was in touch with were so appalled at the results that they agreed to the same being done at their hospital. Staff were told to expect imposters and to rate all admissions with this in mind; 23 out of 193 were suspected by at least one psychiatrist. Of course, Rosenhan had not sent in a single pseudo-patient.

Tough cases like this give some idea of what is at stake. No one could seriously doubt the value of this work, but neither could they deny its dangers. For instance, it is not hard to imagine that the psychiatrists' professional competence would be severely undermined, and their effectiveness with real patients affected negatively. The reaction of some mental health systems to such studies has been to ban social research of any kind from their institutions. What these ethical complications do is to support the case for 'situation ethics' attuned to the specifics of the case, in preference to broad, general principles which collapse when confronted with dilemmas.

This does not mean we are left without rules of thumb. Here are some guidelines. First, all researchers should be honest enough to report their mistakes and failures, and to do so as part of their overall analysis. Second, researchers should not spoil the field for those who may follow. Third, researchers must acknowledge that some groups have virtually no power and are especially vulnerable. They have a right to not be researched, an example being the decision by one ethnographer not to publish a study of American draft resisters during the Vietnam War. Fourth, unless there is a danger of reprisals affecting the physical security of the ethnographer, subjects should be given the right to comment on findings, by being provided with transcripts of interviews and draft publications. This is not just good practice but can yield more data. It should be clear to subjects what comments are legitimate; it is normal to allow points of accuracy and information to be added, while reserving the analysis to yourself.

9.7   Project

This project is an exercise in collecting observational data. The emphasis is on developing your skills of observation and gaining experience of the techniques of recording social events. First, think about a research design before your fieldwork. Decide what research topic is appropriate to study through observation. For instance, you might be interested in the unstated rules that govern queueing behaviour, and go to watch people lining up for buses. Or you might be interested in how people interact when they are engrossed in video games, and find your way to the student union to watch them. Another idea is to watch how people order drinks in the pub, noting gender differences particularly. Several students might work on the same topic so that they can (literally) compare notes.

Second, carry out field observation. Record your observations by writing fieldnotes. Now write a description of the research procedure and the sort of data you gathered. Mention any problems in using the method and evaluate how it went.

The exercise works best if there is someone with whom you can discuss it who has also tried it out. When you are thinking over the experience, or discussing it, here are the sort of questions you need to ask to assess the adequacy of your observations:

• How accurate an observer am I of sequences of action? of dialogue?

- Have I the ability to write 'concretely' or do my notes contain generalisations and summaries?
- Was my research aim realistic? Was it adequately specified at the outset? Was it interesting? Was it 'sociological' ?
- Was I comfortable doing the observation? Did I tell anyone I was researching? If I did not tell anyone I was researching, do I think anyone guessed?
- What other methods could I have used to get this data? Now that I have tried observation, was it the best available method to get this data?

9.8   Further reading

Burgess (1982) is a comprehensive edited collection which serves well as a sourcebook and field manual. It is particularly good on naturalistic and American sources.

Fetterman (1989) offers guidance about every step in the process of conducting an ethnography.

Hammersley and Atkinson (1983) is a thorough treatment of ethnography with particularly good attention to issues of analysis and writing up.

Patton (1980) is particularly good on sampling in ethnography and on the practical application of observational methods.

Yin (1984) provides an excellent introduction to the case study approach.

Exemplar A Becoming a carer

Patricia Taraborrelli

Contents

This chapter is an account of how the author embarked upon an ethnographic expedition, using intensive interviews, observation and the analysis of documents to return with a few new discoveries. Its intention is to use the experiences and findings of one study as an example of some of the more abstract issues covered in the chapters on ethnography and interviewing. It is an account of a study of informal carers: individuals who care for sick or disabled people, usually members of their family, at home. They are referred to as 'informal carers' to distinguish them from people, such as doctors and nurses, who have received some formal training and who care for their patients in hospitals or similar institutions. It has been estimated that in Great Britain there are about 6 million informal carers (OPCS, 1987).

More specifically, the study was concerned with those particular informal carers who care for people suffering from a form of dementia known as Alzheimer's disease. Alzheimer's disease is an irreversible and usually progressive destruction of the brain, which occurs more often in older people but which can affect people as young as their 30s. It is not a normal consequence of ageing, but as yet its cause is still unknown. The speed and extent of deterioration varies, as does the particular manifestation of the disease an individual may experience. For instance, the period of illness may last only 18 months or continue for over 10 years. What is more predictable, however, is the progressive decline in the sufferer's ability to remember, to think and to reason. The illness affects the sufferer's personality, behaviour, intellectual functioning, and in its later stages, can lead to severe physical deterioration. The symptoms of mild dementia include: short-term memory loss, apathy and difficulty in making decisions. The problems of moderate dementia are more apparent; sufferers become lost if in unfamiliar surroundings, forget names of family or friends and may become confused about time and place. For instance, they may go out shopping at night. Common manifestations of severe dementia include failure to recognise family, difficulty in walking and becoming incontinent.

A.1   Formulating the research question

Among sociologists involved in ethnographic research, there is a tradition of 'starting where you are' (Lofland and Lofland, 1984: 9). Numerous projects have been born out of the personal history or experiences of the researcher; this study proved to be one more.

Some six years prior to the study, my godfather had been diagnosed as suffering from Alzheimer's disease and since that time he had been cared for at home by my godmother. Around the same time my mother undertook to care for a frail elderly neighbour, an activity in which I was involved for a time. During this period I observed a number of changes in the lives of both women, but particularly my godmother. As the nature of their caring responsibilities changed, so did their social relationships and attitudes towards their roles as carers. Such observations, together with some of my own experiences of caring, served to spark an interest in informal care and in particular the problems posed by dementia. However, the formulation of a more precise set of research questions owed much to a review of the sociological literature.

The review uncovered a wealth of literature about informal care. Much of the earlier work was concerned with the demographics of informal care and with quantifying the amount and type of care being provided informally in the community. The 1985 General Household Survey, based on a random sample of the population of Great Britain, provided a great deal of data, including that 3.5 million of the 6 million carers were women. Other research was concerned with the economic, social and psychological costs of informal care (e.g. Nissel and Bonnerjea, 1982). Another branch of the literature was concerned with the social foundations of informal care, that is, why individuals, and women in particular, care for family and friends. Qureshi and Walker (1989) and Ungerson (1987) had explored how and why particular individuals come to be selected as carers.

What was absent from all this work was a conceptualisation of the carer's role as dynamic in nature, and an exploration of how carers' experiences, orientations and social relationships may change over time, or according to the different levels of the dependency they experienced. I was interested in the process by which one *becomes* and *maintains* the role of carer.

Within the subdiscipline of medical sociology, I found a number of studies on the process of becoming a formal carer, the classic example being Becker et al.'s ethnographic study *Boys in White* (1961). In this study Becker et al. followed a group of medical students throughout the entire course of their training in order to understand the process by which young medical students became doctors. The principal conceptual framework used in *Boys in White* was that of 'career', a concept developed by Everett Hughes (1958) in his study of the professions. It refers to a sequence of movements from one position to another within a particular institution. Embedded in this concept of 'career' is the notion of career contingencies, the factors on which mobility from one position to another depend. These contingencies may include objective facts or changes in an individual's motivations and perspectives. Career contingencies determine career outcomes.

A review of a number of studies that had employed the concept of career to develop sequential models convinced me of its applicability to the study of informal carers. It also helped me to refine the aim of my research, which I had now narrowed down to charting the careers of the informal carers of Alzheimer's disease sufferers and exploring both objective and subjective career contingencies.

Having established the research question, the next step was to decide on the design of the research study. That is, which methodological tools should I use and how should they be employed in order to collect the kind of data I required.

The aim of data collection was to understand individual perspectives and experiences and how these change over time. Given the research topic, the possibility of direct participation or observation of the research setting for any length of time seemed unlikely. An ideal alternative design might have been a longitudinal study: a group of carers being interviewed repeatedly over a number of years. However, the project had to be completed within a year, there was no budget to cover fieldwork expenses and I alone would be responsible for the data collection and analysis. Given these limitations I decided that a workable and effective design would be one in which people caring for individuals at different stages of the illness were interviewed about their present and past caring experiences.

A.2   Getting started

For the purposes of my small and essentially exploratory study I proposed to interview a sample of about 15 respondents, comprising roughly equal numbers of men and women coping with a range of dependency levels. I was to spend the next two months discovering the problems of identifying and contacting carers in the community and searching for possible solutions.

For the purposes of sampling in social research, informal carers are classified as a 'rare population' (see chapter 5). In addition, as we shall see, they are not an easily accessible group of individuals, particularly for the purposes of drawing a large, representative sample. This is primarily a result of informal care taking place within the private domain of the family home.

Many 'rare populations' are sampled through some third party or institution. For example, Ungerson (1987) obtained her sample of carers from lists held by a social services department. In the hope of imitating Ungerson's example I contacted the local social services department. I was told that no such list was kept and that while it was possible that some staff may be aware of the 'odd case' in the area, it was unlikely that they would be able to offer me any practical assistance with the matter. Following this initial disappointment, I explored the possibility of drawing a sample from the relatives who care for patients attending a local psychogeriatric day hospital, which provides day care for elderly people suffering from some form of dementia, or other psychiatric problems. However, this method of contacting respondents would only have been possible after the receipt of ethical approval from the relevant health authority (see chapter 4), a lengthy process and one which, assuming that approval was given, would have left insufficient time to carry out the study.

Fortunately, the Alzheimer's Disease Society, a non-professional organisation, had established two contact groups and funded a small day centre in the locality. Although these groups presented none of the formal access problems, because they were part of a voluntary organisation, there were informal vetting procedures to be negotiated.

Lofland and Lofland (1984: 25) suggest that when negotiating access to a research setting it is necessary to be 'armed with connections, accounts, knowledge and courtesy'. This was also my experience during this study. My initial contacts with these groups were encouraging. However, the groups were interested in my motives and my knowledge of the practicalities of caring for dementia sufferers. My account of my godfather's illness provided a path through this informal vetting procedure. Access to the carers in contact with these groups was agreed in principle soon after. However one further subtle test to determine my suitability as a potential researcher remained. The chairmen of both groups suggested that I first attend a support group meeting; I suspect this was as much for their information as for mine.

A.3   Lessons from the field

The invitations from the two groups to attend their support meetings were accepted. The two visits proved to be tremendously influential. They challenged a number of my preconceptions, raised a number of issues and resulted in significant changes to the design of the project.

I had expected the two groups to be very similar in their organisation and membership. I was mistaken. The first meeting I attended was held in the evening and run by the staff of the Alzheimer's Disease Society day centre. It was also attended by a community psychiatric nurse and an occupational therapist. Carers and staff formed a circle and individuals were encouraged to raise issues or problems for discussion. The second meeting was held in the early afternoon (attracting carers who could only attend a group while their relatives were at a day hospital) and run by ex-carers. This meeting was smaller and more intimate than the first. People talked together in groups of two or three and on subjects other than caring for their relatives.

I had not expected observation to be a part of my research. However these visits convinced me of the value of my continued attendance at these meetings. At the first meeting, one of the carers pointed out a woman who had recently started caring for a parent suffering with dementia but who had found it difficult to accept the illness. It was hoped that talking with more experienced carers would help her come to terms with her parent's dementia and thus be more able to cope with its implications. This exchange struck me as interesting on two counts. First, it proposed that this (experienced) carer believed that the acceptance of a dependant's illness was a desirable, possibly essential characteristic for a carer; why should this be? Second, it raised questions about the content, value and manner of exchange of information between carers. These issues were later to develop into analytical themes central to the identification and understanding of a number of career contingencies, some of which will be discussed later.

One of the first observations I made about both groups concerned the number of organisers and day centre staff who had previously cared for a relative or friend with Alzheimer's disease. The smaller support group was not only organised entirely by ex-carers whose relatives were now either in residential care or had died, but was also attended by ex-carers. In the course of my introductions to both groups, I was given the same piece of advice: 'If you want to get the full story go and talk to the ex-carers.' After the second meeting I was also particularly interested in why those ex-carers who performed no organisational role attended meetings which I had assumed were of use only to current carers. This interest was later to lead to issues concerning carers' experiences and need for support on ending their caring role. Given my research objectives, the inclusion of carers who had ended their caring careers seemed logical, yet this had been over-looked. The whole matter stands as an example of the value of researchers getting the seats of their pants dirty in real research (see chapter 9).

A.3.1   The observation of support groups

My observation of the two monthly support groups was overt. The leaders of both groups had allowed me to attend, knowing that my main purpose was to study them. However, particularly in the smaller, more informal setting, the boundaries between overt and covert observation occasionally blurred.

I arrived 15 minutes early for my second visit to the smaller group meeting. The only other person present was an ex-carer who had brought the tea and coffee supplies. We chatted and I found that before the meeting had even begun I had gained a good deal of information about her own experiences and the personalities within the group. I continued to arrive early for these meetings, helping to make the tea and arranging chairs about the room. This activity had the advantage of allowing me to meet the carers as they arrived and chat to them individually from time to time. It also served to give me a role in the group, helping to mask my status as an outsider and make me feel more comfortable in the role of observer. After a few months my role of assistant tea maker became the norm and my attendance only commented upon for the benefit of new members.

While the setting did allow me the luxury of carrying a notebook 'in public', most of my notes in the field were made quickly and discreetly. Support groups are settings where individuals come to share often very personal and painful experiences. As an observer, I felt that it was important that I should have as little effect on the setting as possible. I was concerned that my presence might somehow inhibit carers' discussions. Therefore I adopted a passive role in the group, using my discretion when it came to asking questions, introducing myself to members of the group and taking notes. For instance, although the groups were aware of my note-taking, I tried not to be seen to 'take direct dictation' while individuals spoke to a group, so as not to embarrass or inhibit their normal interaction. My notes consisted of memos of comments, events, behaviour or opinions that I felt might be analytically relevant. For instance I recorded a difference of opinion regarding the use of respite care services, which allow carers to take a holiday. I made notes on the composition of the group, the involvement of carers in discussions and patterns of interaction.

A friend of mine who once studied the suicide prevention movement was told that the work required volunteers with 'big ears but little mouths'. Ethnographers are often required to have similar characteristics.

A.3.2   The interviews

As noted earlier, I had proposed to interview a sample of about 15 carers. In fact I interviewed 23 respondents over four months. Decisions about the composition of the sample were informed by theoretical sampling (see section 5.3.2) which aims to sample those who will contribute most to the development of theory. My choice of respondents was directed by my initial research interests, such as the experiences of carers at different stages of their relatives' illnesses, and by questions which arose while I was in 'the field'. Two examples are my decision to include ex-carers in the study and my selection of individual respondents from this group. In the course of field work I became aware of the different types of ex-carer. Some were no longer in a caring role because their relatives had died; others because their relatives were now in some form of residential care. I thought that it would be interesting to examine the experiences of these different types of ex-carer and so I sampled some respondents from each subgroup. This resulted in some findings about the processes by which carers exit from their caring roles and their experiences of these exits. However, my use of theoretical sampling was constrained by the availability and cooperation of respondents in theoretically interesting categories.

All the interviews were carried out in the respondents' own homes, usually while their relatives were at a day centre. This arrangement proved to be the most suitable for both them and me. Carers were free to talk without interruption and some would have felt uncomfortable talking in front of the person being cared for. The interviews lasted for about two hours on average and were tape-recorded (see chapter 8). They were carried out with different interview schedules for carers and ex-carers. These schedules were designed after three months' observation of both support groups. Initially, the interviews had two objectives. First, I needed an objective indicator of the level of care provided by a carer. Second, I needed to observe very sensitive shifts in carers' orientations over time.

I was fortunate that my solution to the first objective provided a framework with which to tackle the second. I assembled a set of questions from a list and scale used by Gilleard (1984) in a study of the stresses and problems faced by people caring for dementia sufferers. The questions covered all aspects of care. An example is 'Does —— require any help washing themselves?' Each response is ranked on a scale from 0 to 4. The scores are then summed to produce a final score.

Within the interview these questions were used both to impose some order and to act as 'gateways' to a range of issues. The questions were used to encourage respondents to talk about what they do, how they learnt to do it and their past and present feelings about it. As is normal in intensive interviews, the ordering of the questions was flexible.

In addition to this section on specific caring activities, the schedule included a 'face sheet' section to collect basic details about the carers, and other sections listing topic headings to be discussed. These topics included: the effects of caring on carers' social and family lives, their experiences of welfare services and future plans for the care of their relatives. I also provided space on the schedule for jotted notes made either during the interview itself or on the bus ride home. Some of these notes turned into analytic memos, which will be discussed later.

Given the subject matter, it is understandable that at times some of the interviews proved quite stressful for both myself and the interviewee. It was not unusual for respondents to cry while discussing certain subjects, such as the hospitalisation of a relative. On such occasions I would try to reassure the interviewee that neither they nor I should be embarrassed, and that I understood their difficulty in discussing such experiences. This appeared to reassure respondents who, given time, were always willing to continue with the interviews.

In chapter 9, it was noted that ethnographers must guard against 'going native'. The phrase conjures up images of them becoming like the soldier in the film *Dances with Wolves* whose fascination with the Sioux Indians leads to his gradual incorporation into their culture. Although my study may appear too mundane to raise such concerns, the problem of 'getting close' without losing one's ability for detached analysis did prove to be a challenge. Given the nature of the setting and the illness, it was difficult to witness some events and listen to some accounts while maintaining an academic interest and outlook. There was also a temptation to take on the role of social worker, counsellor or activist. I volunteered to help in fund raising activities, but strictly avoided giving advice to carers. Some of the respondents initially equated sociologist with social worker. This led them to request clarification of the rules governing welfare benefits, a subject on which I was not qualified to comment. Similarly I avoided any involvement in disputes with medical professionals.

The collection and analysis of ethnographic data is extremely time-consuming. After four months in the field I had to stop seeking out new sources of data. If I was to complete my final research report in time for my deadline, it was time to focus on drawing together existing pieces of analysis and thinking about further analyses.

A.4   Developing a theory

This section is concerned with how I analysed my data and how I gradually developed a theoretical model which would help explain the differences between caring careers. It complements the sections concerning theory construction and data analysis in chapters 2 and 9 (sections 2.2 and 9.4 respectively).

First, however, it is worth reiterating two points concerning ethnographic research. Ethnographic data need not only refer to observational fieldnotes. In this study, data were collected from formal and informal interviews, fieldnotes and various documentary sources. These documentary sources included official 'handbooks' published by statutory and voluntary agencies such as the Alzheimer's Disease Society as well as self-penned accounts of carers' experiences (see chapter 10, section 10.2, on documentary sources in social research).

Data collection and data analysis do not fall neatly into two separate sections of the research timetable. Any researcher who intends to analyse his or her data only after it has all been collected is courting disaster. Ethnography is primarily a reflective occupation. Most sociological data are collected with the express purpose of answering a particular research question; the researcher who indulges in non-reflective note-taking for any length of time is more likely to experience confusion than enlightenment.

So, where, when and how did I begin? Of course I started with the raw data. By raw data I mean the fieldnotes of support group meetings, the transcripts of interviews with respondents and various documents. During the process of writing up fieldnotes or transcripts, or sometime soon afterwards, I would make a separate note of any points of interest or things which puzzled me. I stored these notes or 'analytic memos' (Strauss and Corbin, 1990) in one of the notebooks which I found useful to carry around with me. Many of these notes and comments remained just that. However, as the same comments or questions came up in successive meetings and interviews, some developed into new lines of inquiry or into important analytic themes.

Examples of such themes and issues include: the effect of a formal diagnosis of Alzheimer's disease, the importance and nature of caring routines, and attitudes regarding state welfare services such as day care or visits by medical or welfare professionals.

Many of these themes were later developed into more refined and abstract theoretical concepts. Careful reading of other research is a worthwhile means of sensitising oneself to concepts within the data. Inspiration often derives from the most unexpected sources. The concept of 'dirty work', for example, proved useful in my analysis of carers' management of those elements of their caring activities which they considered unpleasant or repugnant. It had earlier been adopted by Everett Hughes (1958) in his study of doctors' management of the more unpleasant aspects of medicine. The concept originated from Gold's (1952) analysis of how janitors coped with dealing with tenants' rubbish.

Two concepts which began to emerge midway through data collection were 'Initial Innocence' and 'The Carer's Perspective'. The idea of 'Initial Innocence' was borrowed from Fred Davis's (1972) study of student nurses. I used the concept to refer to informants' perceptions of the possible implications of their relatives' illness immediately following a formal diagnosis of Alzheimer's disease. They were ignorant concerning the likely extent and nature of future caring activities; negative, even hostile, in their assessment of residential care and entrenched in their pre-Alzheimer's family roles and relationships. An example of this last characteristic may be found in one woman's refusal to take over responsibility for managing the household finances from her husband, despite numerous problems, because throughout their marriage this activity had always been viewed as the 'man's job'. These carers also failed to draw a distinction between the Emotional (caring about) and Tending (physical work, such as bathing) elements of their caring roles. They either refused or felt very guilty about accepting help with tending tasks from outside the family, from the welfare services, such as daycare or visits from community nurses. It was believed that 'caring about' their relative meant that they should shoulder the responsibility for all tending tasks. To accept help was to neglect their caring obligations in some way. They were also concerned that the use of such services would be interpreted by neighbours or other family members as a negative indicator of their emotional feelings for their relative.

In contrast, the adoption of the Carer's Perspective is characterised by a change in attitude towards their caring activities and obligations, and their relationship with the individuals they care for. A distinction is made between the emotional and tending dimensions of their activities. Carers make a positive decision to avail themselves of the services provided by the National Health Service, Social Services and voluntary agencies. Tending activities become routinised and carried out with a degree of expertise that frequently surprises 'formal' carers, and caring 'timetables' are developed. These 'timetables' concern the timing of a possible exit from the caring role and the relative's entry into full-time residential and formal care.

Having identified a number of issues and concepts, the next step in the analytical process was to attempt to generate an explanation of the relationships between the concepts. The question I now faced, therefore, was the relationship between Initial Innocence and the Carer's Perspective. An early thought was that over a period of time all carers lost their 'Initial Innocence' and developed a 'Carer's Perspective'. The data from the 10 interviews carried out thus far supported such a hypothesis. However, my ideas concerning the possible relationship between these two concepts required further testing and exploration: would data from all my informants provide evidence of a conversion to a 'Carer's Perspective' and, if so, on what factors would this conversion be contingent?

With these questions in mind, I returned to the field and to further analysis of new and existing data. A case-by-case analysis of interviews with another 13 informants revealed an additional five cases of the pattern outlined above, which I was to call 'pattern A'. I had also discovered that these carers had adopted a 'Carer's Perspective' after experiencing some 'turning point'. As the illness progressed, and the nature and amount of help required by the sufferer altered, the dissonance between the realities

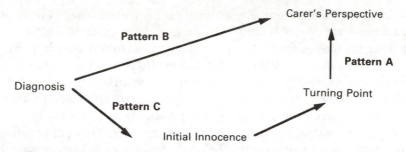

Figure A.1   *The three caring scenarios*

of dementia and a carer's 'innocent' conceptions of the caring role escalated until some 'turning point' was reached. The 'turning points' take a number of forms, but are generally characterised as events occurring at times of mental and physical strain. For example, one carer began to reassess her negative opinion of daycare for her husband after pushing him against a wall in frustration. The turning point marks the start of a carer's search for a more suitable approach to their activities, and their conversion to the 'Carer's Perspective'.

Data from the remaining eight interviews did not support this hypothesis, however. Six of the informants appeared to have by-passed the stage of 'Initial Innocence' following the onset of dementia in their relative and the formal diagnosis of Alzheimer's disease. Instead they immediately adopted a 'Carer's Perspective'. I called this 'pattern B'. The other two of my respondents at the time of the interview were still in the state of 'Initial Innocence' ('pattern C').

At this stage in the analysis I found it useful to record my discoveries, possible leads and unanswered questions in the form of diagrams and flowcharts. The flowchart in Figure A.1 represents the three caring scenarios.

Further analysis was now required to answer questions concerning the possible reasons for the differences between pattern A and pattern B carers. I was also interested in the yet to be converted carers in pattern C and the possible implications of failing to convert to the 'Carer's Perspective'. Once again, I returned to the existing data and continued to ask questions of day centre staff and other informants in the course of my fieldwork. Essentially, I was searching for clues, examining motives, searching for common characteristics and shared experiences.

The flowchart in Figure A.2 represents the final theoretical model which resulted from the particular section of the analysis discussed in this chapter. It is a theoretical model because it claims not only to describe, but also to explain the different career paths of carers. Three career paths were identified corresponding to the career patterns A, B and C mentioned earlier.

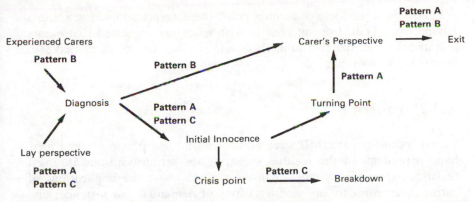

Figure A.2   *A flowchart suggesting a Model of Three Career Paths for Carers*

A.4.1   Pattern A

Prior to the receipt of a formal diagnosis, pattern A and C carers held 'lay' definitions and conceptions of informal care. Caring was perceived in terms of a loving, supportive and essentially reciprocal relationship.

A number of pattern A carers had made plans to care for their parents even before any signs of the illness had manifested itself. In retrospect, these respondents stated that these plans were grounded in naive and idealised images of informal care. They had little or no previous experience or knowledge of the possible implications of their decision. It was frequently said that, 'I never thought it would turn into a 24 hour a day commitment.' Carers had intended to fulfil their kinship obligations or marriage vows, but had also expected to maintain their existing relationships with the relatives for whom they cared. They were prepared to offer practical, financial and emotional support, but had not been prepared for the level of dependency that they were to encounter.

The receipt of a formal diagnosis, and the manner in which it was delivered, had a number of implications for carers' careers. Following a diagnosis, pattern A carers entered a period of initial innocence and what one informant described as either the 'carry-on-as-normal' or the 'I-must-do-it-all' phase. During this stage carers' attitudes regarding their moral obligations and orientations to their caring activities remained closely aligned to the 'lay' perspective.

A great deal of data were collected concerning the manner in which doctors informed the carers of the diagnosis and the sufferer's future needs. These data suggest that many of the carers in this category received very little detailed information about the implications of dementia for the carer. Many said that they were not fully briefed on the possible level of care that their relatives would require. As a result, carers were either unaware of the support services available, or felt that as close relatives they were not entitled to any outside support.

Following some form of turning point these carers adopted a 'Carer's Perspective'. Data from interviews with ex-carers suggested that carers maintain this perspective until their relative dies or the carer makes a planned exit from that role.

A.4.2   Pattern B

Carers following pattern B were all carers who had previously had first-hand experience of the realities of caring for seriously ill and disabled relatives. They held a more realistic attitude about the implications of caring, even prior to any manifestations of dementia. For instance, one carer who had watched her own mother care for her bed-ridden husband for almost 15 years had few 'romantic illusions'. Her domestic situation was such that, even before the onset of dementia, she felt that she would not be able to provide full-time care for her frail mother. As a result she had taken a number of steps to support her mother in her own home, taking advantage of statutory and voluntary support services. Early on in their caring careers, these carers had made a distinction between the emotional and tending aspects of their caring role, another characteristic of the 'Carer's Perspective'. As a result, these carers' reactions to the diagnosis of Alzheimer's disease were the most pragmatic. Daycare was seen as beneficial, providing the relative with added mental stimulation. Carers believed that even a break of a few hours from their responsibilities helped them to cope with their caring commitments and therefore benefited the cared-for.

A.4.3   Pattern C

Finally, the third career path, pattern C, was constructed from data derived from only two interviews, together with observation and second-hand accounts. Consequently it may have flaws and there is a need for further research into this element of the model.

This final pattern was characterised by a traumatic, essentially unplanned exit from the caring role, best described as a breakdown since it is distinct from the planned exits experienced by carers who have followed career paths A and B.

Carers who follow pattern C do not convert to the Carer's Perspective. Accounts of key informants suggest that these carers become increasingly unable to cope with their situation until some major crisis develops and the career then comes to an abrupt and traumatic end. For example, individuals care alone until they suffer an emotional or physical breakdown and are no longer able or willing to continue in their caring role. Given the caring experiences of such individuals, it is perhaps understandable that my attempts to sample further from this particular group came to nothing.

A.5   Applying the research findings

The identification of these three caring careers and their contingencies may have a number of possible applications. For instance, these findings are likely to be of interest to individuals and organisations involved in the provision of social welfare and medical services for carers and the cared-for. They may help professionals working with informal carers: doctors, community psychiatric nurses, social workers and others, to understand better carers' experiences over time. Information concerning the various career contingencies, their implications, and the roles played by different professionals at these junctures will also be of use. The most obvious example of this is the influence of a formal diagnosis as a career contingency. Doctors and other medical staff may not appreciate the extent to which the information they provide about the caring implications of dementia can influence the experiences of carers. Policy makers and managers of existing services may be concerned with how the needs of carers for daycare or support changes over time. Finally, one other group of individuals who may find this work of interest are other social researchers working in the field of informal care and carers.

A.6   Conclusion

The intention of this chapter has been to use the experiences and research findings from one small study to draw together many of the ideas and concerns of the previous chapters. My experiences of this project were responsible for teaching me a number of valuable lessons concerning ethnographic research. First, would-be researchers should think carefully about the data they wish to collect and the value of various methods. You need not confine yourself to any single method of data collection when designing a project. Similarly you should not underestimate the value of any particular method. My study benefited greatly from the use of a number of research methods. Second, my experiences highlighted the flexibility of the ethnographic method. It allows the researcher to redefine existing research questions and explore new lines of inquiry in the course of data collection. In my case, we have seen how it allowed me to study the experiences of ex-carers and observe support group meetings. A third lesson highlighted by this research concerns the degree to which the activities of data collection and data analysis merge in ethnography. The analytic process began with my first foray into the field and ended with the completion of the research report. Finally, my account has shown that while ethnographic research projects are particularly time-consuming, they frequently prove a fascinating and challenging experience for the researcher.

A.7 Further reading

Finch and Groves (1983) address the issues of why women provide informal care and the economic and social costs of doing so.

Parker (1990) provides a valuable review of much of the British research in the field of informal care.

10   Using documents

Keith Macdonald and Colin Tipton

Contents

The methods available to a social researcher are usually thought of as being of two main kinds: either the survey, using questionnaires, or field research in one form or another. But in fact there is a third type of method, whose history is longer and whose importance is scarcely less than the other two, namely documentary research. Documentary research was an important research tool of the founders of the discipline of sociology: Marx was a diligent user of Government statistics and the Civil Service reports known as 'Blue Books'; Durkheim's famous work *Suicide* (1951) was based on the study of official statistics and on the unpublished reports on suicides held by the Ministry of Justice; and Weber's career in sociology was really started by his studies of the Hamburg Stock Exchange and of the 'peasant problem' in eastern Germany: these were basically documentary studies and they led him to conclusions which he felt needed sociological explanations rather than economic ones (Bendix, 1960). The tradition of documentary studies in sociology started by these eminent scholars has not declined over the years; it is rather that sociological work has expanded because advances in technology have enabled researchers to handle large sets of survey material, and to record speech and interaction on audio and video tape. Documentary research remains an important research tool in its own right as well as being an invaluable part of most schemes of triangulation, that is, using an intersecting set of different research methods in a single project (Denzin, 1970).

10.1   What is a document?

Documents are things that we can read and which relate to some aspect of the social world. Clearly this includes those things which are intended to record the social world – official reports, for example – but also private and personal records such as letters, diaries and photographs, which may not have been meant for the public gaze at all. But in addition to the purposeful record, there are those things which may be overtly intended to provoke amusement or admiration or pride or aesthetic enjoyment – songs, buildings, statues, novels – but which none the less tell us something about the values, interests and purposes of those who commissioned or produced them. Such creations may be regarded as 'documents' of a society or group which may be 'read', albeit in a metaphorical sense.

It might appear that documents of this last kind require very different treatment from those in the more conventional form of purposeful written records, but the mere fact that a document has survived for the researcher to read means that in addition to the decision to produce the record in the first place, someone has decided to keep it, possibly deciding at the same time not to keep others, to store it in a particular archive, in a particular order – and so on. In other words, the exercise of interpretation which is so obviously part of reading off the 'meaning' of public statues or a genre of movies is not so very different from the assessment that must be undertaken of any archive or set of records.

The sociologist's emphasis on this point is that while public monuments and 'official' art can readily be seen as social products, documents which are intended to be read as objective statements of fact are also **socially produced**. This is not to imply that all official documents are like the statistics that were published in Stalin's Russia, or the war reports issued in Nazi Germany; they are not propaganda. But they are produced on the basis of certain ideas, theories or commonly accepted, taken-for-granted principles, which means that while they are perfectly correct – given certain socially accepted norms – they do not have the objectivity of, say, a measure of atmospheric pressure recorded on a barometer. This view of official records has been shown most clearly in the case of suicide verdicts (Atkinson, 1978), which cannot tell us exactly how many people killed themselves, but only how many were socially defined as having done so in accordance with the array of social rules and practices used by coroners and police to arrive at a socially acceptable judgement. In a very different context, Hindess (1973) has shown how official census statistics are compiled on the basis of certain categories which are derived from a particular theoretical viewpoint. Attempts to reanalyse the data along other theoretical lines are quite misguided. So, a set of minutes, the accounts of a public company, or official statistics are produced in a socially acceptable form that seems to those involved to give a 'reasonable' account of their actions. When one reads that between 1979 and 1991 the basis for collecting British unemployment statistics has been changed 30 times (*Independent on Sunday*, 11 August 1991), it becomes clear just how unstable this 'reasonableness' can be. To this social production of the documents, must then be added the social production of the archive in which they are stored: what is to be kept, how, where and how long they are to be kept, and what is to be thrown away.

10.2   Types of documents

The term 'documents' includes a vast range of materials to be found in all sorts of places and all that can be done here is to give a review of three broad categories, which though necessarily brief, will exemplify the nature of the materials and the problems encountered by the documentary researcher.

10.2.1   Public records

The oldest writings in existence are public records. Writing was devised by officials in the ancient civilisations to record the taxation and tribute that the state received and the rations it issued to its servants. It is ironic that these early bureaucratic records have only survived by accident, for they were intended as temporary records and were made on soft clay tablets. They exist today because the buildings in which they were stored were burnt down. The tablets were baked in the process, buried under rubble and then built over – thus preserving them for posterity.

The modern state has an enormous apparatus for generating fiscal and economic records. These are usually the province of economists rather than social researchers, but those concerned with matters of social policy and welfare are interested in these materials as well. Because these records deal with financial and other quantifiable matters it tends to be assumed that they have an objectivity that other kinds of documents may lack, whereas in fact a financial or statistical record is a social product just as much as any other. The civil servants who produce these statistics undoubtedly make every effort to follow the scientific canons to ensure the reliability and validity of their work, but that does not alter the underlying fact that any indicator of economic performance or incidence of crime or any of the hundreds of matters that the state sees fit to measure and publish is based on working assumptions, some of which, at least, could have been decided otherwise.

In addition to the need to understand the conventions which surround the compilation of official reports and statistics, one must be aware of the distortions that can arise as a result of the actions of the people to whom the statistics refer. A notable example of this is the under-recording of certain groups in the Census. Recent immigrants, for instance, may not understand the purpose of the Census and evade being recorded because they assume it to be connected with taxation or with legislation regarding overcrowding or some other reason. Similarly, the introduction of the Community Charge in Britain in 1989 and 1990, whereby a 'poll tax' was levied on every individual, led to a significant reduction in the number of registered voters because omission from the Electoral Roll meant that a person would not be taxed (*Guardian*, 19 June 1991).

So what sort of public documents are available to the social researcher? Some have already been mentioned, such as the Census and the UK Electoral Register, while the Registrar General produces annual reports on the vital statistics of the nation. In addition to these, every government department produces national statistics which cover its area of activity, industry, education, crime, housing and so on, summaries of which are published for the United Kingdom in the *Annual Abstract of Statistics* or the *Monthly Digest of Statistics*. Statistics and documents of this kind are published as a matter of course by the government as well as a steady flow of reports from individual departments, from government inquiries and so on. Similar material is published by local authorities, health authorities, nationalised industries and many other bodies which are wholly or partly in the public sector. There are, in addition, many collections of statistics published by international organisations such as the United Nations, the International Labour Organization, the European Commission and numerous others.

Another important kind of official record is the verbatim account of British Parliamentary debates to be found in *Hansard* together with the reports of Parliamentary Committees. Verbatim reports of judicial proceeding are also kept, but these are not so readily available to the public, except that important cases from the point of view of case law are published in the *All England Law Reports* and the *Times Law Reports*.

In addition to these, there are the unpublished papers of government departments, which are deposited in the London Public Record Office and only become available after a period of 30 years. At this point the question of the construction of the archive becomes very significant for the researcher. Even if there is no attempt to hide things from public gaze for ever, the idiosyncrasies of departmental officials can prove extremely frustrating. Many a social or historical researcher has found that the civil servants of yesteryear were interested in preserving the record of their salary negotiations to the exclusion of almost everything else. There are some records which are subject to the Official Secrets Act and these see the light of day even longer after the event than 30 years, and in some cases never.

10.2.2 The media

The *Times Law Reports* are, of course, published by the newspaper of that name, and the selectivity that they display follows well-understood principles. The selectivity displayed by the paper itself is a matter of editorial policy and may be much less readily comprehended. Nevertheless editorial policy is usually fairly clear to a regular reader of *The Times* or of any other paper, at least in regard to what they print. What they leave out is another matter altogether and requires much closer study of the media and current events generally. It is fairly easy to discern that the more serious papers print more foreign news than the popular tabloids, but unless one consults newspapers published in other countries, one can have little idea of the selectivity imposed by a particular editor. The bias and selectivity imposed by editorial policy is only one of a number of areas in which the researcher must be on guard: newspapers are subject to:

- Errors, which may be technical – such as spelling, typing, or printing, when lines or longer sections of print get transposed; or matters of fact – such as people's ages which newspapers are very fond of including in their reports but about the accuracy of which they are often careless.
- Distortion, which may stem from the preferences of the proprietor or editor, or from the journalist producing the copy; on the other hand the distortion may have been in the source – as when a politician is giving his or her account of events or when the journalist relies on the press release of some public body or organisation; yet again distortion can arise quite inadvertently from the actions of a sub-editor who changes the meaning of an item in the process of compressing it into the space available, or who conveys an erroneous impression in the search for a punchy headline. The most fundamental form of distortion is, of course, that of propaganda, where the source of the news is engaged in wholesale creation of a particular view of events, which in the case of war, for example, is undertaken in what is perceived to be the national interest or with the object of systematically deceiving an enemy
- Audience context; this is an aspect that may be easily overlooked, and refers to the fact that the production of any medium of communication is undertaken with an audience in mind, and unless one knows how that audience 'reads' the content, it may be possible that the researcher will fail to grasp the message. Not only cultural norms, but jokes, deliberate mistakes, irony and so on depend on the existence of a common frame of reference between writer and reader, and unless the researcher is

privy to their common understandings, serious misapprehension may result. The claim by a German newspaper to have established that the bagpipes were a German invention aroused fury in Scotland, but merely raised a smile in Germany, where it was regarded as either untrue or unimportant.

Finally, the researcher must remember that in many cases it is not the original document that is under scrutiny, but some form of copy, such as a microfilm or microfiche and that its reliability depends on the work of a copyist. Omissions and transpositions are not unknown.

10.2.3 Private papers

It is not only in the media, operating in the public domain, that the researcher must be cautious, for the documents of a private individual are also open to distortion and manipulation, especially if the person concerned is a public figure or an author whose work is so widely read and discussed as to put them in the public sphere.

For example, the author of a biography of the writer, Rudyard Kipling, examines several earlier biographies and shows that they contain serious distortions and omissions that resulted from the pressures and deceptions emanating from Kipling's widow and family (Seymour-Smith, 1989). Their desire to control the account of his life that reached the public was such that they eventually destroyed a sizeable part of the archive of material on which a biographer might wish to work.

Such attitudes are even more likely to be present in the case of a politician, whose private papers refer not only to matters of interest to critics and academics, but to events that were of consequence to the nation or even to the world. So, some private papers deal with public matters.

There are also, of course, large numbers of private papers that refer to private lives and personal careers. A single individual or family can sometimes throw considerable light on the times in which they live, as in the case of the Paston Letters (Bennett, 1922), which come from a fairly well-off family in the fifteenth century, but are sufficiently voluminous to provide social historians with one of the best sources of material on the late Middle Ages. In a case like this, the researcher is the beneficiary of a careful family who treasured their papers, but is essentially at the mercy of those by whom the archive is created and to whom it is entrusted; it is entirely at their whim what is collected and preserved. It is possible to improve on this state of affairs if one is dealing with the recent past, because then one can purposefully collect the diaries and letters of people in a certain category as in the case of *The Polish Peasant in Europe and America* (Thomas and Znaniecki, 1958). One can take this a step further by actually soliciting the material from informants and asking them to search their memories and give accounts of past events. An outstanding example of this method is the work of Middlebrook (1978, 1983), who selects one day, like the first day of the German Spring Offensive in 1918, or the day of the USAF bombing mission to Schweinfurt and Regensberg in 1943. Starting from the official records and histories, he then seeks out the actual participants still surviving by, for example, advertising in the local papers of the regions from which the regiments involved were drawn and obtains first hand accounts. So *The Kaiser's Battle* (Middlebrook, 1978) draws inter alia on the testimony of over a hundred German participants and several hundred British.

10.2.4 Visual documents

Reference was made above to Seymour-Smith (1989) and his work on Kipling. While this is primarily a study in which the insights of psychology are brought to bear on biography and literary analysis, it also has a sociological angle because it is concerned with the question of whether Kipling deserves his reputation as an ideologue of Empire. In these circumstances the analysis of literary work takes on a sociological role. Other examples can be found in the writings of Quigly (1984) and Fussell (1975, 1989). In these cases literary work is being treated as a 'document' and its analysis needs skills that are more often found in a sociologically-minded critic than in a sociologist. But in *Wartime: Understanding and Behavior in the Second World War*, Fussell (1989) quotes from a comparative analysis of posters in the two World Wars, and thus moves into a field in which some sociologists do feel able to contribute, that is in the study of visual 'documents'.

It was noted at the beginning of this chapter that interpretation seems to be a more obvious requirement when dealing with visual materials, such as photos, advertisements, record sleeves, paintings, posters, statues, buildings, films and so on. Although many of the same problems occur in the use of written documents, with visual materials they appear in a somewhat different form. Photographs present a particular problem, because although they make an automatic claim to authenticity ('the camera cannot lie'), the photographer can leave things out of shot, and negatives and prints can be doctored in various ways (Becker, 1979). There is a celebrated example of a photograph of Lenin addressing a crowd from a platform, at the foot of which could be seen, in the original version, the unmistakable figure of Trotsky. In later versions, when Trotsky had fallen out with Lenin's successor, Stalin, and fled to Mexico, he has been blotted out.

With paintings, sculpture and architecture, however, it is unlikely that the artist is trying to deceive the beholder, but it is often necessary to have some knowledge of the circumstances in which an object was produced before it can be interpreted as a social 'document'. This need is nicely exemplified by Berger (1972: 82–112), who examines a number of seventeenth and eighteenth century paintings to show the way in which patrons of painting of that period were concerned with their possessions, and how this trend can be associated with the emerging power of capital (1972: 86). He even reports a dispute between himself and an art critic about this interpretation. But the point for the present discussion is that Berger and the other authorities that he quotes rely extensively on a wide range of social historical data, and indeed on the comments of the painters themselves. Most sociologists would probably agree that Berger had made his point, but he has not done it on the basis of the paintings alone. That raises the problem of what tests of reliability and authenticity must be applied to the supporting data, a matter that will be considered below. Before leaving this topic mention must be made of the work of Fredrick Antal (1962, 1987). His studies of Hogarth and more especially his *Florentine Painting* (Antal, 1987) are outstanding examples of the bringing together of artistic and sociological analysis.

Another example is provided by Cohen (1989), who studied the political implications of public statues erected in provincial France during the nineteenth century. Once again it is apparent that any 'reading' of the objects themselves would be a risky undertaking, because of the difficulty of being sure of the motives lying behind their erection. However, when combined with analysis of local government records and newspaper reports, the part that statues played in the political conflicts of the period becomes clear and their subject matter, their timing and their location intelligible.

It will be apparent from the examples quoted here that the sociologist conducting this kind of research has to be an expert or at least have a strong enthusiasm for the subject matter of the documents or visual materials under investigation. But the novice researcher should not react by saying 'I don't know anything about sculpture or French nineteenth century politics – I can't do this kind of work!'; any more than one should think 'I can't do field work because I can't play jazz like Howard Becker, or I can't shoot pool like Ned Polsky'. Documentary research, like any sociological endeavour, requires an interest in *some* aspect of social existence; with an interest and a little systematic work, one can usually acquire the grounding needed to make a start on research.

10.2.5 Visual presentation of data

In addition to the use of visual materials as documentary sources, one must note the use of pictorial methods of presenting social data. Until the 1930s it was quite usual for articles in American sociological journals to be accompanied by photographs, but this went out of fashion. There now seems to be some slight signs of a revival of this means of communicating qualitative data, and it is advocated with particular cogency by Harper (1979). Harper carried out research in America on 'Skid Row', which combined photography, interviewing and participant observation. Becker commenting on Harper's work, writes: 'He believes strongly that the basic working unit of sociology is text and image as an indivisible whole: that the long narrative accompanying these photographs informs them, just as it is illuminated by them' (1981: 86).

The research that is described in the next chapter (Exemplar B) made use of photographs when it appeared in *Sociology*, and they were in fact the first to be published in that journal in its 20 years of existence. With research of this kind it is scarcely possible to make a convincing case without the use of visual material, because there is no other guarantee that the text accurately describes the objects in question.

10.3   Evaluation and interpretation

In the above review of the kinds of documents that may be used in research, a number of problems were noted that the researcher may encounter. Many of these questions are about how to evaluate material and these can be grouped under four headings: authenticity, credibility, representativeness and meaning. Scott (1990) gives a valuable treatment of these issues and what follows draws on his ideas.

10.3.1   Authenticity

'A CHECK MAY BE WRITTEN ON A COW' ran a headline in the *Memphis Press-Scimitar* in 1967. It is well known that you cannot believe everything that you read in the newspapers, but this particular article referred to a nineteenth century case in England which allowed this practice and quoted as authority the Chase Manhattan Bank. One cannot tell by what route this supposed legal principle reached the *Memphis Press*, but the original source was the dramatisation on BBC Television of one of A.P. Herbert's (fictional) *Misleading Cases in the Common Law*, originally published in the 1930s (and set in that period, not the nineteenth century). Herbert (1977) recounts a number of other occasions in which his litigious character, Mr Haddock, has escaped into real life, thus illustrating one of the problems of authenticity in documentary research, namely that writers (or copyists) may well quite innocently, or perhaps carelessly, convert fiction into fact or perpetuate the errors or deceptions of others.

The occasions on which the researcher encounters deliberate falsehoods are rare. Cases like the Zinoviev Letter or the Hitler diaries do not come our way very often (Scott, 1990: 43,175). But it is always possible that records or factual accounts may have been falsified for the author's own purposes at the time, and the researcher has always to be suspicious of unexpected changes of paper, ink, typeface, handwriting, and so on, as well as checking consistency and plausibility, internally and externally.

In order to test whether a document is genuine, complete, reliable and of unquestioned authorship, Platt (1981), who has encountered the problem of deliberate deception in documentary research, proposes a set of questions for deciding on the authenticity of a document. These include:

- Does the document make sense or does it contain glaring errors?
- Are there different versions of the original document available?
- Is there consistency of literary style, handwriting or typeface?
- Has the document been transcribed by many copyists?
- Has the document been circulated via someone with a material or intellectual interest in passing off the version given as the correct one?
- Does the version available derive from a reliable source?

10.3.2   Credibility

Credibility refers to the question of whether the document is free from error or distortion. The latter may occur when there is a long time between the event and the account of it being written down, or when the account has been through several hands and the author of the document was not present at the event. Credibility can be affected by the interest of the author, which might, for example, be financial, to enhance a reputation, or to please the readers. Such possibilities should always lead the social researcher to ask who produced the document, why, when, for whom and in what context so as to be assured of the quality of the document.

10.3.3   Representativeness

The next problem is whether the documents available can be said to constitute a representative sample of the universe of documents as they originally existed. If the archive appears to contain all the material produced in that category then the problem does not exist. But once it is established that there is something missing the questions of what is missing, how much, and why it is missing become important. When the survival of documents is quite haphazard as it is with the material from ancient civilisations, then conclusions drawn must always be tentative or at least historians must be prepared to revise their accounts if fresh evidence is unearthed. With more recent archives it must always be a matter of judgement, based on the amount of missing material, whether the blanks have any pattern to them and whether anyone could have had an interest in destroying certain documents. In this, as in the questions of authenticity and credibility, the researcher's approach must be essentially that of the detective, in the sense that everything is potentially suspect and anything may turn out to be the key piece of data, including, as for Sherlock Holmes, the dog that did not bark.

10.3.4 Meaning

Establishing the meaning of a document is usually seen as working at two levels: the surface or literal meaning, and the deeper meaning, arrived at by some form of interpretative understanding or structural analysis. Although there is a clear difference between the extreme forms of these two modes, it is possible to see the two as merging in some instances; for form is only conceptually distinct from content, or the message from grammar, and human beings habitually handle both without any trouble.

Understanding the surface message may be troublesome, although this is more often a problem for historians than for sociologists, who do not in the ordinary way have to decipher hieroglyphics or cuneiform writing. But the social researcher will find that language use varies between different groups, cultures and periods.

The deeper meaning of a document or a text may well prove more troublesome. The simpler kind of question about meaning is exemplified by the problem of how important particular themes are to the author (or the newspaper, or whatever is the unit of investigation) and the answer to this question is usually sought through quantification, by means of content analysis (Weber, 1990). The importance of a topic is measured by the number of times it is mentioned, the number of column inches devoted to it, the square inches of the photographs displayed, the number of times it appears in the index, the number of readers' letters that the editor decides to publish, and so on. This method, being a quantitative one, carries with it a number of technical issues to do with sampling, representativeness, coding, and statistical reliability, which for reasons of space, we must leave to one side.

The measurement of the relative salience of a theme by the frequency of its occurrence is a fairly simple notion or even simplistic, for it would be argued by practitioners of literary and other criticism that a quantitative approach of this kind may do no kind of justice to an author's intentions. It is, of course, the case that most of what social researchers study is not produced by artists, so this criticism of quantitative method loses some of its point. None the less, in dealing with anything more complex than newspapers, content analysis on its own does appear rather unsubtle, and so sociologists for many years have searched for something more sophisticated that would do justice to the more complex kind of document. In the earlier part of the century, the notion of 'interpretative understanding', following the ideas of Dilthey (see Rickman, 1961), achieved some importance, especially among German historians. This emphasised the need to understand the particular techniques and definitions that lay behind the production of the text in order to grasp the author's meaning and intentions. More recently the task of textual analysis has drawn much more on the semiotic approach to be found in the structural linguistics of

Saussure, especially as developed by Barthes (1967). The former defined **semiotics** as 'a science that studies the life of signs within society', the object of which is to get to the underlying message of the text. This is to be found, not only in the words and phrases, but in the system of rules that structures the text as a whole. It is therefore this underlying structure and the rules it embodies that can tell the researcher what its cultural and social message is.

An example of a piece of research which explicitly rejects content analysis in favour of semiotics is to be found in McRobbie (1978, 1991), a study of *Jackie*, a weekly magazine aimed at teenage girls. The author describes magazines as 'specific signifying systems where particular messages are produced and articulated'. Quantification is rejected in favour of the understanding of media messages as structured wholes.

> Sociological analysis proceeds by isolating sets of codes around which the message is constructed. These conventions operate at several levels, visual and narrative, and also include sets of subcodes [in *Jackie*] such as those of fashion, beauty, romance, personal/domestic life and pop music. These codes constitute the 'rules' by which different meanings are produced and it is the identification and consideration of these in detail that provides the basis to the analysis. In short, semiology is concerned with the internal structuring of a text or signifying system, with what Barthes calls 'immanent analysis'. (McRobbie, 1991: 91–2)

From the large range of codes operating in *Jackie*, McRobbie identifies four around which to organise her study, and from this analysis delineates 'the central feature of *Jackie* insofar as it presents its readers with an ideology of adolescent femininity'.

While this method undoubtedly provides a more coherent set of guidelines for the analysis of text than its predecessors, Scott (1990) argues cogently that semiotics still does not give us a means of judging between rival interpretations of a text, and draws on the work of Giddens (1976) and the notion that the study of text, taken in isolation from its social context, is deprived of its real meaning. This is provided by a socially situated author and audience who are necessary for the text to have any meaning at all. 'Texts must be studied as socially situated products' (Scott, 1990: 34). An illustration of this point can be found in the novel *Foucault's Pendulum* (Eco, 1988: 134, 534) where a document is found in circumstances that suggest that it could be a plan, devised in the fourteenth century, to perpetuate a secret society for the next 600 years. To achieve this interpretation a system of rules is worked out to explain the text, just as semiotics proposes. The characters in the book proceed to work on this reading of the text for a sizeable part of the novel, until someone proposes a different, and rather more plausible context for the document, and suggests a new system of rules – whereby the text is read as a laundry list! As the author is a Professor of Semiotica at the University of Bologna, one may judge that Eco is indeed having a joke at the expense of his fellow semioticians.

10.4   The need for triangulation

Throughout this chapter a leitmotiv has recurred: the notion that in documentary research everything must be checked from more than one angle. Nothing can be taken for granted. A document may not be what it appears to be, the archive may have been collected for motives we do not understand, the context may be crucial in determining the nature of the object before us. This makes documentary work very different from, say, survey research, where validity and reliability are secured within the method itself. The layout of the questionnaire, the meaning of the items, the reproducibility of scales, the representativeness of the sample, are all concerned with a particular predefined topic, method and data source. But in other modes of research, the notion of **triangulation** has become a salient feature of research methodology (Denzin, 1970, 1978). In this framework, validity is seen as having both external and internal aspects and the achievement of validity, and indeed of the research task as a whole, requires a triangulation of research strategies.

Denzin (1970) proposes four kinds of triangulation. The first is **data triangulation**, which has three subtypes: time, space and person; that is, data should be collected at a variety of times, in different locations and from a range of persons and collectivities. The second is **investigator triangulation**, that is, using multiple rather than single observers of the same object. The third, **theory triangulation**, consists of using more than one kind of approach to generate the categories of analysis. This is the most difficult kind of triangulation to achieve and it is noteworthy that Denzin (1970: 297–301) can only adduce a hypothetical example, and the three theoretical approaches he draws on are in fact quite closely allied. Finally, the fourth, **methodological triangulation** has two subtypes: within-method, for example using, in a questionnaire, a combination of attitude scales, forced choice items and open-ended questions, and between-method triangulation, which is self-explanatory, and which is probably the more important.

The general approach that he advocates, and to some extent the actual methods he suggests, provide sound guidance for the documentary researcher. It is however, rather more difficult to give a toolkit for this kind of work, because the data materials are so various. But hopefully the principle is clear and its practice can be appreciated from the following quotation from *Belfast in the '30s: an Oral History*

> In the first place we carried out . . . 'investigator triangulation'. That is, each transcript was checked by two or three researchers to ensure that it said what people had meant to say. In the second place, we systematically did a cross-method triangulation, in that every piece of oral evidence that could be, was checked against a range of written sources: newspapers, parliamentary reports, documents etc. Finally, there was a considerable amount of data triangulation possible within the oral sources themselves. (Munck and Rolston, 1987: 12)

10.5   Project

You have been recruited as a Research Officer on a project set up to study financial scandals in the twentieth century.

Outline some ways of tackling this using documentary sources, indicating how you would achieve triangulation.

What sorts of documents do you think could be used in this project?

What sorts of problems would you expect to encounter in getting access to and working with these documents?

10.6   Further reading

Platt (1981) is a pioneering article that highlights the problems of handling documentary evidence.

Plummer (1983) is a readable introduction to the importance of personal documents such as letters, diaries and life histories in social research.

Scott (1990) is an essential book for anyone interested in doing documentary research. It provides a particularly valuable introduction to the problems of evaluating and interpreting documentary materials.

Weber (1990) is a short but clear introduction to the technique of content analysis, with an appendix that deals with the use of computers in text analysis.

Becker (1974) is a very stimulating article, which examines the relationship between sociology and social documentary photography.

Exemplar B   Building respectability

Keith Macdonald

Contents

This chapter describes the research on which the article, 'Building Respectability', published in the journal, *Sociology*, (Macdonald, 1989) was based.

The most exciting problems for a social researcher, as perhaps for any kind of scientist, are those which one comes across in the course of research, but which are not actually what one was investigating at the time. This kind of happy accident is probably more likely to occur when doing documentary research, because in the nature of things one is reviewing a large array of material, only part of which is relevant to the research topic. Now although this kind of thing can be productive, the diversity of data that documentary researchers survey in the course of their work in fact presents a considerable problem; one which requires a highly disciplined approach if things are not going to get out of hand and time is not to be wasted. On the one hand you need to be aware of all the angles to the problem under investigation; so if you are trying to establish the extent to which nineteenth century accountants' practice was concerned with bank-ruptcy, it is important to include the other headings in the index of an accountancy journal which would be relevant besides 'bankruptcy'. If 'liquidations' and 'receivership' and 'insolvency' are not included at the outset, a lot of research time will be wasted and effort will be duplicated. On the other hand the interesting points which flash into one's peripheral vision as one focuses on the research topic must not be ignored: *anything* which seems interesting should be noted down at once. Nothing is more frustrating than hunting through documents or archives for items which at the time of the original scan seemed uninteresting but which later turn out to be important. One such interesting question was . . .

B.1   The question

. . . 'Why are Chartered Accountants so interested in their headquarters building, the Chartered Accountants' Hall?' This was the question that occurred to me as I worked through the List of Members of the Institute of Chartered Accountants in England and Wales (hereafter ICAEW) in the course of researching the structure of the accountancy profession and the distribution of power within it. Power could be said to be associated with membership of the Council of the Institute and from the information published in the List of Members I could discover that the large account-ancy firms had an influence out of all proportion to the actual number of practising members that they contained.

But why, in the pages of information the ICAEW gave about itself – officers, past Presidents, Council and committee members and so on – was about a quarter of the space devoted to the *building* that it occupied? It seemed to me to be out of all proportion, so when the project on the structure of the ICAEW and changes in the profession was complete, I started to investigate this curious enthusiasm of accountants for the building they occupied.

B.1.1   Another angle

My first approach was to find out if the accountants' interest in their building was shared by other people, and so I turned to the great expert on English architecture, Nicholas Pevsner, author of *The Buildings of England*, which runs to about two dozen volumes. On the front cover of *London, Vol.1* (Pevsner, 1973) was the dome of St. Paul's Cathedral; on the back was . . . the Institute of Chartered Accountants. Inside the covers, I found that only three buildings were accorded more than one illustration; St Paul's, Westminster Abbey, and . . . the Institute of Chartered Accountants. Later in my research I had to put in quite a lot of work to ensure the validity of judgements based on reference books of this sort, but for the time being the opinion of Pevsner, revealed in the illustrations and backed up by the text, was a good enough reason to find out more about this well-thought-of building.

B.1.2 'There's nothing ill can dwell in such a temple'

Two documentary sources had already been drawn on and the next step was to try to discover what motives lay behind the ICAEW's actions in putting up a building that so impressed the pundits a century later and that seemed to have considerable significance for the Institute itself. From Pevsner's description it appeared that the architect, John Belcher, was a person with a high reputation in his profession who had been awarded the Gold Medal of the Royal Institute of British Architects and had become their President. However, in 1888, when he designed the ICAEW Hall, he was only starting out on his career and this building, says Pevsner, made his reputation. So how did the Chartered Accountants come to pick on this bright young architect who did so well for them?

The best place to look for an account of the motives of a collectivity, such as a professional body, should be its archives where one would hope to find an account of its deliberations and the reasons for making its decisions. Some researchers are lucky enough to find records of this sort. Halliday (1987), for example, as a researcher attached to the Chicago Bar Association was given access to all their archives and was therefore able to obtain information about the decision-making of that organisation. But these circumstances are relatively rare, because the details of debate are not normally recorded in official minutes of meetings, but only the broadest outlines and sometimes only the decision itself. Any notes taken by participants and even the documents tabled, on the basis of which the decision was made, are unlikely to have survived. This is particularly so in the case of documents prior to 1939 relating to organisations based in cities in Britain, because archives were often drastically pruned before being moved to a safer location, or were actually destroyed in air-raids; such problems would be even more acute in Germany. But even without these hazards the data may be thin; for example, for the first 20 years of its existence, the accounts of the Law Society do not form part of its record, even though they were tabled at its annual general meeting.

In the present case, the Minutes of the Council of the Institute give the researcher the bare minimum, at best, while the absence of documents that were tabled, but not preserved, deprived decisions of much of their meaning. In these circumstances one has to be grateful for the existence of the professional journals, which in those days seemed to take a livelier and more detached interest in the doings of their professional bodies. The ICAEW had only been granted a Royal Charter in 1880, while the journals had been in existence rather longer and therefore perhaps felt it appropriate to keep a paternal eye on the youthful professional body. Be that as it may, the pages of *The Accountant* are a fruitful source of information and opinion about the Institute and its activities. From these it became clear that from the date of its foundation the ICAEW had been searching diligently for an appropriate site for its headquarters; not just any old location, but one which would fit what the Council felt would reflect the standing and the nature of their profession. After several years they took the opportunity to purchase a site in a relatively tranquil spot for the City of London (Great Swan Alley), but just off a newly constructed thorough-fare (Moorgate) and only 200 yards from the hub of the City, containing the Bank of England, the Stock Exchange and those places for the display of City pride, Mansion House and Guildhall. The Institute's Building Committee organised a competition supervised by the president of the Royal Institute of British Architects. When Belcher's design was pro-nounced the winner in December 1888 it was greeted with praise in the architectural journals – 'more than ordinary excellence' said the *British Architect*, for example. The completed building cost £32,000, but nearly 10 per cent of that figure – £3,000 – was for the sculptured frieze around the exterior at second floor level. There seems to be little doubt about the kind of building the Institute wanted: one that displayed the conspicuous consumption characteristic of late nineteenth century architecture. Nor is there any doubt about why they were spending their money in this fashion.

> It is our pious hope [wrote the Editor of *The Accountant*] that as the new building rises, so will the reputation of the profession gradually ascend in public estimation, and that both may be established on equally solid foundations. . . . It is the actual and visible embodiment of the astonishing growth of a profession, young but already of commanding power, and capable of almost unlimited extension. May men say with Shakespeare 'There is nothing ill can dwell in such a temple'. (*The Accountant*, 12 July 1890, p. 365)

> Before long the Institute will be lodged in quarters worthy the importance of so necessary profession. (*The Accountant*, 5 July 1890, p. 353)

The President, in laying the foundation stone, spoke in less florid terms but to much the same effect. He referred to its 'central and eligible position' and to how the hall 'will be eminently substantial, convenient, useful and ornamental and will form a not unimportant addition to the many noble edifices that adorn this great city'. (*The Accountant*, 12 July 1890, p. 37)

When the building was completed some three years later *The Accountant* repeated the message, expressing its pleasure that 'the completion of the new building should afford so favourable an opportunity of publicly demonstrating the power and solidarity of the profession.' Others were of the same opinion:

> The Institute has obtained those outward and visible signs of respectability which are of so much importance in England, although they are too often neglected. . . . They have gained the means to impress everybody who gazes on the building that the business of Chartered Accountants has been underrated. Instead of the

commonplace affair . . . [that] might be supposed from its practitioners, it is now shown to be a great power of which the relations are worldwide. (*The Architect and Contract Reporter*, quoted in *The Accountant*, 2 September 1893, p. 753)

The hall also received favourable comment from *The St James Budget*, *The Strand Magazine* and *The Architect*. The building made Belcher famous and Pevsner (1973: 246) describes it as 'eminently original and delightfully picturesque' (see Figures B.1 and B.2). Its elaborate neo-Baroque design includes a frieze of statues over the first floor windows, representing such themes as Crafts (Figure B.2), Education, Commerce and Mining (John Belcher himself is actually represented in the section devoted to Architecture). The statuary accounted for 10 per cent of the cost of the building.

The building was considerably extended in 1930 by Joass, the partner of Belcher (who died in 1913), in the same style, and between 1964 and 1970 it was enlarged still further to the design of William Whitfield. This time the style was mid-twentieth century concrete and glass, and this audacious grafting of new on to old was strikingly successful. 'Here is proof', writes Pevsner (1973: 247) 'that the uncompromisingly old can go with the new, if handled by an appreciative and imaginative architect.' In the past decade even this large increase in floor space has proved insufficient and the Institute has had to expand again – this time in Milton Keynes, 40 miles away.

B.1.3   'Sentence first – verdict afterwards'

It may seem that, like the Queen of Hearts at the trial in *Alice in Wonderland*, I am getting things in the wrong order, in that I am describing how I collected my data before setting out any theoretical position that would have guided my research. But I am not a mindless empiricist nor was I a novice in research on professional organisations. I had been drafting an outline of my findings and I had been working along certain theoretical lines, some of which were continuities of those in my previous work, while others derived from distinct, but not altogether unrelated themes. The published form of this research follows the accepted academic format and sets out a theoretical framework in which the linchpin is Larson's (1977) concept of 'the professional project'. As an epigraph at the head of the article there is a quotation from Veblen (1970) which reads 'To be respectable it must be wasteful', and this was a line of thought that I used to elaborate part of Larson's scheme which referred to 'traditional' sources of professional prestige. It also tied in with my own earlier work on Scottish accountants (Macdonald, 1984) which showed the emphasis that they placed on 'respectability'.

In brief, my theoretical framework is based on the concept of conspi-

Figure B.1   *The exterior of the Institute of Chartered Accountants*

Figure B.2   *The exterior of the Institute of Chartered Accountants –
detail of frieze*

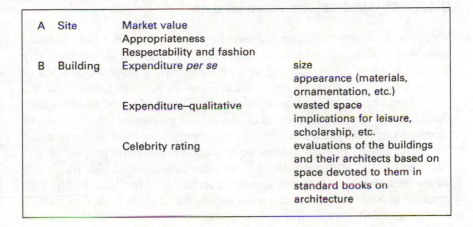

A   Site   Market value
              Appropriateness
              Respectability and fashion
B   Building   Expenditure *per se*   size
                                              appearance (materials,
                                              ornamentation, etc.)
              Expenditure–qualitative   wasted space
                                              implications for leisure,
                                              scholarship, etc.
              Celebrity rating   evaluations of the buildings
                                              and their architects based on
                                              space devoted to them in
                                              standard books on
                                              architecture

Figure B.3

cuous consumption seen as part of the 'professional project' and applied in particular to the contribution to professional prestige made by head-quarters buildings of professional bodies in London. That is, accountants and other bodies of professionals need to work at the difficult task of convincing the public, both that they have the knowledge that they claim to have, and that they can be trusted to use that knowledge for the benefit of their clients or patients. Assurance that they in fact possess the knowledge and skills they lay claim to is achieved by such means as certification (degrees, diplomas, and other examinations), but trust, in the British context at least, is often sought by an emphasis on respectability and the display of those things associated with respectable people. So my thesis is that English professional bodies drew on the 'traditional' and 'gentlemanly' characteristics of the patronage of architecture and art, and that the 'gentlemanly' pursuits of learning and leisure are embodied in the buildings they commisioned or bought.

The theoretical framework required to examine this thesis draws on Larson (1977), Veblen (1970) and Baltzell (1962) and may be summarized as in Figure B.3.

To conclude, it should be noted that what appears to be an unorthodox approach to the research task may be explained by the circumstances of the case: namely, that the starting point was an observation of an anomaly in the material that the ICAEW used to present itself to the outside world and to its own members. So the first task was an exploration of that anomaly and a preliminary definition of what it actually was that had caught the sociological eye. Those procedures automatically brought in theories and concepts, as well as involving an excursion into the documen-tary sources which were to constitute an important part of the research data.

B.1.4   Physical objects as social data

My research design rested on documentary material which I hoped would show that professional bodies did what I said they did and the reasons why they did it. I was also concerned with physical objects which I described as possessing certain qualities and features. But there is no reason why my word should be accepted about features of the physical world and how they should be judged, any more than about the actions or motivations of members of professions. For this reason my project as originally conceived (and executed) involved taking large numbers of photographs of the buildings I was studying. In this way my audience could judge for themselves whether a building appeared ornamented or plain, whether an entrance hall contained wasted space, or whether a room looked as though it was intended for leisure or for work. In fact the original form of publication of my results was a presentation of 40 slides at the Annual Conference of the American Sociological Association, over two years before the article appeared in *Sociology*.

But material of this kind might be thought to be rather different from what are normally regarded as data. With survey data, for example, certain parameters are set, certain questions are asked, and by this means a data set is generated which the research community can inspect for themselves, if they wish. Similarly, findings drawn from documents can be verified. Are photographs, in which the subject matter, the angle, the lighting, the wide-angle or the telephoto lens, are all at the discretion of the researcher, really of the same order? In spite of being in quite a different medium, photos are no more subject to selectivity and bias than any other means of collecting data. It may not be easy for another researcher to obtain an entrée to the Law Society or the Royal College of Physicians, but it can be done; and presenting visual data must surely be an advance on just taking my word for it – which is what you will have to do for the ethnography of any tribal society!

B.2   Method

The strategy adopted was to take as a critical case an occupation which had established itself in a relatively short space of time, and to compare those findings with occupations of established professional standing.

The critical case: Accountancy

Accountancy in England emerged remarkably slowly as a coherent occupation, in view of the rapid development of the commercial and industrial enterprises which might be thought to require its services. In Scotland the profession obtained its first Royal Charter in 1853, but this did not occur in England until 1880, when the ICAEW was formed. Even then it failed to obtain the practical and legal monopoly in the provision of services that professional occupations aim for, and within five years of its foundation the ICAEW was challenged by another body, the Incorporated Accountants, and subsequently by various other groups, which have now amalgamated into the Certified Accountants. These three bodies constitute the 'critical case'.

Comparable cases

The first is the Law Society. From the start, accountants were in competition with solicitors, but in important respects modelled themselves on them and in Scotland a number of the founding members were actually lawyers. The Law Society therefore seemed a potentially comparable body. Second, the Royal College of Physicians and the Royal College of Surgeons were chosen as examples of old established bodies of the highest prestige, with a very different kind of practice and place in society from accountants, which could therefore be regarded as contrasting cases.

B.3   Data collection

Once the general theme had been formulated, and the cases for investigation had been chosen, a plan for data collection was worked out.

The first step was to make contact with the professional body. As this was a documentary study, first contact was made with the person keeping the archives, namely the librarian, by making a phone call. This is often a good tactic because the whole thing can be kept in a low key, by explaining that you want to find out who to ask for permission to use the library for historical research (which most people find less threatening than sociology). At this stage requirements were stated at the minimum, with the explanation that the library would be the most convenient place to find histories that had already been published. Then, if necessary, a follow-up letter was sent, permission was obtained and an appointment made to visit the library.

The second stage was to establish an entrée by explaining a bit more about the project; in this research, as in other projects of this kind, librarians proved to be extremely cooperative. On the whole the presence of a researcher gives librarians an opportunity to exercise their skills and to display their archives to someone who shares their interest in them. The librarians who were so helpful in finding documents were often able to help in another vital matter for this project, namely the freedom to photograph. This might not seem a serious matter at first sight, but in fact most of the buildings in this research contained valuable objets d'art and photos of them would be exactly what art thieves, working to order, would want.

Then, maintaining access is essential because it is only too likely that a source may have been overlooked, one's notes may be ambiguous or the camera flash may have failed to go off – and a return visit is needed. Another aspect of this is that it may be proper, as well as politic, to offer those who have helped the project a copy of the report or part of it, as a way of allowing them some participation in the research and of giving them something in return for their cooperation.

So at the end of my visit to the headquarters of a professional body I would have the following data in my bag.

1. Visual:
   - observations and photographs of the building from the outside, and its location;
   - observations and photographs of the interior and its contents;
   - booklets or other publications which referred specifically to the building, together with any postcards and other such material which in any way reflected the profession's interest in its building.
2. Records:
   - published histories, including those privately published;
   - professional journals;
   - accounts and account books;
   - minutes, annual reports, etc.
3. Informal interviews with anyone who happened to be around. This cannot be regarded as a systematic means of data collection, but rather as a readiness to pick up information from any source that may be available. I spoke to librarians, their assistants, hall porters and other library users; in one location this actually happened to include the author of the official history of the institution, who was working in the library on his next project.

B.4 Assessment

Evaluation, interpretation and triangulation were discussed in chapter 10 as distinct elements of the research process and, analytically, indeed they are. In practice the researcher has to have these questions in mind all the time, otherwise it would be necessary to scan documents several times over with different purposes in mind. Even so, some aspects of these processes have to be carried out as separate tasks, and in order to review the mechanics of the project it is necessary to take them one at a time.

B.4.1 Authenticity

In a study of collegiate bodies of the kind under scrutiny here, one would not expect authenticity to be a serious problem, because their affairs are in principle, if not always in practice, run by the members and therefore difficult to manipulate or to falsify. None the less, there were two instances where the source of funding for the construction of new buildings was not entirely clear; and while there was no reason to suspect any malpractice, there was some reason to suppose that the organisations in question were being given financial advantages that they would prefer to keep out of the public domain for reasons of avoiding envy, if nothing more. Even this conclusion, I should add, could only be reached because, as an erstwhile accountant I had the necessary skill and interest to be able to pursue this kind of topic.

It was also my training in accountancy which enabled me to discover that the eighteenth century bookkeeper of one of my subjects of investigation did not properly understand double-entry bookkeeping. Although this had no significance for that particular investigation it is illustrative of the point that documents can be plain wrong, and of course, if something like this is taken as a model by succeeding clerks the error can become quite significant. Another error I encountered was perpetrated by a professional journal: the Institute of Chartered Accountants decided just before Christmas in 1898 to hold a vote on a major matter of policy and conducted it with less than the stipulated period of notice. Both these points caused uproar among the members, but in spite of the seriousness of the whole business, *The Accountant* recorded the proposal as carried, when in fact it was defeated! Needless to say the record was put right in the next issue, but once again one can see the need to verify and to follow up, because an incomplete review of the documents or a copy missing from the archive could produce a mistake of fact.

B.4.2   Credibility

This was probably even less of an issue in this project than authenticity. Given the public nature of the matters under investigation and the immediacy of the records of them, there was little room for doubt on this score. The most likely way in which a problem might have arisen would have been from the actions of a journal editor with a particular bee in his or her bonnet or an axe to grind, which led him or her to be highly selective over the letters and articles published. So before taking such material as an accurate reflection of the views of the members of a profession a researcher would need to check (i.e. triangulate) against other sources.

B.4.3   Representativeness

This question was rather more problematic. In many cases the record was complete – all the issues of a journal, the minutes of all the meetings, copies of all the annual reports. The problem was rather that the record was minimal, in the sense that documents tabled and referred to in the minutes were missing, thus rendering the official record baffling rather than informative. As mentioned above, the Law Society in its early years failed to file the accounts with the annual report, making it impossible to understand fully the way in which their new building had been financed. Likewise with the Institute of Chartered Accountants; practically none of the papers and discussion documents tabled at meetings during the periods under investigation have survived. So the problem was more the absence of the interesting detail rather than unrepresentativeness.

In one respect the question of representativeness overlapped with that of meaning, because as we shall see, one aspect of assessing the significance of a building is the importance of its architect, which depends on the assessment of his work; and if his work has been demolished, then any quantification of his reputation becomes problematic. This turned out to be the case with the architect of the Law Society's building, Vuilliamy, who seems to have suffered disproportionately at the hands of the developers – and the Luftwaffe. As a result his work does not feature as largely as it otherwise might in the standard works on London architecture. In particular, a mansion that he designed was pulled down in the 1930s to make way for the Dorchester Hotel.

B.4.4   Meaning

In a sense the topic of the project was precisely 'meaning', in that talking of 'traditional' sources of prestige (Larson) and of 'respectability' and 'aristocratic' values (Veblen), my theoretical sources are partly explicitly and partly implicitly referring to the meanings that are attached to certain modes of social behaviour and to the purchase and display of certain objects. In practical research terms, this came down to two broad areas. First, did the professional bodies act in a way which is consistent with the theoretical model – did they go for buildings with more than the functional requirements of an office block and did they actually say anything about what they were doing? Second, what evidence is there that the buildings, the architects, the locations and so on, did and do have the social significance that the theory requires them to have? Or to put it another way, what did a professional body mean or intend when it acquired a building of the kind in question; and what do the public, or the members of the profession, or the architecture buffs think of them?

B.5   Buildings, motives and public esteem

The illustrations in this chapter show pretty unambiguously that the buildings occupied by professional bodies in London are not ordinary office blocks. They are quite clearly in the tradition of the kind of architecture to be found in public buildings – Parliament, town halls, churches etc. – or in the mansions of the very wealthy. Furthermore, the statements of accountants and their journal, quoted above, are examples of the kind of evidence that was available about the motives of a professional body embarking on the construction of its headquarters building. There was other evidence including pamphlets published by the profession, statements in their official histories and even in one case a television documentary about the building as an example of a particular style of architecture. The commentator in this case, himself an architect and son of a Fellow of the institution in question, could not have been more explicit about the non-functional purposes of the structure. Figure B.4, for example, shows the main building of the Royal College of Physicians. This elegant 'cubist' building has been carefully designed by Sir Denys Lasdun using the best materials, so that after 30 years it shows none of the deterioration and staining usually found in concrete buildings. The front two thirds of the structure are occupied by the ceremonial stairway and library, while the entire front section at ground level is a void. The Regency terrace that comprises the 'Medical Precinct' can just be glimpsed through the trees on the right. At the end of the 'Medical Precinct' stands a Palladian villa (Figure B.5) designed by John Nash as part of the whole Regents Park and Regents Street development in the 1820s. It is designated as the official residence of the President and Secretary of the College, but in practice serves other purposes as well.

The other aspect of meaning is whether the buildings in the study are located in areas and are designed by architects that do in fact stand high in public esteem (or at least in the esteem of that section of the public that matters to a professional body) and whether the buildings themselves are well thought of by those in a position to evaluate architecture. So far as area is concerned, there is one kind of measure that is quite explicit, namely the market values of the other properties to be found there. However, when talking of prestige, market value is only part of the story, and the researcher has to evaluate other aspects of location, and in particular to pull together the various strands which go to make up 'appropriateness'. In some instances this might be quite difficult, but in this case the proximity of institutions such as the Bank of England (for accountants) or the Law Courts (for solicitors) would probably be enough on their own to give the appropriate aura to a district so far as those professions were concerned, although in fact there were several other institutions nearby to reinforce their influence.

There is clearly a danger in the researcher relying on his or her own 'common sense' knowledge to interpret the 'meaning' to be attached to a particular site, but this interpretation did not stand alone. On the one hand, there was documentary evidence of the professions themselves making these judgements, and on the other, use was made of a technique employed by social psychologists, namely a panel of experts. The panel consisted of a sociologist with an interest in architecture, an environmental psychologist and an architect, all with a good knowledge of London. Matters of evaluation and meaning such as location of site were checked out with them.

Figure B.4   *The Royal College of Physicians, main building*

Figure B.5   *The official residence of the President and Secretary of the Royal College of Physicians*

The panel was also important in validating the results obtained from a content analysis of works on architecture. It might have been possible to have been more sophisticated about this aspect of the research and to have used semiotics rather than content analysis on the architecture texts, but that would have been so time consuming as to have constituted a project in its own right. So the somewhat mechanical method of adding up number of words, number and size of pictures, number of entries etc. was employed, in order to arrive at assessments of the relative importance of buildings and their architects. Tables showing the results of this work can be found in the article in *Sociology* (Macdonald, 1989).

Meaning, as Denzin (1970) and his followers are aware, can be elusive. The research described here has attempted to follow his precepts. The result is not an empirical fact that can be physically nailed down, but an accumulation of plausible conclusions, all pointing in the same direction and with no contrary instances.

B.6   Triangulation

Two kinds of triangulation have *not* featured in this research, theoretical and observer. Rather than using more than one theoretical approach, an attempt has been made to link together strands from Larson (1977), Veblen (1970) and Baltzell (1962) into a model that fits in with the Weberian tradition. As this was a one-person project there was no triangulation of observers either, although the use of a panel of assessors to validate judgements about meaning, in the sense of the value attached to the reputations of locations, buildings and architects, is based on the same principle.

Data triangulation, on the other hand, does feature to some extent. The choice of cases cannot really be described as triangulation, although the idea of taking the three accountancy bodies as the critical case and then going on to parallel but contrasting cases, is certainly not at variance with it. What is to be found in the study is differentiation by time. The accountancy case is set in the late nineteenth century, and its parallel in law occurs in the 1820s. But the best comparison over time involves the Royal College of Physicians, which in the 1960s acted in a way which was if anything even more oriented to tradition than the accountants, thus providing very strong confirmation of the research hypothesis. Although it does not appear in the paper, triangulation by space was also valuable, because a visit to the United States showed that the strongly anti-tradition and anti-aristocratic culture of that society seems to have entirely inhibited the development of any form of display of the kind discovered in Britain. Two cases in point were the headquarters of the Certified Public Accountants, who occupy a floor in an office block in mid-Manhattan – impressive, but just an office block; and the American Medical Association, which has an ordinary-looking building in a district of Chicago that rather makes you wish that you had stayed on the bus.

Triangulation of methods, however, was a fundamental feature of the project. The main methods were documentary and observational, with interviewing as a minor component. The details of these are set out above so they will not be recapitulated here; documents included records, journals and books, while the observations were recorded both by conventional methods and by photography. What can usefully be noted is that two pieces of data cropped up after the research was complete that act as nice confirmatory examples. One occurred in the journal *Accountancy*, which in 1989 ran for some months a 'Members' Section' for which they had an illustrated title page. The photo used on this page was always of some elaborate or impressive feature of the Institute's Hall. Even more telling was the documentary on BBC2 about the building of the Royal College of Physicians, which showed far more effectively than my photographs just what a splendid waste of space it was, and with a commentary which stated explicitly that the greater part of the building had been designed for ceremonial purposes. Add to this the information (not available to the viewers) that a sizeable part of the funds for this celebration of non-functional traditionalism had come from a charitable foundation and we not only have confirmation of Veblen's dictum, 'To be respectable it must be wasteful', but we may also conclude that if a charity (or the state) can be persuaded to pay for such extravagance, the respectability achieved is surely copper-bottomed.

PART III

Back home

11 Coding and managing data

Jane Fielding

Contents

Once you have collected your research data, you will need to start the process of making sense of the material, whether it be a pile of completed questionnaires, a bulging notebook or a stack of interview tapes. The next step involves organising the information into a form that will facilitate your understanding of its meaning, using whatever modern technology is appropriate.

First, I will review the possible pathways that you may have passed through to arrive at this point.

1. You designed a questionnaire, which may have been self-completion or interview-aided or even completed over the telephone (see chapter 6). Hopefully, you gave some thought to how your respondents might have answered your questions and you may have pre-coded the

questionnaire so that they have already ticked appropriate boxes. If that is the case, then your next task, coding your questionnaire, has almost been completed. However, you may have only just picked up this book, hoping to find a way out of a sea of completed questionnaires which have not been coded in any way. Or maybe you have something somewhere in between these two scenarios. In any case, if you have collected more than 20 questionnaires and have asked more than five questions then you should be using a computer to help analyse the results.

2. You conducted an in-depth face-to-face interview and either recorded it on cassette tape or made notes (see chapter 8).
3. You observed a social situation or setting and made covert or overt fieldnotes (see chapter 9).
4. You collected administrative details from records (see chapter 10), possibly noting the information on a questionnaire.
5. You collected articles or newspaper cuttings about your research topic (as suggested in chapter 10).
6. A combination of these methods.

Whatever data collection you carried out, whether it was of a quantitative or qualitative nature, you will now be faced with some kind of sorting task which by its very nature will impose a discipline on this stage of the research. As Silvey (1975: 16) says:

> Research ultimately must be based on comparisons, whether it be comparisons between different groups of cases, between the same cases at different points in time, or even between what is and what might have been.

In order to make comparisons you will have to access your data and organise it into categories or instances of occurrence. You will have to 'code' your data, be it a survey questionnaire or an interview transcript. You will find that even a 'quantitative' survey has qualitative elements and similarly a qualitative transcript has quantitative aspects. For instance, many questions in a pre-coded survey will resort to a catch-all 'other, please specify' category as a safety net for those responses not anticipated in the original questionnaire design. Very often these responses are the most interesting, as exceptions to the rule, and will need particularly careful consideration and coding. Another common type of question is one which explores why a particular response was chosen for a previous question. For instance respondents may be asked to pick one answer from a list and then the next question may be 'Why did you choose that answer?' This 'open response' will also have to be coded. With qualitative data such as an interview transcript, preliminary analysis may resort to such quantitative methods as frequency counts of occurrences of certain phrases or words.

The discussion that follows begins by considering the quantitative coding of a questionnaire with pre-coded questions and then follows with a discussion of the coding of open questions. This may be seen as qualitative coding and many of the considerations for this activity apply equally to the coding of interview transcripts. The differences lie not in the activity of coding but in the treatment of the resulting categories or codes.

The result of coding a survey questionnaire is a data matrix stored in a computer file. Computer software is now available which will help with data entry although entering data can also be done with a word processor.

The result of coding an interview transcript has usually been a stack of file cards each containing a segment of the text. The file cards are then sorted manually in various ways to generate and explore theoretical categories. However, computer programs for qualitative research are now becoming available to aid the sorting process and the chapter concludes with a discussion of what can be achieved with this software.

11.1   The coding process

In order to put the coding process into perspective, let us consider the following question: 'Do you agree or disagree that capital punishment should be completely abolished?' Respondents will also be asked how old they are, whether they are male or female, and if they are married or single. In the following sections we will explore what is involved in coding these questions, but first I will describe the result of the coding exercise and then go through each step of both quantitative coding and qualitative coding. The steps are:

- Developing the coding frame for both pre-coded and open questions.
- Creating the code book and coding instructions.
- Coding the questionnaires.
- Transferring the values to a computer.
- Checking and cleaning the data.

11.1.1   The result: the data matrix

A survey questionnaire is designed to gather information from a number of cases about various topics of investigation. By **cases**, we typically mean people, but a case could equally be a country or a school or even an observed incident. The information that we collect about each case, such as the sex and age of an individual, birth and death rates of a country, time of incident and number of people present, are the **variables**. The aim of coding is to assign a **value** to each piece of information. Each individual *case* will then consist of a complete set of *values* for each of the *variables* under investigation.

The result of such a coding exercise will be the production of a **data file** which should consist of numbers (or sometimes letters and spaces) such

Variables (columns)

	Question 1	Question 2	Question 3	Question 4
Case 1	Age of person 1	Sex of person 1	Marital status of person 1	Attitude to capital punishment of person 1
Case 2	Age of person 2	Sex of person 2	Marital status of person 2	Attitude to capital punishment of person 2
Case 3	Age of person 3	Sex of person 3	Marital status of person 3	Attitude to capital punishment of person 3

Cases (rows)

The boxed part of the diagram will form the data file

Figure 11.1   *A data matrix*

that the rows correspond to each case and the columns correspond to each variable.

Notice how the boxed part of Figure 11.1 will form a block of numbers and/or letters once each variable has been assigned values. Even if the respondent has not replied to a particular question, or the question was 'not applicable' to the respondent, a value is still usually assigned to the variable for that case. And if we make sure that each value is placed in the same column for each variable, for each case, we will end up with a **rectangular data matrix**. This sort of data file is known as a **fixed format** data file.

Generally, this rectangular data matrix does not exceed 80 columns in width. This is so the whole data file can be seen on a computer monitor with no lines 'wrapping round' to the next line. If you have many variables then you can use more than one line of data for each case.

11.1.2   Developing the coding frame

As you develop the **coding frame** you need to understand the different sorts of variables that you may come across. If you ask people how much they earn in a year you could compare someone earning £10,000 with someone earning £20,000, since this variable is measured on an **interval** or continuous scale. The former earns half as much as the latter.

If you ask the question, 'How well do you manage on your income?', allowing the respondent to tick one of a selection of answers ranging from 'not at all well' to 'doing very well', you would have some basis for comparing someone who said they were managing 'very well' with someone who said they were 'not managing at all well'. However, you would not know the difference between 'doing very well' and 'doing well'. And one person who thinks that they 'are doing very badly' may not mean the same as another who gives the same answer. This variable is being measured on an **ordinal** scale since the responses are ordered.

If you ask what religion someone belongs to, you would receive a response that merely nominates a particular religion (or no religion). There is no intrinsic ordering between religions. Religion is being measured on a **nominal** scale.

There is a special kind of nominal variable, called a **dummy** variable, where the measurement is either the presence of an attribute or its absence. For instance, instead of asking people what religion they belong to, creating a nominal variable, you could have asked people if they were Protestant. Then all those people who said they were Protestant could be coded with the value 1 and all the rest with the value 0. Similar dummy variables could be created if you had asked people if they were Catholic, or if they were Jewish, and so on. The essential feature of a dummy variable is that it is a binary coded variable, having a value of either 1 or 0.

The sequence of levels of measurement is from nominal, the lowest, through ordinal, to interval. Each higher level possesses all the properties of the lower levels. With the increase in level of measurement comes greater flexibility and power in the statistical methods that can be employed in analysis.

In Figure 11.1 there are four questions corresponding to four variables which illustrate these levels of measurement. Age is measured at the interval level. Attitude to capital punishment is, as we shall see in the next section, measured at the ordinal level. Sex and Marital Status are measured at the nominal level.

We will start by coding the pre-coded questions. This should ideally be carried out before the questionnaire is administered so that the anticipated responses and their codes can be printed onto the questionnaire.

It is usual to assign a unique ID or case number to each questionnaire, so that, if necessary, you can refer back to the original questionnaire once all the data are on the computer. This is very often the first variable and therefore is often put into the first columns. So you must make sure that you have reserved enough columns for the maximum number of cases. For instance, if you expect no more than 99 filled-in questionnaires (99 cases), you only need to reserve columns 1 and 2 for the ID values. However, if you expect over a hundred completed questionnaires, but no more than 999, you need to reserve columns 1, 2 and 3 for these ID values. These column assignments lead to variables being referred to as 'single column variables', 'two column variables' and so on.

If the questionnaire asked people how old they were, you could assign two columns, assuming there is no one older than 99, and then code the actual age into those columns, thus creating age as an interval variable. However, you may decide you do not need to retain all this information

Age	Code
Under 20	1
21–35	2
36–50	3
51–65	4
66–80	5
Over 81	6

Figure 11.2 *Coding for the variable, Age*

and are only interested in the distinctions between certain age groupings. In other words, code age as an ordinal variable. Another reason why you might code age as an ordinal variable is that people are often reticent about their age and feel happier if they just have to tick an age range on a questionnaire (see chapter 6). So your coding frame for age as an ordinal variable may resemble Figure 11.2.

Some people in your sample may have refused to answer this question and you need to decide what code to assign to these 'non-responses'. By convention 9, 99 or 999 are reserved as **missing values** to be used to code non-responses. The code 9 would be used for single column variables and 99 for double column variables. So if you coded age as a continuous variable, you would assign the value 99 to those people who did not respond. If there was a possibility of a respondent being 99 years of age, you could use the value 999 for the missing value, or you could use 98 for all those who are 98 or older. If you decide to code age in age groups, you could use the code 9 as the non-response code.

While on the subject of missing data, there are other possible reasons for data to be missing for a particular case. For instance, a respondent may not know the answer to a particular question and respond with a 'don't know'. Or a question or set of questions may be inapplicable. For instance, one would not ask for the salary of an unemployed person. Again there are conventions to follow. 'Don't know' responses are often coded with an 8 or a 98 and 'not applicable' responses are often coded with a 0. If you have a large number of non-responses in your questionnaires, it is acceptable to leave blanks in the data file.

In coding a question about a respondent's sex you might assign the value 1 for those who responded 'male' and a 2 for those who responded 'female'. You could equally well have coded 'female' as 1 and 'male' as 2, but, whatever you decide, you must stick to it for the rest of your cases. You could have coded sex with a letter, for example 'm' and 'f', but it is

Marital status	Code
Married	1
Living as married	2
Separated/divorced	3
Widowed	4
Not married	5
No response	9

Figure 11.3   *Coding for the variable, Marital Status*

Attitude to capital punishment	Code
Strongly agree	1
Agree	2
Neither agree nor disagree	3
Disagree	4
Strongly disagree	5

Figure 11.4   *Coding for the variable, Attitude to Capital Punishment*

more usual to use a number since the use of alphabetic coding sometimes imposes restriction on subsequent analysis.

A possible scheme for marital status is shown in Figure 11.3. Marital status is a nominal variable. It is important that when the questionnaire is administered, it is made clear that this question refers to the current marital status of the respondent, and that 'married' means married at the moment, rather than 'ever been married'.

A common method of coding attitudinal questions is seen in Figure 11.4. Coded in this way, this variable is an ordinal variable. For a fuller discussion of this kind of coding see chapter 7.

So, after coding, the data file for three respondents might look like Figure 11.5. Here case 1 is a 23 year old man who is living as married and agrees that capital punishment should be completely abolished. Once again the data file is boxed.

Variables

	ID (identification number)			Question 1 (age)		Question 2 (sex)	Question 3 (marital status)	Question 4 (Attitude to capital punish- ment)
variable type:				*interval*		*nominal*	*nominal*	*ordinal*
column:	1	2	3	4	5	6	7	8
Case 1	0	0	1	2	3	1	2	2
Case 2	0	0	2	4	1	2	1	3
Case 3	0	0	3	9	9	2	4	5

Cases (label to left of Case rows)

Figure 11.5 *The coded data matrix*

11.1.3 Rules for coding

The following are some basic rules for coding:

1. Codes must be mutually exclusive. Any particular response must fit into one, and only one category. Someone cannot be both married and single at the same time.
2. Codes must be exhaustive. You must have covered all possible coding options and allowed for them in your scheme.
3. Codes must be applied consistently throughout.

You should be consistent within your questionnaire for the values you use for similar responses in different questions. For instance, if you decide to code a 'yes' responses with the value 1 and a 'no' responses with the value 2, use those values throughout the questionnaire for other yes/no questions. Similarly, code all non-response categories with a 9, 99, or 999, all 'don't know' responses with the values 8, 98, or 998 and all 'not applicable' categories with either a blank or a zero.

11.1.4 Comparability

When selecting categories for closed questions it is a good idea to be consistent with the codes that have been used in other surveys. The *Standard Occupational Classification* (1990) is a manual which indexes occupations according to qualifications, training, skills and industry and is widely used by labour market researchers. Other sources of coding for standard variables such as household composition, education, age, gender, race and leisure are described by Stacey (1969) and Burgess (1986). Using the same codes as other surveys makes it easier to compare results.

Questionnaire

ID number

□ □ □   1–3

Please provide the following details:

Q.1   Age: □ □   4–5

Q.2   Sex:
Please tick one box: Male   □¹   Female   □²   6

Q.3   Marital status:
Please tick one box:

Married   □¹   7

Living as married   □²

Separated/divorced   □³

Widowed   □⁴

Not married   □⁵

Q.4   Do you agree or disagree with the following statement:
        Capital punishment should be completely abolished

Please tick one box:

Strongly agree   □¹   8

Agree   □²

Neither agree or   □³
disagree

Disagree   □⁴

Strongly disagree   □⁵

Figure 11.6   *Sample questionnaire with pre-codes*

So far this chapter has discussed the coding of closed questions in which codes have been assigned to each of the responses on the actual question-naire. It is often a good idea to type these codes onto the questionnaire so that respondents only have to tick boxes or circle numbers when filling out the form. This often leads to a better response because it is quicker for someone to tick a box than write out their response. Also, the next stage of transferring the data onto a computer is considerably quicker if as much pre-coding as possible has been done beforehand. In addition to the numerical codes that you assign to each response, the column number is often also written onto the questionnaire, often under a heading such as 'For office use only'. So the above set of questions could have been laid out as shown in Figure 11.6.

11.2   Qualitative coding

Often a pre-coded question will offer the option of an 'other (please specify)' category to act as a 'safety net' to catch additional responses which may be encountered infrequently. There are also questions which qualify previous responses such as 'Why did you say that?', for which pre-coding is not possible. These represent qualitative elements in an otherwise quantitative analysis. Whether one is coding these kinds of questions, open questions in which verbatim responses are recorded, or interview transcripts or fieldnotes, the process of coding is the same.

The first step is to develop the set of categories into which the data will be coded. The categories may come from theory, intuition or from the data themselves. If the research is designed to test a hypothesis, the categories should be derived from the theoretical framework and the data made to fit the categories. This is termed 'coding down'. However, if the aim is to describe data in order to generate theory, you can develop the categories from the data: 'coding up'. The process of coding up involves the following steps.

- Either take the first 20 or so questionnaires or the interview transcript or fieldnotes.
- Use filing cards to note down each response from the questionnaire or each significant feature or quote from the interview/fieldnote. Use a new filing card for each new response or concept.
- With survey questionnaires, code question by question (i.e. across all 20 questionnaires), not case by case. This leads to greater consistency in coding each variable. It also reduces the possibility of a build-up of any preconceived picture of the respondent which could lead to a bias in the coding of any ambiguous response.
- For an interview or transcript, code a paragraph at a time.
- Sort the filing cards into related categories.
- Continue with another 20 questionnaires or another interview/fieldnote.
- Repeat the sorting exercise.
- Repeat the last two steps until no new categories are generated.
- Create coding instructions in order to define category membership.

11.2.1   An example of coding a fieldnote

Turner (1981) offers a clear example of coding up a fieldnote. In the example shown in Figure 11.7, the fieldnote describes an aspect of the queuing system at a cement factory. Turner generates a number of potential ways of coding the fieldnote through a 'brainstorming' session where as many plausible accounts of its meaning are listed as possible. These form possible codes which are then compared to other fieldnotes in

A. First paragraph from a set of fieldnotes

A row of lorries varying between 30 and 50 queue up every morning in front of the factory to obtain cement. All lorry drivers and owners place great importance to be first in the queue as this means getting served first. This has added importance in times of cement shortages when the cement outflow from the factory to the private sector is rationed and when the prices of cement are high. In addition to cement customers, there is also a set of lorry owners stationed at H. . . who act as transport agents for other customers. Porcelli is one of these transport agents.

Source: Former factory manager who is embarking here upon a discussion of Porcelli's activities in the area.

B. Categories generated (to be placed on cards)

Cement shortage
Competitive behaviour among lorry drivers
Many agents transporting cement
Greater intensity of competition caused by cement shortage
Customers transporting their own cement
Role of factory
Significance of queue system as a means of distributing scarce resources
Economic context of scarcity
Porcelli's role
Significance of time in relation to the queue
Routinised pattern for the distribution of goods
Importance of priority position in queue

Source: Turner (1981)

Figure 11.7   *Coding a fieldnote*

the set. Some will be discarded because they do not resonate with the other data, while others will be seen to relate to each other and so will be combined. Thus, several codes are likely to end up being applicable to the fieldnote shown. For each code an attempt is made to 'define' it by writing it up in formal, abstract terms. Another important aspect of the procedure is that, once stated in formal terms, an effort should be made to identify parallel codes or processes in other, documented social phenomena. For example, if 'power' emerges as a code applicable to the data you should try to think of other situations in which 'power' governs the course of interaction. This will help to identify elements of the operation of power which you can then look for in your own data.

Pfaffenberger (1988) has described some coding strategies for qualitative data, some of which apply equally well to open questions in a survey or interview (see Figure 11.8). Note that 'strip' refers to a discrete segment of coded data.

11.2.2   Coding open questions in a survey questionnaire

Having created a workable coding frame for the open questions in a survey, there are several points to consider before you can go ahead and

Prefer inclusive codes to exclusive code

> The point of coding is to interlink units of data. The interlinkages thus created will play a major role in data analysis. To maximise the number of such interlinkages, use inclusive codes – codes that link at least two (and preferably more) strips together. The point is, that in any subsequent sifting of data, such codes will be more likely to include a relevant item than to leave it out. Try to code each strip, moreover, with two or more codes.

Let coding categories emerge from the data

> Mark off coherent stretches of the field notes by the topical focus expressed in them. Question the a priori, exogenous categories developed before field research. If such categories obscure indigenous ones, and if the indigenous ones fit the data better, replace the exogenous categories with those recognised and used by the culture or organisation.

Develop abstract categories

> The exclusive use of indigenous categories makes it difficult to compare your data with cases derived from other contexts. While developing indigenous categories, therefore, strive also to find abstract categories that do fit the data, and apply them to all relevant instances.

Classify data and create typologies

> Using both indigenous and exogenous categories, subdivide and classify the data. Develop a framework that links the codes together typologically.

Change and refine the categories as understanding improves

> The achievement of a workable framework of codes, one that is sensitive to patterns in the data and does the best possible job of linking related data, is itself a form of theoretical discovery.

Source: Pfaffenberger (1988)

Figure 11.8   *Some coding strategies*

code the rest of the questionnaires. For a survey questionnaire, you will be converting responses to numbers to be collated later by a statistical computer program. Each response category could be assigned a different value, the first category coded 1, the second coded 2 and so on. So if 15 categories were developed from the responses, the values will range from 1 to 15. However, before you decide on this scheme you need to consider how many answers to each question you are going to accept. For instance, to the question 'Why did you say that?', the respondent may offer one reason or many. You will need to decide whether to accept only the first mentioned reason or several. For instance, you may decide to code the first three mentioned reasons. In the latter case, you will need to allow three variables, one for each reason. Of course, data from some respondents may be missing for one or more of these variables. Alternatively, you may decide that you want to code all responses, each one as a separate variable, in which case you would have as many variables as categories. Each variable would then be coded as either, 'yes, the reason is mentioned' and given the value 1, or 'no, not mentioned' and given the value 0.

These points are considered in the example which follows.

In 1982, Social and Community Planning Research conducted a national survey of 1,195 members of the public about their attitudes to industrial, work-related and other risks. The respondents were asked the following, rather cumbersome question:

> Thinking of all the sorts of risks there are, at the present time what risks are you particularly worried or concerned about because they could happen to you or a member of your family?

The interviewers were instructed to 'probe and record fully' and therefore each individual might have mentioned more than one risk (Prescott-Clarke, 1982). With such an open question you could not possibly anticipate all responses and therefore need to develop a coding scheme after the questionnaires have been filled out. In the original survey the answers to this question were left uncoded and unanalysed. The opportunity arose of carrying out a secondary analysis of this and other open questions from the survey (Brown et al., 1984). This involved designing a coding frame for the first 72 questionnaires and trying to define theoretically relevant distinctions between responses. A list of 23 different risks were elicited, although nearly 25 per cent of respondents did not proffer a risk at all. This list formed the basis of the coding frame used to code the rest of the questionnaires.

Because respondents could mention more than one risk, there was a problem in deciding how to code the answers. Figure 11.9 outlines three possible coding schemes.

We could have decided to code only the first mentioned answer on the assumption that it would be the most important (see coding scheme 1 in Figure 11.9.). However, we would have lost a lot of information from respondents who made multiple answers. Alternatively, we could have decided to code the first 3 responses from each respondent, each with the same coding scheme (see coding scheme 2 in Figure 11.9.). However, this might still lead to a loss of information from those respondents offering more than three responses. The third coding scheme in Figure 11.9 involved creating 23 different variables, each one coded either 1 to indicate that it was mentioned or 0 to indicate that it was not mentioned. Obviously, this final scheme coded all the data, but the data may be more difficult to analyse.

The choice of which coding scheme to adopt should depend on the needs of the subsequent analysis. Schemes one and two lend themselves to a more descriptive account of people's responses. Scheme three would be more appropriate if the data were going to be analysed further. In fact, scheme three was employed in the study and the data was analysed using Smallest Space Analysis computer software. This provided a two dimensional 'map' of people's responses such that those risks most frequently mentioned were located towards the centre of the 'map' and those risks mentioned together were located close to one another. From such a two dimensional map, clusters of risks located in proximity were identified as conceptually similar and given group names.

Another common method of dealing with multiple responses in open

Type of worry	Coding scheme 1: First mentioned risk only coded in one variable called RISK	Coding scheme 2: Code the first three mentioned risks into three variables called RISK1, RISK2, RISK3			Coding scheme 3: Each risk mentioned is a variable and coded with a 1 if mentioned, otherwise 0. Therefore 24 variables are required.		
	Variable name RISK code	Variable names			Variable name	code if mentioned	code if not mentioned
		RISK1 code	RISK2 code	RISK3 code			
None	1	1	1	1	RISK1	1	0
Car	2	2	2	2	RISK2	1	0
Crossing road	3	3	3	3	RISK3	1	0
Fire	4	4	4	4	RISK4	1	0
Other specific hazards	5	5	5	5	RISK5	1	0
Traffic	6	6	6	6	RISK6	1	0
Other health	7	7	7	7	RISK7	1	0
Falling	8	8	8	8	RISK8	1	0
Steam	9	9	9	9	RISK9	1	0
Work	10	10	10	10	RISK10	1	0
Electric current	11	11	11	11	RISK11	1	0
Children in traffic	12	12	12	12	RISK12	1	0
Military nuclear power	13	13	13	13	RISK13	1	0
Mugging	14	14	14	14	RISK14	1	0
Vandalism	15	15	15	15	RISK15	1	0
Other crime	16	16	16	16	RISK16	1	0
Unemployment	17	17	17	17	RISK17	1	0
Lightning	18	18	18	18	RISK18	1	0
Pollution	19	19	19	19	RISK19	1	0
Uneven pavements	20	20	20	20	RISK20	1	0
Civil nuclear war	21	21	21	21	RISK21	1	0
Smoking	22	22	22	22	RISK22	1	0
Stress at work	23	23	23	23	RISK23	1	0
Poor housing	24	24	24	24	RISK24	1	0

Figure 11.9   *Three coding schemes for risk responses*

questions is to code only one that satisfies certain criteria. For instance, if you ask respondents what qualifications they have, perhaps offering them a list of pre-coded responses, they may tick more than one box. You may in this instance decide only to code the highest education qualification.

11.2.3   Storing verbatim responses

You may prefer to use the open responses as verbatim comments in your report to illustrate certain points, rather than reducing them to numerically coded categories. Obviously, if you have not quantified them, you will not be able to do any statistical analysis on these responses, but you will still have to read and sort them. You could just type a list of responses and then pick those that are useful for a particular point. Or you could use a database program to store the verbatim comments (this was done in the research described in chapter 3). For example, Dbase III+ will allow you to store textual comments (not exceeding 4,096 characters) as memo fields. Database programs have the advantage that you can save certain 'face-sheet' variables, such as the age and sex of the respondent, along with the verbatim comments. This would enable you to select, say, only those quotes for a particular question from all females aged over 65.

Some statistical packages, such as SPSS, can also store textual comments. However, many statistical programs limit the length of each comment. For example, with SPSS, quotes can be no more than 255 characters in length.

11.3   Creation of the code book

Having created your coding frame and written your coding instructions, you can now create the **code book**. This is often usefully done before you carry out coding of the questionnaires. A code book is a form in which the following information is recorded for each variable:

- Question number and wording.
- Variable name for use by computer programs to refer to the variable (often restricted by the analysis software to 8 characters).
- Column location of that variable.
- Values that the variable can take and what these values represent.
- Missing value(s).
- Range of valid values.

An example of a code book is shown in Figure 11.10.

11.3.1   Coding the questionnaires

Having created the coding frame, written the coding instructions and created the code book, you are now ready to code the rest of the questionnaires. This means going through each questionnaire and writing on the ID number, if it is not already marked, checking for missed questions, marking the appropriate missing value, and marking the values for each open question.

At this stage, the importance of a pilot survey becomes apparent. Any unanticipated responses to your questionnaire may lead to the reorganisation of the coding frame. For instance, you may find during your pilot that you had not anticipated a frequent response that should be added to the pre-coded answers in the main questionnaire.

Question/ variable label	Variable name	Column location	Value labels	Values	Missing values	Range of valid values
Identifi- cation number	ID	1–3	–	–	–	1–450*
Age	AGE	4–5	–	–	99	18–91
Sex	SEX	6	Male Female	1 2	9	1,2
Marital status	MARSTAT	7	Married Living as married Separated/divorced Widowed Not married No response	1 2 3 4 5 9	9	1–5
Attitude to capital punishment	ATTCAP	8	Strongly agree Agree Neither agree nor disagree Disagree Strongly disagree No response	1 2 3 4 5 9	9	1–5

* assuming no more than 450 completed questionnaires

Figure 11.10   *The code book*

11.3.2   Transferring the data to a computer

As mentioned in the introduction to this chapter, if you have more than 20 questionnaires in which you asked more than 5 questions, it makes sense to use a computer to do the analysis. The software that you use will often depend on what is available or within your budget. Software is available that can help you not only with the statistical analysis but also with the data entry process.

There are many statistical programs for analysing survey data. The most popular and widespread is SPSS which is available in several different versions for mainframe and microcomputers. There is also a cheap 'studentware' version which only allows you to use 20 variables and has fewer statistical routines than the full version. Software for data entry includes Data Entry II, which can be used in parallel with SPSS or as a stand alone package. The SocInfo Software Catalogue (1990) has a comprehensive list of software used in the social sciences.

Data entry software will help you enter your data from a coded questionnaire. Generally, whatever software you use, you will need to set up the program to recognise your variables. This usually involves giving a name to each variable, telling the program whether its values are numeric or alphanumeric and stating how many columns it occupies. Having set up the program with this initial information you can then enter the data. Some programs allow you to create an entry screen to resemble the original questionnaire with guidance notes to help the data entry process. Some allow you to define each variable to accept only data within a certain range (e.g. ages between 18 and 65) and some allow you to skip non-applicable questions to speed up data entry. For instance, if someone is asked if they have any children and reply that they do not, then subsequent questions asking for the number of children under 5 will be skipped. On completion of data entry, some programs will allow you to create files which can then be input into statistical programs. Others allow simple statistical procedures to be carried out for each variable.

If you do not have access to software to help you enter the data, other options are available. At some institutions, the computer centre will type your data into the computer directly from your questionnaire. However, you must indicate the column locations of all your variables in order for the 'data entry' staff to know where each variable's values are to be placed. This usually involves typing the column locations onto the actual questionnaire before it is administered. You should have anticipated how many columns all the open questions would occupy and reserved them on the questionnaire.

Another option is to transfer all your values from the questionnaire onto coding sheets. These are A4 sheets of square-lined paper printed with column numbers measuring 80 columns wide by about 22 lines. Each computer centre generally prints its own coding sheets with any special coding instructions, such as whether a zero is to be written with a line through it to distinguish it from a capital letter O. If you go for this option, your questionnaire need not be printed with column numbers, although the numbers will help to guide you when you transfer the data onto the coding sheets. However, it is important that you have your code book prepared before this stage, so that you have a reliable guide for the column locations of each of the variables. Having filled in the coding sheets, your computing centre should be able to enter the data onto the computer for you.

The choice of using either coding sheets or entering data directly from your questionnaire will often come down to whether your computing centre offers a direct entry service, and if it does, how long it takes. It is considerably more time consuming to enter data from a questionnaire than from a coding sheet, even for experienced data entry staff. In addition, to use the direct data entry service, you have to spend more time at the questionnaire design stage in order to satisfy their requirements. It is a good idea to show your completed questionnaire to the direct data entry staff, before you administer it. They can then advise you of any possible problems they might encounter in entering your data.

Instead of relying on a data entry service, you could type in your own data from a coding sheet or even directly from the questionnaire using a text editor or a word processor. Most statistical software provides a text editor for you to type in your own data and this usually indicates the column location of the cursor to help in such a task. However, while it may be convenient to type in your own data, it is easy to make typing mistakes and so this should be undertaken only if other options are not available.

The result of direct data entry using coding sheets or of manual data entry will be a data matrix, stored on the computer.

11.4   Data cleaning

The first statistical operation you should carry out on your data is a frequency count for each variable. For instance, this will tell you for the variable 'sex', how many men and how many women there are in your sample. It should also calculate the percentages of men and women. The main function of this frequency listing is to alert you to any 'wild codes' in your data. These are codes that may have been miscoded during the coding operation or been wrongly entered at the data entry stage. For instance, you might find there were some respondents coded with the value 3 for sex. You should check the frequency listing for such inconsistencies and then identify the cases where these problems occur. Then you must return to the questionnaire to check the original coding.

11.5   Computer analysis of qualitative data

Although the methods used in quantitative surveys and qualitative interviews are often seen as fundamentally different, there are many areas of overlap, especially, as we have seen, in the process of coding. Of course, although the process of coding may be similar, the objectives of coding are different. With a quantitative survey, we try to allocate a value to each category which can then be manipulated statistically, even if only by a simple frequency count. However, categories obtained from interviews and fieldnotes are not normally allocated values but maintain their contextual position. Co-occurrences of categories are explored and themes elicited. This process of comparing similarly coded segments of text is called 'analytic induction' (Manning, 1982).

Software for the analysis of qualitative data has been reviewed and described in detail by Tesch (1990) and by Fielding and Lee (1991) and so only some of the possibilities for qualitative analysis will be outlined here.

Traditionally analysis of similarly coded segments or strips of interviews or fieldnotes (Agar, 1986) is carried out using a cut and paste technique where a copy of the transcript is literally cut up into strips and pasted onto file cards before rearranging them according to co-occurring categories (see chapter 9). Similar procedures can be carried out more easily and accurately with the help of a computer. Computers are ideally suited for sorting, but it is up to the researcher to instruct the program to perform the appropriate analysis. The first step towards analysis is to transfer the interview transcript or fieldnotes to computer-readable form, generally using a word processor.

The word processor program itself can perform basic search procedures which will provide evidence of co-occurrence of concepts and words marked in the text. However, this can be quite tedious unless one is fairly expert at using the software to create 'macros' to simplify the repeated running of the same search procedure. There are automatic indexing programs which will perform the searching more quickly and simply. When a code word is found they will retrieve the paragraph that contains the code. However, you lose the context of the coded segment outside the paragraph boundaries. The ETHNOGRAPH (Seidel and Clark, 1984) will allow you to create the 'boundaries of the coded segment' and to attach codes (i.e. labels of 10 characters) to lines of text, and upon retrieval will find the whole of the coded segment. This software allows you to code text with one or several code words in straight, overlapping or even nested segments of text. These segments can then be retrieved. Retrievals can be made according to the presence of just a single code word or more complicated retrievals based on certain code words being present together or in other combinations can be performed.

For a study of police recruits during their induction period interviews, transcripts were coded with the label FRIENDS for any mention of former friends and with the codeword SHIFT for any reference to shift work. One might be interested in mentions of shift work in relation to the problems of maintaining contact with former friends. A compound retrieval of the co-occurrence of the code words SHIFT **AND** FRIENDS will retrieve all segments which have been coded with both these code words, in all interviews. In this way a comparison can be made between interviewees. You can also attach face-sheet variables to each interview or fieldnote so that in subsequent search and retrieval tasks you can retrieve coded segments from, for example, just those male recruits aged between 19 and 21.

11.6 Conclusion

This chapter has shown the steps involved in coding data from survey questionnaires and unstructured interviews. The methods used for both types of data collection overlap in many ways and emphasis has been placed on the similarities at this stage of the research process. The differences between 'quantitative' and 'qualitative' methods are more marked in the treatment of the resulting coded data. The next chapter discusses in detail how to go about the analysis of quantitative data. The analysis of qualitative data has often been seen as being dependent on the individual researcher and is certainly not as formalised as the analysis of quantitative data. However, with the emergence of new computer software, even the process of qualitative analysis is becoming more amenable to formalisation.

11.7 Project

You have been asked to investigate people's beliefs in the paranormal through administering a questionnaire in the street to the general public. From such a study you can begin to investigate people's understanding of scientific knowledge.

Decide whether you are going to administer a survey questionnaire or carry out a structured interview. Design your interview schedule or your interviewer-administered questionnaire to include the following questions. Try to pre-code the questions where possible and mark your questionnaire with response codes and column numbers in order to simplify data entry.

1. What kinds of things come to mind when you think of the paranormal? (This is an open question to which people may offer more than one answer. Allow several lines on the questionnaire in which to write the answers.)

2. Do you think that any of the following are true?:
    (a) It is possible to make someone turn round just by looking at them.
    (b) Prayers can sometimes be answered.
    (c) It is possible to know what someone else is thinking or feeling even if they are hundreds of miles away and out of touch by ordinary means.
    (d) Some houses are haunted.
    (e) The Earth has been visited by beings from outer space.
    (f) Dreams can sometimes foretell the future.
    (g) Some people can remember past lives (i.e. reincarnations they may have lived).
    (h) It is possible to get messages from the dead.
    (You should expect people to respond with either a positive or negative answer, although it is likely that there will also need to be a 'Don't know' category.)

3. Are you a religious person? (Decide whether to use a yes/no answer or an ordinal scale with responses ranging from very religious to not at all religious.)

4. Age. (Decide whether to use age ranges or to ask people their actual age.)

5. Sex.

6. Social class.

7. Ethnic group.

Remember to include columns for an identification number.

After designing your questionnaire, select a small sample to interview and administer it to them. Create a code book and then code the open question. Finally you could create the data file.

11.8   Further reading

For a discussion of coding survey questionnaires, Silvey (1975) is an early but comprehensive text.

For a discussion about collecting and coding data for computer analysis, chapter 2 in Frude (1987) is a very good introduction.

Coding qualitative data is covered by Pfaffenberger (1988).

12 Analysing survey data

Michael Procter

Contents

Statistical analysis is seen as one of the more frightening and mysterious (some would even say 'mystified') stages of the survey research process. This reputation is unfair – to the other stages. At least as much intellectual effort is needed to conceptualise the problem, to design the sample, and to devise the interview schedule, not to mention the often enjoyable but always demanding task of writing the final report. Perhaps the reason for the special status of data analysis is that you *know* when you do not understand the technical details.

To try to take some of the fear away, this chapter goes through a small-scale example of a real-life analysis.

'Real-life' means real data, which in turn means more than you could hope to deal with equipped only with a pencil and paper and a calculator. It is not sensible to try to analyse a survey of a reasonable size except with a computer and a suitable program. The most commonly used computer software for survey analysis is SPSS, the Statistical Package for the Social Sciences. My examples are produced by the personal computer version, SPSS/PC+.

You can run SPSS on two main kinds of small computer: 'IBM-compatibles', and Apple Macintoshes. In either case you need a machine equipped with a hard disk. An absolutely minimal computer of this kind costs only about £500 – about the same as a television and video cassette

recorder – though for serious work on a full-scale data set you would have
to spend twice that.

12.1   Programs for data management

A program like SPSS (comparable products include SAS, Minitab, P-Stat,
and Systat) has two main components: the statistical routines, which do the
numerical calculations that produce tabulations and summary measures of
various kinds, and the data management facilities. Perhaps surprisingly, it
was the latter that really revolutionized quantitative social research. This is
best clarified by a few examples.

Age is usually measured by asking respondents their date of birth
because this is harder to misremember. Then 'age last birthday' is
calculated from date of birth and the date of the interview using a special
formula. This converts each date into the number of days since 15 October,
1582 (the first day of the Gregorian calendar), and the difference is
converted back into whole years. So far so good; but for many purposes
you may want to use broader categories of age than whole years, for
example the two categories up to 39 versus 40 or over. All these
manipulations count as simple kinds of data management.

The General Household Survey is an annual survey carried out by a UK
Government agency, the Office of Population Censuses and Surveys. The
basic unit of analysis is the household: roughly, a group of people who live
together and share catering arrangements. Variables that describe the
household include the kind of housing tenure (private rented, public
rented, owner-occupied, etc.) and whether it has central heating. Information is gathered about each individual in the household, too: his or her
age, sex, health record, smoking habits, etc. Looking at the relationship
between central heating and housing tenure is fairly straightforward
(presumably we would find that owner-occupiers are more likely to have
the benefit of this feature than are public sector housing tenants) because
both measures are household-level characteristics. It is just as easy to see
whether smokers have more respiratory disease than non-smokers – this
time both measures apply to individuals. But determining whether central
heating is good for your lungs involves looking simultaneously at variables
from different levels of analysis, household and individual. This would be
done by copying the information about central heating down from the
household to all its individual members. Even more complicated, the
question whether you can suffer from the smoking of other people in the
household involves first carrying each household member's smoking up to
the household level and aggregating it, and then transferring household
smoking back down to the individual and relating it to his or her health. All
of this would be extremely difficult to do without the right kind of data
management tools.

DEGREE   HIGHEST DEGREE,RESP

Value Label	Value	Frequency	Percent	Valid Percent	Cum Percent
LT HIGH SCHOOL	0	1072	35.0	35.2	35.2
HIGH SCHOOL	1	1482	48.4	48.6	83.8
JUNIOR COLLEGE	2	68	2.2	2.2	86.0
BACHELOR	3	278	9.1	9.1	95.1
GRADUATE	4	148	4.8	4.9	100.0
	9	12	.4	Missing	
	Total	3060	100.0	100.0	

Figure 12.1   *Marginal frequency distribution for* DEGREE

Having pointed out the importance of data management, there simply is not space to say anything more about it here, although the topic is discussed further in chapter 13. You can start to acquire the necessary skills by reading *The SPSS Guide to Data Analysis* (Norusis, 1988) or a similar guide to another data management program.

12.2   An analysis

12.2.1   Frequency distributions

The first stage in the analysis of a new data set is almost always to get the 'marginal frequency distributions'. The origin of this term will be explained later; all that it means is that we count the number of respondents who answer each question in each of the possible ways. Actually, this is not quite accurate: as chapter 11 explained, sometimes answers will be processed before they are entered into the computer – for instance, a verbatim answer to a question about your job will be coded into one of a number of occupational categories – and it is the coded categories rather than the verbatim responses that will be tabulated.

Here, interspersed with a lot of commentary, is some printout from SPSS, showing the frequency distributions for three variables. Other programs will produce similar tables. The data I have analysed comes from an American survey, the General Social Survey (GSS) carried out every year by the National Opinion Research Center (NORC).

The information reported here (Figure 12.1) came from a sequence of four questions which asked the respondents whether they had graduated from high school and, if so, what higher qualifications they had. The highest qualification mentioned was then coded, so that, for instance, someone with a first degree and a Master's would be put only in category 4. The original researchers have chosen to call this variable 'DEGREE', so that subsequent analysts will have a reasonable chance of remembering the name without having constantly to look it up in a manual. The other labels

MARITAL   MARITAL STATUS

Value Label	Value	Frequency	Percent	Valid Percent	Cum Percent
MARRIED	1	1950	63.7	63.7	63.7
WIDOWED	2	330	10.8	10.8	74.5
DIVORCED	3	206	6.7	6.7	81.2
SEPARATED	4	124	4.1	4.1	85.3
NEVER MARRIED	5	450	14.7	14.7	100.0
	Total	3060	100.0	100.0	

Figure 12.2   *Marginal frequency distribution for* MARITAL

have been assigned in the same way: the program uses all of this information without 'knowing' what any of it means.

We can read from the table that the value '0' occurs with a frequency of 1,072: these are all the people who did not graduate from high school (LT here means 'less than'). A rather larger number, 1,482, did graduate from high school but got no further, and so on. Each of the 'Percent' figures is the corresponding Frequency divided by the total, 3,060. Notice that twelve respondents are coded as 9, which has no label, but which is marked as 'missing'. Data can be missing for a variety of reasons, and a specific numerical code is set aside to mark it (see section 11.1.2); then the program is told that cases with that value are not normally to be included in numerical calculations. For instance, the code for a missing income figure will not be used in the calculation of the average income. In the present example the total for percentaging should not include individuals for whom no data are available: hence the column headed 'Valid Percent', which is based on 3,048 not 3,060. Of course, it makes very little difference to the calculations here, but if there were more missing data it would be a different story.

Finally, the 'Cum Percent' (short for Cumulative Percentage) column gives partial sums of the previous one: 35.2 + 48.6 = 83.8, + 2.2 = 86.0, and so on down the column. Thus we can see immediately that 95.1 percent have a qualification up to and including a first degree. For this cumulation to make sense the order of the categories must be meaningful: DEGREE is an example of an ordinal scale variable (see chapter 11).

Marital status (see Figure 12.2), on the other hand, is said to be measured at the nominal scale, because there is no intrinsic order: it would be hard to argue that 'widowed' is intermediate between 'married' and 'divorced', for instance. So here the cumulative percentages are not meaningful, although SPSS calculates them regardless.

Age has not only a meaningful order (from youngest to oldest or vice versa) but equal scale intervals: (as Gertrude Stein might have said) a year is a year is a year, and the difference between 27 and 28 is numerically identical to that between 33 and 34. This is not true of DEGREE: despite the numerical values (chosen for convenience) there is no reason to suppose that the difference between junior college and high school is in any sense

AGE

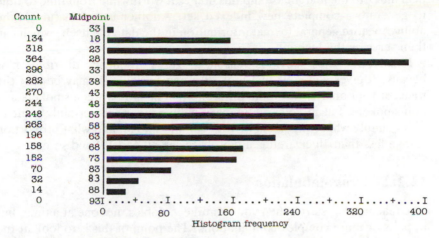

Count	Midpoint	
0	33	
134	18	
318	23	
364	28	
296	33	
282	38	
270	43	
244	48	
248	53	
268	58	
196	63	
158	68	
152	73	
70	83	
32	83	
14	88	
0	93I	

```
     I....+....I....+....I....+....I....+....I
     0       80      160     240     320     400
              Histogram frequency
```

Figure 12.3   *Frequency distribution of* AGE

equivalent to the difference between a doctorate and a bachelor's degree. AGE is referred to as an **interval scale** variable.

AGE is also a **continuous** variable, whereas the others examined here have discrete categories. Age as recorded does in fact have a limited number of categories, since we content ourselves with 'age last birthday', but even this has so many categories that the form of frequency distribution table presented so far is rather cumbersome. As a special option SPSS displays what the manual refers to as a histogram, in which the almost continuous variable is split into a number of convenient groupings, and the relative frequency is represented by the length of a bar (see Figure 12.3). The class midpoint of 28, say, represents ages of 26, 27, 28, 29 and 30.

There are two main reasons for 'getting the marginals'. As mentioned in section 11.4, the first is to look for errors in the data. The second is that this is generally the best way of keeping tabs on the state of the data set, which necessarily gets modified during the process of analysis. This becomes especially necessary as research in general and data analysis in particular become cooperative enterprises: the costs of the field-work phase of a survey are so great that it makes sense to get the resulting data thoroughly analysed, often by a whole team of social scientists. As was explained earlier, practically every data set will go through repeated modifications as the analysts conceptualise new variables and new analytical frameworks. Of course, it is essential that these modifications are carefully documented, especially if a derived variable is to be used by workers other than the one who has created it. One way to do this is to keep a logbook (either a physical volume or in the form of a text file on the computer system being used). But in addition, it makes sense to generate a frequency table for every new variable and add it to the set you will have made at the beginning of the analysis process. Some programs will produce an alphabetical index to the marginals, and this makes it worthwhile from time to time to generate a complete new indexed set. Another useful feature is the ability to store general textual information in the data file itself, which can then serve as the logbook.

Finally, the most obvious reason to get a frequency distribution is because it gives you your first look at a new variable. It may be that the focus of your analysis is on the differences in health between smokers and non-smokers, but in your preliminary analysis you will certainly want to know simply what proportion of your sample smoke, and what proportion smoke less than 10 cigarettes a day, between 10 and 19, and so on.

12.2.2   Cross-tabulation

The real analysis starts when you examine variables, not one at a time, but in pairs or more complex combinations. The point of this is to look at the relationship between variables, usually in order to explain differences on one variable in terms of differences on the other. As a simple example, if we find that workers with different jobs tend to have different health records, whereas workers with the same job are similar in their health, then we might say that differences in occupation at least partly explain differences in health or, more concisely, that occupation explains health. 'Explains' is here being used rather differently than in everyday language: it refers to a statistical relationship that may or may not lead to increased understanding.

What follows is the record of a run using SPSS. No attempt is made to define systematically what this requires; luckily, it is not difficult to acquire a reading knowledge of SPSS, so you should be able to follow what is going on. The main thing to understand is that the researcher types in commands that look like a version of English, and the program displays the results on the computer's screen or on a printer. The method of use and the output from other programs will differ, but the general principles of analysis are the same.

The question chosen to be explored is: 'To what extent is a man's occupation determined by his father's?' This is perhaps one of the central questions in the study of social mobility. A legitimate preliminary question is: 'Why only men?' The simple answer is 'because our society is patriarchal, and the patriarchy pervades sociology just as it does other spheres of life, so that this survey doesn't ask about the respondent's mother's work'.

The first command to SPSS is to fetch the General Social Survey: thus

get file 'gss'.

A small subset of the data is provided as an example data set with the SPSS program, but variables from the full survey have been chosen. In creating an SPSS-readable file, NORC provided standard variable names, and the two principal variables used here are called occ and PAOCC16.

The first of these is formed by asking an elaborate series of questions designed to find out exactly what job the respondent does (or did, if they are retired), and then classifying every employed person into one of nearly 1,000 occupational categories defined by the US Bureau of the Census. The second is formed in the same way, except that the questions are asked about the respondent's father 'While you were growing up' ; the mnemonic name suggests that this means 'When you were about 16'.

Social mobility usually means occupational mobility, which in turn means roughly 'having a job of a different status from your father'. A number of different status rankings have been suggested, but the simplest possible one, which is adopted here, simply differentiates between non-manual and manual occupations. Census codes 1 to 399 are non-manual occupations; 400 to 995 are manual. So in order to restrict the analysis to men (the variable SEX is here coded 1, male and 2, female) and then divide the occupation variables into two groups, the following was typed in

```
select if (SEX = 1).
recode OCC, PAOCC16
      (0 thru 399 = 1)
      (400 thru 995 = 2).
```

SPSS will print helpful labels on output tables, provided it 'knows' what labels to print. So the program was given the necessary information by typing in

```
value labels OCC, PAOCC16
      1 'non-manual'
      2 'manual'.
```

Finally, an instruction was typed in to generate the table of results:

```
crosstabs tables = OCC by PAOCC16
      /cells = count, column.
```

The first line specifies the variables to be used in forming the table. The only thing that needs attention is the order of mentioning the variables. The customary procedure is to ask if we can establish a causal order between the variables. Here it is straightforward: a father's job can influence his son's, but not vice versa (except, no doubt, in a few eccentric cases where, for instance, junior becomes a tennis star or rock singer and takes on Dad as manager). This being so, OCC, which is dependent on PAOCC16, is called the **dependent variable**, while PAOCC16 is referred to as the **independent** variable. Then the order is conventionally *dependent* by *independent*, which SPSS interprets as instructions to lay out the table as it appears in Figure 12.4, that is, with the dependent variable as the rows and the independent as the columns.

The second line, beginning with the '/' symbol (called 'slash' by computer users) is a subcommand: what it does will be explained in a moment.

OCC   RESP:S CENSUS OCCUPATION CODE
by PAOCC16   FATHER:S CENSUS OCCUPATION CODE
                PAOCC16   Page 1 of 1

Count Col Pct		non-manual	manual	Row
OCC		1	2	Total
non-manual	1	194 63.4	248 27.4	442 36.5
manual	2	112 36.6	656 72.6	768 63.5
Column Total		306 25.3	904 74.7	1210 100.0

Figure 12.4   *Respondent's occupation by father's occupation*

Figure 12.4 is a typical cross-tabulation as produced by SPSS. To understand the table we must first name the parts. The total number of 'cases' (in this context, people) on which the table is based is printed at the bottom right: it is 1,210. Above this are the numbers in each of the categories of the variable that defines the rows of the table: there are 768 respondents with manual occupations and 442 with non-manual jobs. The relative numbers are given, too, in the form of percentages: 63.5 per cent of respondents are manual workers. The column totals give the corresponding numbers for the respondents' fathers.

The first substantial point to notice is that the respondents are more likely to be in a non-manual occupation than their fathers were. This is an example of structural mobility: the occupational structure has changed, so necessarily some sons must be in a different occupational group than their fathers. However, this could have been discovered by examining the simple frequency distributions, without arranging them in this sort of table. Here we see why those simple distributions are called marginals: they appear in the margins of a cross-tabulation.

The special interest of a table of this sort comes when we examine the conditional distributions: the distributions of one variable under particular conditions of the other. Here, we are interested in the distribution of respondents' occupations under different conditions of the fathers' occupations. The findings are clearest in terms of the percentages. Specifically, among the 306 respondents whose fathers had non-manual jobs, 112, or 36.6 per cent, were in manual occupations and therefore the remainder, 63.4 per cent, were in non-manual jobs. On the other hand, if the father was in a manual job there was a 72.6 per cent chance that the respondent would be a manual worker, too, and only a 27.4 per cent chance that he would be in a non-manual job.

The subcommand /cells count, column can now be explained: it means 'each cell is to contain a count of the number of respondents with that combination of characteristics, together with that number expressed as a percentage of the column total'.

This is already quite a lot to take in, so we can concentrate on just two numbers: for manual fathers 72.6 per cent of their sons were in manual jobs; for non-manual fathers it was 36.6 per cent. An even simpler summary might be: the chance of being in a manual job was 36 per cent (i.e. 72.6 − 36.6) greater for sons of manual workers. Notice that it does not matter which row you choose: 63.4 − 27.4 = 36, just as before. In bigger tables (with more rows and columns) it is impossible to summarise the findings quite so simply, but in a 2 × 2 (two rows and two columns) table the standard procedure can be summed up as follows.

- If possible, decide on the causal ordering of your variables.
- Then tell your data analysis program to produce a table of the dependent variable against the independent variable.
- Ask for column percentages.
- Compare a pair of percentages in the same row.

12.2.3 Interpreting the figures

What do these figures really mean? Simply that your father's occupation seems to have a substantial influence on your own, at least if you are an American man. One other reservation is necessary: we have only sample data, but we want to be able to make statements about the population as a whole. The justification for doing this – the general idea is called **statistical inference** – is a complicated one, and cannot really be dealt with in less than a whole book, although some of the issues were introduced in chapter 5; some suggestions for further reading are given at the end of this chapter. It is sufficient to say here that it can be proven that, provided we really have got a random sample, our best guess for any percentage in the population is the corresponding sample percentage: in the United States as a whole, as in this table, about 63.5 per cent of all men are in manual jobs. Why 'about' ? Because if we took another sample just as carefully we would not be surprised to find a slightly different set of numbers, simply because of random sampling variability. The obvious consequence of this is that we should not draw strong conclusions from small differences based on small samples. Here, though, we have a reasonably large sample (the public opinion polls whose results are discussed with such interest by politicians are typically based on only 1,000 interviews or so), and the difference is very large, so common sense suggests that the influence must be real, even if not necessarily of precisely the magnitude that we have found.

What about 'provided we really have got a random sample' ? Almost certainly we have not. NORC designs its sampling procedure to produce a random sample, but a problem with all survey research is non-response: people who were included in the sample design but not actually interviewed, because they were never at home when the interviewer called, or because they thought the details of their life were no business of the survey organisation's (see section 5.9). These non-respondents are almost bound to be different in interesting but often unknowable ways from those who did take part. At best, then, we have a random sample of those adult male Americans who are not always out and who are not hostile to pollsters. This must introduce some distortion into the results, which is another reason for caution, and which is potentially more dangerous than the intrinsic sample-to-sample variability that the theory of statistical inference is all about.

This all appears very pessimistic about survey methods. Years of experience by thousands of researchers suggest that we get more useful results than we are perhaps entitled to expect. So from this point on the results still to be presented in this chapter will be interpreted without constantly worrying about what may have gone wrong.

12.2.4   Correlation and causation

Let us consider another interesting question. To what extent are we justified in making causal statements, such as that one's occupational status is influenced by one's father's, on the basis of statistical findings alone? The simple answer is that we are not. For instance, there is no statistical reason why we should not consider PAOCC16 as the dependent variable and OCC as the independent. The reason this has not been done so far is that there is a good non-statistical reason against it: a father's occupation 'happens' before his son's, and it is universally accepted that (in this explanatory paradigm) an effect cannot precede its cause. So although OCC cannot (except exceptionally) influence PAOCC16, PAOCC16 can influence OCC. 'Can', not 'must'. Another possibility is that both may be influenced by a third variable.

A good example of this is the discovery of a marked correlation between the price of rum in Barbados and the level of Methodist ministers' salaries: in any given year either both are high or both are low. There are two simple explanations of this, according to what you think the causal direction is. One says that ministers have a (secret) addiction to rum; when they get a pay rise they can afford to buy more liquor, and the price goes up in response to the increased demand, as can be predicted from elementary economics. The alternative version is even more conspiratorial: the Methodist Church is secretly financed by the distillers of rum and when the distillers' finances improve they can afford to give a bigger subvention.

You should not read on without trying to find a more sensible explanation in terms of a third variable which could reasonably be expected to influence both salaries and rum prices. Yes, it is general price levels, or the result of inflation. Over time the value of money falls, so both the price of rum and ministers' salaries have to rise to compensate. Here

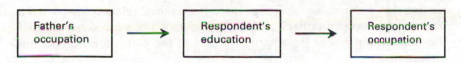

Figure 12.5   *Causal model to explain occupational mobility*

general price level is referred to as the **antecedent** variable that accounts for the primary relationship between the price of rum and salary.

In other circumstances it is useful to introduce a third variable, not in order to explain away the primary relationship, but in order to explain how it works, and this will be done in the case of the occupational mobility table. It would be quite legitimate to look for an antecedent variable, but for present purposes it is better to think about an **intervening** variable. This time we start by assuming for the time being that a father's occupation really does influence the son's, and ask how it exerts that influence. The two possible general answers are, first, that the influence is direct (a nepotistic mechanism) or, second, that some third variable acts as a causal link.

Of course, nepotism does operate to some extent. A large proportion of 'company directors' get their start from their father's position. The best way to get to be a farmer, or a doctor, or even a docker may still be to arrange to be born to a father in the same line of work. But these are special cases, which cover only a relatively small number of workers. So it may make more sense instead to look for a third factor which is influenced by a father's occupation and in turn influences the son's. An obvious candidate is education. A father in a higher status job is likely to improve his son's educational chances in a number of ways: by paying for private schooling, or by moving house to a good school district, or just by knowing the ropes and pushing hard. And, of course, on the whole, the better the son's education the higher the status of his eventual job. Figure 12.5 represents the causal model implied by this.

In an ideal world (ideal from the point of view of a power-crazy social scientist, that is) we would set up a randomised trial to check this idea. A cohort of children would be assigned to schools at random, so that the causal flow would be interrupted: father's occupation would no longer influence education, so that this path would no longer be available for transmitting an effect from father's job to son's job. If this were indeed the only path through which father's occupation influenced son's, then the apparent effect of PAOCC16 on OCC would disappear; if other paths were operating then the effect would persist.

Alas, such a research design is hardly practicable. However, we can simulate at least part of what it implies. Instead of artificially assigning children to schools at random we can examine subgroups in which there is naturally no variation in schooling. If there is no variation then, necessarily, there can be no covariation, so the causal flow is interrupted. Then, if we find that within these subgroups there is a reduced relationship (or even none at all) between father's and son's occupation, we can conclude that the relationship was at least partly a result of the path via differences in education.

To do this with existing survey data we tell SPSS to repeat the original tabulation within all education level groups – those who had one year of schooling separated from those with two years, three years, etc. (This seems to assume that everyone completes a whole number of years at school, which is no doubt not true, but the inaccuracy seems unlikely to be of crucial importance.) With any practicable sample size this will not quite work, because the sample will have to be divided across too many subgroups, so we compromise by using broader education categories. In this example a compromise is made by using only three categories and, since these are US data, the men are divided into those who had at least some college education, those who have a high school diploma but no more, and those who did not graduate from high school. Where to make that split will depend on what the investigator knows of important thresholds in the local education system.

First, then, it was necessary to create my education variable. You have already seen the distribution of the variable, DEGREE (Figure 12.1). The three highest categories contained quite small numbers of men, so it was decided to group them into a single one. The following SPSS commands did the grouping, relabelled the variable, and requested the necessary tables:

```
recode DEGREE
     (0 = 0)
     (1 = 1)
     (2 thru 4 = 2).
value labels DEGREE
     0 '< high school'
     1 'high school'
     2 'college'.
crosstabs tables OCC by PAOCC16 by DEGREE
     /cells = count column.
```

The 'crosstabs' command produces an OCC by PAOCC16 table for every category of degree: three separate tables in each of which education is 'held constant'. It may help to think of this as a three-dimensional table: a stack of two-dimensional tables, in which the stacking axis is the third variable. What you actually get is Figure 12.6.

What are we to make of this? First, note a caveat: some of these conditional tables are rather short of cases, especially in certain subgroups. In particular, there are only 42 non-manual fathers in the table of non high school graduates. This really means that we should be quite cautious about drawing firm conclusions. Having made this point, we shall put it on one side.

First, some further points of terminology. The variable DEGREE is called the **control variable**, and we are investigating the relationship between

OCC   RESP:S CENSUS OCCUPATION CODE
by PAOCC16   FATHER:S CENSUS OCCUPATION CODE
Controlling for..
DEGREE   HIGHEST DEGREE,RESP   Value = < high school
         PAOCC16   Page 1 of 1

OCC	Count Col Pct	non-manual 1	manual 2	Row Total
1 non-manual		10 23.8	40 10.7	50 12.0
2 manual		32 76.2	334 89.3	366 88.0
	Column Total	42 10.1	374 89.9	416 100.0

OCC   RESP:S CENSUS OCCUPATION CODE
by PAOCC16   FATHER:S CENSUS OCCUPATION CODE
Controlling for ..
DEGREE   HIGHEST DEGREE,RESP   Value = 1 high school
         PAOCC16   Page 1 of 1

OCC	Count Col Pct	non-manual 1	manual 2	Row Total
1 non-manual		64 50.0	104 25.9	168 31.7
2 manual		64 50.0	298 74.1	362 68.3
	Column Total	128 24.2	402 75.8	530 100.0

OCC   RESP:S CENSUS OCCUPATION CODE
by PAOCC16   FATHER:S CENSUS OCCUPATION CODE
Controlling for ..
DEGREE   HIGHEST DEGREE,RESP   Value = 2 college
         PAOCC16   Page 1 of 1

OCC	Count Col Pct	non-manual 1	manual 2	Row Total
1 non-manual		120 88.2	104 83.9	224 86.2
2 manual		16 11.8	20 16.1	36 13.8
	Column Total	136 52.3	124 47.7	260 100.0

Figure 12.6 *Respondent's occupation by father's occupation controlling for education*

occupation and father's occupation **controlling** for education. You will recall that the distribution of OCC on its own is called the marginal distribution, while the distributions of OCC within categories of PAOCC16 are called the conditional distributions. By analogy the original OCC by PAOCC16 table is called a **marginal table**, and the three new tables are called **conditional tables**: they show the relationship between OCC and PAOCC16 under specific conditions of DEGREE. Similarly, we sometimes speak of marginal and conditional relationships; and the process of **elaborating** a table, as it is classically called, consists in essence of comparing a marginal relationship with its conditional counterparts. Sometimes the several conditional associations are summarised into a single **partial association**; in practice this is done by calculations based on the **correlation coefficients** rather than by working on the conditional tables.

The marginal association here can best be summarised by the percentage difference already established: 36.6. In the marginal table it really did not matter (apart, perhaps, from convenience in the wording of the verbal description of the findings) which row we chose to make the comparison. Now, however, it is important that we be consistent with that earlier decision: since we used the second row of the table and subtracted the first column from the second we must treat each conditional table in the same way; otherwise we might not notice if the sign of the difference (positive or negative) changes between marginal and conditional tables. In practice this will seldom happen, but it would not do to miss it.

So we find the same percentage difference in each conditional table, and get respectively

$89.3 - 76.2 = 13.1$

$74.1 - 50.0 = 24.1$

$16.1 - 11.8 = 4.3.$

The sign does, in fact, remain positive, so in every conditional table there is still a tendency for manual fathers to have manual sons. However, in every case the conditional association is weaker than the marginal 36.6. So the overall conclusion is that when education is held constant the relationship between father's and son's occupation is substantially weaker. A plausible causal interpretation is that, if non-manual fathers were not able to get a better education for their sons, there would be greater intergenerational mobility. But beware: there may be other variables involved whose inclusion in the analysis would lead to a quite different conclusion – for instance, IQ is quite highly correlated with education, and it is consistent with the results obtained here (though we have no direct evidence whatsoever) that non-manual fathers tend to have genetically brighter sons, who get better education through meritocratic selection rather than through father's efforts. (For an attempt to throw some light on this question, see Jencks (1973).)

Of course, almost as obvious as the difference between marginal and conditional associations is the variation *among* conditional associations, a phenomenon known in the traditional literature as **specification**, because education specifies the conditions that determine whether and to what extent the primary relationship holds. (In more recent literature, the term **interaction** is used in exactly the same sense.) In the present example, the association remains quite strong among those who just graduated from high school (the second conditional table), but is considerably weaker in the other two, especially among those who have some college education. An interpretation of this would be along the following lines.

- Without a high school diploma having a non-manual father does not help very much.
- Once you have a college education a manual father is no longer an important handicap.
- If you are in the middle band of education your father's occupation can have more influence.

It has to be recognised that all this is at best true only in terms of the rather crude educational and occupational classifications that have been used. These have been to an extent necessitated by the rate at which multidimensional tables can generate cells if they have too many categories per variable, but a measure of education which fails to take account of the *quality*, both real and perceived, of the school is hard to justify as a basis for 'holding constant'. Probably if a better measure of education were available the conditional associations would be even weaker – but the opposite is possible.

The problem of too many cells can sometimes be solved by using a different statistical method (multiple regression, for instance); the problem of measurement demands a constant alertness on the part of the researcher, so that measures can be developed that more closely approximate the often carefully explicated theoretical constructs. But the basic logic of causal analysis remains the same however technically advanced the methods used to implement it.

12.3   A general approach to survey analysis

In the words of Poul Anderson, the science fiction writer, 'there is no situation, however complex, which on careful examination does not become more complex'. The main application of this idea to the analysis of survey data is that the world is multivariate: every effect has not one but several causes. So to find a relationship between two variables is not the end but little more than the beginning of the analysis. It is the researcher's job to be sceptical about the causal interpretation that might be made from such a relationship, to think carefully, in a theoretically sensitive way, about what 'nuisance factors' might be involved in the system of variables, and to find ways of testing alternative explanatory hypotheses. The approach exemplified in this chapter has a long and distinguished history, and incorporates the logical principles – in particular the idea of holding constant the suspected nuisance factors – which underlie more statistically advanced methods, such as multiple regression and loglinear analysis.

12.4   Project

If you have access to a computer with almost any version of SPSS you will almost certainly be able to use the small subset of the General Social Survey which is included with the package. Ask your local SPSS coordinator how to do this, and how to get a frequency count for all the variables. Having got this far, browse through the variables until you find one that looks interesting as a dependent variable: you could start with *satjob*, *hapmar* or *life* (roughly satisfaction with job, marriage and life generally). Try to find out what sort of people are happiest with their lot. What marital status is most conducive to general life satisfaction? What truth is there in the assertion that men get more out of marriage than women? All these questions can be addressed by cross-tabulating a satisfaction variable by one or more background factors, possibly after recoding.

12.5   Further reading

An excellent introduction to SPSS/PC, which will also get you started in statistics, is *The SPSS Guide to Data Analysis for SPSS/PC+*, by Marija J. Norusis (1988). Norusis has also written several other more advanced books on SPSS and on statistics. Her *SPSS/PC+ Advanced Statistics* (Norusis, 1991) provides a clear, relatively non-technical explanation of, for instance, multiple regression and loglinear analysis, which has the advantage of being directly related to the details of the program printout.

There must be hundreds of books on statistical methods for social scientists, but relatively few of them deal adequately with cross-tabulation methods. By all means browse through the shelves of your library and bookshop; one of the best is Loether and McTavish (1992). Marsh (1988) provides an accessible introduction to exploratory data analysis.

A very clear treatment of survey methods in general, from problem formulation to finished report, is to be found in De Vaus (1990).

Finally, when you get seriously interested in quantitative methods, the publishers Sage have a comprehensive series of short books called *Quantitative Applications in the Social Sciences* which is an excellent starting point.

13 Analysing other researchers' data

Michael Procter

Contents

Having read the earlier chapters you have perhaps realised by this point that to use the word 'data' is something of a misnomer. *Data* is the Latin word for 'things given'; it might be more appropriate to call it (it collectively, or them, if you are thinking about individual items of information) *capta*: 'things taken', or, indeed, wrested with a great deal of effort from a recalcitrant social world.

In ethnographic research that effort is often entirely expended by the lone researcher, because the total immersion in the research act is essential to its success. Professional survey research is practically always on too large a scale for one or two people to carry out the data collection without help, and the effort is usually translated into payment to a survey organisation, or at least to a sizeable force of directly employed interviewers. Of course, this restricts the data that can be collected to the kind that can be handled in the context of a structured interview, but all research designs involve compromises. The funds for such a study come typically from a charitable foundation or from a government research council, and we are talking serious money here: say £50 per interview as an order-of-magnitude figure; or £900 to have one question included in the OPCS Omnibus Survey.

It is a truism of social research that almost all data are seriously underanalysed: unless the data collection is tightly designed to test a specific hypothesis the original researcher will explore only a fraction of its potential. (The reason for this is that it is seldom possible to state precise hypotheses in a discipline whose theories are relatively weakly structured, and the data collection has therefore to be planned to cover a wide range of rather imprecise ideas.) In ethnography it is difficult for further analysis to be delegated, just as the fieldwork cannot easily be farmed out. Survey data, however, are rather easier for an adoptive researcher to understand almost as well as the natural parent – or, indeed, parents, because much survey research is in any case planned and executed in the first place by several researchers rather than one.

For this reason, secondary analysis of survey data is fast growing in importance. Most developed countries have centrally funded data archives, in which are deposited the data from hundreds or thousands of surveys, in order that they may be reanalysed by other researchers who have new ideas to test out on the old data. The data are often available at no cost (apart, perhaps, from a small fee to cover the costs of distribution) and with minimal restrictions.

In this way, then, Jay Ginn, whose contribution follows this chapter (Exemplar C), was able to get access to the UK government's General Household Survey (GHS), an annual survey of all the members of around 10,000 households, a data set which virtually no researcher could imagine generating for themselves.

13.1   The pros and cons of secondary analysis

It may be helpful to summarise here the advantages and limitations of secondary analysis, even though many of these points will also be made later. As you might expect, the overall conclusion is in favour of this methodology, but a number of warnings are offered.

Surely the most obvious advantage of secondary analysis is **cost**. For many researchers there is no possibility of obtaining funding at the level required for survey work.

In addition, it is argued, a great deal of **time** can be saved. First, if the data already exist, then new analysts can get to work almost as soon as they think of the idea, instead of having to face years of preparation and fieldwork if they are to be responsible for their own data collection. Second, if one is primarily employed as a teacher, as most academic researchers are, one may never be able to find the time to run one's own project from start to finish – unless one can cut out a whole section of the work by starting at the point where the data have been collected. Similar considerations apply to student researchers, who have, in addition, externally imposed deadlines to cope with.

On the other hand, it cannot be denied that a rather rosy picture has just been painted. The process of obtaining the data and knocking them into shape on one's own computer can take many months and, though this is unlikely ever to approach the time needed to carry out a substantial survey in the field, it can still sometimes be more time than is allowed by, for instance, an undergraduate dissertation deadline. Probably the best advice is not to commit oneself to this form of research without first discussing its pitfalls with a more experienced adviser.

At its best, the **quality** of data obtained in this way is likely to be higher than a relatively inexperienced researcher can hope to obtain unaided. Government survey organisations, in particular, have great expertise in their chosen method, and because their clients are usually government departments they can often bring to bear the political pressure that is needed to legitimise the relatively expensive technology they employ: nationally representative probability samples, highly trained and closely supervised interviewers, the necessary sequence of pilot studies, etc.

On the other hand, all this technical excellence is completely beside the point if the questions asked are not relevant to your research problem. There is always a temptation for the subject of research to be determined by what is convenient rather than by what is scientifically important, and the balance of effort between data collection and data analysis makes this particularly dangerous in planning secondary analysis.

Widely used data sets often receive special support from the agency through which they are made available. For instance, in the United Kingdom the Economic and Social Research Council (ESRC) Data Archive runs a variety of 'data use' workshops for people working on material such as the General Household Survey and the National Child Development Study. These can be wonderful opportunities for lone researchers to get the intellectual support they need, and especially for beginners to benefit from the often uncodified wisdom of more experienced workers.

Even though the original purpose of a survey may not have been connected with the particular subgroup you wish to focus on, sample sizes are often so large that otherwise **inaccessible populations** can be reached, especially if it is legitimate to merge successive years' samples. For instance, Hornsby-Smith and Dale (1988) were able to study recent Irish immigrants to the United Kingdom in this way. To collect their own data, they would first have had to obtain a list from which to sample, a substantial project in itself.

However, there can be pitfalls in the **sample design**, into which one would be unlikely to fall in planning the project from scratch. To cite a classic example, the UK Family Expenditure Survey, which is a survey of private households and thus excludes people living in pubs and bars, has proved to be entirely inappropriate as a source of information about alcohol consumption.

It is often unrealistic for a researcher, especially a relatively junior one, to plan to collect data over a period of years, if only because one's career requires that one 'publish or perish' over a relatively short **time span**. And yet data collected over an extended period of time is often precisely what is required by the logic of the research problem. For instance, a cross-sectional analysis (in which all the data are collected at one point in time) shows that heavy drinkers are healthier than light drinkers and teetotallers. To some extent the relationship can be clarified (using the approach outlined in the previous chapter) by showing that drinking generally declines with age, for the most part, because of life cycle changes, and that of course older people tend to be less healthy. However, until we follow the same individuals through time we fail to realise that reduction in drinking often follows and, presumably, is a result of declining health rather than preceding and causing it.

The solution may be to make use of an existing **longitudinal** data set, so that the waiting period has already taken place when the researcher gets to work.

Social researchers have long been concerned about a variety of **ethical issues** raised by their research. Many of these issues are concerned with the intrusive nature of research on individuals. Secondary analysts might therefore think that, since they are not directly involved in data collection, they are exempt from such concerns. This is not so. There is not sufficient space here to attempt a full discussion of the ethical problems faced in secondary analysis (see Dale et al., 1988), but mention should be made of the continued need for maintaining anonymity – perhaps even more important than in the primary analysis, because the respondents are not in general aware of the uses to which their answers will be put in subsequent work. In practice responsible researchers will ensure anonymity when depositing their data at the data archive, and secondary analysts will have the necessary restrictions imposed on them, but they should remain aware of their responsibilities in this respect.

13.2   Descriptive and explanatory research

When considering the kinds of research which give rise to data that may be subsequently made available for secondary analysis, an important general distinction to make is that between descriptive and explanatory designs (though, like most distinctions of this kind, it is far from watertight).

A **descriptive** research design is intended to provide an accurate factual characterisation of its subjects. For instance, the General Household Survey (OPCS, 1990) supplies the Department of the Environment with annual estimates of the extent of overcrowding in housing, including its variation across region, and subdivided by family type (such as whether or not small children are involved). If these estimates are to be useful it is obviously important that the sample should be nationally and regionally representative.

On the other hand, although Brown and Harris (1978) in their famous study, *The Social Origins of Depression*, could not avoid producing basic descriptive information about their sample, they did not attempt to use a nationally representative sample design and concentrated instead on interviewing women in social circumstances which were thought, on prior theoretical grounds, to be relevant to an **explanation** of depression. Implicit here (though not always stated in quite such bald terms) is a crucial assumption: that the causal laws which link traumatic life events to clinical depression in the absence of protective social circumstances such as the support of a partner are broadly invariant, at least within a modern urban setting. If this assumption is true, the results could be replicated in a wide range of locations other than Camberwell in South London. Of course, the essence of an assumption is that it is not adequately supported by direct evidence; but this particular belief in one form or another underpins almost all research, in astrophysics as much as in sociology.

Researchers in general, and secondary analysts in particular, are seldom content with merely descriptive conclusions, and a good deal of the challenge of secondary analysis lies in squeezing an ostensibly descriptive data set until it yields up explanatory possibilities. Jay Ginn gives a full account of such an analysis in Exemplar C which follows this chapter.

13.3   Data sources

13.3.1   Government data

An important source of high quality data is government work in many forms. For the most part those discussed here will be UK data sets, but equivalent materials are available in many industrialised countries.

The decennial Census of Population gives rise to a number of data sets. Until recently this has been restricted to data aggregated at various levels: parliamentary constituency, enumeration district, etc. Data in this form are known as the **small area statistics**. Analysis of such material requires specialised software (data are initially extracted by a package called SASPAC before conventional statistical analysis) and, indeed, specialised skills. With data in this form it is possible to find out, for instance, how *rate* of owner occupation differs across areas of the country. However, to preserve confidentiality no information about individuals' housing tenure is available.

Individual data (sometimes in this context called **microdata**) from the

Census have been made available in a restricted way. A one-in-four sample from the files of the 1971 Census was chosen, and additional information added to the records of the selected individuals by tracking them through the registration of deaths and through certain statutory health registration systems. Because the data are continually updated they represent a particularly powerful resource. However, because of the impossibility of assuring perfect anonymity the data cannot be released to individuals. Instead, approved researchers specify the analyses required for a particular project, and these are carried out by a special service made available through City University in London. In this way individual information is hidden in the summary statistics that come out of the analysis.

The UK Census is the responsibility of the Office of Population Censuses and Surveys (OPCS) which, as the name implies, also carries out surveys. These can conveniently be divided into two categories: continuous and ad hoc.

The most important example of a **continuous survey** is the General Household Survey (GHS). The GHS has been carried out every year since 1971. The basic unit of analysis, as the title implies, is the household: roughly, people living at the same address who share catering. Most commonly they are members of the same family, although a household may also include any lodgers and servants. The contents of the interview are mainly determined by the interests of government departments – health, housing, education, employment, etc. Because the data are 'hierarchical', so that, for example, a household consists of one or more people, each person's record contains details of a variable number (which may be zero) of visits to the doctor, and so forth, there are special analytical problems, which will be discussed in section 13.6.2.

The OPCS uses the term **ad hoc surveys** to designate studies which, in contrast with the GHS, are carried out just once, in response to a specific request from a client government department. Important examples include the Women and Employment Survey (Martin and Roberts, 1984) and the Family Formation Survey (Dunnell, 1979).

13.3.2 Academic sources

A great deal of data are collected by academic social scientists. There would be very little point in doing this kind of work without the assumption that the findings will be communicated, mainly through the medium of books, articles in academic journals, and conference papers (see chapter 16). But this idea is now extended, at least in the case of survey research, to making the raw data available to other competent researchers, and it is usually deposited at the national data archive. So when you read an account of survey-based research and wonder why the researcher did not analyse it differently, it may be possible for you to contact the archive and see if the data are available for reanalysis.

A special case is the growing body of data sets collected specifically in order to make them available for secondary analysis. The first example of this was the General Social Survey (GSS) of the National Opinion Research Center at Chicago. This project was first planned at the end of the 1960s by social scientists representing the entire US academic community, who designed an interview covering a wide range of factual and attitudinal questions, many of them taken from classic studies which were thought worth replicating. One example of this is Stouffer's series of civil liberties studies (Stouffer, 1963), carried out at the time of the McCarthy witch-hunts. It is extremely illuminating to be able to compare the results obtained in successive years with the original findings. The GSS has been carried out every year since 1971, and its director, James A. Davis, has gone as a 'missionary' to other national survey agencies with the result that the International Social Survey Programme (ISSP) now covers around a dozen countries. As well as a common core of mainly factual questions which appear annually, every year a special theme is chosen to occupy a section of the interview – examples have so far included the role of government, social support networks, and religion.

The ISSP is not the only cross-national project: within Europe there is the annual Eurobarometer series; and the European Values System Study Group has carried out surveys in 1981 and 1990, initially with data collection in most of the member countries of the European Community, but subsequently spreading to a number of other countries, including the United States, so that missionary work is operating in both directions.

13.4 Getting your data

The first place to try to obtain data is your national Data Archive; in the United Kingdom this is located at the University of Essex. It holds mainly UK data, but, like other national archives, it has reciprocal arrangements which will allow you to obtain data held in other countries. For instance, UK researchers can obtain data via their own Data Archive from the ICPSR archive in the United States and the Zentralarchiv in Germany.

Archives all publish catalogues of their holdings, and this should be your starting point. In general terms, the catalogue will provide information for each dataset including

- The size and design of the sample
- The broad areas covered by the interview, possibly with considerable detail on the questions asked
- The availability of the data, and information about restrictions on use
- The format in which the data is available, including an SPSS self-describing system file
- Availability of detailed documentation, including the interview

schedule and instructions to interviewers and coders, and the costs of
these
- A brief bibliography of published work resulting from the data
- How to order the data, including the physical medium (disk format,
  etc.) and costs.

Having drawn up a shortlist of interesting data sets you should probably
not make a final decision without obtaining more detailed information of
the kind just mentioned, for which you will typically have to pay the cost of
photocopying and postage. Finally you order the chosen file, which may be
sent to you in the form of magnetic disks (or tape, if it is to be used on a
mainframe computer) or sent electronically via a data network. You will be
asked for information about the kind of computing hardware on which the
data are to be analysed, because several mutually incompatible formats are
in common use. The archive will normally be equipped to provide data in
any reasonable format that its customers ask for. Charging arrangements
vary, but academic users seldom have to pay more than the actual cost of
the disk or tape and postage.

13.5   Conceptualising in secondary analysis

What has been discussed so far is essentially mechanical stuff. The real
challenge in secondary analysis lies in finding ways of forcing the data,
collected by someone else, quite often with entirely different theoretical
and analytical intentions, to answer your questions.

According to Stewart (1984) a secondary analyst should try to get
answers to the following questions about the data.

- What was the purpose of the original study? Was it designed around a
  specific hypothesis which limits its usefulness for a researcher with
  different ideas?
- What information was collected? Were key variables defined in such a
  way as to be compatible with the new analyst's ideas?
- What was the sample design and what sample was actually achieved? Is
  it adequately representative of those groups that play a key part in the
  new researcher's theory?
- What are the credentials of the data? Can the original researchers be
  assumed to be competent? What evidence is available about the
  reliability and validity of the data?
- When were they collected? Is topicality important, or is it reasonable to
  assume that the relationships being studied are relatively invariant
  across time?
- Are the data nationally representative? Is this crucial, or is it reasonable to assume, as under the last point, that the relationships hold
  across a wide range of geographical localities?

Type of variable	Example of variable	Description
ABSOLUTE	age; sex; region; marital status; housing tenure	Absolute variables do not need to be derived; they exist as direct answers to survey questions
SUMMARY	average hourly pay; attitude score derived from a number of individual items; quality of housing score	Summarises the information from a number of existing variables by means of an arithmetic operation
CONSTRUCTED	typology of labour market status; typology of housing tenure	Combines information on a number of variables to represent a concept not in the original data set
COMPARATIVE	income quartile by comparison with all in sample, either individual or household	Uses information from one variable to establish a comparative ranking on that variable for each case

Figure 13.1   *Types of variables that may be used with secondary data*

13.5.1   Derived variables

Whether working with your own or someone else's survey it will almost always be necessary to recast the data in order to represent concepts not considered at the time the interview schedule was designed. Indeed, questions are often included in the full knowledge that answers will need some preliminary processing before the statistical analysis can be tackled. Dale et al. (1988: 142) offer a typology of variables, shown in Figure 13.1.

The mechanics of deriving the new variables using SPSS (a typical survey analysis program) are hinted at in chapter 12, under the general heading of data management. Two facilities are mentioned in that chapter: the ability to select a subset of cases (not really a way of defining new variables, but nevertheless important when theory requires disaggregating the sample into distinct subgroups); and the recode command for amalgamating categories. Two other commands will be illustrated, again using SPSS for the examples, although the principles are similar for all survey analysis programs.

Sometimes it is necessary to combine variables according to an arithmetic formula. The compute command is the way to do it. For instance, suppose each respondent has been asked a series of questions about their income from various sources, such as main employment, supplementary work ('moonlighting'), lodgers, investment income, occupational pension and welfare benefits, all of which have been read into the data file under names chosen to be relatively easy to remember. At certain points in the subsequent analysis the details about the sources of income may be unimportant, and the analyst only needs to know the total income. A command like the following might be needed:

```
compute totinc = empinc + mooninc + lodginc + invinc +
    pensinc + welfinc.
```

All kinds of complications can be imagined, which might require refinements in the working. For instance, the various items might be paid at different intervals: weekly rent, monthly salary and quarterly dividends. Perhaps the solution would be to begin by multiplying weekly amounts by 13 and monthly payments by 3, so that each becomes a quarterly amount. Then the total can be divided by the appropriate value to bring it back to the standard interval – divide it by 3 to make all the totals equivalent to a monthly amount. Another common problem is that if, for instance, it has already been established that the respondent has no lodgers, the question about income from this source will not have been asked, and the missing value code will have been applied. Now the built-in rule that SPSS follows is for the compute command to ignore any case which includes missing data (otherwise it might do arithmetic with perfect precision on what in the context are nonsense values, such as 99, which have been chosen to flag missing observations). Since practically no respondents will have income under every single heading, almost everyone will be eliminated from the calculations. To avoid this, missing values must be recoded to zero before the compute command – while ensuring that anyone for whom an item is really unknown is treated differently.

You can see that this requires a good deal of careful and logical thought. Because it is easy to make errors in defining new variables, it is very good practice to use the SPSS list command, which can be set to print out the variables involved for the first 20 cases or so, in order that the analyst can check 'by hand' that the data modifications have been done in the way intended. In the present example, one can check that the various income items really do add up to the value of the newly derived variable.

The other command to be mentioned is in effect a conditional compute, though it is simply called if. This allows a formula to be applied to a specified subgroup of cases. For instance, in the United Kingdom, men (coded sex = 1 in a hypothetical survey) may claim their government pension from the age of 65, while women (coded sex = 2) can get theirs at 60. To define a new variable which codes each respondent as being of pensionable age or not, the following sequence is necessary:

```
compute pension = 0.
if ((sex = 1 and age > 64) or
    (sex = 2 and age > 59))
    pension = 1.
value labels pension
    1 'yes'
    0 'no'.
```

You can see that the first part of the if command sets conditions in just the same way as select if, but then instead of merely filtering out the specified cases, it applies a formula to them. Before that can be done the compute command **initializes** the new variable PENSION by setting it to zero for everyone. Then, as each case in turn is processed by the if command, it is checked against the complex condition. If the current case is either male and over 64 or female and over 59 then PENSION is reset to one; otherwise it remains at zero. Finally, the value labels command ensures that tables using this new variable will be correctly labelled.

You will have noticed that combinations of conditions may be assembled by using parentheses. Such combinations may become very complicated, in which case it is especially useful to list a few cases to check that the derivation has worked correctly.

13.5.2 Multi-level analysis

Statistical analysis is almost always carried out on a rectangular table of numbers, in which each **observation** (case, respondent, subject, etc.) occupies a given **row**, and each **variable** (characteristic, sometimes corresponding to a single question) occupies a **column**. So, to take a very simple example, the percentage of respondents saying they vote Green would be found by counting the total number of individuals with a non-missing value in the vote column, counting the number who are coded with the value representing Greens, dividing the second count into the first and multiplying by 100. At the next higher level of complexity, the relationship between vote and gender would be explored by counting combinations of codes in those two columns. This rectangular format (sometimes known as a **flat file**) is not, however, always the form in which the data are collected.

The General Household Survey is one counter-example. The sample design of the GHS is, like almost any large, nationally representative study, a complex multistage one, but this gives rise to no problems in the analysis (except that the usual formula for the standard error has to be modified by the design effect – see chapter 5). The extra complication arises as follows.

The units selected within this design are households: approximately, people living at the same address (not an institution) who share common catering. One person is then asked a series of questions about characteristics of the household, including physical features of the dwelling itself, and basic information about household composition. Next, each adult is interviewed about a wide range of matters which apply to an individual – his or her age, education, occupation, health, etc. (Information about children aged under 16 is obtained by proxy, typically from a parent.) Of course, the number of individual interviews will differ from one household to the next. The health section of the interview asks, among other things, whether the respondent has visited the doctor in the last two weeks. For every visit within the specified period a standard set of questions is asked.

Again, the number of visits will vary from none (in most cases) to perhaps a dozen.

This multi-layered data structure does not form a neat rectangle. Instead, we will find something like this:

```
Household 1
    Person 1
    Person 2
        GP visit 1
    Person 3
Household 2
    Person 1
Household 3
    Person 1
        GP visit 1
        GP visit 2
    Person 2
  etc.
```

with a different meaning to each column, according to whether the record being considered is a household, a person or a GP visit.

This is a natural structure for data collection, but an inconvenient one for data analysis. For instance, a cross-tabulation of health (a variable which records whether or not a person suffers a long-standing illness) by household tenure (owned, rented, etc.) will have as many health values as there are individuals, but only as many tenure values as there are households – quite simply, it will not work. The solution is to copy the tenure variable from the household *down* to the record for each individual within that household. As a second example, the relationship between tenure and household income can be examined only by first aggregating individual incomes *up* to the household level. Another quite reasonable request might be for a table showing the relationship between wife's and husband's education – as measured by, for instance, the age that each left school. This looks at first sight logically similar to a table of, say, respondent's occupational class by education. The big difference is this: the class by education table refers to two variables which coexist in every individual's record, so that combinations of codes can easily be counted. But wife's education appears on her record, and husband's education appears on his, and in flat-file analysis there is no way of linking them. The solution here is to copy all individual education variables up to separate variables at the household level, and do the cross-tabulation at that level. Actually it is even more complicated than it sounds, because of the problem of ensuring that couples are paired off correctly, but the principle is as described.

A full account of the types of variables that can be derived in hierarchical data sets appears in Dale et al. (1988: ch. 9).

How all this extra data management is achieved in practice depends on the software available. Using SPSS, the best approach is to set up a series of flat files, one for each level of the structure. Then variables are transported up the structure using a procedure called aggregate, and down using the join command, with subcommand match, and an option which SPSS refers to as a **table lookup** procedure. To explain the details would take at least another chapter: this is intended only to hint at what is required.

For completeness it should be mentioned that this kind of complex non-rectangular file management is often approached using specialised database management programs, such as SIR/DBMS: Scientific Information Retrieval.

13.6 Conclusion

The survey method itself, like all research methods, is fraught with dangers and difficulties. Secondary analysts can, if they are fortunate, avoid some of those dangers by 'standing on the shoulders of giants', even if they aspire to more modest goals than Newton's. At the same time, they lose the opportunity to make their own decisions, perhaps crucially related to their research aims, which may be very different from those of the original researchers. Still, as in so many situations, both in research and in other aspects of life, it is inadvisable to let the best be the enemy of the good: the acknowledgement that you cannot attain perfection should not prevent you from doing the best you can in the circumstances.

13.7 Project

Of course, the only way to become competent at secondary analysis is to do it. A full-scale project may be too large for an initial exercise, but you can operate at a smaller scale by dividing the whole history of such a project into smaller chunks.

One thing to do is to get hold of the current catalogue of your national archive and scan it so as to get an idea of the range of holdings. Almost certainly you will find some data sets which have been specially prepared for teaching purposes, and one of these could be a good focus for this exercise.

The first step is to scan the code book or data dictionary (depending on how the data is documented), this time to get an idea of the range of variables. Work out some ways of combining variables to operationalise a concept not provided for in the raw data – it could be something as simple as an index of parental education to add to the father's and mother's education variables.

If you can get access to the data set in the form required by your data analysis software then you can try out your ideas in practice; if not, try writing the necessary data transformation commands, either in the command syntax of an actual program (you may by now have some idea of how to do this in SPSS), or else in English.

If you have managed to work through these steps, the final suggestion is to consider how differently you might have proceeded if you had had the opportunity to plan and carry out the data collection yourself.

13.8 Further reading

This chapter is heavily based on a full-length book on secondary analysis by Dale et al. (1988). It provides a comprehensive guide through every stage of secondary analysis of survey data, including conceptualisation of the research problem, use of flat and hierarchical data files and the construction of new variables. Detailed discussion of the benefits and costs of using secondary analysis of government surveys is provided in chapter 3, pp. 44–60.

The Economic and Social Research Council Data Archive's *Bulletin*, produced quarterly and available from the ESRC Data Archive, Essex University, Colchester, provides news about the recurrent government data sets and all newly acquired data sets, as well as articles on methods of analysis.

The General Household Survey *Newsletter*, produced twice yearly by the ESRC Data Archive, Colchester, Essex, contains articles by researchers on their use of the GHS and other large government data sets. The reader will find examples of creative and ingenious ways of using the data.

Hakim (1982) provides a detailed and comprehensive guide to British official census and survey data and also reviews the potential for secondary analysis of selected academic surveys. The practical and methodological problems encountered in secondary analysis are considered and examples provided of solutions developed by researchers.

Hyman (1972), an American text, is organised in terms of the major types of problems that can be studied through secondary analysis of surveys. Through case studies, it shows how the principles and procedures of analysis have been applied by researchers to particular problems and how difficulties have been resolved. Cross-national comparisons, cohort analysis and the identification and explanation of trends are all discussed.

You cannot really make much progress in secondary analysis without some understanding of statistics, data management and computing, usually integrated into knowledge of a particular computer data analysis program. If at all possible you should approach this by going on specialised courses – perhaps at a summer school if there is nothing suitable within your main programme of study. Chapter 12 will get you started, and you can follow the reading suggestions at the end of that chapter.

Take local advice on which software to learn: most institutions provide only one or two packages, and it would be perverse to try to use a system which is not part of the local culture. SPSS has been the focus only because it is widely used; it will be perfectly satisfactory for most purposes.

Exemplar C   No jam tomorrow: why women are disadvantaged in occupational pensions

Jay Ginn

Contents

This chapter will describe a practical example of secondary analysis using the General Household Survey 1987. The research forms part of a project funded by the Economic and Social Research Council (ESRC) which I carried out in 1991 jointly with Sara Arber. I show how the research question arose and consider the advantages and problems of using a large government data set to address it. The example illustrates the process of research using secondary analysis, including operationalising concepts, preliminary analysis to guide the formulation of specific hypotheses and the use of cross-tabulation to test these.

C.1   The research question

Sociological theory and research on stratification have traditionally been predominantly concerned with work in the formal economy and with class as the main structural basis of inequality, while gender and the domestic economy have been relatively neglected. Recently, feminist sociologists have highlighted gender as an equally important basis of structured inequality, arguing that the concentration of women in jobs which are characterised by low pay, insecurity, lack of opportunities for promotion and poor working conditions (often referred to as the secondary labour market), is related to patriarchal power and the sexual division of domestic labour (Crompton and Mann, 1986; Walby, 1986). Secondary analysis by Joshi (1984) of the Women and Employment Survey (Martin and Roberts, 1984) confirmed the influence of women's family roles on their participation in the labour market.

However, one aspect of gender inequality in employment which has received little attention is occupational welfare benefits, or 'fringe' benefits, such as paid sick leave and holidays, company cars and occupational pensions (Mann, 1989). Because women are concentrated in the secondary labour market (Barron and Norris, 1976), we would expect that their wage disadvantage is compounded by lack of fringe benefits.

A previous secondary analysis project on elderly people had shown the income disadvantage of elderly women and the crucial role of occupational pensions in transmitting structured income inequalities into later life (Arber and Ginn 1991; Ginn and Arber 1991). Marital status, as well as class and gender, affected pension income; whereas single elderly women had higher pensions than single men, marriage or previous marriage reduced women's pension income drastically. This indicated that elderly women's pension disadvantage was due not only to sex segregation and discrimination in the labour market, but also to the disruptive effect of domestic responsibilities on women's employment histories. Pension scheme rules favour those with full-time continuous employment, first by often excluding part-timers or by having a minimum service requirement (Labour Research Department, 1988) and second through the difficulty in transferring pension rights when changing jobs.

Having established that women's greater poverty in later life was due mainly to their lack of access to occupational pensions, we wished to undertake a more detailed study of the nature and extent of gender inequality in occupational pension scheme membership during working life. We wished to understand how women's domestic role, in terms of marriage and children, and their position in the labour market, in terms of type and level of occupation, hours of work, and industrial sector, influenced their acquisition of pension rights.

C.2   Using the General Household Survey

The research problem required data from a large nationally representative probability sample of people about their domestic circumstances, age and employment, as well as detailed information on their occupational pension scheme membership. Secondary analysis is a suitable way of addressing the research question since the General Household Survey (GHS) provides much of the relevant information and is readily accessible.

A probability (or random) sample was needed in order to be able to infer, with a known degree of certainty, that the associations and mean values found in the sample apply generally in the population, and are not due to bias in the selection of the sample (see chapter 5).

A large sample was necessary in order to compare subgroups (for example by age, sex, marital status and class) without the numbers in the subgroups becoming so small that there might be distortion due to sampling error. When the research requires comparisons within statistically rare groups, such as ethnic minorities, women in the highest occupational positions, or divorced and separated people, a large sample is particularly important.

The GHS, an annual survey carried out since 1971 by the UK government's Office of Population Censuses and Surveys (OPCS) on a two-stage probability sample, has a response rate of over 80 per cent and provides high quality information on over 25,000 people living in over 10,000 private households in Britain. All adults in a sampled household are interviewed and the information is coded and stored on a computer in a way which preserves information about the household and family to which each individual belongs, and data on each individual may be analysed in relation to data on other family and household members (see section 13.6.2 and Dale et al., 1988: ch. 4). The number of cases is sufficient to allow comparison of the effect of several factors simultaneously, and to provide an accurate estimate of the rate of pension scheme membership for small population subgroups. The data are of high quality and from a random sample, allowing inference to be made to the whole population.

The 1987 GHS provides information which allows the effect of family circumstances and labour market position on women's and men's pension scheme membership to be explored. On the other hand, there is no information in the GHS as to the *amount* of pension entitlement, so that those who are likely to receive a substantial pension on retirement cannot be distinguished from those who expect a negligible amount.

A further limitation of the GHS for this research is that it is cross-sectional: the information has been collected at one point in time. Ideally the process of gender differentiation in occupational pension entitlements through the working life would be traced using data on the same individuals as they grew older. This would also show whether gender differences in pension acquisition are diminishing with successive cohorts, reflecting more equality of opportunity for women since the 1970s. When comparing people of different ages it is difficult to separate the effect of age (or stage in the life course) from differences due to being in an earlier or later cohort. Large-scale longitudinal data sets on adults in Britain are available (for example, the National Child Development Study and the OPCS Longitudinal Survey) but they do not include information on occupational pensions.

Although secondary analysis of the GHS has these limitations compared with a specially designed survey, they are outweighed by the advantages of using an existing data set.

C.3   The initial stages of research

In order to analyse the GHS, permission must first be obtained from the ESRC Data Archive and the OPCS. The GHS, or more usually a subset of cases and selected variables, may be received from the Data Archive either in its original hierarchical format which links individuals to their family and household, or as a flat file (a case by variable matrix) at the household or the individual level (see section 13.6.2). For a flat file at the individual level, it may be necessary to request that the specific linkages you need between household information and individual records are preserved. Once the flat system file has been mounted on your local mainframe computer or PC, it can be analysed using a software package such as SAS, SPSS^x or SPSS/PC.

C.3.1   Operationalising concepts

Although secondary analysis may appear to short cut the task of operationalising concepts, since the questions have already been designed, it is important to understand the exact wording of the questions and how they could be interpreted by respondents, the sequence of questions, the definitions used in coding responses, and how each new (or 'derived') variable has been constructed from original ones. Documentation is available from the Data Archive to assist in this. For example, in distinguishing between employment in the public and private sectors, the OPCS defines the 'public sector' as comprising nationalised industries, public corporations, central or local government and armed forces; universities are defined as 'private sector', a categorisation which is by no means obvious.

Since your aim as a researcher is different from that of the originators of the survey, the questions asked and the respondents to whom they were applied are unlikely to be exactly as you would wish. Construction of additional derived variables, as described in section 13.6.1, may provide improved indicators and facilitate analysis.

The questions in the GHS about current pension scheme membership were only asked of employees, as the remainder (whether self-employed, unemployed or economically inactive) would have had no opportunity to join a scheme. Those whose employer had a pension scheme were asked whether they were a member and if not, why not.

The major concepts of interest to us were the likelihood of benefiting from occupational welfare provisions, position in the domestic economy

	Concept	Indicators in GHS
Occupational welfare position	Pension status	Current scheme membership
		Reasons for non-ship
Domestic roles	Marital history	Marital status
	Current parental role	Child living at home
	Fertility history	Child ever born
Labour market position	Type of job	Own occupational class
	Level of job	Usual gross earnings
	Job stability	Years in job
	Commitment to employment	Hours of work*
	Type of employer	Industrial sector, public/ private
Life course stage		Age group

* full time employees are defined by OPCS as those working over 30 hours per week, but pension scheme rules may define full time as over 35 hours a week.

Figure C.1   *Concepts and the variables used as indicators*

and position in the productive economy. The indicators used are set out in Figure C.1.

The age of individuals is clearly crucial to their pension status and affects most of the other independent variables, directly or indirectly. In particular, age is associated with life course stage, in terms of the likelihood of marital, reproductive and parental roles, and with the potential length of time in employment. It is therefore essential to 'control' for age in all the analyses, that is, to hold age (or age group) constant when investigating the relationships between other variables (see section 12.2.4).

We carried out a preliminary analysis to determine whether pension scheme membership did vary in a patterned way with age for women or men, and if so whether age ranges emerged which corresponded to typical life course stages, as we expected would occur for women.

C.3.2   Preliminary, descriptive results

In order to analyse the rates of pension scheme membership and the immediate reasons for non-membership among different groups of employees aged between 20 and 59, we constructed a new variable combining information from several original variables: whether the person was employed, self-employed or economically inactive; for employees, whether the employer ran a pension scheme; if so, whether the respondent belonged to it; and if there was a scheme but they were not a member, the reason for this. The constructed variable was cross-tabulated by sex for all individuals and by hours of work for employees.

Over twice as many men were members of a scheme as women, 46 per cent compared with 21 per cent (see Figure C.2). The reasons for lack of

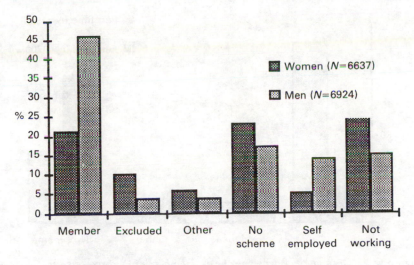

Figure C.2   *Occupational pension scheme membership, men and women aged 20–59, Britain, 1987*

occupational pension scheme membership were different for men and women. Women were less likely to be economically active (65 per cent compared with 85 per cent of men) which not only diminishes their chance of ultimately receiving a pension, but also the amount of pension entitlement they can accumulate over the working life. In addition a larger proportion of women than men worked for an employer who had no scheme (23 per cent compared with 17 per cent) and women were more likely to be excluded from membership by rules of eligibility such as length of service or a minimum hours requirement (10 per cent compared with 4 per cent of men). A small percentage of both men and women whose employer operated a scheme had other reasons for not belonging. Self-employment was the only reason for non-membership given more often by men than women.

Among employees, nearly two thirds of those who worked full time were members of a pension scheme, compared with only 13 per cent of part-timers, and the higher proportion of women than men who worked part time is clearly a major reason for their being more likely to be excluded from pension schemes (see Figure C.3).

These preliminary results confirmed our initial expectations: in spite of women's increasing employment rates since the 1960s, by the late 1980s they were still much less likely than men to belong to an occupational pension scheme. Employed women were less likely than men to work for an employer who had a pension scheme, and where there was a scheme they were more likely to be excluded by the rules.

Pension scheme membership varied with age in different ways for men and women. For men, the membership rate increased with age until 40, when it stabilised, but for women, a more complex pattern emerged: the

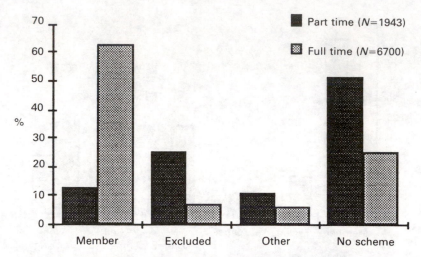

Figure C.3 *Occupational pension scheme membership and reasons for non-membership by hours of work, employees aged 20–59, Britain 1987*

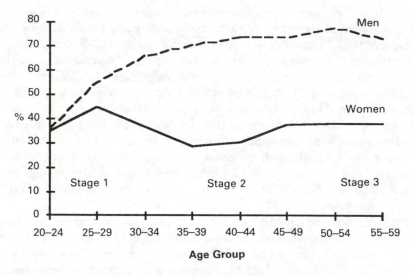

Figure C.4 *Occupational pension scheme membership among men and women whose employer operates one, by age group, Britain 1987*

membership rate rose until around age 29 (stage 1), fell to a substantially lower rate between 30 and 44 (stage 2) and recovered only slightly in the later part of the working life (stage 3) (see Figure C.4). Thus a gender gap in the membership rate opened up before age 30, reaching 40 per cent in stage 2 and diminishing slightly to 35 per cent in stage 3.

This analysis of membership rate by age group and sex showed that women's disadvantage is related to their stage in the life course, and indicated the age grouping most appropriate to use as a control in further cross-tabulations.

The pattern of steep decline and slight recovery of the membership rate among women suggests that the variation was not solely due to later cohorts of women employees enjoying greater equality than their predecessors, but was strongly influenced by life stage events, such as reproductive roles. Further analysis by marital status and fertility was needed to confirm our supposition and this could most easily be carried out by formulating a set of hypotheses to guide the research.

C.4   Explanatory analysis

Since occupational pension scheme membership is only available to employees, only they were included in subsequent analyses. We expected that for women, the characteristic features of the secondary labour market – part-time hours, low pay, lack of opportunities for promotion and lack of job stability – would contribute to low rates of pension scheme membership, but that the effect of gender alone would be less important than domestic roles.

We examined the following hypotheses, for employees within each age group.

A.   Pension scheme membership is less likely for married women than single, for those with a child at home than those without, and less likely for women working part time than full time.
B.   Among full-time employees, likelihood of membership is higher in the public than the private sector.
C.   Among full-time employees, likelihood of membership is directly related to the level of the occupation, as indicated by average usual gross earnings.
D.   Length of time with their present employer is likely to be shorter for women who are married or who have a child, and likelihood of pension scheme membership is directly related to the length of time an employee has been in a job.

C.4.1   Grouping of variables

At this stage of the analysis, cross-tabulation is the most appropriate way to examine relationships among variables. It enables the testing of bivariate relationships by the introduction of selected, theoretically relevant, control variables. Interpretation of the results is relatively straightforward provided the values of variables are suitably summarised or grouped. For the cross-tabulation we grouped variables as shown.

• Age: we used age groups 20–29, 30–44, and 45–59.

- Marital status: we grouped married and cohabiting people together as married for the purpose of analysis, because domestic role rather than legal status was the concept of interest. We also grouped widowed, divorced and separated people together; divorced and separated people were relatively few and, like widows, they had experienced a period of marriage and domestic responsibility.
- Parenthood: the GHS provides information for both men and women about whether they have had any children living with them in the household. Only women were asked whether they had ever borne a child, so we constructed a new five category variable: men with a child at home, men without a child at home, women who had never borne a child, women who had borne at least one child but had none living at home, and women with at least one child living at home.
- Job stability: we grouped individuals according to whether they had been with their present employer less than five years or not, this being the period after which employees had the right to preservation or transfer of accumulated pension entitlements as alternatives to a refund of their own contributions (in 1987; the period is now two years).
- Earnings: we took the OPCS derived variable of usual gross weekly earnings, and calculated the mean value for each population subgroup. Ideally we would have obtained the median as this is less sensitive to extreme values, but the computation would have been far more lengthy.

C.4.2   Results

Cross-tabulation confirmed that the overall disadvantage of women in pension scheme membership did not apply to all women, but was related to their domestic responsibilities and labour market position.

Our first hypothesis (A), was that pension scheme membership is less likely for married women than for single women, less likely for those with a child than for those without and less likely for women working part time than full time. The results confirmed these suppositions. Among employees who were married or cohabiting, 70 per cent of men were members, but only a third of women. The gender difference between married employees (see the first two columns for each age group in Figure C.5) was greatest between ages 30 to 44, the reproductive life phase, and persisted up to women's normal retirement age at 60. In contrast, among single employees, a higher proportion of women than men belonged to a pension scheme until age 45. The results for widowed, divorced and separated employees were similar to those for married employees.

Parental roles also affected pension scheme membership rates, but not in the same way for men and women. For men, having a child in the family slightly increased the likelihood of occupational pension scheme member-ship in each life cycle stage (see Figure C.6), but, for women, having a

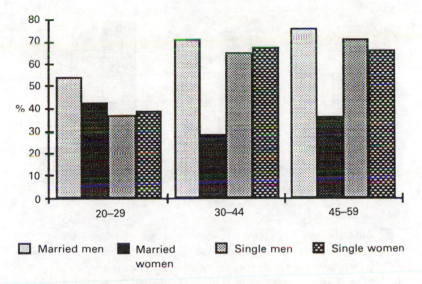

Figure C.5   *Occupational pension scheme membership, men and women employees, by marital status and age group, Britain 1987*

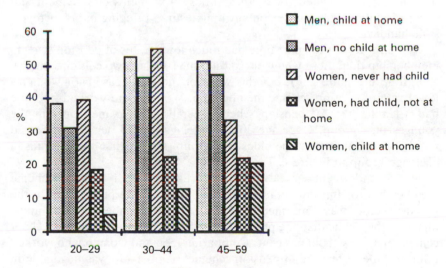

Figure C.6   *Occupational pension scheme membership, men and women aged 20–59 by age group and parental status, Britain 1987*

child in the family was associated with the lowest rates of membership, especially among those aged under 30, whose children were likely to be most dependent. Comparing men and women with a child in the family, the difference in pension scheme membership rates (first and last columns) was nearly 40 per cent in the 30–44 age group. Women who had never borne a child had much higher membership rates than those who had had a

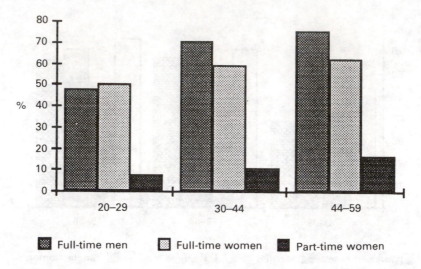

Figure C.7 *Occupational pension scheme membership, men and women employees aged 20–59, by hours of work and age group, Britain 1987*

child, even when they had no child still living in the family. This suggests that the effect of childcare responsibilities on women's employment and occupational welfare entitlements is long-lasting, bringing largely irreversible handicaps.

Women who worked part time had much lower rates of pension scheme membership than those who worked full time (see last two columns in each age group in Figure C.7), but this was not the only reason for women's lower rate of pension scheme membership. Women who worked full time had a similar rate of pension scheme membership to men only in the youngest age group. Over age 30 a gender gap of 13 per cent emerged which was maintained in the oldest age group (see the first two columns in each age group in Figure C.7).

Our second hypothesis (B), that the likelihood of pension scheme membership for full-time employees was higher in the public than in the private sector, was confirmed. Pension scheme membership was much higher in the public than the private sector for employees of all ages, 74 per cent compared with 40 per cent. Comparing men and women who worked full time, the difference in pension scheme membership was negligible in the public sector, but in the private sector there was a substantial gender gap among those employed full time (see Figure C.8).

The reasons for non-membership differed between the public and private sectors. In the public sector very few employees worked for an employer who had no pension scheme (6 per cent) but in the private sector this proportion was nearly half (43 per cent). The difference between the industrial sectors was particularly marked for women working part time (see Figure C.9); in the private sector their low rate of pension scheme membership was due mainly to lack of a scheme (71 per cent), but in the

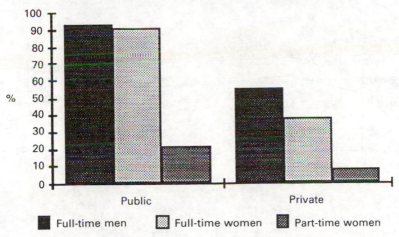

Figure C.8 *Occupational pension scheme membership, men and women employees aged 20–59, by industrial sector and hours of work, Britain 1987*

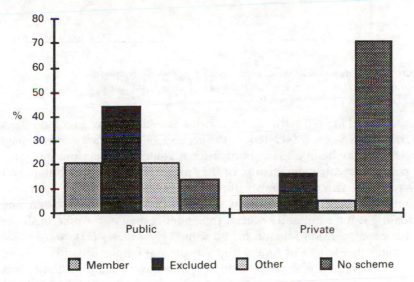

Figure C.9 *Reasons for non-membership by industrial sector, women employed part time aged 20–59, Britain 1987*

public sector it was mainly due to the scheme's rules excluding part-timers (44 per cent).

Even among full-timers in the private sector, women over age 30 were more likely than men of the same age to work for an employer with no pension scheme.

Turning to hypothesis (C), it was confirmed that employees' likelihood of pension scheme membership is related to their earnings (see Figure C.10). Among all full-time employees, those who belonged to an occupational pension scheme had higher average earnings than non-members,

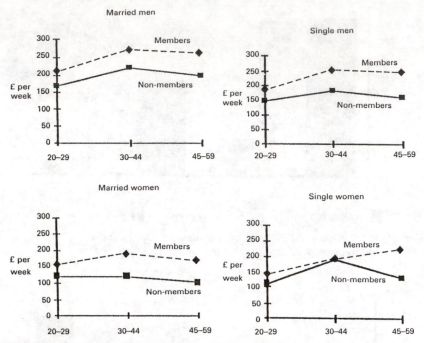

Figure C.10 *Mean usual gross earnings in £ per week, by pension scheme membership, by marital status and age group, full time employees aged 20–59, Britain 1987*

irrespective of marital status and age group. Level of earnings could reflect several differences associated with occupational welfare; lower paid employees may be in a lower occupational grade and therefore ineligible for pension scheme membership, or they may work for a smaller employer or have been with the employer for a shorter time.

Domestic roles may affect job stability, reducing it for women and increasing it for men, and reduced job stability may in turn diminish the likelihood of pension scheme membership. Hypothesis (D), whose first part states that length of time with their present employer is likely to be shorter for women who are married or who have a child at home, was confirmed by our results. The percentage of employees who had been in their present job more than five years was higher for men than for women, 58 per cent compared with 44 per cent (Figure C.11(a)). There was little difference between single women and single men, although in the oldest age group men were more likely to have changed jobs in the last five years. The gender difference for married and previously married employees was greatest in the 30 to 44 age group, the second life stage.

Where there was no child in the family, there was no gender difference in the percentage who had been in their job more than five years, but the presence of a child reduced the likelihood of a woman having been in her job more than five years and increased it for men under age 45 (Figure C.11(b)).

Although job changes can sometimes be advantageous to the individual,

Age group	Men				Women			
	20–29	30–44	45–59	All	20–29	30–44	45–59	All
All	31	65	76	58	23	40	69	44
a) *Marital status:*								
Married	40	65	76	64	26	38	69	46
Widowed, divorced, or separated	67	61	79	70	26	39	67	52
Single	22	64	73	35	21	63	85	33
b) *Parental status:*								
Child at home	42	66	76	66	16	34	64	41
No child at home	28	61	76	49	25	60	76	47

Figure C.11   *Percentages of men and women employees in their present job more than five years, by marital status, parental status and age group, Britain 1987*

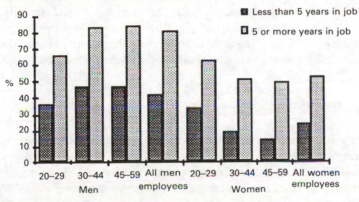

Figure C.12   *Occupational pension scheme membership, men and women employees, by length of time in their job and age group, Britain 1987*

they are often involuntary, and reduce the chance of pension scheme membership if the rules require a minimum length of service. This is expressed in the second part of hypothesis (D), that the likelihood of pension scheme membership depends on the length of time an employee has been in their job. Men and women who had been with their current employer over five years were more likely to belong to a pension scheme than more recently recruited employees, within each age group (see Figure C.12). For example, only a quarter of all women who had been with their employer less than five years belonged to a pension scheme, compared with over half of those who had been employed in the same job for five years or more. For men the corresponding proportions were two fifths and four fifths.

The length of time in a job affected not only the chance of pension scheme membership but also the employee's right to the accumulated funds. Until 1987, an employer was under no obligation to preserve or transfer the pension entitlement of employees who changed jobs with less than five years' service (now two); such employees could receive a refund of their own payments, but lost the benefit of the employer's contributions.

There are other labour market factors which are likely to be related to pension scheme membership, such as class and size of organisation. However, further elaboration, that is, the detailed examination of a relationship between two variables through the introduction of additional control variables (see chapter 12), becomes complex and cumbersome when there are more than three or four variables involved. The proliferation of subgroups entailed in further elaboration, especially when variables cannot reasonably be grouped into a few categories, would also result in unacceptably small cell sizes in cross-tabulations, even with a data set as large as the GHS. In order to control simultaneously for a number of independent variables, we would use multivariate analysis as the next stage in this research. This would enable us to assess the relative importance of two aspects of family circumstances (marital status and fertility) and several aspects of labour market position (hours of work, occupational class, industrial sector, length of time in the job, size of organisation and earnings) in influencing occupational pension scheme membership.

C.4.3   Discussion

Women's disadvantaged pension position is partly accounted for by their lower rate of economic activity, but even those who are employed are much less likely than men to be in a pension scheme. The results of cross-tabulations confirmed our hypotheses, A to D: women employees' relative disadvantage in pension scheme membership was greater if they were married, worked part time, were employed in the private sector or had low earnings. Within the private sector, women who worked part time were more likely than full-timers to work for an employer with no pension scheme, while in the public sector part-timers were often excluded from membership.

There were several immediate reasons why women employees' pension disadvantage arose in the child-rearing phase of the life course: after age 30, the proportion of women working part time increased, but in the private sector even women working full time were more likely than men to work for an employer with no pension scheme. For women employees, marriage and the presence of a child increased the likelihood of having been with their employer for under five years, but for men the reverse was true. The features which characterise the secondary labour market all contribute to reducing the chance of pension scheme membership for both men and women, and gender appears to be relatively unimportant in itself.

We conclude that women's disadvantage in membership is mainly due to the impact that childbearing and the gendered division of domestic labour have on the type of employment women are able to undertake. We cannot find out from cross-sectional data whether women's disadvantage is diminishing with successive cohorts, but the pattern of gender differences with life stage suggests that domestic responsibilities will continue to reduce elderly women's occupational pension income into the next century. Not only is there no jam today in women's wages, but there will be no jam tomorrow in their pension income.

Women's disadvantage in terms of fewer and lower occupational pensions due to their role in marriage and childrearing will be an increasingly important issue as the value of the state pension relative to occupational pensions and to average incomes declines. The situation of the increasing number of elderly divorced women, who are likely to have lost the opportunity to build an adequate occupational pension of their own, yet will have no access to their ex-husbands', is particularly bleak. If elderly women in the future are not to suffer poverty as a result of their reproductive and nurturing roles, policies are needed which minimise the effect of marriage and family on women's employment, and ensure an adequate income from the state for those who have undertaken unpaid caring responsibilities.

By disseminating our research through academic journals and elsewhere (see chapter 16), we can add to the growing literature which demonstrates how women's financial disadvantage in later life is the result of socially structured arrangements. Achieving policy change is more difficult, since it depends on the political and economic climate.

C.5   Conclusions: research as a process

We have shown how secondary analysis can be used to contribute to understanding the effect of women's domestic roles and employment on their acquisition of an occupational pension. We have illustrated the strengths and limitations of secondary analysis of a large government data set and traced the process of analysis through several stages.

Each stage of the research affected the way in which we treated the data subsequently. Our own interests and previous experience affected the choice of research problem. Use of the 1987 GHS for secondary analysis influenced the hypotheses which we could test, because these were constrained by the questions asked and definitions used in this data set. Preliminary analysis established an overall picture of pension scheme membership and confirmed our expectations drawn from theory about the factors which affected membership. It also enabled us to use an appropriate age grouping.

Although the work of other researchers had shaped our expectations about the reasons for women's disadvantage in pension scheme membership, the results were not wholly predictable. For example, we did not anticipate that the high overall rate of membership in the public sector would also eliminate the gender gap for full-time employees. We did not expect to find that the low rates of membership among part-timers in the public and private sectors, although similar, arose in different ways, nor did we foresee the extent of exclusion of part-timers by pension scheme rules in the public sector.

The research drew our attention to areas which needed further examination. We found that married men's pension advantage over single men was due to their better labour market position, yet the reason why married men are in better jobs than unmarried men of a similar age is not yet clearly understood (Payne, 1991). Another puzzle concerns older women: we can explain the lower pension scheme membership of married women employees in the middle age group – the reproductive phase – as reflecting the downward occupational mobility associated with the demands of rearing children. But the failure of employed married women over 45 to reach the rates of membership of the youngest age group also requires explanation. It may reflect differences between cohorts in married women's attitudes to employment, or discrimination against older women with interrupted employment, but we require data on women's work histories to test these and other possible explanations.

The research we have described here represents an early stage in our two-and-a-half year project on Older Women's Working Lives in which we shall examine the social factors affecting the nature and extent of labour force participation of older women, using secondary analysis of the Social Change and Economic Life Initiative (SCELI) employment histories. As such it can be seen as a small piece in a jigsaw which will, we hope, make a contribution to a wider body of research and theory.

14 Analysing accounts

Robin Wooffitt

Contents

Language use permeates and infuses all those aspects of society that are conventionally regarded as the core topics for sociological research. For example, everyday language is the medium through which society social-ises young children; institutional norms and values are transmitted through a variety of forms of discourse; family life is rife with words, jokes and arguments; society's gender inequalities may resonate in patterns of conversation between women and men; the education of young people rests in part upon the verbal skills of teachers to interest, enthuse or cajole their students; and legal declarations are administered in courtroom trials which involve the verbal interrogation of witnesses and defendants for the benefit of an overhearing jury. Yet the sociological study of language-use has not yet emerged as one of the central core topics of the discipline along with the study of class, gender, ethnicity, deviance, education, the family, and so on. Perhaps it is because 'people talking to each other' is so commonplace and taken for granted that for the majority of the twentieth century it has not been treated as a central topic in social scientific research.

The analytic approach to be described and illustrated in this chapter seeks to rectify this deficiency by focusing primarily on language use. It shares many features of two other contemporary approaches to the study of language: conversation analysis in sociology and discourse analysis in social psychology.

14.1   Language: descriptions as actions

In the last 30 years sociological interest in the use of language has been influenced by the philosophy of Wittgenstein (1953) and Austin (1962), and the sociological research of Garfinkel (1967; and see Heritage, 1984) and Sacks (1992).

In his early research, Wittgenstein examined language to explore how it represented objects and states of affairs in the world. In his later work, however, he rejected the theory that language is a medium which merely reflects or describes the world, and emphasised instead the importance of language use. He urged that we consider language as a tool box, and focus on the ways that people use these tools. His primary contribution was to propose that language is a central feature of the social and cultural milieu in which it was used, and not merely a logical system of symbols with which we can represent the world 'out there'.

Austin's (1962) work also emphasised the social and dynamic character of language, but his work focused on instances of specific types of sentences. He began by distinguishing between two types of utterances: constative utterances, which report some aspect of the world; and performative utterances, which perform a specific action. An example of a performative is 'I suggest you do this', where saying these words is to perform the action of suggesting. Other examples are promises, warnings, declarations, and so on. He termed such utterances, speech acts. Austin subsequently rejected the distinction between performative and constative utterances: his investigations convinced him that all utterances could be treated as performative. He concluded that any use of language, regardless of what else it might be doing, was a series of actions.

A renewed interest in the sociological study of language was stimulated by the sociological approach that came to be known as ethnomethodology. Pioneered by Harold Garfinkel (1967) the fundamental tenet of ethnomethodology is that the sense of social action is accomplished through the participants' use of tacit, practical reasoning skills and competencies. (These skills are referred to as 'tacit' and 'practical' because they are not the kinds of 'rules' or norms of behaviour which we could consciously articulate, or on which we would routinely reflect. Instead, they inhabit the very weave of social life, and thereby become invisible and unnoticeable.) As so much of social life is mediated through spoken and written communication, the study of language was placed at the very heart of ethnomethodology's sociological enterprise.

Harvey Sacks was a colleague of Garfinkel, and their work shares many concerns. However, Sacks's work was focused exclusively on the communicative competencies that informed ordinary, everyday conversation. Sacks and his colleagues conducted detailed and repeated analyses of tape recordings of everyday telephone conversations, and produced transcripts which tried to capture the messiness and complexity of the exchanges. This research led to the discovery of systematic properties in the way that conversation is organised. The study of the structure of conversational organisation has come to be known as conversation analysis, or CA, and is one of the pre-eminent contemporary approaches to the study of language use. (Conversation analysis is described in more detail in chapter 15.)

Finally, discourse analysis is an analytic method which grew out of the sociological study of scientific knowledge (Gilbert and Mulkay, 1984), but which developed principally in social psychology (Potter and Wetherell, 1987). Unlike conversation analysts, discourse analysts examine all forms of verbal and textual materials: spoken and written accounts, letters, scientific journals, newspaper reports and so on. The object of empirical study is to describe the way that such texts are constructed, and to explore the functions served by specific constructions at both the interpersonal and societal level.

This has been a brief and partial review of some of the most important intellectual ideas and research which have influenced the way in which we can conceptualise language use and its relation to social life (but see also Mills, 1940; Scott and Lyman, 1968; Coulthard, 1977; Brown and Yule, 1983). As a consequence of these developments, it is now untenable to retain conceptions of language as a merely neutral medium for the transmission of information, values, and beliefs about a world 'out there'. Instead, we can examine language use as a form of social action, the systematic properties of which can be described and rigorously analysed.

14.2 Data

To illustrate the study of language use as a form of social action, it is useful to describe 'work-in-progress', rather than present a polished analysis in which the empirical technique is obscured by the presentation of specific findings. Therefore, some preliminary analytic remarks will be generated through an initial consideration of a single, short data extract. It is important to keep in mind, however, that these remarks are presented only as a collection of illustrative 'first observations', and their presentation here is not representative of the more formal reports of analytic conclusions which appear in the research literature.

The data extract we are going to examine was recorded during an informal, conversational interview (see chapter 8). This interview was conducted as part of a social psychological investigation of adolescent youth subcultures: punks, skinheads, rockers, gothics, hippies, and so on (Widdicombe and Wooffitt, 1990). The extract comes from a conversation between three punk rockers and a research colleague, recorded on the pavement in a back street of London's Camden market area. In the interview from which the following extract has been taken, the speaker, a male punk, has been describing in general terms the police's hostile attitude to the concerts of punk rock bands. In this sequence he begins to describe what happened at the end of one specific concert.

(1)
And the police were all outside there at the concert. There wasn't a bit of trouble, apart from say one or two wee scraps, you know. But that happens . . . every gig there's a scrap – there's always somebody that doesn't like somebody else. It doesn't matter what it is, it's always happening, you know you cannot stop that. And we go outside and there they are – fucking eight hundred Old Bill, just waiting for the chance – riot shields, truncheons, and you're not doing nothing – you're only trying to get down to the tube and go home. So what do they do? You're walking by and they're pushing you with their truncheons and they start hitting the odd punk here and there. And what happens? The punks rebel – they don't like getting hit in the face with a truncheon, nobody does. So what do you do? You push the copper back and what happens? Ten or twelve of them are beating the pure hell out of some poor bastard who's only trying to keep somebody off his back. Now that started a riot.

In this chapter we have two related concerns. The first will be to examine some of the descriptive resources used by the speaker to warrant the claim that the punks were not responsible for the violence. The second will be to investigate the way that the speaker's account is organised to address the likelihood that negative stereotypical knowledge about punks may be drawn upon to inform a sceptical response to the factual status of his claims.

14.3   Some methodological issues

In conversation analysis, and, to a lesser extent, in discourse analysis, it is customary to produce a detailed transcription of the taped interview. In this case, however, the tape was transcribed by a professional transcriber who was not asked to include all the 'uhms', 'errs' and complexities of speech production. In one sense, this is to our advantage: the transcript is relatively straightforward to read. It is important to realise, however, that many important details of the talk may have been lost in this transcription, and thus it is a good methodological practice always to produce as detailed a transcription as possible. (The Introduction to Atkinson and Heritage's (1984) edited collection of conversation analytic studies argues persuasively for the importance of detailed transcriptions. Some of the more common transcription conventions are described in the Appendix to this chapter.)

Before we examine the data extract, some warning notes need to be sounded. First, the mode of analysis illustrated in this chapter is not conducted according to a set of hard and fast rules, and there are no prespecified statistical techniques which can be used to manipulate data to furnish a set of results or findings. This analytic approach thus has little connection to the kinds of quantitative analyses described in some of the other chapters, but resembles most closely the ethnographic research tradition discussed in chapter 9. In common with anthropologists and ethnographers, the study of language use advocated here requires the development of an 'analytic mentality': a repertoire of craft skills acquired through practical experience (rather than from the perusal of research methods textbooks).

This analytic approach gives rise to some difficult methodological problems. For example, how can an analyst warrant the validity or accuracy of specific empirical observations? However, we will not address such difficulties in this chapter, as they receive a more comprehensive treatment in section 15.3.

Second, it needs to be stressed that the analytic approach outlined in this chapter is informed by very different assumptions to those which underpin many other empirical methodologies employed in sociological research. Indeed, it will become clear that some of the arguments in this chapter will seem incompatible with assumptions which inform other research strategies described in this book. A plurality of competing and, at times, incompatible research approaches is to be expected in a discipline as theoretically diverse as sociology. In this chapter, however, there will be no attempt to track in detail the relationship between different research methods.

The first thing to be done to the data extract is rearrange it so that it is easier to refer to specific sections when assembling analytic observations. Organising the data prior to analysis is not the most crucial phase of the analytic process. But be warned: it is unwise to try to arrange the data to highlight what you anticipate will be the significant passages. At this preliminary stage it is sensible to be agnostic about what the data may reveal because, before getting to grips with the material, one simply does not know which passages will yield interesting phenomena worthy of more detailed inspection. Any pre-analytic guesswork might only lead the analyst to overlook some detail which, although significant, does not fit in with intuitive speculation about 'what is really important'.

(2)
1   And the police were all outside there at the concert.
2   There wasn't a bit of trouble,
3   apart from say one or two wee scraps, you know.
4   But that happens . . . every gig there's a scrap –
5   there's always somebody that doesn't like somebody else.
6   It doesn't matter what it is, it's always happening,

```
7   you know you cannot stop that.
8   And we go outside and there they are –
9   fucking eight hundred Old Bill,
10  just waiting for the chance –
11  riot shields, truncheons, and you're not doing nothing –
12  you're only trying to get down to the tube and go home.
13  So what do they do? You're walking by
14  and they're pushing you with their truncheons
15  and they start hitting the odd punk here and there.
16  And what happens?
17  The punks rebel – they don't like getting hit
18  in the face with a truncheon, nobody does.
19  So what do you do?
20  You push the copper back and what happens?
21  Ten or twelve of them are beating
22  the pure hell out of some poor bastard
23  who's only trying to keep somebody off his back.
24  Now that started a riot.
```

The decision to make line breaks in these places rather than any others is in this case partly determined by the transcriber: note that in many cases the transcript has been broken where commas, full stops and question marks have been introduced.

The empirical observations focus on three features of the data segment. First, we shall examine some properties of the varying ways in which the actions of the punks and the police are described. This is to introduce the concept of the 'linguistic repertoire', a methodological tool central to many discourse analytic studies. This in turn highlights the sociological relevance of examining accounts. Second, we focus on the ways in which specific descriptive sequences have been assembled. So, the description, 'one or two wee scraps' (line 3) will be analysed. Third, we examine the statement 'every gig there's a scrap – there's always somebody that doesn't like somebody else. It doesn't matter what it is, it's always happening' (lines 4 to 6). This is to emphasise that descriptive practices are not random or idiosyncratic events, but have systematic properties.

14.4   Linguistic repertoires

The notion of the **linguistic repertoire** (Halliday, 1978) was developed by Gilbert and Mulkay in their (1984) study of scientists' accounts of their own scientific work, and the work of other scientists. A linguistic repertoire is simply a set of descriptive and referential terms which portray beliefs, actions and events in a specific way. According to Potter and Wetherell, a repertoire is: 'constituted through a limited range of terms used in particular stylistic and grammatical constructions. Often a repertoire will be organised around specific metaphors and figures of speech (tropes)' (1987: 149).

It is useful to describe Gilbert and Mulkay's (1984) study to show how they came to argue for the importance of linguistic repertoires.

Gilbert and Mulkay began by studying one scientific dispute in an area of biochemistry. This dispute was about the correct way to understand the mechanisms by which chemical and other kinds of energy are stored within cell structures. To study this dispute, Gilbert and Mulkay collected taped interviews with the various biochemists involved in the dispute, read relevant research papers and obtained informal communications between the participants, such as letters and notes. However, these data presented them with a problem: within these accounts there were a variety of plausible and convincing versions of the dispute. Furthermore, they noted that any one feature of the debate, such as the significance of a series of experimental studies, could be described and accounted for in a number of different ways. Gilbert and Mulkay argued that it is imperative to attend directly to the variability in accounts, and not simply to employ techniques which purge it from the data. Consequently, they advocated the study of participants' discourse (or use of language) to reveal the interpretative practices, embodied in discourse, by which accounts of beliefs and actions are organised to portray events in a certain way. So, they did not examine their accounts to furnish definitive sociological statements about a specific state of affairs. Instead, they explicated the systematic properties of language use through which scientists constructed their accounts. Chapter 1 of Gilbert and Mulkay's 1984 study discusses these methodological issues in more depth.

The concept of the linguistic repertoire was adopted as a consequence of Gilbert and Mulkay's emphasis upon the study of variability in language use. For example, in the various accounts about the biochemistry dispute, they noted that there were two ways in which scientists could characterise their own experimental results and those produced by other scientists. Through the use of what Gilbert and Mulkay called the 'empiricist' repertoire, scientists characterised experimental results, and the experimental method more generally, as merely reflecting the properties of an objective world. This repertoire was used regularly to describe the experimental results or theoretical work of a scientist with whom the speaker/author agreed. The 'contingent' repertoire, however, was used to emphasise that scientific work is not necessarily constrained exclusively by empirical reality, but is subject to a range of personal motivations and social influences. Such a repertoire occurred on occasions in which scientists, who supported one theoretical explanation, were describing or commenting on the work of those other scientists who held an opposing position. Through the use of the contingent repertoire the actions and scientific practices of some scientists could be characterised as reflecting their own personal interest in their specific theories and experimental methods, rather than being motivated by the (more 'scientific') pursuit of objective knowledge.

Gilbert and Mulkay considered linguistic repertoires to be sets of

discursive resources with which people constructed versions of the world
for specific social purposes in specific social settings. Having established
the dynamic and functional character of linguistic repertoires, let us
reconsider the punk's description of some incidents following a punk rock
gig.

1   And the police were all outside there at the concert.
2   There wasn't a bit of trouble,
3   apart from say one or two wee scraps, you know.
4   But that happens . . . every gig there's a scrap –
5   there's always somebody that doesn't like somebody else.
6   It doesn't matter what it is, it's always happening,
7   you know you cannot stop that.
8   And we go outside and there they are –
9   fucking eight hundred Old Bill,
10 just waiting for the chance –
11 riot shields, truncheons, and you're not doing nothing –
12 you're only trying to get down to the tube and go home.
13 So what do they do? You're walking by
14 and they're pushing you with their truncheons
15 and they start hitting the odd punk here and there.
16 And what happens?
17 The punks rebel – they don't like getting hit
18 in the face with a truncheon, nobody does.
19 So what do you do?
20 You push the copper back and what happens?
21 Ten or twelve of them are beating
22 the pure hell out of some poor bastard
23 who's only trying to keep somebody off his back.
24 Now that started a riot.

In lines 2 to 7 there is a short sequence in which the speaker describes
some violent incidents which happened at the concert. (This part of the
account is examined in a later section.) Then the speaker begins a series of
descriptions of the actions of the punks, and the actions of the police. So in
lines 8 to 12 the speaker says 'And we go outside and there they are –
fucking eight hundred Old Bill, just waiting for the chance – riot shields,
truncheons, and you're not doing nothing – you're only trying to get down
to the tube and go home.'

Note that the first reference to the punks' behaviour is a very minimal
description of what they did after the concert: 'And we go outside'. The
second reference provides a further characterisation of the unexceptional
nature of their behaviour: 'doing nothing' and simply 'going home'. It is
interesting to note that the speaker's reference to the punks changes in the
course of the segment. He says firstly that 'we go outside' but then he
reports their subsequent behaviour as '*you're* only trying to [go home]'.
There is a sense in which 'we' clearly marks the speaker as a member of a
specific group or collectivity. But the characterisation of their attempt to go
home as '*you're* only trying . . .' does not invoke such a clear affiliation.
Indeed, it appeals to 'what everybody does' or 'what anybody would do'.
Initially, we might assume that this is simply an idiosyncratic and 'one-off'

way of engendering a recipient's sympathy for the events that befell the punks on the night of the concert. As we progress through the rest of this account, however, we shall see that the character of this specific segment is tied to the broader organisation of the whole account of the incidents.

There is a contrast between the way that the behaviour of the punks is described, and the way in which the speaker reports the presence of the police. The speaker provides a numerical evaluation of the police officers in attendance after the concert which, regardless of its 'accuracy', portrays the police presence as 'excessive'. Furthermore, he reports that the officers came equipped for violent confrontation. So, he builds a contrast between the actions of the punks and the subsequent response by the police: the behaviour of the punks is portrayed as quite unexceptional and routine, whereas the response of the police is portrayed as extreme.

In lines 13 to 15 the speaker reports 'You're walking by and they're pushing you with their truncheons and they start hitting the odd punk here and there.' As in the previous extract, there is firstly a description of the punks' behaviour and then a description of the actions of the police. And, like the previous segment, the behaviour of the punks is reported in minimal, everyday terms: they are simply 'walking by'. By contrast, the police are portrayed as initiating violence in that they start 'hitting the odd punk'. Note also that the violence is portrayed as being indiscriminately inflicted, rather than directed at specific individuals, or as part of the police response to a particular contingency. This serves to undermine the warrant for such police behaviour. Furthermore, it portrays the police's actions as being propelled not by any 'rational' motives or plan of action, but as an irrational and prejudiced response. Thus, the speaker's description in this segment further emphasises the contrast between the behaviour of the punks and the police.

In lines 16 to 22 the speaker then recounts the events which culminated in what he describes as 'a riot', and provides a characterisation of the punks' contribution to the escalating violence. Note, firstly, that this issue is raised via his posing the rhetorical question 'And what happens?' as a consequence of the police indiscriminately hitting the punks.

Note also that the use of the verb 'rebel' portrays the punks' first active involvement in the violence as being responsive to, and a consequence of, police provocation, oppression, and so on. Furthermore, this response is warranted by an appeal to 'how any one would respond in these circumstances': '[the punks] don't like getting hit in the face with a truncheon, nobody does'.

Finally, the speaker provides the first reference to violent actions actually perpetrated by the punks after the concert: 'You push the copper back'. It is clear that he is not describing one specific event, or any number of specific incidents; rather, he describes a general response, which is again warranted by an appeal to what 'anyone would do in this situation'. There are two interesting features of the description of the punks as 'pushing back'. 'Pushing' is not a particularly aggressive act, and its use here portrays the punks' behaviour as being defensive, rather than offensive. Also, the characterisation of the punks as pushing back demonstrates that their actions are a form of resistance to an ongoing physical assault, rather than any attempt to initiate conflict.

One short data extract is simply insufficient to make any strong claim about the use of different linguistic repertoires through which the speaker describes the actions of the punks and the police. But some interesting differences are emerging. So, for example, the behaviour of the punks is described as entirely mundane: they are characterised as simply doing what any 'ordinary' person might do. They are also portrayed as passive recipients of violence, rather than aggressive perpetrators; even when they are actively involved in violence the punks are portrayed as using physical force to effect the most minimal form of self-defence. The description of the behaviour of the police, however, is couched in terms of their orientation to, and pursuit of, aggressive confrontation: their presence is excessive and they engage in random physical assaults. Thus, the speaker uses a repertoire to portray the ordinary and mundane activities of the punks, but formulates the behaviour of the police through a series of descriptions which emphasise the aggressive and extraordinary behaviour of the police. Studies by Sacks (1984[1970]), Jefferson (1984) and Wooffitt (1992) also consider the ways that an individual's identity as an 'ordinary person' can be made relevant as an interactional resource.

We have noted that the speaker builds a series of **contrasts** between the behaviour of the punks and that of the police. In this the speaker is using a rhetorical and interactional resource which occurs in a variety of occasions of natural language use. For example, they occur regularly in political speeches (Atkinson 1984; Heritage and Greatbatch, 1986), in market pitchers' selling techniques (Pinch and Clark, 1986), and in an account of mental illness (Smith, 1978). These studies have shown that contrast structures are employed as a persuasive device. In political speeches, for example, it is found that these structures are regularly followed by audience applause. In this case the speaker uses contrastive organisation to emphasise the extreme nature of the police response. Indeed, the inference that the presence of the police and their subsequent behaviour was unwarranted in part rests upon the juxtaposition of police action with the seemingly inconsequential and ordinary behaviour of the punks.

It is important to remember that we are not assessing this account to try to discover whether the speaker's description is accurate, or whether he is distorting 'what really happened'. Rather, we are interested in the descriptive resources which are used to construct this version, and to sketch what dynamic and functional properties this version has. Indeed, it is quite possible that the same linguistic resources could be used to achieve the opposite ends. It is not hard to imagine how the punks could be described to portray their extraordinary and potentially aggressive demeanour, thereby warranting the appropriateness of the police response.

14.5 Assembling descriptions

In this section we are going to attempt a more detailed consideration of a much smaller data segment: 'one or two wee scraps' (line 3). A short utterance like this seems an unpromising target for detailed examination. To indicate why even apparently minor statements such as this merit close attention, we need to discuss some salient features of the practice of 'describing'.

The first step in examining descriptive sequences is to ask why these specific words have been used in this specific combination. Initially, this might seem a trivial task with a self evident answer: this description has been provided because it captures, represents or reflects the state of affairs in the world being described. But we have seen that there are a variety of philosophical and sociological arguments which suggest that descriptions are designed not merely to *represent* the world, but to do specific tasks *in* the world.

Similarly, it is important to keep in mind that any actual description, however sensible or accurate it may appear, has been assembled from a range of possible words and phrases. Schegloff (1972) has illustrated the necessary selectivity of descriptions by illustrating the various ways that one state of affairs could be reported.

> Were I now to formulate where my notes are, it would be correct to say that they are: right in front of me, next to the telephone, on the desk, in my office, in the office, in Room 213, in Lewisohn Hall, on campus, at school, at Columbia, in Morningside Heights, on the upper West Side, in Manhatten, in New York City, in New York State, in the North east, on the Eastern seaboard, in the United States, etc. Each of these terms could in some sense be correct . . . were its relevance provided for. (Schegloff, 1972: 81)

The point is that any description or reference is produced from a potentially inexhaustible list of possible utterances, each of which is 'logically' correct or true. So when we pose the analytic question 'why this specific description?' we need also to ask 'what *tacit practical reasoning* informs the design of this description?' (see also the discussion in Heritage, 1978).

Let us consider the word 'scrap'. Of all the ways which could be used to describe two people hitting each other – 'fighting', 'violence', 'a punch up' – the word 'scrap' clearly minimises the seriousness of the incident. Indeed, 'scrap' evokes images of schoolboy tussles in playgrounds rather than incidents in which people may incur severe physical damage. The characterisation of the incidents as 'wee scraps' further portrays the relative insignificance of the incidents.

Consider also the numerical evaluation 'one or two wee scraps'. A first point is that 'one or two' clearly registers the 'occurring more than once' character of the incident being described. Referring to a *number* of violent incidents could easily be used by a sceptic to undermine the general thrust of the speaker's claim that the police presence after the concert was

unwarranted. However, 'one or two' provides the most *minimal* characterisation of 'more than one'. Secondly, note that the speaker does not say
'one' or 'two', but 'one or two'. In one sense, this marks the speaker as 'not
knowing' the precise number of incidents. More important, however, is
that the display of 'not knowing' marks the precise number as not *requiring*
clarification, and therefore as being relatively unimportant. Thirdly, in this
sequence the speaker concedes that violent disturbances occurred at the
gig. Thus the speaker makes an admission which could be damaging to his
overriding claim that the punks were not to blame for the subsequent 'riot'.
However, conceding such a potentially delicate point is one method by
which the speaker can minimise the likelihood that his account will be seen
as a biased version of events. This in turn augments his implicit claim to be
an accurate reporter of 'what really happened'. So, although the speaker
does reveal that indeed there were *some* violent incidents at the concert, he
does so in such a way as to portray the 'more than one' number of incidents
as minimally as possible, while at the same time registering the relative
insignificance of these events, and portraying himself as an 'honest
observer'.

14.6　The organisation of descriptive sequences

In this section we will consider lines 4 to 6.

4　But that happens . . . every gig there's a scrap –
5　there's always somebody that doesn't like somebody else.
6　It doesn't matter what it is, it's always happening,

A first preliminary observation: note the instances on which the speaker
uses the words 'always' and 'every'.

Pomerantz (1986) has studied the use of words like 'always' and 'never'
in ordinary conversation. She provides a technical identification of this,
referring to words such as 'always' and 'every' as **extreme case formulations**. Other examples are 'never', 'brand new', 'nobody', 'everybody',
'completely innocent' and 'forever'. Such formulations serve to portray the
maximum (or minimum) character of the object, quality or state of affairs
to which they refer.

A second preliminary observation: note that the speaker provides three
discrete descriptions of some characteristics of violent incidents, and, in
each case, he uses an extreme case formulation.

These two aspects of the sequence in lines 4 to 6 warrant further
inspection. We will begin by posing two (related) questions. How is this
sequence organised, and what is it organised to do?

An initial answer to the first of these questions is, the sequence has been
organised as a list: the speaker produces a series of three descriptions
which focus on some underlying cause or feature of violent activities.

The study of everyday conversation has discovered that three partedness in list construction is a common occurrence (Jefferson, 1991). For example:

(3)
while you've been talking tuh me,
I mended,
two nightshirts,   **1**
a pillowcase?   **2**
enna pair'v pants.   **3**

In ordinary conversation three part lists can be used to indicate a general quality common to the items in the list. In (3) above, the speaker provides a summary of the items she has mended. By virtue of their placement in a list, the reference to these items is hearable as the speaker indicating 'look how much I've done'. Furthermore, listing these items displays to the recipient their **occasioned co-class membership**: that is, the way that they are used conveys the general class of objects to which the speaker's activity has been directed – mending household linen. This feature of listing is often employed as a resource in political speeches. For example (Atkinson, 1984: 60):

(4)   Tebbit, UK General Election, 1983.
1   Labour will
2   spend and spend   **1**
3   borrow and borrow   **2**
4   and tax and tax   **3**

In the extract above the speaker is not concerned with spending, borrowing and taxing as separate features of the Labour Party's policies; rather, by listing these three features he is able to convey the *general* point that their economic policy is inherently flawed.

The sequence below is a three part list of events that the speaker claims happen at rock concerts.

4   But that happens . . . every gig there's a scrap –
5   there's always somebody that doesn't like somebody else.
6   It doesn't matter what it is, it's always happening,

It is apparent that the speaker is using his own 'lay' knowledge of the practices of listing to furnish a description which is recognisably complete. Also, this reference is designed so that the characteristics he indexes will not be heard as specific particulars, but are hearable as pointing to general features of violent incidents.

Investigation of the *organisation* of the speaker's utterances in lines 4 to 6 only provides us with a partial understanding of what sort of pragmatic work is being addressed in this sequence. To obtain a more sophisticated understanding of the actions being accomplished here, it is necessary to examine in more detail the use of the extreme case formulations, 'always' and 'every' in this passage.

Initially these items might appear to be a case of simple exaggeration, with little indication that there is something systematic about their use. But let us return to Pomerantz's (1986) analysis of extreme case formulations in everyday conversation. She discovered that speakers use extreme case formulations to influence the judgement or conclusions of co-interactants, *especially in circumstances in which the speaker may anticipate that the account, story or claim being made will receive an unsympathetic hearing.*

This is illustrated in the following extract, which comes from a call to a suicide prevention centre in the United States (Pomerantz, 1986: 225). (The transcription symbols are explained in the Appendix.)

```
(5)
 1   D   Do you have a gun at home?
 2       (.6)
 3   C   A forty fi:ve,
 4   D   You do have a forty fi:ve.
 5   C   Mm hm, it's loaded.
 6   D   What is it doing there, hh Whose is it.
 7   C   It's sitting there.
 8   D   Is it you:rs?
 9       (1.0)
10   D   It's Da:ve's.
11   C   It's your husband's hu:h?=
12   C   =I know how to shoot it,
13       (.4)
14   D   He isn't a police officer:r,
15   C   No:.
16   D   He just ha:s one.
17   C   Mm hm, It-u-Everyone doe:s don't they?
```

A gun is the type of possession for which an explanation may be sought. Indeed, the member of staff tries to find a reason for the caller's possession of a gun by asking whether her husband was a police officer. In this extract C describes the practice of keeping a gun by using the extreme case formulation 'Everyone does', thereby proposing that this is a common practice and therefore something for which she does not have to offer a mitigating explanation.

Let us consider this example further. In the United States gun ownership is far more common than in Europe. So we might expect that the mere fact that the speaker possesses a gun is not the kind of thing that requires some special justification. But keep in mind that this is a call to a suicide prevention agency, and that the caller has just admitted that she has a gun. In this situation, ownership of a gun is a slightly more sensitive issue, simply because it presents one immediate method by which the caller can end her life. This casts light on the defensive character of the caller's statement that 'everyone' has a gun. She is displaying a sensitivity to what the recipient might infer about her ownership of a gun: that she will use it to kill herself. Her use of an extreme case formulation is thus designed to portray her specific possession of a weapon as a normal matter, and not related to her status as 'someone calling the suicide prevention agency', with all that that might imply. Thus we may say that by using 'everyone does' the caller attempts to circumscribe the range of inferences that the agent of the suicide prevention agency might arrive at. This is the inferential work that the statement 'Everyone doe:s don't they?' is designed to do.

To understand this extract, note that it was necessary to invoke a form of 'common sense reasoning', or 'what everybody knows' about the category, 'potentially suicidal persons': that is, possession of a gun may be a very serious matter for someone who can be legitimately assigned to this category.

From our examination of the example of an extreme case formulation, we have three kinds of useful information which we can bear in mind when we return to the punk extract. First, extreme case formulations are, broadly, a device: a resource for doing things in spoken interaction. Second, we know that they are used in circumstances in which the recipient of the speaker's claim may attempt to undermine the accuracy or legitimacy of that claim. Third, we have seen that it has been necessary as a methodological resource to draw upon stereotypical or common sense knowledge which is, in principle, applicable to the kind of person who is speaking (in this case, the relevant category is 'potentially suicidal person'), and the circumstances in which they are speaking (in this case, 'ringing a suicide prevention agency').

We can now return to the instances of extreme case formulations in the punk extract. Recall that the speaker has just revealed that there was a spate of violent activity at the concert he had attended. He then says:

4   But that happens . . . *every* gig there's a scrap –
5   there's *always* somebody that doesn't like somebody else.
6   It doesn't matter what it is, it's *always* happening,

Observe the work that the use of extreme case formulations does here. 'Every gig there's a scrap' portrays violence as being related to a general kind of social occasion, namely, rock concerts. Note that he does not say that these violent incidents occur at every *punk* rock gig. Rather it is the 'gigs' that are associated with the disturbance, and not the gigs of bands whose following comes from a specific youth subculture. The second extreme case formulation 'there's *always* somebody that doesn't like somebody else' characterises violence as arising inevitably from inter-personal conflict. Such conflicts are portrayed as having their roots in idiosyncratic clashes of personality, irrespective of the social groups to which individuals may belong. Finally, 'it's *always* happening' marks such conflicts as a recurrent and consistent feature of human existence, and not peculiar to specific sections of the community.

In reporting the violence which occurred at the concert, the speaker makes no reference to the fact that the combatants were punks. Indeed, he does considerable work to portray the incident as something which occurs routinely at rock gigs generally, or which arises from two people's dislike for each other, and which is endemic in human society. In so doing, he minimises the relevance of the social identity of the combatants as 'punk rockers', and thus implies that their subcultural membership is merely incidental to this violence and not the reason for it.

To develop our understanding of this sequence, it is necessary to consider the range of culturally available stereotypes about the category 'punks'. As punks and punk rock emerged in the mid-1970s, tabloid press coverage focused on and glorified the more extreme characteristics of their lifestyle and the music: rejection of societal convention, self-mutilation as decoration, violence, uncleanliness, rebellion, and so on. The sometimes violent exploits of bands like the Sex Pistols and some of their followers ensured that the punk subculture was ideally suited to be the subject of a media-initiated 'moral panic' (Cohen, 1972).

These stereotypical representations of the punk lifestyle permeate our culture, and constitute a powerful set of lay assumptions and common sense knowledge. It is always possible that the behaviour of someone who seems to fit the category 'punk rocker' can be explained and interpreted by reference to this largely negative stock of knowledge.

Throughout the passage, the speaker is making the claim that the 'riot' which followed the concert was a consequence of the unwarranted presence of the police, and their subsequently provocative behaviour. However, the occurrence of a spate of violence at the concert could easily be interpreted in the light of negative stereotypical knowledge about punks: namely that their lifestyle and attitudes lead them to seek rebellion, confrontation with authority and violence. The mere fact that there was some disturbance could warrant the inference that the violence was another instance of 'typical punk behaviour'. Clearly, such a conclusion would severely undermine the validity of the speaker's (implied) claim that the problems after the concert were a consequence of the police presence. The design of the speaker's descriptions in lines 4–6 displays his sensitivity to precisely these kinds of alternative interpretations. He uses extreme case formulations as a rhetorical device to minimise the likelihood that his account of the violence following a punk rock concert may be called into question by reference to 'what everyone knows about punks'. Also, the speaker uses a three part list, a form of conversational organisation which permits the speaker to portray further general characteristics of violent incidents, thereby augmenting his implicit claim that the disturbance was not a specific consequence of the presence of punk rockers. This sequence, then, has been designed as an interactional resource through which the speaker warrants the factual status of his account in the light of potentially sceptical responses.

14.7 Conclusion

This has been a brief examination of three features of the data extract: the asymmetrical use of linguistic resources in the way that the speaker formulates the behaviour of the punks and the police; the speaker's description of some actual violent incidents; and the use of extreme case formulations. There are many further points which could be investigated in this extract. However, this exercise has been useful in that it has revealed some of the *design features* of the speaker's descriptive reports, and has indicated the kind of work his words are doing. In short, he is guarding against potentially sceptical responses to his account of the events following the punk rock concert, and warranting the authority and factual status of his own version of those events.

In the introduction to this chapter it was noted that the study of language use has not emerged as one of the central topics of sociological research. In part, this rests on a traditional commitment to the sociological study of specific social processes, rather than the investigation of talk about those processes, or the study of discourse which inextricably permeates social life. This chapter, however, has tried to illustrate that language use is a form of, and a vehicle for, social action. As such, it merits serious sociological attention.

However, there are additional methodological arguments which suggest the need for the systematic study of language use in sociology. To address these arguments, we can return to Gilbert and Mulkay's (1984) study of scientists' accounts of a scientific dispute in biochemistry.

Recall that Gilbert and Mulkay developed their discourse analytic approach as a consequence of their recognition of variation in the scientists' accounts. However, they realised that the variability they observed in scientists' discourse was not peculiar to their project, but is a constituent feature of any sociological (and social psychological) research which relies on accounts of behaviour, events, mental states, attitudes, beliefs and so on. Of course there are customary procedures by which sociologists can produce a single 'definitive' analytic version from the multiplicity of accounts which constitute their data. They can examine their data to look for broad similarities between the statements, and any similarities between accounts can be taken at 'face value', that is, as if they reflect accurately 'what really happened'. The analyst is then at liberty to construct a generalised version of participants' accounts and present these as analytic conclusions.

However, Gilbert and Mulkay question the role of the researcher when confronted by a variety of accounts of ostensibly the 'same' event or circumstances. In particular, they address the argument that, on account of sociological 'expertise', the analyst can recognise the difference between accurate accounts and inaccurate or irrelevant ones. They argue that this methodological strategy rests on the assumption that any social event has one 'true' meaning. They indicate, however, that social activities are the 'repositories' of multiple meanings, by which they mean that the 'same' circumstances can be described in a variety of ways to emphasise different features. (Indeed, earlier in this chapter we illustrated the way that the 'same thing' can be variously described by referring to Schegloff's illustrative formulation of where he was at one particular time.) So, Gilbert and Mulkay argue that there is no privilege for the analyst's decision as to what constitutes an 'objective' or 'accurate' version of the world, simply because any state of affairs can be described in a series of different ways.

For these reasons, Gilbert and Mulkay rejected the attempt to recon-struct 'what actually happened' from accounts. Instead, they began to examine the ways that accounts are organised through certain sets of interpretative practices to construct and warrant particular versions of 'what actually happened'. The implication of their argument, therefore, is that the study of discourse may be necessarily prior to, if not a replacement for, traditional forms of analysis.

> Given that participants' use of language can never be taken as literally descriptive, it seems methodologically essential that we pay more attention . . . to the systematic ways in which our subjects fashion their discourse. Traditional questions . . . will continue to remain unanswered, and unanswerable, until we improve our understanding of how social actors construct the data which constitute the raw material for [sociologists'] interpretative efforts. (Gilbert and Mulkay, 1984: 15)

14.8   Project

Collect a video or tape recording of a discussion between representatives of the major political parties, or an in-depth interview with one politician. Examine the ways in which specific positions and policies are described. What are the devices used to make specific policies seem reasonable and sensible? How do these devices work?

Go back over this chapter and try to identify the devices, techniques and descriptive resources through which have been warranted the importance of studying accounts.

14.9   Further reading

Atkinson and Heritage (1984) is the best single collection of conversation analytic studies, and contains two chapters which are based on lectures given by Harvey Sacks.

Heritage's (1984) book is by far the most accessible and insightful introduction to ethnomethodology; it also provides an excellent introduction to the principles of conversation analysis.

Potter and Wetherell (1987) is a clear introduction to discourse analysis, and its implications for social psychology.

Wooffitt (1992) is a study of the ways that people describe personal encounters with paranormal and supernatural phenomena, and discusses in more detail many of the methodological issues raised in this chapter.

Appendix: transcription conventions

(.5)	The number in brackets indicates a time gap in tenths of a second.
(.)	A dot enclosed in a bracket indicates pause in the talk less than two tenths of a second.
'hh	A dot before an 'h' indicates speaker in-breath. The more h's, the longer the inbreath.
hh	An 'h' indicates an out-breath. The more 'h's the longer the breath.
–	A dash indicates the sharp cut-off of the prior word or sound.
:	Colons indicate that the speaker has stretched the preceding sound or letter. The more colons the greater the extent of the stretching.
( )	Empty parentheses indicate the presence of an unclear fragment on the tape.
.	A full stop indicates a stopping fall in tone. It does not necessarily indicate the end of a sentence.
,	A comma indicates a continuing intonation.
?	A question mark indicates a rising inflection. It does not necessarily indicate a question.
Under	Underlined fragments indicate speaker emphasis.
CAPITALS	With the exception of proper nouns, capital letters indicate a section of speech noticeably louder than that surrounding it.
=	The 'equals' sign indicates contiguous utterances.

A more detailed description of these transcription symbols can be found in Atkinson and Heritage (1984: ix–xvi).

15 Explicating face-to-face interaction

Christian Heath and Paul Luff

Contents

> If society is conceived as interaction among individuals, the description of the forms of this interaction is the task of the science of society in its strictest and most essential sense. (Simmel, 1950: 21–2)

Sociology has long been concerned with developing a naturalistic and observational discipline which can deal rigorously with the details of social conduct. Underlying this concern is the classic problem of *verstehen* or interpretative understanding discussed in Weber's methodological writings (Weber, 1947). Indeed the 'problem of understanding' and the ways in which different methodological and conceptual orientations attempt to solve or even by-pass its implications form one of the most differentiating and intriguing elements of methodology in the social sciences. In this chapter we develop the discussion of the distinctive approach to the study of social action; an approach which places the situated and interpretative character of human conduct at the forefront of the methodological agenda and which is concerned with discovering the social organisation underlying the production and intelligibility of ordinary, everyday social actions and activities.

The pioneering research of Harvey Sacks and his colleagues, Emanuel Schegloff and Gail Jefferson, led to ethnomethodological studies becoming increasingly concerned with language use and social interaction. It was recognised that the analysis of social interaction, in particular talk-in-interaction, could provide the possibility of developing a 'naturalistic observation discipline which could deal with the details of social action(s) rigorously, empirically, and formally' (Schegloff and Sacks, 1974: 233). Since these early beginnings, a substantial body of empirical studies have emerged which have explicated the systematics underlying a wide variety of social activities within conversation and within a range of other interactional environments (see, for example, Atkinson and Heritage, 1984; Button and Lee, 1987; Conein et al., 1989; Boden and Zimmerman, 1991; Drew and Heritage, in press). In his recent collection of key contributions to conversational analysis, Coulter (1990) includes a bibliography of ethnomethodological and conversational analytic studies containing more than 1,400 citations to articles in five different languages. In this chapter we will briefly discuss the methodological considerations underlying conversational analysis and in particular the analytic orientations of recent work concerned with the study of face-to-face interaction. This work has begun to explicate the organisation of visual as well as vocal conduct (for example, Goodwin, 1981; Heath, 1986; and related work such as Kendon, 1979, 1982, 1990).

15.1 Data

Alongside a concern for gathering materials of ordinary conversation there has been a growing interest in exploring the organisation of interaction in various institutional environments such as courts of law, medical consultations and emergency control rooms. The primary sources of data for these studies are audio and audio-visual (mainly video) recordings of 'naturally occurring' interactions. On occasions these recordings are augmented by field observation. For the analysis of language use and social interaction, audio and video recordings have considerable advantages over more conventional forms of data used in the social sciences, such as fieldnotes or the responses to questionnaires. Recordings of human interaction provide the researcher with access to the richness and complexity of social action, allowing particular events to be scrutinised repeatedly and subjected to detailed inspection. They provide raw data to which a range of analytic interests can be applied, unconstrained by the concerns of a particular research project. Moreover, audio and video recordings enable other researchers within the scientific community to evaluate the strength of particular analyses with respect to the raw data and thus provide an important constraint on the quality and rigour of findings and explanations. Audio and video recordings give researchers a cheap and reliable technology which provides *repeatable* access to specific details of real world actions, activities and events; a microscope with which to study human life. As Heritage and Atkinson suggest:

> In sum, the use of recorded data serves as a control on the limitations and fallibilities of intuition and recollection; it exposes the observer to a wide range of interactional materials and circumstances and also provides some guarantee that analytic considerations will not arise as artifacts of intuitive idiosyncrasy, selective attention or recollection, or experimental design. (Heritage and Atkinson, 1984: 4)

Although access to gather data in a particular setting can prove difficult (see chapter 4), a wide range of real world environments, including potentially sensitive domains such as medical interviews and crisis management centres, have provided researchers with access for recording data (Heath, 1986; ten Have, 1991; Heath and Luff, 1991). There can be additional problems associated with video recording, particularly since it is more difficult to preserve the anonymity of participants. However, it has been found that people in a wide variety of settings are often willing to allow researchers to record both the audible and visual aspects of their conduct if they are guaranteed a final veto on whether the recordings should be preserved. Where possible, it is preferable to secure written permission from the participants. In the publication of papers and reports, it is essential to preserve the anonymity of the participants and events in question.

While it might be thought that the process of recording, particularly the use of video cameras, would be intrusive, it can have less effect on the character of the interaction than having a human observer, whether participant or non-participant in the scene. As Goffman (1981) suggests, and recent studies have shown (Goodwin 1981), the production of social activities may be deeply sensitive to the ways individuals participate within 'perceptual range of the event', even where these individuals are apparently not attending to the action in progress. Thus, where possible, the researcher should set up the equipment prior to the events being recorded and try to avoid focusing and operating the camera equipment during the events. Of course it will be necessary for the researcher to return to the scene to change cassettes, but normally it is possible to manage these practicalities between events. For example, when gathering data of a reception desk in a local police station, it was possible to change tapes and make adjustments to the camera and recording equipment at times when there were no callers in the reception area. In gathering audio-visual data it is important to try to position and focus the camera and the microphone so that the visual and vocal contributions of all the participants to the interaction are on the recording. It can be extremely difficult to analyse material if the researcher has inadvertently excluded participants from the recording. In some multiparty interactions such as in classrooms or even political speeches, it is difficult to generate recorded data which can provide sufficient access to the interactional organisation of the participants' visual and vocal conduct.

Despite the advantages of audio and video recordings of naturally occurring interaction, it can be helpful, especially in cases where the investigation is directed towards highly specialised forms of social interaction and language use, to generate field observations as well as recorded data. Augmenting recorded data with field observation has become increasingly relevant in recent years as researchers have begun investigations of complex activities in a range of organisational and institutional environments, including studies of crisis management centres, airport operations and control rooms on urban railway networks. The observations generated through fieldwork may not only provide an important resource in deciding how to focus the collection of recorded materials, but may also provide a vehicle for becoming familiar with highly specialised tasks and activities which occur within such environments. However, recorded materials prove critical in generating a detailed analysis of the interactional organisation of social actions and activities which is sensitive to orientations and procedures utilised by the participants' themselves.

15.2   Transcription

The analysis of recordings of naturally occurring interaction requires some form of transcription system to help the researcher both retrieve and inspect the details of the participants' conduct. The process of transcription is an important analytic tool, providing the researcher with an understanding of, and insights into, the participants' conduct. It provides the researcher with a way of noticing, even discovering, particular events, and helps focus analytic attention on their socio-interactional organisation. Conversational Analysis and allied approaches to the analysis of language use and interaction use a transcription system for capturing the details of talk which has been developed by Gail Jefferson over a number of years and which continues to evolve in response to particular research interests and findings. Like any transcription system, it is selective (Ochs, 1979) and focuses on the interactional and sequential features of talk. It delineates the location and interrelationship of speakers' utterances within talk by indicating, for example, where those utterances overlap, and it pays close attention to the way in which talk is articulated by indicating, for example, where talk is stressed by a speaker. Thus, in transcribing talk the aim is not simply to present an improved and more legible version of events. The level of detail in the transcriptions may appear puzzling to social researchers, although perhaps not to linguists and psychologists. However, as soon as one begins to work closely with recordings of actual social activities and notice the complexity of the participants' conduct, it becomes clear why so much trouble should be taken in transcribing the fine details of the interaction.

Consider the Fragment 15.1. It is drawn from a medical consultation in general practice. We enter the scene as the doctor begins to manipulate the patient's foot in order to determine the location of her pain.

Fragment 15.1   Transcript 1

```
 1   Dr:   You've got some varicose veins haven't you?
 2         (.)
 3   Dr:   a bit.
 4   Dr:   (manipulates foot) (2.3)
 5   P:    arghhh°hhh    (°hm)=
 6   Dr:   =is that sore when I do ⌐that?
 7   P:                            ⌊mhm hhum
 8         (0.5)
 9   Dr:   Where do you feel: it?
10   P:    Her:agh:
11         (0.4)
12   Dr:   °um
13         (2.5)
14   Dr:   °hhh (.) just stand up (.) Missus Delft,
15         (.) will you?
```

It can be seen that the talk is laid out sequentially, utterance by utterance. A silence or pause, either between utterances or within a particular speaker's turn, is measured in tenths of a second and bracketed, so for instance '(2.5)' is a silence of two and a half seconds. The bracketed single dot '(.)' indicates a 'minipause' of about a tenth of a second. When one speaker's contribution overlaps with another's, the point of overlap is indicated with a left hand bracket. So, for example, the patient's 'mhm hhum' begins during the doctor's utterance '=is that sore when I do that?', following the word 'do' (lines 6–7). The equals sign '=' at the beginning of '=is that sore.' indicates that the doctor's utterance is 'latched' to the prior utterance; there is no discernible gap between the two contributions. Aspects of the articulation of talk are also captured. Colons indicate that the prior sound is stretched, the number of colons being used to capture the length of the sound. The underlinings indicate points of emphasis and punctuation marks capture intonation: a question mark indicates rising intonation; a full stop, falling intonation; and a comma, falling intonation that is less well marked, as when a speaker pauses in an incomplete utterance prior to a next phrase. Audible inhalations '°hhh' and aspirations 'arghhh' are also indicated, the number of hhhs capturing the length of the sound. Descriptions in double brackets, for example '((manipulates foot))', are used to insert a transcriber's description of some feature of the action or activity. Further details about the transcription system and an explanation of the notation can be found Atkinson and Heritage (1984) and Boden and Zimmerman (1991).

Transcribing the talk in this way provides the researcher with a way of seeing the interrelationship between the actions of different speakers and focusing on their emergent properties. It also provides the researcher with the opportunity to examine aspects of the production of talk that are frequently hidden in more conventional ways of representing talk. Let us take a seemingly trivial instance in the fragment above, the patient's reply to the doctor's query concerning the location of the pain, on line 10 in Fragment 15.1. It is apparent from the transcript that the speaker does not simply utter 'here', but rather 'Here:agh:'. The utterance, a single word, is articulated by the speaker so that it not only provides a lexical component which indicates the location of the pain, namely 'Here', but includes in the second syllable of the word, a conventional sound used to display suffering, namely 'agh'. The patient is not only cooperating with the doctor's enquiries in determining the location of pain she has been suffering, but also through the way in which she articulates the response displays, then and there, the pain she is experiencing. It is interesting to observe that immediately following the patient's response, the doctor ceases to manipulate the foot and pursues an alternative, perhaps less painful way of discovering the actual location of the difficulties. He asks the patient to stand and observes the way in which she moves her foot. Despite the apparent awkwardness of transcribing 'Here:agh:', rather than the more conventional 'Here', the distinction might prove critical to the way in which we understand the developing course of the talk and the organisation of the diagnostic activities at hand. It also demonstrates how small variations in the articulation of a single word may be of interactional significance.

More generally, conversational analytic research has demonstrated through numerous empirical studies the ways in which seemingly trivial aspects of talk and bodily comportment can be critical to the organisation and sequential development of social activities in interaction. Whether it is the location of laugh particles within the delivery of an utterance, the selection of 'uh huh' or 'yeah' in encouraging a speaker to continue, or a momentary gesture towards a potential recipient, it has been found that participants systematically organise their conduct with respect to the conduct of their co-participant(s) and the potential sequential implications of particular activities. In consequence, it seems wise to assume that no object or event, however trivial it might initially appear, should be treated as irrelevant to the interaction or to the developing course of the activity. Underlying this assumption is the more general orientation that the researcher should focus analytic attention on the indigenous socio-organisational properties of situational conduct. Indeed, a strength of conversational analytic research is its ability to provide rigorous and generative explanations of in situ human conduct which do not rely on extraneously formulated analyses or theoretical models of actions or activities.

15.3 Analytic orientations

To speak of a 'method' for conversational or interaction analysis, in the ways methods are proposed in some areas of the social sciences, would be misleading. There is no method per se, no set of clearly formulated techniques and procedures which if properly followed will unambiguously provide rigorous explanations of interactional conduct. There are however, some wider methodological orientations which underpin the analytic stance that conversational and interaction analysis adopts towards its 'data', and a body of practice for ways in which analyses of phenomena are articulated and warranted.

As suggested earlier, conversational or interaction analysis is not concerned with language per se, but rather it recognises that talk is a primary vehicle for the accomplishment of social actions in human society. Its primary concern is with the social organisation of ordinary, naturally occurring, human conduct, particularly in explicating the resources that members of society rely upon in the production and recognition of social activity. In numerous studies, Garfinkel (1967) demonstrates how social actions are embedded in and inseparable from a body of common sense knowledge and practical reasoning which renders human conduct, 'account-able'. The production and intelligibility of social action are two sides of the same coin; the resources relied upon in the accomplishment of conduct are the self-same resources through which sense of the action(s) is assembled. Societal members presuppose and rely upon a common body of resources for producing their social actions and rendering actions intelligible, for all practical purposes. These resources, this common sense knowledge and practical reasoning, which forms the foundation to social life is systematically masked, taken for granted, 'seen but unnoticed'. These resources are unavailable to unguided intuition, introspection or theoretical imagination, but as Garfinkel (1967) and Sacks (1992) demonstrated, they can be made accessible through the detailed, case by case analysis of in situ conduct.

Therefore analytic attention can be directed towards the in situ accomplishment of social actions and activities and the resources that participants utilise in producing, recognising and coordinating their conduct with others. Nowhere is the 'ongoing accomplishment' of social action and activity more clearly apparent than in human sociability and interaction. A glance at a transcript or a review of a recording reveals how talk, and the social actions and activities that it embodies, progressively emerge step by step, the interactants producing their contributions moment by moment in the light of the conduct of their co-participants.

Conversational Analysis has focused on the socio-interactional organisation which underlies the production of talk, and the ways in which turns at talk accomplish specific actions by virtue of their location and design. In contrast to some theories of language use and linguistic analysis (e.g. speech act theory), it is assumed that a turn at talk and the action it accomplishes is thoroughly embedded in and dependent upon the context of its occurrence. The intelligibility of an utterance is produced in the immediate context at hand and itself forms an integral part of that context; the meaning or sense of the utterance is inextricably embedded in the circumstances of its production. It has been demonstrated that to treat a turn at talk in isolation from its context leads to unwarranted and frustrating attempts to assert that the utterance has a literal meaning which remains stable through time and space. Thus, conversational analysis focuses on the situated organisation of human conduct and is derived from the detailed inspection of the organisation of particular actions and activities from within the situation in which they are produced and rendered intelligible. Through these analyses it is able to derive generalisable descriptions of the resources through which specific forms of conduct are systematically accomplished.

Although it has a general concern with the situated character of human conduct, conversational analysis places rigorous constraints on the way in which talk-in-interaction can be explicated with respect to the 'context-at-hand'. All too often 'context' in the social sciences is treated as a realm of local variables which can be invoked to explain the character of a particular activity within some particular occasion. By contrast, in conversational analysis, the detailed inspection of in situ human conduct is concerned with the identification of 'features of context' which are oriented to by the participants themselves. The idea of context, therefore, is not simply concerned with a frame within which an action or activity occurs, but rather an analysis seeks to specify, and provide evidence for, the relevance of features of context which inform the very accomplishment of the participants' conduct. The 'problem of relevance', particularly the development of analyses which seek to systematically locate and warrant the procedures, practices, knowledge and reasoning used and oriented to by the participants themselves, forms the foundation of the detailed investigation of situational conduct in conversational analysis.

It is not surprising that within conversation the immediately preceding utterance(s) or action(s) recurrently form an object within the context to which subsequent action and activity is oriented. Telephone conversations, in which visual conduct is clearly not relevant to co-participant action, provide a clear example of the way in which a next utterance, or action, is produced in the light of the immediately prior turn(s). In general, talk and aspects of bodily comportment in interaction are organised locally, step by step, utterance by utterance, with each next action oriented to the immediately preceding action(s) and activity(ies). Indeed, speakers design their talk and bodily movement with regard to the immediately prior action(s), and co-participants rely upon the local design of conduct and its sensitivity to prior action in order to render intelligible particular contributions. It is also clear that, while a next utterance or action is produced with respect to the immediately preceding action(s), it simultaneously contributes to the context-at-hand, forming the framework to which subsequent actions will be addressed. Consider, for instance, the organisation of the talk between the Counsellor and the Caller in Extract 6 in the previous chapter, and the ways in which each utterance projects a range of possibilities for the next action. Moreover the next action, while sensitive to the prior action and the possibilities it makes relevant, generates its own distinctive implications for a subsequent action or activity by the co-participant. As Heritage (1984) suggests, the conduct of participants in interaction is doubly contextual, both 'context shaped and context renewing'. In consequence, the character of an action or activity and its organisation can only be determined, both by participants and by researchers, with reference to its location within the local framework of conduct. Schegloff and Sacks write that:

> a pervasively relevant issue [for participants] about utterances in conversation is 'why that now,' a question whose . . . analysis may also be relevant to find what 'that' is. That is to say, some utterances may derive their character as actions entirely from placement considerations. (Schegloff and Sacks, 1974: 241)

Audio and video recordings provide researchers with a medium through which they can repeatedly inspect social activities in the context of their occurrence, and in particular the location of specific actions within the developing course of the interaction. Thus, researchers can begin to assess the character and social organisation of these activities. We can consider an utterance or bodily movement with respect to the circumstances of its production and its significance for subsequent action. By repeated inspection of the data, we can begin to assess how the participants display an understanding of, and act upon, each other's actions and activities. Through this analysis we can slowly begin to develop insights into the socio-interactional organisation of the ways in which the participants produce their own conduct and recognise the actions of their co-participant(s). In other words, the researcher, in inspecting the data and deriving observations, is utilising the sequential character of the participants' conduct as a resource for developing an understanding of the organisation of the various actions and activities. By inspecting the ways in which the participants respond to and display an understanding of each other's conduct in subsequent actions and activities, the researcher can begin to develop observations concerning the character of an action and its organisation which is sensitive to the orientations of the participants' themselves. Sacks, Schegloff and Jefferson suggest:

> [It] is a systematic consequence of the turn taking organisation of conversation that it obliges its participants to display to each other, in a turn's talk, their understanding of the other turn's talk. More generally, a turn's talk will be heard as directed to a prior turn's talk, unless special techniques are used to locate some other talk to which it is directed . . . . But while understandings of other turns' talk are displayed to co-participants, they are available as well to professional analysts, who are thereby provided a proof criterion (and a search procedure) for the analysis of what a turn's talk is occupied with. Since it is the parties' understandings of prior turns' talk that is relevant to their construction of next turns, it is their understandings that are wanted for analysis. The display of those understandings in the talk in subsequent turns affords a resource for the analysis of prior turns, and a proof procedure for professional analyses of prior turns, resources intrinsic to the data themselves. (Sacks et al., (1974: 728–9)

Talk and interaction therefore, and the use of audio and video recordings, provide the researcher with the possibility of using the participants' own contributions to assess their understanding of the immediately preceding action or activity, and to discern how the co-participant(s) address(es) the others understanding of their own contribution. The turn and sequential organisation of talk and interaction provides an important resource for establishing the relevance of particular characterisation of the participants' conduct and for generating and warranting an explanation of its organisation.

With some of these issues in mind, let us return to Fragment 15.1 and begin to consider the ways in which the interaction and the diagnostic activities emerge with respect to both the talk and bodily conduct of the participants. As the doctor begins the manipulation and draws the foot backwards, the patient utters a cry of pain 'arghhh°hhh(°hm)'. The cry entails a conventional expression of pain, namely 'argh', coupled by sharp audible breathing, firstly out, 'hhh', and then in, '°hhh'.

Fragment 15.1   Transcript 2

```
    4  Dr:  (Manipulates foot) (2.3)
 →  5  P:   arghhh°hhh    (°hm)=
    6  Dr:  =is that sore when I do ┌that?
    7  P:                           └mhm hhum
    8        (0.5)
    9  Dr:  Where do you feel: it?
   10  P:   Her:agh:
   11        (0.4)
   12  Dr:  °um
   13        (2.5)
   14  Dr:  °hhh (.) just stand up (.) Missus Delft,
   15        (.) will you?
```

Ordinarily we might think of a cry of pain as a relatively unfettered expression of bodily experience lying outside the realm of social and interactional organisation. However, even such apparently idiosyncratic and 'natural' expressions as these cries of pain may arise in, and be organised with respect to, the emergent activities and interaction at hand.

In Fragment 15.1 the cry of pain arises in response to the manipulation of the foot by the doctor; the doctor's actions momentarily inflict suffering on the patient. The cry of pain does not, however, occasion sympathy or appreciation from the doctor, nor is the actual suffering experienced by the patient addressed as a topic in its own right. Rather, in next turn, and in response to the cry of pain, the doctor produces a query in which he attempts to locate the actual element of the action which gave rise to the suffering expressed by the patient. As the doctor produces this enquiry, he manipulates the foot, repeating the movements which inflicted the pain on the patient. In response to the doctor's enquiry, the patient produces 'mhm hhum' which in turn engenders a more general attempt by the doctor to locate the area of difficulty, to which the patient responds with 'Here:agh:' briefly discussed earlier.

Despite the potential suffering incurred by the patient as the doctor manipulates the foot, she cooperates with the practical enquiries at hand, retaining her foot in his hands and responding to his queries. The way in which the patient participates in the activity allows the practitioner to pursue his diagnostic enquiries into the location of the pain. The way in which the doctor responds to the patient's initial expression of suffering, producing a query which addresses the location of the pain, rather than appreciating the actual suffering, encourages her to adopt an analytic stance towards the foot and its malfunction. The immediate juxtaposition of the query and the continued manipulation of the foot establishes a particular orientation towards the activity from the co-participant which allows the diagnostic enquiries to continue. A sympathetic alignment by the doctor towards the patient's suffering immediately following the cry would temporarily suspend diagnostic enquiries and might well undermine the possibility of inflicting further suffering on the patient.

It is clear that before we can proceed further with a discussion of this fragment we need to have a closer understanding of the ways in which participants' visual conduct features in the developing course of the talk and interaction.

15.4   The transcription of talk and bodily movement

The transcription of visual conduct has long been a vexed question, and it is unlikely that a general orthography will emerge that serves the range of disciplines which investigate bodily movement, including dance, physical education and social psychology. Among researchers concerned with the naturalistic analysis of social interaction, a transcription system for capturing aspects of visual conduct, in particular its relation to talk, has been developed. This system involves mapping or charting the visual and vocal conduct of the participants, so that the researcher can see where the various actions within a particular fragment occur in relation to each other. It provides a rough and ready guide to the interaction within a particular fragment which is used alongside the actual data, the video recording, to facilitate analysis.

The following transcript is a simplified map of part of Fragment 15.1.

This transcript captures some aspects of the participants' conduct surrounding the initial cry of pain. Talk is transcribed using the system we discussed earlier. However, the talk is laid horizontally across the page, so that each speaker's contribution follows on from the prior. In the example, the participants' talk has been presented in the centre of the page, but in multiparty interactions it will be necessary to divide the page vertically so that space is left to transcribe their visual conduct either above or below each speaker's talk. So that silences or pauses are represented spatially as

Fragment 15.1   Transcript 3

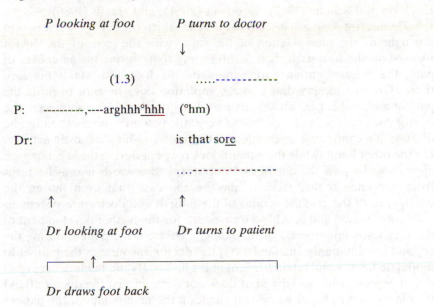

well as descriptively, a gap is transcribed by dashes, '–'. A single dash is a
tenth of a second, so that in the gap of (2.3) prior to the patient's pain cry,
we find 13 dashes. In cases where there is no talk occurring within the
interaction, a timescale in tenths of a second may be drawn at the bottom
of the page.

The visual conduct of the participants is then located in relation to the
talk and/or timescale. Gaze is transcribed using a system developed by
Goodwin (1981). A continuous line indicates that the participant is gazing
at the co-participant, a series of dots ('.....') that one party is turning
towards another, and a series of commas (',,,,,') that one party is
turning away from the other. In the transcript we find the patient turning
towards the doctor on completion of her pain cry and immediately
following the onset of his shift of gaze towards her. In certain circumstances it may be helpful to use a series of spaced dashes ('– – –') to
indicate gaze is directed towards an object, such as the patient's knee in
Transcript 3. Other features of the participants' visual conduct are
indicated on the transcript according to where they occur within the talk or
timescale. The researcher should at least indicate the onset and completion
of particular movements, such as gestures, postural movements, and in the
case at hand, the manipulations of the foot by the doctor. It is also useful to
indicate any critical junctures within the development of a particular
movement. Movements are represented by a continuous line, although in
fact a whole range of ad hoc signs and symbols are often used to represent
particular aspects of movement. A more detailed discussion of these and

related issues can be found in Scheflen (1973), Kendon (1979, 1982, 1990), Erickson and Schultz (1982), Goodwin (1981), and Heath (1986).

In Transcript 3 we can discern the way in which the cry itself emerges in the light of the manipulation of the foot, with the gaze of the doctor focused on the foot itself. It is worth noting that, during the actual cry of pain, the doctor continues to manipulate the foot and retains his gaze there. Only as the cry draws to a completion does he turn towards the patient and, as his gaze arrives, delivers the question. In consequence, the doctor does not see, and is not seen to see, the patient's suffering; rather he displays his continuing orientation to the foot and his diagnostic activity. On the other hand, while the patient does reorient during the cry, her gaze appears to by-pass the doctor and only turns to towards him as he turns from her knee to her face. It may be the case that even during the emergence of the cry, the actions of the patient and doctor are systematically coordinated and provide a framework for the further development of the diagnostic enquiry. By 'withholding' gaze from the patient during the cry and continuing the manipulation, the doctor encourages the patient to modulate her cry and retain her foot in his hands. By modulating her cry so that it expresses her suffering but does not demand that the doctor attend to it in its own right, or worse still abandon the manipulation, the patient cooperates with the actions of her co-participant and his diagnostic activity. Even the way in which the patient constructs her reorientation during the cry itself, by-passing the doctor and looking into the middle distance, may be designed to diminish the potential demands on the other to abandon the activity at hand. In this way we can begin to discern how diagnostic activity is produced in and through the interaction of patient and doctor.

As with examining talk, the process of transcribing the visual and vocal conduct within a particular fragment is an important analytic aid. As in Transcript 3, it helps the researcher to identify the details of participants' conduct and interaction which remain inaccessible even after repeated viewings of the data. Indeed, it is often only during the process of mapping out data that one begins to discover the ordering of actions, and in many cases one discovers conduct during transcription which previously remained unnoticed. Once complete, the map provides a sketch of the local geography of the participants' conduct, particularly the position of actions in relation to each other. It provides a resource with which the researcher can explore the interaction within a relatively brief moment in time and consider how specific actions may be organised with respect to each other. The map is simply a way of capturing some details of the participants' conduct and should always be used analytically alongside the data itself, the video recording of the actual event.

A complex map of the visual and vocal conduct within a particular fragment should be seen as a device to support individual analysis, rather than a way of presenting material. Ideally, the researcher needs to present the transcript with the actual extract to which it refers, but until we are able to incorporate video cassettes or video discs within journals and books it is not practically feasible. Moreover, in presenting data in text, as in Transcript 3, it is often necessary to highlight certain features and exclude others to enable the reader to make sense of the action. Photographs and illustrations of particular frames can help, but remain unsatisfactory. Despite these difficulties, video recordings can be viewed at colloquia and conferences by members of the research community, providing an important resource for the evaluation and development of analyses.

15.5   The interdependence of visual and vocal conduct

It is clear from the foregoing that the ways in which visual conduct are addressed within conversational or interaction analysis stand in marked contrast to more traditional studies of non-verbal behaviour. In the first place, non-verbal behaviour is not treated in isolation from the co-occurring or surrounding verbal behaviour of the participants; indeed, visual and vocal conduct are treated as various means through which social actions and activities are accomplished. Secondly, behaviour in interaction, whether visual, vocal or a combination of the two, is addressed in terms of the actions it performs in situ within the local configuration of activity and the developing course of the interaction. This is in direct contrast with considering the way such behaviour reveals, expresses or represents the psychological or emotional dispositions of actors. Thirdly, the meaning or, better, the sense of a particular piece of conduct, is embedded in the context at hand, accomplished in and through a social organisation which provides for the production and intelligibility of the social action or activity it performs.

The following fragment offers an opportunity for discussing in a little more detail the way in which we might explore the interrelationship of talk and visual conduct. The material is drawn from video recordings of the Bakerloo Line Control Room on London Underground. The Line Control Room houses the Line Controllers (Ci and Cii), the Divisional Information Assistant (DIA) and the Signal Assistants. These personnel are responsible for the day-to-day running of the service and providing passengers with information. We join the fragment as one of the Controllers fails to make contact with a driver through the radio telephone. He turns to the DIA and, very unusually, asks him use the Public Address system to make an announcement on the platform to tell the driver to go if there is a green signal.

At first glance the exchange looks relatively straightforward. The Controller produces a request (line 9) which the DIA accepts. In accepting, the DIA begins the activity which allows him to deliver the announcement to the station; he sets the PA system to allow him to make an announcement to the southbound platform at Oxford Circus. The

Fragment 15.2   Transcript 1 (simplified)

```
   1              ((Attempts for a third time to contact the driver
   2              on the radio telephone ......))
   3    Cii:      Control(ler) to the train at Oxford Circus South
   4              (.) Driver do you receive:, over?
   5              (1.1)
   6              ((replaces one receiver and picks up another to
   7              contact Station Manager))
   8              (2.5)
→  9    Cii:      Tell him to go: (.) if you've (got) a clear sig ⌐nal
  10    DIA:                                                      ⌊Yeah
  11              (6.3) ((sets PA system))
  12    DIA:      This is a staff announce:men:t ↑
  13              (0.2)
  14    DIA:      to the train operator (.) if you have a::
  15              Green Signal: ↑ you may proceed .........
```

request and its acceptance embodies an organisation found throughout a range of activities within interaction, where a first action, the request, establishes the sequential relevance for a next action, an acceptance or rejection of the request. In other words, the first action projects one of two alternative actions to be undertaken by the co-participant in immediate juxtaposition with it; and if the relevant response is not forthcoming then that response is noticeably or accountably absent. Of course, in the case at hand the vocal acceptance, uttered in overlap with the Controller's request, makes it incumbent upon the DIA to produce the requested action, namely, to tell the driver to go if there is a green signal. Even before the DIA utters 'yeah' his hand reaches for the buttons which operate the Public Address system. He thereby displays, prior to the completion of the request, that he is beginning the sequentially relevant activity, allowing the Controller to turn to complete this momentary interaction and deal with some other unrelated business.

The design of the request by the Controller raises some interesting issues. Even though the DIA and the Controller have been occupied with quite distinct activities and the DIA has had no direct contact with the Controller concerning the driver at Oxford Circus, the request is designed in such a way that it presupposes that it is clear who the 'him' is and what the reasons are for 'telling him to go'. The Controller's request however, appears to operate unproblematically; the DIA delivers the correct announcement to the relevant driver. It may be that the participants' visual conduct immediately prior to and during the request provides a partial explanation for its design and its success.

In the gap following the third attempt to call the driver on the radio telephone and before he produces the request to the DIA, the Controller turns to the telephone panel and looks for a number. Roughly two seconds into the silence, the DIA turns from a large line diagram on the wall of the

Fragment 15.2   Transcript 2

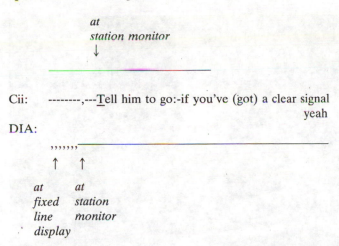

at
station monitor
↓

Cii: --------,---T̲ell him to go:-if you've (got) a clear signal
                                                                yeah

DIA:

,,,,,,,
↑   ↑

at   at
fixed   station
line   monitor
display

Control Room to the closed circuit television (CCTV) monitors directly in front of him. His shift of orientation appears to engender action from the Controller, who immediately turns towards the same screen as the DIA. As they are both looking at the CCTV screen, an image of Oxford Circus southbound platform appears and the Controller produces the request. Figure 15.1 shows two photographs which give a sense of the action: one taken immediately before the DIA glances towards the CCTV monitor (a), and one as the Controller begins the request (b).

As the Controller produces the request, both he and the DIA are oriented towards the same object; the platform at Oxford Circus. Thus, the DIA is able to make sense of the request in the light of the Controller's orientation, inferring that 'him' is the driver of the train they are both looking at and that the request entails asking this particular train to leave if there is a clear signal. So, the utterance's ability to engender an appropriate response from the DIA relies, in part, upon the participants' momentary, common orientation towards the same object. Mutatis mutandis necessary change, the utterance serves reflexively to invoke a common referent and make it an integral feature in both the production and the recognition of the activity. The utterance and the participants' visual conduct are thoroughly interdependent, each elaborating and dependent upon the other.

It appears, therefore, that both the response to the request and its ability to engender the appropriate action from the recipient are embedded in the visual conduct of the participants. We can discern how the visual orientation of a potential recipient may occasion the production, and inform the design of, a particular action and how a shift of gaze towards a particular object can serve to engender it being noticed by another. In the space available it is not possible to discuss the further complexities of this

(a) *immediately before the request*

(b) *at the beginning of the request*

Figure 15.1   *In the control room*

fragment. However, by focusing on the moment at which the two colleagues establish mutual engagement during the production and acceptance of the request, we can begin to develop an analysis that addresses the ways in which participants' actions may be oriented to features of the emergent context. In particular, their conduct could be sensitive to the preceding attempts to deal with the developing problem that the request is designed to solve. It is, however, only by detailed and repeated observation of a fragment that the researcher can begin to build an analysis of the ways in which the participants' conduct orientates to each others' actions. The analysis must establish empirically, a demonstrable case for the 'contextual features', primarily the conduct of the co-participants, to which specific actions and activities are oriented.

The naturalistic analysis of interactional conduct entails bringing particular methodological considerations to bear upon the fragments of 'naturally occurring' encounters captured on audio or video recordings. The technology provides the analyst with the ability to scrutinise the recording repeatedly with the assistance of conventional transcription procedures. The methodological considerations treat talk and visual conduct with respect to the activities they perform in situ and use the interaction as a medium through which to detect the conventions used by the participants themselves in producing and coordinating their conduct. In particular, the analysis explicates the sequential organisation between particular actions which informs the production and intelligibility of mundane, real world, human activity. We can utilise recordings of real world interactions as a way of developing insights into the organisation of human conduct and as a resource for warranting descriptions of particular phenomena and their organisation. Thus, we can begin to develop explanations of the social organisation of human conduct which are sensitive to the orientations and practices utilised by the participants' themselves and which are empirically generative and cumulative. (See for example the studies collected in Atkinson and Heritage, 1984.)

In the light of the assumptions discussed earlier, particularly the assumption that no object or event should be treated as inconsequential to the interaction, it is inevitable that interaction analysis is a methodological orientation dedicated to the detailed analysis of single cases. As we have seen, analysis begins with the discussion of particular fragments of interaction and charts the character of the conduct and the relations and practical reasoning that pertain between particular activities. The identification of a particular phenomenon and the characterisation of its organisation derives from the detailed interaction analysis of a particular fragment of data, where the central focus of the analysis is concerned with delineating the orientations of the participants to each others' conduct and building an explanation of the procedures and reasoning which inform the production and recognition of an activity.

The investigation of a phenomenon may begin by forming 'candidate' collections of particular instances, and then proceed by undertaking detailed analysis of these cases and comparing and contrasting the organisation of an activity across multiple instances. These instances could involve different participants on different occasions in very different situations. Through the investigation of multiple instances the analysis can begin to identify recurrent features of a particular action or activity. A description of the activity's organisation can then be developed which accounts for the ways in which it is systematically accomplished by participants within specific occasions.

Through the detailed analysis of particular instances, coupled with a concern to examine specific phenomena across multiple cases, the naturalistic analysis of conversation and interaction has developed a substantial body of findings which delineate the interlocking social organisation of a wide range of 'ordinary' social actions and activities.

One final point: potentially 'deviant' or complex cases play a particularly important part in developing the analysis, providing further evidence for a body of practice and reasoning which features in the production and recognition of an action or activity. In first place, such cases can throw into relief incongruities or difficulties with a candidate analysis of particular phenomena, encouraging the researcher to reconsider or even abandon a provisional sketch of the organisation of an activity. Indeed, deviant or complex cases may often help the researcher to search for a more general socio-interactional organisation, which can deal with the specifics of the case at hand while preserving the integrity of related cases. Secondly, deviant or complex cases are often used to demonstrate how a procedure or practice is oriented to even when a feature or action, recurrently provided for by the organisation, is either absent or uncharacteristic.

15.6   Summary

Like other forms of qualitative social science the naturalistic analysis of face-to-face interaction does not consist of a set of methods which can be mechanically applied to data. Rather, the approach discussed in this chapter, consists of an analytic orientation which is primarily concerned with using naturalistic data to explicate the 'methodology', the common sense knowledge and practical reasoning which underlies the in situ production and intelligibility of social actions and activities. Gaining familiarity with this analytic standpoint can be helped by reading studies in ethnomethodology, conversational and interaction analysis. However, it is only by dealing with data, and addressing the specifics of in situ social action and activity, that a researcher can begin to develop analytic skills. Indeed, it is often suggested that to undertake interaction analysis, students need to take an apprenticeship through which they work on materials with a more experienced researcher. By collecting and handling data one can progressively learn to reason with action and interaction and develop the sorts of analytic orientation which inform a cumulative body of studies found in conversational analysis.

It is worthwhile summarising a few of the central concerns which underlie this analytic orientation and which provide a foundation for explicating the social organisation of naturally occurring interactional activities and events.

First, human conduct is contextual and situated. The accomplishment of an action or activity, its sense, impact, and accountability is embedded within the local configuration of activity and the particular situation in which it occurs. There is no necessary correspondence between the lexicon or syntax of an utterance or the physical form of a movement and the action it performs. The meaning or sense of an action or activity is 'indexical'; systematically accomplished by the participants within the practical circumstances at hand.

Second, social action and activity rely upon a body of common sense knowledge and reasoning, a 'methodology', which informs their real world accomplishment in actual situations of choice. Participants (or societal members) utilise and orientate to this 'methodology' both in the production and in the recognition of situationally embedded ordinary conduct. It is their practices and the mundane reasoning these entail which form the focus of analytic attention.

Third, talk and visual conduct are the primary vehicles for the production of social action and activity in face-to-face interaction. The sequential organisation of talk and the interactional coordination of visual and vocal conduct provide the researcher with an important resource for identifying the participants' orientations to each others' conduct, and generating insights into the organisation of particular actions and activities.

Through the detailed case-by-case analysis of human conduct in the situations of its occurrence, particularly of talk and bodily conduct in interaction, we can begin to explicate the social organisation utilised by the participants in producing their own actions and recognising the actions of others. In this way, we can shift analytic attention away from the presupposition of stable meanings of conduct in different situations to the resources utilised by societal members in producing and generating the in situ sense of social action and activity, a concern which, as Weber pointed out, lies at the heart of sociological enquiry.

15.7 Project

Record on video some naturally occurring interaction between people, for example a casual conversation, a dinner party or a potentially more formal encounter such as a service transaction. Select one or two brief fragments and transcribe the participants' actions and activities, firstly by transcribing the talk and then by mapping out the visual conduct. Generate some preliminary observations concerning the character of the participants' conduct and the actions produced through their talk and body movement. Assemble evidence indigenous to the interaction itself for potential relationships and procedural connections holding between specific actions.

15.8   Further reading

Garfinkel (1967) is a difficult but an extremely rewarding book, which forms the foundation to ethnomethodology and related research in conversational analysis.

Sacks (1992) is a collection of transcribed lectures; they not only provide an extraordinary insight into the analysis of conversation and the ways in which phenomena can be discovered through detailed naturalistic analysis, but a rich collection of highly insightful observations concerning language use and interactional organisation.

Atkinson and Heritage (1984) is an important collection of papers that provides an introduction both to the methodological assumptions of conversational analysis and to the substantive areas of interest such as topic, preference organisation and non-vocal conduct.

Boden and Zimmerman (1991) is a recent set of papers that draws together an interesting body of conversational analytic studies of institutional interaction which address some of the current important debates within sociology.

Button (1991) is an ethnomethodological respecification of foundational topics in the human sciences including: the social actor, logic, cognition, epistemology and methods of measurement, inference and evidence.

Heath (1986) examines talk and visual conduct within the medical consultation which also includes analyses of the manipulation and inspection of such objects as the patient's body, medical records and computer systems in the encounter.

Heritage (1984) is a clear introduction to the background to ethnomethodology and to current areas of related research including conversational analysis and studies of work.

Kendon (1990) is a collection of fascinating empirical studies concerned with the organisation of face-to-face interaction, coupled with a useful methodological discussion concerning the naturalistic and contextual analysis of human conduct.

PART IV

Endings

16   Writing about social research

Nigel Gilbert

Contents

Until research has been published, available for all to read, it barely counts as social science at all. In science and social science, publication is an essential final step of the research process. There are good reasons for this. First, knowledge is itself a social creation. If you believe something, it remains a mere belief until you can persuade others that it is true; then it becomes knowledge that is shared. Second, as you will probably already have experienced yourself, it is not until you try to write down the results of your work in a way that is accessible to others that things become clear. Writing is a process of discovery as well as a process of clarification and of communication.

This last chapter is about writing and publishing social research. In the first section, we discuss some ways of thinking about the communication of research findings. The next section examines the origin and form of the research literature. This is followed by the dissection of a journal article published in the *American Sociological Review* to show how such articles are organised. In the final section, we discuss some of the difficulties of getting social research to influence social policy.

16.1   Truth and persuasion

There are several ways of thinking about sociological writing. At first sight, you might think that such writing merely records the facts for all to see. The ideal social scientific paper or book should be objective, setting out as clearly and precisely as possible what has been discovered. However, this view of scientific writing does not stand much scrutiny. It leaves un-examined several crucial questions: what do we mean by 'objective'?, what counts as a 'fact'?, why do research reports contain arguments as well as statements of fact?

A more sophisticated view of scientific writing recognises that writing is a form of rhetoric; that is, writing aims to persuade the reader of a position. It can be done well or badly. Over the years, writers have evolved stratagems for persuasion and have devised 'tricks of the trade'. Good writing is persuasive partly because of its use of these rhetorical devices, but also because it dares to go beyond them to invent new ways of putting arguments together.

A third view of scientific writing locates writing within the social structure of science. Sociological articles and books are written for and mainly read by other sociologists, who form a community with its own customs and beliefs. The shape of a journal article or the ways in which arguments are presented in sociological books are designed by writers for this community and in turn modify the community and its beliefs. Individually, sociologists write for the community because they prize the rewards it offers them, not financial rewards (often minimal or non-existent) but rewards of status, or 'recognition' of their labours and their abilities.

16.2   The research literature

One way to get a better understanding of the relationship of writing to the sociological community is to look at the history of the research paper in the natural sciences. The sociological literature has grown in much the same way as the scientific literature. This history has been well documented by Bazerman (1988).

16.2.1   The history of the scientific paper

The first scientific journal to be published in English, *The Philosophical Transactions*, was founded in 1665 by the Secretary of the Royal Society. It had its origins in the correspondence which members of the Royal Society wrote to each other to record their observations and ideas on topics of mutual interest, mainly about what today would be called natural science.

Initially, the editor treated the journal much like a club newsletter: picking out interesting titbits from the correspondence and inviting the readers to send in further information. Gradually, however, the contributors were left to speak for themselves, and within a few years, the editor was reprinting letters verbatim, with only a few lines of editorial introduction.

The editor had to have a steady flow of correspondence coming to the journal to keep it afloat. Among the lures for authors were recognition of ideas, public acknowledgement of who was first to propose an idea or make a discovery, and the feeling that one was cooperating in a significant undertaking.

Over time, members began to write their letters, not as private correspondence to the editor which then happened to get published, but as public documents with an increasingly formal structure. Although many of the readers of the early *Transactions* were attracted by the tales of the curious and extraordinary which were reported there, there was a central circle of contributors who tended to be much more knowledgeable and much more sceptical, comparing what they read with what they believed and observed. As the journal also printed critical commentary, scientists for the first time had to defend themselves and their opinions in public.

According to Bazerman, this led to role conflict for the authors, who were torn between publicising their own work in the terms which would most appeal to the general reader, and defending their work from the criticisms of knowledgeable fellow scientists. A strategy for avoiding disputes with the other scientists was to present the work in the clearest possible way, anticipating possible objections. Gradually, standardised methods for presentation evolved.

Over the next century, several other scientific journals were started. These had to compete for readers and contributors. One way to get subscribers was to publish articles which were more carefully tuned to the particular interests of their readers. In addition to *The Philosophical Transactions*, which covered the whole of science, more specialised journals appeared for particular disciplines. In order to maintain its position in the face of this competition, there were increasing efforts to improve the articles in the *Transactions*, as first the editor excluded information only of interest to amateur scientists, and then kept out work judged to be of relatively low quality.

The use of the editor as a 'gatekeeper' who rejected some articles as unsuitable for the journal imposed obvious strains on the post holder who had to fend off the disappointed contributors. After conflict erupted in the 1750s, an editorial board was created and later, the editor's decisions began to be made on the recommendation of 'referees', scientists chosen for their specialist knowledge who read and commented anonymously on papers.

Nowadays, when a paper is sent to an academic journal for publication, the editor first scans it to see whether the subject matter fits within the journal's scope. Then the editor sends it to two or three referees who write a commentary on it, indicating any weaknesses, and recommend whether it should be published as it stands, revised to take account of the criticisms, or rejected as unsuitable for publication. The editor, acting on this advice, writes back to the author, usually enclosing the referees' comments. If the verdict is that changes need to be made, the author is invited to resubmit and, depending on the scale of the amendments required, may either have the revised paper accepted forthwith or sent to referees again for further consideration. In the social sciences somewhere between 50 and 80 per cent of articles submitted are rejected, depending on the journal (although rejected articles may then be accepted by other journals which have less rigorous standards) (Hargens, 1988).

As the quality and prestige of the early scientific societies and their journals increased, so the advantages for the scientists of publishing in them increased also. Presenting work before the Royal Society and contributing to the *Transactions* identified one as a natural philosopher, as scientists were then called.

The task of natural philosophers was to persuade the scientific community of the truth and originality of their discoveries. In the earliest days, this was a matter of showing other scientists what one had found, in a public demonstration before the assembled Royal Society; later it depended on persuasion through the written word. Various rhetorical devices for increasing the persuasive power of scientific writing were invented. These included de-emphasising the presence of the scientist by writing in the passive, so making it seem that the results could have been obtained by 'anyone', and using plain, rather than literary language, to emphasise the objectivity of the research.

One way of defending one's procedures and arguments against potential criticism was to make it clear that they were the same procedures and arguments which others, more illustrious than oneself, had themselves already used. As Newton once said, 'If I have seen further, it is by standing on the shoulders of giants' (this famous quotation is the starting point for a fascinating book by the sociologist, Robert Merton (1965)). This is one of the functions of citations, references to previously published work which gradually came to be a standard ingredient of scientific papers. Thus, by the late nineteenth century, the 'scientific paper', a social invention of enormous significance, had been born.

16.2.2 The modern sociological literature

The sociological literature is not as dominated by the research paper published in an academic journal as the natural scientific literature is, although journal articles are important as a method of communication. Sociologists also write books, reports and conference papers, as well as making occasional contributions to the mass media. Books are getting harder to get published as publishers merge and publishing is increasingly big business. Academic books, such as you might find on a reading list, rarely sell more than 2,000 copies and specialised monographs often sell only a few hundred. The economics of publishing in such small quantities means that the books tend to be very expensive (reducing sales still further) and publishers are choosy about what they will take on. Thus considerations about the size of the potential market become much more important than the originality or quality of the research being reported.

The process of selection of books to be published is very different from that of the selection of articles to be printed in a journal. An author will approach a publishing house (or, often, several at once) with a brief proposal for a book. If the publisher likes the idea, they will usually ask for a sample chapter, to see whether the tone and style of the writing is to their liking. This may be sent out to 'readers', academics who are paid a small fee for commenting on the proposal and estimating the likely market for the book. If the publisher's editor is happy with the readers' advice, a contract will be issued which specifies when the complete manuscript is to be delivered, the length of the book in words and the percentage of the revenue which the author will receive (the 'royalties', usually between 7 and 10 per cent for an academic book). When the publisher gets the manuscript, it is copy edited by a professional who checks it for grammatical and spelling errors and it is then sent to the printer. Between six months and a year after the manuscript arrives at the publisher, the book is released to bookshops.

At the other end of the continuum in terms of time to publication is the conference paper. All professional societies, such as the British Sociological Association in the United Kingdom, organise conferences and there are many subgroups which arrange meetings on specific topics. Researchers are invited to submit papers to these conferences and attend them to 'read' (or more usually, lecture on the general topic of) the paper. Sometimes the papers are collected together and published as a book, but more usually, they are only available as photocopied typescript by writing to the author. The time lag between writing and circulation is much shorter for such papers, but they are of course not so readily available as reports which have been more formally published.

16.3   Reporting research

We have seen that writing is an essential part of the research process, and that the object of writing is both communication and persuasion. This and the following section offer some advice about how to organise writing about social research. Suppose that you were just embarking on a research project – it might be for a dissertation as part of a course, or a thesis for a postgraduate degree, or a full-time, large-scale funded project. What preparations are needed for reporting such work?

Getting down to writing is difficult for almost everyone, but particularly for researchers, because research is a mixture of very sociable activities (organising access, interviewing, and so on) and the very unsociable act of writing. Once one has got used to the sociable side of research it is sometimes hard to move to the writing up stage, where one is often working alone, just you and a word processor. A consequence of the differences between these two kinds of activity is that many people put off writing until it is far too late.

You should be thinking about the organisation of your research report at the very beginning of the project. As the project continues, the shape of the report ought to become clearer. Some parts can even be written before any data are collected – accounts of the previous work on which your research is based and the theoretical grounding of your own work can both be drafted before data collection has been completed. One advantage of writing as you go along is that if you spend a long time not writing you can get 'rusty'. The act of writing, of trying to put down your thoughts as clearly as possible, can suggest new issues and new ideas and these can go back to influence data collection and analysis.

There are several steps you need to take before setting pen to paper. First, if you are working with colleagues, you need to decide who will be listed as the authors and the order of names. This may seem a trivial point, but some excellent research teams have come to grief because this issue was not settled before the writing began. Second, it helps if you can map out the reports, papers and other publications you hope to write and where these will be published. If you think your work would best go into an academic journal, you will need to think about which journal is most appropriate and look through some back issues to see the style and type of article it publishes. If you are writing a thesis or dissertation, or to satisfy course requirements, it is worth looking at previous dissertations to see what length, style and format is expected.

Once you have decided on where to publish, there are further decisions to make about what to write. Usually, the temptation is to put too much in, so that the overall message gets confused. A single paper (or a chapter in a thesis or book) should only carry one message. It requires great skill to keep even two balls in the air at once and unless you are an expert, you should decide before you start what *the* one point you want to make will be, and then stick to it ruthlessly. Of course, to arrive at one specific conclusion, you will need to cover many supporting issues. But everything should be there because it is needed to argue the one basic message; if there is anything in the paper which cannot be justified in that way it should be cast out (perhaps to become the seed of another publication).

A journal article in sociology is normally between 4,000 and 7,000 words in length and this is also the typical length of a book chapter (the chapters in this book average about 7,000 words). But no one other than under-graduate course tutors ever worries about a report being too short; it is much more likely that the complaint will be that it is too long. Perhaps this is because clarity and conciseness are harder to achieve than verbosity. Length also comes from the writer not having a clear plan of how the report will be organised before the writing starts, so making yourself an 'outline' of the structure of the report (as you may have been taught to do at school when writing essays) is an excellent way of preparing to start writing.

Even if you take this advice and begin writing drafts as early as you can, you may find it hard to get started. It is not necessary to write a chapter or article by starting at the beginning and working through to the end, although some people do that. Try beginning with whatever section seems easiest to get you started. The Introduction and Conclusion are best written last because they need to be composed with knowledge of what the rest of the piece is about, and this may change and develop as you write.

It often helps to have someone in mind to whom you can aim your writing. For an academic paper or dissertation, you should be writing for another researcher, but not one who is a specialist in your area. For more popular work, you will need to decide what kind of person is likely to read your report, what they are likely to be interested in and what they are likely to know already. No matter who you are writing for, however, keep your sentences short and straightforward and, whenever you can, use ordinary words in preference to technical terms. Convoluted sentences and complex constructions merely confuse the reader (and might lead to the suspicion that you, the writer, are not thinking clearly, either).

The first draft is often the hardest. After it is completed, you should put it away for a few days and then read it through critically, trying to look at it from the point of view of someone who is coming to it fresh. You will certainly find much that is wrong, from sentences which need phrasing more clearly to major omissions and repetitions. These problems should be put right in a second draft. This second draft can then be shown to colleagues with a request for comments. Their suggestions can be incorporated into the third draft. As this sequence suggests, writing about research always involves much rewriting and refinement and you should plan for at least three times round the comments and redrafting loop.

16.3.1   The shape of a journal article

When writing a report, it helps to know how other people have organised their work, so that you can see what arrangements are clear and persuasive. In this section, we examine in some detail how one particular article published in the *American Sociological Review* was constructed. There is nothing special about the article we shall be looking at; it is typical of a particular style of quantitative sociology and there are many hundreds of similarly structured papers in the sociological literature. It does, however, have the merit of displaying its structure especially clearly. Other papers written in a more discursive style and those based on ethnographic

Title
Author
Abstract
Introduction
Theory
Data and methods
Results
Conclusions
References

Figure 16.1 *The conventional structure of a sociological research paper*

data often do not reveal their structure so immediately, but you will usually find that more or less the same types of material are included in more or less the same order.

This section will therefore be about the standard, conventional structure for an article. Almost the same structure is typically used in project reports, Masters' and Doctoral theses and in research reports written for sponsors and funders, rather than for publication. It is a structure which has been devised through much experience and it will usually serve you well. But it is just a convention. If, when you come to report on your research, you find that the conventional structure does not fit what you have to say, no one will stop you from breaking the convention. (At least not in sociology; other disciplines are rather stricter. For example, it is almost impossible to get articles published in certain psychology journals unless they precisely follow the conventional structure.)

So what is this structure? The main sections of a research paper are listed in Figure 16.1. Let us look at each of these sections in turn and see how the authors of the *American Sociological Review* article dealt with them.

The **Title** (in Figure 16.2, 'Sex segregation in voluntary associations') is the best advertisement that the article will get. Most readers will be attracted to the article by noticing the title on a journal's Contents page or in the list of references in another paper. The same applies to book titles: remember how often you have picked up a book in a bookshop just because the title made it seem interesting. The title needs to be short, snappy and above all, accurately descriptive of the content.

The **Abstract** (from Figure 16.2, 'We analyze the sex composition . . . networks they generate') is expected to summarise the content of the paper. Abstracting journals (e.g. *Sociological Abstracts*) will reprint just the abstract, together with those from all the other articles which have been published that quarter, under a subject classification which makes it fairly easy to track down articles on a particular topic. The abstract therefore has a double function: it serves as an overview for people who are reading the article in a journal and as a self-standing summary for people who are reading an abstracting journal. Because for most readers the most interesting part of an article is the conclusion, it is wise to put this

SEX SEGREGATION IN VOLUNTARY ASSOCIATIONS*

J. MILLER MCPHERSON   LYNN SMITH-LOVIN

University of South Carolina

We analyze the sex composition of 815 face-to-face voluntary associations in 10 communities to determine the extent of sex integration produced by voluntary affiliation. The sex segregation in these groups is substantial; nearly one-half of the organizations are exclusively female, while one-fifth are all male. Instrumental organizations (business-related and political groups) are more likely to be sex heterogeneous, while expressive groups are likely to be exclusively male or female. From the point of view of the individual, the typical female membership generates face-to-face contact with about 29 other members, less than four of whom are men. Male memberships, on the other hand, produce contact with over 37 other members on the average, nearly eight of whom are female. Men's contacts are both more numerous and more heterogeneous. We conclude that there is little support for the sex integration hypothesis in these data, although the sex heterogeneity of instrumental groups (especially those which are job-related) indicates that this pattern may change as women move into the labour force in increasing numbers. The paper explores some consequences of segregation for the organizations and the social networks they generate.

The integration hypothesis has been a main theme of research on voluntary organizations since Toqueville (1969) first raised the issue in the nineteenth century. From Durkheim's (1902) and Kornhauser's (1959) notion of voluntary organizations as mediators between the mass and the elite, to Babchuk and Edwards' (1965) view of voluntary groups as multi-level integrators, researchers have argued that voluntary groups serve as a sort of interstitial glue. Yet the details of exactly what is integrated with what has remained remarkably unclear over the years. What emerges from the literature is a picture of voluntary groups which may represent the emergent interests of unspecified publics in the political domain, provide resources for useful contacts in the economic domain, allow the expression of altruistic impulses in the charitable domain, and provide a variety of peripheral and ephemeral services (Smith and Freedman 1972).

In contrast to this integrative view of voluntary groups, many of the early community studies emphasised that voluntary associations were sorting mechanisms (Hughes, 1943; Anderson, 1937). As Gans (1967:61) noted, the groups "divided and segregated people by their interests and ultimately, of course, by socio-economic, educational, and religious differences". Of course, the integrating and sorting perspectives on voluntary associations are . . .

*   Address all correspondence to J. Miller McPherson, Department of Sociology, University of South Carolina, Columbia, SC 29208.

Work on this paper was supported by National Science Foundation grants SES-8120666 and SES-8319899, Miller McPherson, Principal Investigator. The authors would like to thank John McCarthy of Catholic University and the members of the structuralist group at the University of South Carolina for their helpful comments: Charles Brody, Michael Kennedy, Bruce H. Mayhew, Patrick Nolan, Jimy Saunders, Eui-Hangl Shin, and John V. Skvoretz. Data were collected through the facilities of the Bureau of Sociological Research of the University of Nebraska, Helen Moore, Director. The authors bear full responsibility for the interpretation of the data.

Figure 16.2   *The first page from McPherson and Smith-Lovin (1986)*

near the beginning of the abstract. Then specify the sample or setting to indicate the scope of the findings. Finish with a brief account of the method used to collect and analyse the data. Abstracts should never include citations to other work.

The **Acknowledgements** (from Figure 16.2, 'Work on this paper was supported . . . for the interpretation of the data.'): it is conventional to acknowledge the assistance of the people who funded the research, anyone who made a significant contribution to the research but is not an author, and colleagues who commented on drafts of the paper and helped to improve it. If you are a student writing a thesis, it may be appropriate to acknowledge your supervisor.

The paper proper starts with an **Introduction** which should indicate the topic of the paper, demonstrate why this topic is interesting and important, and show how the approach taken in the paper is an advance on previous work. In brief, the purpose of the Introduction is to get the reader hooked. That means starting from the reader's present knowledge and leading him or her on to see that the topic is worth spending time investigating. Notice how McPherson and Smith-Lovin in their introduction locate their research immediately into 'classical' sociology, with references to Toqueville and Durkheim in the first sentence. Notice also how in the space of two paragraphs they introduce a potentially interesting controversy in the existing literature – is the function of voluntary groups that of integration or sorting? One of the objects of the paper is to offer evidence which might resolve this controversy. In these few lines of introduction, the authors have mapped out a domain of research, have suggested that there has been much sociological interest in the domain, have identified a gap in the research concerning the integrative versus sorting issue, and have implied that the paper will go some way towards filling that gap.

The hallmark of a good introduction is that it locates a 'hole' in the research literature which the rest of the paper will fill. This particular paper offers a very good example. But the same principle applies generally, not only to papers, but also to books and theses. A thesis or dissertation usually begins with a chapter intended to 'review the literature'. But in writing such a review, one needs to remember that the purpose is not to catalogue the available literature for its own sake, but rather, as with this introduction, to show that there is some research which has yet to be done – and here it is!

Notice also that, as a matter of convention, the text starts without any preceding subheading: there is no heading, 'Introduction'.

On the page after the one shown in Figure 16.2, the authors observe that the integrative and sorting mechanisms are not as opposed as they might seem, because both may operate simultaneously, producing homogeneity on some dimensions and heterogeneity on others. They argue that the question then becomes 'which social dimensions are integrated and which are sorted, and in what types of organisations?' (McPherson and Smith-Lovin, 1986: 62). They then move on to discuss sex segregation in

Sample size
Sample design
Sampling frame
Date of data collection
How settings selected for observation were chosen
Response rate achieved
Limitations of and possible biases in the data
Sources of secondary data (e.g. statistics from government surveys)
Basic demographic characteristics of the sample
Explanation of any special data analysis techniques used

Figure 16.3   *Items for inclusion in the Data and Methods section*

voluntary organisations, which has previously been considered mainly in terms of the sorting view, and review the literature on this topic. This brings them to the second major section, headed 'Network Implications of Sex Segregation in Organizations', which is as close as this paper gets to a section devoted to 'theory'.

The **Theory** section is the place to introduce the concepts you will be using in your analysis. Although called the Theory section, it is not 'grand theory' that is needed here, but what Merton (1968) called 'Middle range theory': the specific concepts and ideas that you will use to explain your findings. In McPherson and Smith-Lovin's paper, this leads to the statement of a number of propositions which they then go on to test later in the article. For example, they write,

> Based on our earlier discussion of the changing rôle of women, we would expect that working women, more highly educated women, and younger women would be less likely to participate in organizational environments which are single sex (all women's clubs) and more likely to participate in mixed sex groups (although they may often be in the minority there). (McPherson and Smith-Lovin, 1986: 63)

This is a proposition that they will compare with the data they have collected. But before we reach these results, there is a section on Data and Methods.

The **Data and Methods** section is often the most standardised and least interesting part of a research article, because it has to convey a lot of strictly factual information. The ideal is to provide just enough detail that another researcher could find everything needed to repeat the work. That means that you must specify here the decisions you made about matters such as how you selected the respondents, how you collected the data and any special methods you used. Figure 16.3 lists the important characteristics which you should consider mentioning in this section; include only those which are relevant to the research design you have chosen.

In the McPherson and Smith-Lovin study, the design was complicated by the fact that they wished to sample, not individuals, but voluntary organisations. This they did by asking a representative probability sample

of adults from 10 communities in Nebraska about the organisations to
which they were affiliated. They write, in the section headed 'Data and
Methods':

> In the first stage, a representative probability sample of 656 non-institutionalized
> adults was interviewed from the 10 communities. In the interviews, we obtained
> a list of all the organizations with which each individual was affiliated. We used a
> technique known as aided recall (Babchuk and Booth, 1969) to insure that all
> organizations were reported. Respondents were encouraged to report even
> small, relatively informal groups if these groups had an identifiable membership.
> A total of 2091 organizational names were generated, representing an affiliation
> rate of about 3.2. (in smaller communities, of course, some names represented
> multiple reports of the same organization). Of the 2091 organizations, 815
> groups which met face-to-face in the local community constitute the sample for
> this analysis. (1986: 64)

In this brief excerpt from a much longer description of their methods of
sampling and data collection, note how the authors take pains to be precise
about the way in which their sample was obtained and the criterion (face-
to-face meetings) which they used to select those organisations chosen for
further study. Note also how, rather than describe in detail the way that
they maximised respondents' recall of all the organisations they belonged
to, they just reference another article (Babchuk and Booth, 1969) where
the technique is described.

After outlining the methods used to collect data, the typical paper
discusses the **Results**, which in the McPherson and Smith-Lovin article are
described as the 'Analyses and Findings'. When writing this part of the
paper, the problem is usually to know which of all the analyses you have
done should be included and which should be left out. The primary rule is:
be relevant. Remember that the Introduction has already stated what the
paper is about and that the purpose of this Results section is to provide the
findings on which your conclusions will be based. This means that data
which may be very unexpected or significant, but which is not related to the
point of the paper, should be excluded (it could form the basis of another
paper). For a similar reason, this section needs to focus around your
findings, not the way in which you came to reach the results. In particular,
this is not the place for an account of the process of research, nor of the
dead-ends which all researchers encounter, nor the disasters and difficulties which you have overcome.

The Results section will probably contain summaries and analyses of the
data you have collected, in the form of statistical tables (if your data are
quantitative) or characteristic quotations or descriptions of observations (if
your data are qualitative). McPherson and Smith-Lovin use the statistical
technique called regression and present the results in tables which
summarise the relative importance of marital status, employment status,
education and age on being involved in voluntary organisations. They find
overall that the voluntary groups they have studied are very segregated:
almost one half are all female and one fifth are all male. Large organisations are less likely to be all-female and those that recruit from the labour

force are likely to be mixed, while those which are expressive in character are more likely to be segregated. Their Results section concludes:

> At the individual level, single males are more likely to belong to sex-segregated groups, while widowed or separated women are more likely to be in all-female groups. The effects of work status are quite different for men and for women. Employed women are very much less likely to belong to all-female groups than employed men are to belong to all-male groups. (McPherson and Smith-Lovin, 1986: 75)

Notice that these results are closely tied to the data and are more or less devoid of theory. The above quotation consists of little more than the output of the statistical analysis put into words. In this article, the interpretation of these results is left to the next section. However, it is usual to link the results and their theoretical interpretation more closely together than they are here, with both data and interpretation included in the Results section.

Relating the results back to the issues raised in the Introduction and the Theory sections is the job of the **Conclusion**. In the McPherson and Smith-Lovin article, the Introduction posed the question of whether voluntary groups fulfil a sorting or integrative function. Now is the time for the authors to answer that question. In the previous section they reported that, overall, voluntary associations are very segregated. In this section they conclude that these organisations reaffirm sex distinctions rather than creating ties between the sexes: 'The sorting function, then, clearly dominates the integrative function with regard to sex' (McPherson and Smith-Lovin, 1986: 75). This is a good example of the way in which the Conclusions should relate back to the issues raised in the Introduction, thus closing the circle and tying up the article neatly. This is also the section in which you can speculate a little, going beyond the strict confines of the data, and where you can point to further issues which the research has raised.

The last paragraph of the Conclusion is one of the most difficult to write because it ought to summarise what the main findings of the research were, in a succinct and interesting way. This is because many readers will look first at the end of the article to see whether it has anything interesting to say, before they start at the beginning. And it is as well to anticipate this.

Lastly, there is the list of **References**. This is a list of the full bibliographical details of the books and articles cited in the text. ('References' are the list of details at the end of an article; 'citations' are the (Author, Year) pairs in the body of the text.) Citations are important in a sociological article for a number of reasons. First, they situate the article within existing research. We saw citations used in this way in the Introduction (see Figure 16.2) where the particular topic of this paper is located within the sociological literature. Second, references act as a kind of shorthand. It was pointed out that in the Methods section, instead of describing the technique of 'aided recall', a citation to Babchuk and Booth (1969) was provided. This sort of citation saves space, because the details of the technique need only be printed once in the original article, rather than being rolled out again and again in reports of every piece of research that uses it. Thirdly, citations to reports which have come to the same or similar results can help to give an article some authority, for the citations imply that the conclusions reproduce those found elsewhere by independent investigators.

For all these reasons, sociological books and papers are always sprinkled with citations. Each citation must be linked to a reference which provides the full details about where to find the work cited. There are several standard conventions for references. Sometimes the citation is a superscript number in the text, leading to a numbered reference at the end. More usually, as in this book, citations are given as the name of the author and the year of publication, and the references are listed alphabetically at the end. This is known as the Harvard convention and is probably the easiest for authors to use. Unless you are using a clever word processor which can do it for you, using numbered superscripts makes for difficulties if you change your mind and want to add or delete a citation; you then have to renumber all the citations following.

Ensuring that all the necessary details are correct and included in the References is part of intellectual good manners. It means that, for example, if you read a book that you might want to refer to later, you should take careful note of the author, the author's initials, the date of publication, the title, the city of publication and the publisher. With articles in journals, you should note the author, the author's initials, the date of publication, the title of the article, the name of the journal, the volume number of the journal in which the article is printed, and the starting and ending page numbers of the article. Keeping a record of these ought to become second nature. They are the standard data which librarians will want if you need to find the book or article again. One more item is needed if you copy out a direct quotation from a book or paper: the page number from which the quote is taken (how else will you be able to check that you've got the wording exactly right if you do not have the page number?).

16.3.2 Breaking the rules

So ends our tour of one sociological article. The general shape of this article is a good one to follow, not only for research papers, but also for more informal reports and for dissertations and theses. Often when research is funded by an agency or is commissioned, those sponsoring the research will demand a specially written report about the results. Such reports can keep to the conventional structure which we have seen in the previous section, but with some modifications to suit the audience for which it is intended. The Abstract is often replaced by a somewhat longer preliminary section headed 'Summary', in which the findings of the research are laid out as clearly as possible, perhaps as a list of the main conclusions. If the sponsors of the research are mainly interested in social policy, the summary might also indicate the policy implications of the research. Within the body of the report, it is usual to have less about the research design than is needed for an academic article, with further details relegated to an Appendix.

Dissertations written as part of a degree also often follow the standard structure, modified slightly. A doctoral thesis will typically have at least one chapter corresponding to each of the main sections of Figure 16.1. The Abstract will again be replaced by a Summary, usually about one page in length. The Introduction will probably include a rather more exhaustive literature review than would be appropriate for a published report.

McPherson and Smith-Lovin's paper was chosen for detailed examination because it follows the standard and conventional shape of a social research article very closely. It is a good example of following the 'rules'. But, of course, not all sociological articles do keep to the 'rules' and they are none the worse for that. Breaking the rules is fine, so long as the message you want to convey is nevertheless communicated effectively. There are some rules you should break only with the greatest of caution and others which should not give you a moment's worry. For example, it is almost always a bad idea to miss out either the Introduction or the Conclusion. These two sections tell the reader what to expect and what to take from the research. A rule which *can* be broken for many research reports is the one which says that you should divide the middle of the report into separate 'Theory', 'Methods' and 'Results' sections. Often, some other form of organisation will suit what you have to say much better. For example, it is possible to interweave theory and findings by telling a 'story' about your respondents (Richardson, 1990), or select themes which emerge from your data and devote one section to each theme. The best way of learning about these alternative structures is to look carefully at how the books and articles which you think communicate effectively have been constructed by their authors.

16.4   Conclusion

All through this chapter, it has been emphasised that social research is only completed when its results have been published. Most research is published in the academic literature, in journals or in books aimed at the academic reader. However, social scientific knowledge is not only valuable for its own sake, to increase our understanding of the social world; much research is conducted in order to inform or to influence the making of public policy. Should not research findings be made available ('disseminated' is the jargon) to the wider public as well?

Of course, the answer to this question must be, yes. But the process by which this dissemination generally occurs is much more complicated and less open to intervention by social researchers than one might imagine. When one thinks of the 'use' of research, the traditional view is that policy makers ought to read and understand the research, consider its implications and then translate the findings into practice as soon as possible. In fact, policy making is rarely done in this way and research findings, no matter how significant they may appear to be, rarely influence the policy making process so directly. A number of studies have been undertaken on how research findings do influence social policy (Weiss, 1980; Wenger, 1986) and these have shown that policy making, especially government policy making, is itself a complex process with its own momentum. Findings from individual research projects tend not to be influential unless they happen, by chance, to impinge on this process at just the right moment. Sometimes, policy research is commissioned by governments merely to delay the need to take action.

Social research does, however, have an indirect effect on policy. Individual research results add to a broad pool of work which accumulates over time and which raises new issues, provides new perspectives, and asks new questions. There is a slow seepage of ideas from the academic literature into the policy process, working its way through indirect channels such as professional and trade journals, textbooks and university education as well as directly when policy makers find themselves needing to obtain a broad understanding of a policy topic. And pressure groups and voluntary groups also use the research literature directly to press their case, often taking advantage of the authority which publication in the academic literature bestows on the research. This indirect influence can be very powerful, although sometimes in unexpected ways. For example, terms like deviance, ethnicity, institution, labour market, dependency and gender are now part of the common vocabulary of educated people, but were originally given their meaning by the social scientists who used them in reporting their research findings in the academic literature.

16.5 Project

As was noted in section 16.2.1, every academic paper is reviewed before publication by at least two referees, chosen from among the academic community by journal editors for their knowledge of the paper's topic. Referees (who are rarely paid for their labours) receive a copy of the paper in typescript and a letter (or sometimes a form) from the editor which requests them to comment on the paper's suitability for publication in terms of its clarity, originality and the adequacy of its argument. The referee has between two and six weeks to respond with a verdict (one of: accept, accept with minor revisions such as spelling or stylistic errors, accept but require major revisions, or reject) and a report. The report, which is always anonymous and will often be forwarded to the author, explains the referee's verdict, commenting on the overall strengths and weaknesses of the paper and making suggestions for improvements. Despite the care which many referees put into the task, editors often find that they get contradictory recommendations from referees and it is very common for two referees to make quite different suggestions for improvements.

The first step in this project is to identify a research area in which you have an interest (the sociology of health, or deviance, for example). Look through the library current journals shelves and find a recent issue of a journal publishing in your area. Choose one paper from that journal. If possible, make a photocopy of it.

You should imagine that you have received a typescript copy of this paper from a journal editor to referee. Examine the paper closely. Is it clear? Is it well organised? Can one quickly identify the main conclusions? Are the justifications for those conclusions soundly based? Are the data appropriate to the topic of the paper? Are the methods of data collection and analysis described in sufficient detail that someone else could repeat the study? Are there plausible alternative interpretations of the data or of the results which the author has not noticed? Does the abstract adequately describe the contents of the paper? Are there passages which could be rewritten to make them clearer? Has the author referenced all the relevant literature?

It is surprising how often even published papers will wilt under careful scrutiny of this kind. In about 300 words, write a report about the article. Your criticisms should be phrased so that they are constructive, polite and encouraging – the aim of a referee's report is to encourage the author towards a better article, not to damage the author's ego.

16.6   Further reading

Becker (1986) is excellent on writing about social science. Mullins (1977) is also good, especially about the processes involved in getting published.

Mulkay (1985) is a fascinating exploration of the textual forms which are, or could be, used by sociologists to report on the social world.

Richardson (1990) includes a reflective account of how she, as a sociologist, came to write a book intended for the lay person about her research, as well as offering wise words about writing. Wolcott (1990) concentrates on the particular problems of reporting on qualitative research.

If you are writing a dissertation for a research degree, Phillips and Pugh (1987) should be essential reading.

Bibliography

Abbott, P. and Wallace, W. (1990) *An Introduction to Sociology: Feminist Perspectives*. London: Routledge.

Adler, P. (1985) *Wheeling and Dealing: an Ethnography of an Upper Level Dealing and Smuggling Community*. New York: Columbia University Press.

Agar, M. (1986) *Speaking of Ethnography*. Beverly Hills: Sage.

Antal, F. (1962) *Hogarth and his place in European Art*. London: Routledge and Kegan Paul.

Antal, F. (1987) *Florentine Painting and its Social Background*. Cambridge, MA: Harvard University Press.

Arber, S. and Ginn, J. (1991) *Gender and Later Life: A Sociological Analysis of Resources and Constraints*. London: Sage.

Arber, S. and Sawyer, L. (1979) *Changes in the Structure of General Practice. The Patients' View*. Report to DHSS, University of Surrey, unpublished.

Armstrong, D. (1983) *Political Anatomy of the Body: Medical Knowledge in the Twentieth Century*. Cambridge: Cambridge University Press.

Aron, R. (1967/1968) *Main Currents in Sociological Thought*. (Volumes I and II). Harmondsworth: Penguin.

Ashworth, P. (1979) *Social Interaction and Consciousness*. Chichester: Wiley.

Atkinson, J.M. (1978) *Discovering Suicide*. London: Macmillan.

Atkinson, J.M. (1984) *Our Master's Voices: the Language and Body Language of Politics*. London: Methuen.

Atkinson, J.M. and Heritage, J. (eds) (1984) *Structures of Social Action: Studies in Conversation Analysis*. Cambridge: Cambridge University Press.

Austin, J.L. (1962) *How To Do Things With Words*. Oxford: Oxford University Press.

Baltzell, E.D. (1962) *Philadelphia Gentlemen*. Glencoe: The Free Press.

Bandura, A. (1977), *Social Learning Theory*. Englewood Cliffs, NJ: Prentice Hall.

Barnes, B. (1991) 'Non-response on Government Household Surveys', *Survey Methodology Bulletin*, 28: 34–44.

Barron, R. and Norris, G. (1976) 'Sexual divisions and the dual labour market', in D. Barker and S. Allen (eds), *Dependence and Exploitation in Work and Marriage*. London: Longman.

Barthes, R. (1967) *Elements of Semiology*, trans. Annette Lavers and Colin Smith. London: Jonathan Cape.

Bauman, Z. (1990) *Thinking Sociologically*. Oxford: Blackwell.

Bazerman, C. (1988) *Shaping Written Knowledge*. Madison: University of Wisconsin Press.

Becker, H. (1971) *Sociological Work*. London: Allen Lane.

Becker, H. (1974) 'Photography and Sociology', *Studies in the Anthropology of Visual Communication*, 1: 3–26.

Becker, H. (1979) 'Do photographs tell the truth?', in T. Cook and C. Reichardt, (eds), *Qualitative and Quantitative Methods in Evaluation Research*. London: Sage.

Becker, H. (1981) *Exploring Society Through Photography*. Chicago: North Western University.

Becker, H.S. (1986) *Writing for Social Scientists*. Chicago: University of Chicago Press.

Becker, H.S., Greer, B., Hughes, E.C. and Strauss, A. (1961) *Boys in White*. Chicago: University of Chicago Press.

Bell, C. (1978) 'Studying the locally powerful: personal reflections on a research career', in C. Bell and S. Encel (eds), *Inside the Whale*. Sydney: Pergamon. pp. 14–40.

Bell, C. and Encel, S. (eds) (1978) *Inside the Whale: Ten Personal Accounts of Social Research*. Sydney: Pergamon.

Bell, C. and Newby, H. (eds) (1977) *Doing Sociological Research*. London: Allen and Unwin.

Bell, C. and Roberts, H. (eds) (1984) *Social Researching: Politics, Problems and Practice*. London: Routledge and Kegan Paul.

Bell, H. (1987) *Doing Your Research Project: A Guide to First-Time Researchers in Education and Social Science*. Milton Keynes: Open University Press.

Bendix, R. (1960) *Max Weber: an Intellectual Portrait*. London: Heinemann.

Bennett, H.S. (1922) *The Pastons and their England*. Cambridge: Cambridge University Press.

Berger, J. (1972) *Ways of Seeing*, Harmondsworth: Penguin.

Blalock, H.M. (1969) *Theory Construction*. Englewood Cliffs, NJ: Prentice Hall.

Blau, P.M. (1964) *Exchange and Power in Social Life*. New York: Wiley.

Boden, D. and Zimmerman, D.H. (eds) (1991) *Talk and Social Structure*. Cambridge: Polity Press.

Boudon, R. (1981) *The Logic of the Social Sciences*. London: Routledge and Kegan Paul.

Braithwaite, J. (1981) 'The myth of social class and criminality reconsidered', *American Sociological Review*. 46: 36–57.

Brannen, J. and Moss, P. (1988) *New Mothers at Work: Employment and Childcare*. London: Unwin Hyman.

Brannen, P. (1987) 'Working on directors: some methodological issues', in G. Moyser and M. Wagstaffe (eds), *Research Methods for Elite Studies*. London: Allen and Unwin. pp. 166–80.

British Sociological Association (1973) *Statement of Ethical Principles and Their Application to Sociological Research*. London.

British Sociological Association (1991) *Statement of Ethical Practice*. London.

Brown, G. and Yule, G. (1983) *Discourse Analysis*. Cambridge: Cambridge University Press.

Brown, G.W. and Harris, T.O. (1978) *Social Origins of Depression: A Study of Psychiatric Disorder in Women*. London: Tavistock.

Brown, J., Fielding, J. and Lee, T. (1984) *Perception of risk – a secondary analysis of data collected by S.C.P.R.* Report for the HSE, University of Surrey.

Bruyn, S.T. (1966) *The Human Perspective in Sociology*. Englewood Cliffs, NJ: Prentice Hall.

Bulmer, M. (1980) 'Why don't sociologists make more use of official statistics', *Sociology*, 14(4): 505–23. (Reprinted in M. Bulmer (ed.) (1984) *Sociological Research Methods: An Introduction*, 2nd edn. London: Macmillan.)

Bulmer, M. (1982a) 'The research ethics of pseudo-patient studies', *Sociological Review*, 30 (4).

Bulmer, M. (1982b) 'The merits and demerits of covert participant observation', in M. Bulmer (ed.) *Social Research Ethics*. London: Macmillan. pp. 217–51.

Bulmer, M. (ed.) (1982c) *Social Research Ethics: An Examination of the Merits of Covert Participant Observation*. London: Macmillan.

Burgess, R.G. (1982) *Field Research*. London: Allen and Unwin.

Burgess, R.G. (ed.) (1986) *Key Variables in Social Investigation*. London: Routledge.

Bury, M. and Holmes, A. (1991) *Life After Ninety*. London: Routledge.

Butcher, B. and Dodd, P. (1983) 'The Electoral Register – two surveys', *Population Trends*. 31: 15–19.

Button, G. (ed.) (1991) *Ethnomethodology and The Human Sciences*. Cambridge: Cambridge University Press.

Button, G. and Lee, R.E. (eds) (1987) *Talk and Social Organisation*. Clevedon: Multilingual Matters.

Campbell, D.T. and Fiske, D.W. (1955) 'Convergent and discriminant validation by the multitrait-multimethod matrix', *Psychological Bulletin*, 56: 81–105. (Reprinted in Summers, 1970.)

Cassell, J. (1988) 'The relationship of observer to observed when studying up', in R.G. Burgess (ed.), *Studies in Qualitative Methodology*. Greenwich, CT and London: JAI Press.

Catford, R. and Parish, J. (1989) ' "Heartbeat Wales": New horizons for health promotion in the community – The philosophy of Heartbeat Wales', in D. Seedhouse and A. Cribb, (eds), *Changing Ideas in Health Care*. London: Wiley. pp. 127–41.

Champion, A. and Green, A.E. (1985) 'In search of Britain's booming towns', *CURDS Discussion Paper*, University of Durham.

Cicourel, A. (1964) *Method and measurement in Sociology*. New York: Free Press.

Clegg, S. (1990) *Frameworks of Power*. London: Sage.

Cloward, R.A. and Ohlin, L. (1960) *Delinquency and Opportunity*. New York: Free Press.

Cohen, S. (1972) *Folk Devils and Moral Panics*. Oxford: Oxford University Press.

Cohen, S. and Taylor, L. (1977) 'Talking about prison blues', in C. Bell and H. Newby (eds), *Doing Sociological Research*. London: Allen and Unwin. pp. 67–86.

Cohen, W. (1989) 'Symbols of power: statues in nineteenth century France', *Comparative Study of Society and History*, 31(3): 491–513.

Conein, B., de Fornel, M. and Quere, L. (eds) (1989) *Analyse de L'Action et Analyse de la Conversation. Volume 1 and II*. Paris: Reseaux CNET.

Corcoran, M.P. (1991) 'Ethnic Boundaries and Legal Barriers: The Undocumented Irish Community in New York City'. Unpublished PhD thesis, Columbia University.

Coulter, J. (ed.) (1990). *Ethnomethodological Sociology*. Bibliography compiled by B.J. Fehr and J. Stetson with the assistance of Y. Mizukawa. Aldershot: Edward Elgar Publishing.

Coulthard, M. (1977) *An Introduction to Discourse Analysis*. London: Longman.

Crompton, R. and Mann, M. (1986) *Gender and Stratification*. Cambridge: Polity Press.

Cronbach, L.J. (1951). 'Coefficient alpha and the internal consistency of tests', *Psychometrika*, 16: 297–334.

Cronbach, L.J. and Meehl, P.E. (1955). 'Construct validity in psychological tests,' *Psychological Bulletin*, 52: 281–302.

Cross, M. and Arber, S. (1977) 'Policy and practice in paramedical organisations: the case of family planning agencies', in R. Dingwall, C. Heath, M. Reid and M. Stacey (eds), *Health Care and Health Knowledge*. London: Croom Helm. pp. 185–208.

Cuff, E.C., Sharrock, W. and Francis, D.W. (1990) *Perspectives in Sociology*, 3rd edn. London: Unwin Hyman.

Dale, A., Arber, S. and Procter, M. (1988) *Doing Secondary Analysis*. London: Unwin Hyman.

Dalton, M. (1964) 'Preconceptions and methods in *Men Who Manage*', in P.E. Hammond (ed.), *Sociologists at Work*. New York and London: Basic Books. pp. 50–95.

Daniels, A.K. (1967) 'The low-caste stranger in social research', in G. Sjoberg (ed.), *Ethics, Politics and Social Research*. Cambridge, MA: Schenkman. pp. 267–96.

Davis, F. (1972) *Illness, Interaction and The Self*. Belmont, CA: Wadsworth.

Davis, J.A. (1977) *General Social Survey*. Chicago: National Opinion Research Center.

Davis, J.A. and Smith, T.W. (1992) *The NORC General Social Survey: a User's Guide*. Newbury Park, CA: Sage.

De Vaus, D.A. (1990) *Surveys in Social Research*, 2nd edn. London: Unwin Hyman.

Denzin, N.K. (1970) *The Research Act in Sociology*. London: Butterworths.

Denzin, N.K. (1978) *Sociological Methods: A Sourcebook*, 2nd edn. New York: McGraw-Hill.

Deutscher, I. (1973) *What we say/what we do*. Glenview: Scott Foresman.

Devault, M. (1990) 'Talking and listening from women's standpoint: feminist strategies for interviewing and analysis', *Social Problems*, 37(1): 96–116.

Dillman, D.A. (1978) *Mail and Telephone Surveys: The Total Design Method*. New York: Wiley.

Ditton, J. (1977) *Part-time Crime: An Ethnography of Fiddling and Pilferage*. London: Macmillan.

Dodd, T. (1987) 'A further investigation into the coverage of the postcode address file', *Survey Methodology Bulletin*, 21: 35–40.

Dohrenwend, B. (1964) 'A use for leading questions in research interviewing', *Human Organization*, 23: 76–7.

Dohrenwend, B. and Richardson, S. (1956) 'Analysis of the interviewer's behaviour', *Human Organization*, 15 (2): 29–32.

Douglas, J.D. (1976) *Investigative Social Research: Individual and Team Field Research*. Beverly Hills, CA and London: Sage.

Drew, P. and Heritage, J.C. (eds) (in press) *Talk at Work*. Cambridge: Cambridge University Press.

Dunnell, K. (1979) *Family Formation Survey*. London: HMSO.

Durkheim, E. (1897) *Le suicide: étude de sociologie* (trans J.A. Spaulding and G. Simpson). London: Routledge and Kegan Paul, 1952.

Durkheim, E. (1951) *Suicide*. Glencoe: The Free Press.

Eco, U. (1988) *Foucault's Pendulum*. London: Pan Books.

Elias, N. (1979) *What is Sociology?* London: Hutchinson.

Empey, L. and Erickson, M. (1966) 'Hidden delinquency and social status', *Social Forces*, 44: 546–54

Encel, S. (1978) 'In search of power', in C. Bell and S. Encel (eds), *Inside the Whale*. Sydney: Pergamon. pp. 41–66.

Erickson, F. and Schultz, J. (1982) *The Councillor as Gatekeeper*. New York: Academic Press.

ESRC (1991) 'Noticeboard', *ESRC Data Archive Bulletin*, Spring, No. 47: 22, Colchester: University of Essex.

Festinger, L., Riecken, H.W. and Schachter, S. (1964) *When Prophecy Fails: A Social and Psychological Study of a Modern Group that Predicted the Destruction of the World*. New York: Harper Torchbooks.

Fetterman, D. (1989) *Ethnography: Step by Step*. London: Sage.

Fielding, N. (1981) *The National Front*. London: Routledge and Kegan Paul.

Fielding, N. (1982) 'Observational research on the National Front', in M. Bulmer (ed.), *Social Research Ethics*. London: Macmillan. pp. 80–104.

Fielding, N. (1988) *Joining Forces*. London: Routledge

Fielding, N. (1990), 'Mediating the message: affinity and hostility in research on sensitive topics', *American Behavioral Scientist*, 33(5): 608–20.

Fielding, N. and Fielding, J. (1986) *Linking Data*. Beverly Hills, CA: Sage.

Fielding, N. and Lee, R. (eds), (1991) *Using Computers in Qualitative Research*. London: Sage.

Finch, J. and Groves, D. (eds) (1983) *A Labour of Love: Women, Work and Caring*. London: Routledge and Kegan Paul.

Fishbein, M. and Ajzen, I. (1975) *Belief, Attitude, Intention and Behavior: An Introduction to Theory and Research*. Reading, MA: Addison-Wesley.

Forcese, D.P. and Richer, S. (eds) (1970) *Stages of Social Research: Contemporary Perspectives*, Englewood Cliffs, NJ: Prentice Hall.

Form, W.H. (1973) 'Field problems in comparative research: the politics of distrust', in M. Armer and A.D. Grimshaw (eds), *Comparative Social Research*. New York: Wiley. pp. 23–113.

Fox Keller, E. (1990) 'Feminist criticism of the social sciences', in J. McCarl Nielssen, (ed.), *Feminist Research Methods: Exemplary Readings in the Social Sciences*. Boulder, CO: Westview.

Frude, N. (1987) *A Guide to SPSS/PC+*. London: Macmillan.

Fussell, P. (1975) *The Great War and Modern Memory*. London: Oxford University Press.

Fussell, P. (1989) *Wartime: Understanding and Behaviour in the Second World War*. Oxford: Oxford University Press.

Garfinkel, H. (1967) *Studies in Ethnomethodology*. Englewood Ciffs, NJ: Prentice Hall.

Gash, S. (1989) *Effective Literature Searching for Students*. Aldershot: Gower.

Giddens, A. (1976) *New Rules of the Sociological Method*. London: Hutchinson.

Giddens, A. (1990a) *The Consequences of Modernity*. Cambridge: Polity.

Giddens, A. (1990b) *Sociology: A brief but critical introduction*, 2nd edn. Basingstoke: Macmillan.

Gilbert, G.N. and Mulkay, M.J. (1984) *Opening Pandora' s Box: A Sociological Analysis of Scientists' Discourse*. Cambridge: Cambridge University Press.

Gilleard, C.J. (1984) *Living with Dementia: Community Care of the Elderly Mentally Infirm*. London: Croom Helm.

Ginn, J. and Arber, S. (1991) 'Gender, class and income inequalities in later life', *British Journal of Sociology*, 42(3): 369–96.

Glaser, B.G. and Strauss, A.L. (1967) *The Discovery of Grounded Theory*. Chicago: Aldine.

Goffman, E. (1959) *The Presentation of Self in Everyday Life*. New York: Anchor Books.

Goffman, E. (1961) *Asylums*. New York: Doubleday.

Goffman, E. (1981) *Forms of Talk*. Oxford: Blackwell.

Gold, R. (1952) 'Janitors vs tenants: a status-income dilemma', *American Journal of Sociology*, 57: 487–93.

Goldthorpe, J. (1980) *Social Mobility and the Class Structure in Modern Britain*. Oxford: Oxford University Press.

Goodwin, C. (1981) *Conversational Organisation: Interaction between a Speaker and Hearer*. London: Academic Press.

Gorden, R. (1980) *Interviewing: strategy, techniques and tactics*. Homewood, IL: Dorsey.

Gray, P. and Gee, F.A. (1972) *A Quality Check on the 1966 Ten Per Cent Sample Census for England and Wales*. London: HMSO.

Grene, D. (ed.) (1959) *Thucydides' History of the Peloponnesian War*. New York: Cape.

Guttman, Louis (1944). 'A basis for scaling qualitative data', *American Sociological Review*, 9: 139–150. (Reprinted in Summers, 1970.)

Hakim, C. (1982) *Secondary Analysis in Social Research*. London: Allen and Unwin.

Halliday, M.A.K. (1978) *Language as Social Semiotic*. London: Edward Arnold.

Halliday, T.C. (1987) *Beyond Monopoly*. Chicago: University of Chicago Press.

Hammersley, M. and P. Atkinson (1983) *Ethnography: Principles in Practice*. London: Tavistock.

Hammond, P.E. (ed.) (1964) *Sociologists at Work: Essays on the Craft of Social Research*. New York and London: Basic Books.

Hargens, L.L. (1988) 'Scholarly consensus and journal rejection rates', *American Sociological Review*. 53: 139–51.

Harper, D. (1979) 'Life on the road' in J. Wagner (ed.), *Images of Information: Still Photography in the Social Sciences*. London: Sage. pp. 25–42.

Harvey, L. (1990) *Critical Social Research*, London: Unwin Hyman.

Health Promotion: an international journal (1986), vol 1.

Heath, A. (1981) *Social Mobility*. Glasgow: Fontana.

Heath, C.C. (1986). *Body Movement and Speech in Medical Interaction*. Cambridge: Cambridge University Press.

Heath, C.C. and Luff, P. (1991) 'Collaborative activity and technological design: task coordination in London Underground control rooms. *Proceedings of E-CSCW 1991*. Amsterdam, 1991.

Hedges, B.M. (1979) 'Sampling minority populations', in M. Wilson (ed.) *Social and Education Research in Action*. London: Longman. pp. 244–61.

Herbert, A.P. (1935, 1977) *Misleading Cases in the Common Law*. London: Eyre Methuen.

Heritage, J. (1978) 'Aspects of the flexibilities of language use', *Sociology*, 12 (1): 79–104.

Heritage, J. and Greatbatch, D. (1986) 'Generating applause: a study of rhetoric and response at party political conferences', *American Journal of Sociology*, 92(1): 110–57.

Heritage, J. (1984) *Garfinkel and Ethnomethodology*. Cambridge: Polity Press.

Heritage, J. and Atkinson, J.M. (1984) 'Introduction' in J.M. Atkinson and J. Heritage (eds), *Structures of Social Action: Studies in Conversation Analysis*. Cambridge: Cambridge University Press. pp. 1–15.

Hindess, B. (1973) *The Use of Official Statistics in Sociology*. London: Macmillan.

Hoinville, G. and Jowell, R. (1977) *Survey Research Practice*. London: Heinemann.

Homan, R. (1980) 'The ethics of covert methods', *British Journal of Sociology*, 31: 46–59 (with a comment by M. Bulmer, pp. 59–65).

Homan, R. (1991) *The Ethics of Social Research*. London: Longman.

Homan, R. and Bulmer, M. (1982) 'On the merits of covert methods: a dialogue', in M. Bulmer (ed.), *Social Research Ethics*. London: Macmillan. pp. 105–21.

Hornsby-Smith, M.P. (1987) *Roman Catholics in England: Studies in Social Structure Since the Second World War*. Cambridge: Cambridge University Press.

Hornsby-Smith, M.P. and Dale, A. (1988), 'The assimilation of Irish immigrants in England', *British Journal of Sociology*, 39(4): 519–44.

Horowitz, I.L. and Rainwater, L. (1970) 'On journalistic moralizers', in L. Humphreys *Tearoom Trade*. Chicago: Aldine. pp. 181–90.

Howard, K. and Sharp. J.A. (1983) *The Management of a Student Research Project*. Aldershot: Gower.

Hughes, E.C. (1958) *Men and Their Work*. Chicago: Free Press.

Hughes, J.A. (1976) *Sociological Analysis: Methods of Discovery*. London: Nelson.

Humphrey, C. (1983) *Karl Marx Collective: Economy, Society and Religion in a Siberian Collective Farm*. Cambridge: Cambridge University Press.

Humphreys, L. (1970) *Tearoom Trade: Impersonal Sex in Public Places*. Chicago: Aldine.

Hunt, J. (1984) 'The development of rapport through negotiation of gender in field work among police', *Human Organization*, 43(4): 283–96.

Hyman, H. (1954) *Interviewing in Social Research*. Chicago: University of Chicago Press.

Hyman, H. (1972) *Secondary Analysis of Sample Surveys*. New York: Wiley.

Irving, B. and McKenzie, I. (1988) *Regulating Custodial Interviews*. London: Police Foundation.

Jefferson, G. (1984) ' "At first I thought": a normalizing device for extraordinary events', unpublished manuscript, Katholieke Hogeschool Tilburg.

Jefferson, G. (1991) 'List construction as a task and resource', in G. Psathas and R. Frankel (eds) *Interactional Competence*. Hillside, NJ: Lawrence Erlbaum Associates.

Jencks, C. (1973) *Inequality*. London: Allen Lane.

Johnson, J.M. (1976) *Doing Field Research*. New York: Free Press.

Johnson, M. and Cross, M. (1984) *Surveying Service Users in Multi-Racial Areas: The Methodology of the Urban Institutions Project*. Research Papers in Ethnic Relations No. 2, Coventry: Centre for Research in Ethnic Relations, University of Warwick.

Joshi, H. (1984) *Women's Participation in Paid Work: Further Analysis of the Women and Employment Survey*, Department of Employment Survey Research Paper No. 45. London: HMSO.

Jowell, R., Brook, L. and Prior, G. (eds) (1992) *British Social Attitudes: The Ninth Report*. Aldershot: Dartmouth.

Kalton, G. (1983) *Introduction to Survey Sampling*, Sage Quantitative Applications in the Social Sciences, No. 35.

Kendon, A. (1979) 'Some theoretical and methodological aspects of the use of film in the study of social interaction', in G.P. Ginsburg (ed.), *Emerging Strategies in Social Psychological Research*. New York: Wiley. pp. 67–91.

Kendon, A. (1982) 'The organisation of behaviour in face-to-face interaction: observations on the development of a methodology', in K.R. Scherer and P. Ekman (eds), *Handbook of Methods in Nonverbal Behaviour Research*. Cambridge: Cambridge University Press. pp. 440–505.

Kendon, A. (1990). *Conducting Interaction: Patterns of Behaviour in Focused Encounters*. Cambridge: Cambridge University Press.

Kish, L. (1965) *Survey Sampling*. New York: Wiley.

Kitsuse, J.I. and Cicourel, A.V. (1963) 'A note on the uses of official statistics', *Social Problems*, 11: 131–9.

Klatch, R.E. (1988) 'The methodological problems of studying a politically resistant community', in R.G. Burgess (ed.), *Studies in Qualitative Methodology*. Greenwich, CT and London: JAI Press. pp. 73–88.

Kuhn, T.S. (1962) *The Structure of Scientific Revolutions*. Chicago: University of Chicago Press.

Labour Research Department (1988) *The LRD Guide to Pensions Bargaining*. London: LRD Publications.

LaPiere, R.T. (1934) 'Attitudes vs actions', *Social Forces* 13: 230–7.

Larson, M.S. (1977) *The Rise of Professionalism*. London: University of California Press.

Lee, R.M. (1992) 'Access: the politics of distrust', in C.M. Renzetti and R.M. Lee (eds), *Researching Sensitive Topics*. Newbury Park: Sage.

Lee, R.M. and Renzetti, C.M. (1990) 'The problems of researching sensitive topics: an overview and introduction', *American Behavioral Scientist*, 33(5): 510–28.

Liddle, J. and Joshi, R. (1986) *Daughters of Independence: Gender, Class and Caste in India*. London: Zed Books.

Likert, R. (1932) 'A technique for the measurement of attitudes', *Archives of Psychology*, No. 140. (Reprinted in Summers, 1970.)

Lodge, M. (1981) *Magnitude Estimation*. Sage Quantitative Applications in the Social Sciences, series no. 07–025. Beverly Hills, CA and London: Sage.

Loether, H.J. and McTavish, D.G. (1992) *Descriptive and Inferential Statistics: An Introduction*, 4th edn. Boston: Allyn and Bacon.

Lofland, J. (1971) *Analysing Social Settings*. Belmont, CA: Wadsworth.

Lofland, J. and Lofland, L.H. (1984) *Analysing Social Settings*, 2nd edn. Belmont, CA: Wadsworth.

Lurie, A. (1987) *Imaginary Friends*. London: Abacus.

McCall, G. and J. Simmons (1969) *Issues in Participant Observation*. New York: Addison-Wesley.

Lynn, P. and Lievesley, D. (1991) *Drawing General Population Samples in Great Britain*. London: Social and Community Planning Research.

McCann, K., Clark, D., Taylor, R. and Morrice, K. (1984) 'Telephone screening as a research technique', *Sociology*, 18 (3): 393–402.

Macdonald, K.M. (1984) 'Professional formation: the case of Scottish accountants', *British Journal of Sociology*, 32(2): 174–89.

Macdonald, K.M. (1989) 'Building respectability', *Sociology*, 23(1): 55–80.

Macfarlane Smith, J. (1972) *Interviewing in Market and Social Research*. London: Routledge and Kegan Paul.

McPherson, J.M. and Smith-Lovin, L. (1986) 'Sex segregation in voluntary associations', *American Sociological Review*, 51: 61–79.

McRobbie, A. (1978) *'Jackie': an Ideology of Adolescent Femininity*. Birmingham: Centre for Contemporary Cultural Studies.

McRobbie, A. (1991) *Feminism and Youth Culture: From Jackie to Just Seventeen*. London: Macmillan.

Mann, K. (1989) *Growing Fringes: Hypotheses on the Development of Occupational Welfare*. Leeds: Armley.

Manning, P. (1982) 'Analytic induction', in R. Smith and P. Manning (eds), *Qualitative Methods (Vol II of Handbook of Social Science Methods)*. Cambridge, Ballinger. pp. 273–302.

Mansfield, P. and Collard, J. (1988) *The Beginning of the Rest of your Life? A Portrait of Newly-Wed Marriage*. London: Macmillan.

Marsh, C. (1988) *Exploring Data. An Introduction to Data Analysis for Social Scientists*. London: Polity Press.

Martin, J. and Roberts, C. (1984) *Women and Employment: A Lifetime Perspective*. Department of Employment/Office of Population Censuses and Surveys, London: HMSO.

Martin, J., Meltzer, H. and Elliot, D. (1988) *The Prevalence of Disability among Adults*. OPCS Surveys of Disability in Great Britain, Report 1, London: HMSO.

Mason, V. (1989) *Women's Experience of Maternity Care: A Survey Manual*. OPCS, London: HMSO.

Medhurst, K. and Moyser, G. (1987) 'Studying a religious elite: the case of the Anglican Episcopate', in G. Moyser and M. Wagstaffe (eds), *Research Methods for Elite Studies*. London: Allen and Unwin. pp. 89–108.

Merton, R. and Kendall, P. (1946) 'The focused interview', *American Journal of Sociology*, 51 (6): 541–57.

Merton, R.K. (1965) *On the Shoulders of Giants: A Shandean Postscript*. New York: Harcourt Brace Jovanovich.

Merton, R.K. (1968) *Social Theory and Social Structure*. New York: The Free Press.

Middlebrook, M. (1978) *The Kaiser's Battle*. Harmondsworth: Penguin.

Middlebrook, M. (1983) *The Schweinfurt–Regensburg Mission*. Harmondsworth: Penguin.

Miles, M. and Huberman, A. (1984) *Qualitative Data Analysis*. London: Sage.

Mills, C.W. (1940) 'Situated actions and vocabularies of motive', *American Sociological Review*, 5: 904–13.

Mills, C.W. (1959) *The Sociological Imagination*. Oxford: Oxford University Press.

Mishler, E. (1986) *Research Interviewing*. Cambridge, MA: Harvard University Press.

Morley, D., Rhode, J. and Willams, G. (1987) *Practising Health for All*. Oxford: Oxford University Press.

Moser, C.A. and Kalton, G. (1971) *Survey Methods in Social Investigation*, 2nd edn. London: Heinemann.

Mulkay, M. (1985) *The Word and the World*. London: Allen and Unwin.

Mullins C.J. (1977) *A Guide to Writing and Publishing in the Social and Behavioural Sciences*. New York: Wiley.

Munck, R. and Rolston, W. (1987) *Belfast in the 30's: an Oral History*. Belfast: Blackstaff Press.

Newby, H. (1977) 'In the field: reflections on a study of Suffolk farm workers', in C. Bell and H. Newby (eds), *Doing Sociological Research*. London: Allen and Unwin. pp. 108–29.

Nissel, M. and Bonnerjea, L. (1982) *Family Care of the Handicapped Elderly. Who Pays?* London: Policy Studies Institute.

Norris, M. (1983) *A Beginner's Guide to Repertory Grid*. Guildford: University of Surrey, Department of Sociology.

Norusis, M. (1988) *The SPSS Guide to Data Analysis for SPSS/PC+*. Chicago: SPSS Inc.

Norusis, M. (1991) *SPSS/PC+ Advanced Statistics 4.0*. Chicago: SPSS, Inc.

Oakley, A. (1974) *The Sociology of Housework*. Oxford: Martin Robertson.

Ochs, E. (1979). 'Transcription as theory', in E. Ochs and B. Shieffelen (eds), *Developmental Pragmatics*. New York: Academic Press. pp. 43–72.

OPCS (1980) *Classification of Occupations 1980*. Office of Population Censuses and Surveys, London: HMSO.

OPCS (1984) *Population Census, National Report*. Office of Population Censuses and Surveys, London: HMSO.

OPCS (1987) *The General Household Survey, 1985*. Office of Population Censuses and Surveys, London: HMSO.

OPCS (1989) *The General Household Survey, 1987*. Office of Population Censuses and Surveys, London: HMSO.

OPCS (1990) *The General Household Survey, 1988*. Office of Population Censuses and Surveys, London: HMSO.

Oppenheim, A.N. (1966) *Questionnaire Design and Attitude Measurement*. London: Heinemann.

Owen, D. and Green, A.E. (1989) 'Spatial aspects of labour mobility in the 1980s', *Geoforum*, 20(1): 107–26.

Parker, G. (1990) *With Due Care and Attention: A Review of Research on Informal Care*. Occasional Paper No.2. London: Family Policy Studies Centre.

Patton, M. (1980) *Qualitative Evaluation Methods*. London: Sage.

Patton, M. (1987) *How to Use Qualitative Methods in Evaluation*. London: Sage.

Payne, G. (1987) *Mobility and Change in Modern Society*. London: Macmillan.

Payne, J. (1991) 'Does unemployment run in families? some findings from the General Household Survey', *Sociology*, 21(2): 199–214.

Pearson, G. (1983) *Hooligan: A history of respectable fears*. London: Macmillan.

Pettigrew, J. (1981) 'Reminiscences of fieldwork among the Sikhs', in H. Roberts (ed.), *Doing Feminist Research*. London: Routledge and Kegan Paul. pp. 62–82.

Pevsner, N. (1973) *The Buildings of England: London*, 3rd edn. Vols I and II. Harmondsworth: Penguin.

Pfaffenberger, B. (1988) *Microcomputer Applications in Qualitative Research*. Qualitative Research Methods Series 14, CA: Sage.

Phillips, M. and Pugh, D.S. (1987) *How to get a PhD*. Milton Keynes: Open University Press.

Pinch, T.J. and Clark, C. (1986) 'The hard sell: "patter merchanting" and the strategic (re)production and local management of economic reasoning in the sales routines of market pitchers', *Sociology*, 20(2): 169–91.

Plant, M. (1975) *Drugtakers in an English Town*. London: Tavistock.

Platt, J. (1981) 'Evidence and proof in documentary research', *Sociological Review*, 29 (1): 31–66.

Plummer, K. (1983) *Documents of Life: An Introduction to the Problems and Literature of a Humanistic Method*. London: Allen and Unwin.

Polsky, N. (1971) *Hustlers, Beats and Others*. New York: Anchor Books.

Pomerantz, A.M. (1986) 'Extreme case formulations: a way of legitimizing claims', in G. Button, P. Drew, J. Heritage (eds), *Human Studies* 9 (Special Issue on Interaction and Language Use), 219–29.

Potter, J. and Wetherell, M. (1987) *Discourse and Social Psychology: Beyond Attitudes and Behaviour*. London: Sage.

Prescott-Clarke, P. (1982) *Public Attitudes towards Industrial, Work-related and other Risks*. London: Social and Community Planning Research.

Psathas, G. (ed.) (1979). *Everyday Language: Studies in Ethnomethodology*. New York: Irvington.

Punch, M. (1986) *Politics and Ethics of Fieldwork*. London: Sage.

Quigly, I. (1984) *The Heirs of Tom Brown: the English School Story*. Oxford: Oxford University Press.

Quinney, R. and Wilderman, J. (1977) *The Problem of Crime*, 2nd edn. New York: Harper and Row.

Qureshi, H. and Walker, A. (1989) *The Caring Relationship: Elderly people and their families*. London: Macmillan.

Richardson, L. (1990) *Writing Strategies*. Newbury Park, CA: Sage.

Rickman, H.P. (1961) *Meaning in History: Wilhelm Dilthey's Thought on Society and History*. London: Allen and Unwin.

Robb, J. (1954) *Working class antiSemite*. London: Tavistock.

Roberts, H. (ed.) (1981) *Doing Feminist Research*. London: Routledge and Kegan Paul.

Roth, J. (1966) 'Hired hand research', *American Sociologist*, 1: 190–6. (Reprinted in N.K. Denzin (ed.) (1978) *Sociological Methods: A Sourcebook*, London: Butterworths.)

Sacks, H. (1984) 'On doing "Being Ordinary" ', in J.M. Atkinson and J. Heritage (eds), *Structures of Social Action: Studies in Conversation Analysis*. Cambridge: Cambridge University Press. pp. 413–29. (Edited by. G. Jefferson from unpublished lectures: Spring 1970: lecture 1.)

Sacks, H. (1992) *Lectures on Conversation*. (Edited by G. Jefferson and E.A. Schegloff.) Oxford and Cambridge, MA: Blackwell.

Sacks, H., Schegloff, E.A. and Jefferson, G. (1974). 'A simplest systematics for the organisation of turn taking in conversation', *Language*, 50: 696–735.

Saunders, P. (1984) 'Beyond housing classes: the sociological significance of private property rights in the means of consumption', *International Journal of Urban and Regional Research*, 8(2): 202–27.

Saunders, P. (1986) *Social Theory and the Urban Question*, 2nd edn. London: Hutchinson.

Saunders, P. (1990) *A Nation of Home Owners*. London: Unwin Hyman.

Savage, M., Watt, P. and Arber, S. (1990a) 'The consumption sector debate and housing mobility', *Sociology*, 24 (1): 97–117.

Savage, M., Watt, P. and Arber, S. (1990b) 'Housing mobility and social stratification: an analysis of council tenants in Guildford', *Surrey Occasional Papers in Sociology and Social Policy*, No. 20.

Savage, M., Watt, P. and Arber, S. (1991) 'Social class, consumption divisions and housing mobility', in R. Burrows and C. Marsh (eds), *Consumption and Class: Divisions and Change*. London: Macmillan. pp. 52–70.

Scheflen, A.E. (1973). *Communication Structure: Analysis of a Psychotherapy Transaction*. Bloomington: Indiana University Press.

Schegloff, E.A. (1972) 'Notes on a conversational practice: formulating place', in D. Sudnow (ed.), *Studies in Social Interaction*. New York: Free Press. pp. 75–119.

Schegloff, E.A. and Sacks, H. (1974) 'Opening up closings', in R. Turner (ed.), *Ethnomethodology: Selected Writings*. Harmondsworth: Penguin. pp. 233–64.

Schuman, H. (1966) 'The random probe: a technique for evaluating the validity of closed questions', *American Sociological Review*, 31: 218–23. (Reprinted in Forcese and Richer, 1970.)

Schur, E.M. (1971) *Labeling Deviant Behaviour*. New York: Harper and Row.

Scott, J. (1990) *A Matter of Record*. Cambridge: Polity Press.

Scott, M.B. and Lyman, S. (1968) 'Accounts', *American Sociological Review*, 33: 46–62.

Seidel, J. and Clark, J.A. (1984) 'The ETHNOGRAPH : a computer program for the analysis of qualitative data', *Qualitative Sociology*, 7: 110–25.

Sellin, T. and Wolfgang, M.E. (1964) *The Measurement of Delinquency*. New York: Wiley.

Selltiz, C. and Jahoda, M. (1962) *Research methods in social relations*. New York: Methuen.

Seymour-Smith, M. (1989) *Kipling*. London: Papermac.

Shapiro, S. and Eberhart, J. (1947) 'Interviewer differences in an intensive survey', *International Journal of Opinion and Attitude Research*, 1(2): 1–17.

Shipman, M. (1988) *The Limitations of Social Research*. London and New York: Longman.

Short, J. Jr and Nye, F.I. (1958) 'Extent of unrecorded juvenile delinquency: tentative conclusions', *Journal of Criminal Law and Criminology*, 49: 296–302.

Silverman, D. (1985) *Qualitative Methodology and Sociology*. Farnborough: Gower.

Silvey, J. (1975) *Deciphering Data: The analysis of social surveys*. London: Longman.

Simmel, G. (1950) *The Sociology of George Simmel*. (ed.) K. Wolff. Glencoe, IL: The Free Press.

Smith, C. (1981) 'How complete is the electoral register?', *Political Studies*, 29: 275–8.

Smith, D.E. (1978) ' "K is mentally ill": the anatomy of a factual account', *Sociology*, 12: 23–53.

Smith, H.W. (1975) *Strategies of Social Research: The Methodological Imagination*. Englewood Cliffs, NJ: Prentice Hall.

Smith, N. and Williams, P. (1986) *Gentrification of the City*. Boston: Allen and Unwin.

Social Research Association (1990/91) 'Ethical Guidelines', in *Directory of Members*, London. pp. 73–87.

SocInfo Software Catalogue (1990) University of Stirling, Scotland.

Spencer, G. (1973) 'Methodological issues in the study of bureaucratic elites: a case of West Point', *Social Problems*, 21(1): 90–103.

Spiegelberg, S. (1980) 'Phenomenology and observation', in B. Glassner, (ed), *Essential Interactionism*. London: Routledge and Kegan Paul

Stacey, M. (1969) *Methods of Social Research*. Oxford: Pergamon Press.

Standard Occupational Classification (1990) *Structure and Definition of Major, Minor and Unit Groups, Volume 1 and Coding Index, Volume 2*. London: HMSO.

Stewart, D.W. (1984) *Secondary Research: Information Sources and Methods*. Beverly Hills, CA: Sage.

Stinchcombe, A.L. (1968) *Constructing Social Theories*. Chicago: University of Chicago Press.

Stouffer, S.A. (1963) *Communism, Conformity and Civil Liberties*. Gloucester, MA: Peter Smith.

Strauss, A. and Corbin, J. (1990) *Basics of Qualitative Research*. London: Sage.

Sudman, S. and Bradburn, N.M. (1974) *Response Effects in Surveys*, Chicago: Aldine.

Sudman, S. and Bradburn, N.M. (1983) *Asking Questions*. San Francisco: Jossey-Bass.

Summers, Gene F. (ed.) (1970), *Attitude Measurement*. Chicago: Rand McNally.

ten Have, P. (1991). 'Talk and institution: a reconsideration of the asymmetry of doctor–patient interaction', in D. Boden and D.H. Zimmerman (eds), *Talk and Social Structure*. Oxford: Polity Press. pp. 138–63.

Tesch, R. (1990) *Qualitative Research: Analysis Types and Software Tools*. London: Falmer.

Thomas, W.I. and Znaniecki, F. (1918–20, 1958) *The Polish Peasant in Europe and America*. New York: Dover Publications.

Thompson, K. (1985) *Readings from Emile Durkheim*. Chichester: Ellis Horwood.

Thurstone, L.L. (1928). 'Attitudes can be measured', *American Journal of Sociology*, 33: 529–54. (Reprinted in Summers, 1970.)

Turner, B. (1981) 'Some practical aspects of qualitative data analysis: one way of organising the cognitive processes associated with the generation of grounded theory', *Quality and Quantity*, 15: 225–47.

Ungerson, C. (1987) *Policy is Personal*. London: Tavistock.

Van Maanen, J. (1982) *Varieties of Qualitative Research*. Beverly Hills, CA: Sage.

Van Maanen, J. (1988) *Tales of the Field*. Chicago: University of Chicago Press.

Veblen, T. (1970) *The Theory of the Leisure Class*. London: Unwin Books.

Vidich, A.J., Bensman, J. and Stein, M.R. (eds), (1971) *Reflections on Community Studies*. New York, Evanston, San Francisco and London: Harper Torchbooks.

Wagstaffe, M. and Moyser, G. (1987) 'The threatened elite: studying leaders in an urban community', in G. Moyser and M. Wagstaffe (eds), *Research Methods for Elite Studies*. London: Allen and Unwin. pp. 183–201.

Walby, S. (1986) *Patriarchy at Work*. Cambridge: Polity Press.

Wallis, R. (1976) *The Road to Total Freedom: A Sociological Analysis of Scientology*. London: Heinemann.

Wallis, R. (1977) 'The moral career of a research project', in C. Bell and H. Newby (eds), *Doing Sociological Research*. London: Allen and Unwin. pp. 149–69.

Walton, H. (1986) *White Researchers and Racism*, Working Papers in Applied Social Research No. 10, Manchester: University of Manchester.

Weber, M. (1947). *The Theory of Economic and Social Organisation*. Glencoe, IL: The Free Press.

Weber, R. (1990) *Basic Content Analysis*, 2nd edn. London: Sage.

Weiss, C.H. (1980) 'Knowledge creep and decision accretion', *Knowledge: Creation, Diffusion, Utilisation*, 1: 381–404.

Wenger, C. (ed.) (1986) *The Research Relationship: Practice and Policy in Social Policy Research*. London: Allen and Unwin.

WHO (World Health Organisation) (1990) *World Health Statistics Annual*. Geneva: WHO.

Whyte, W.F. (1955) *Street Corner Society: The Social Structure of an Italian Slum*. Chicago and London: University of Chicago Press.

Widdicombe, S. and Wooffitt, R.C. (1990) ' "Being" versus "doing" punk (etc.): on achieving authenticity as a member', *Language and Social Psychology*, 9: 257–77.

Williams, B. (1978) *A Sampler on Sampling*. New York: Wiley.

Wilson, P. and Elliot, D. (1987) 'An evaluation of the postcode address file and its use within OPCS', *Journal of the Royal Statistical Society*, Series A, 150(3): 230–40.

Winkler, J.T. (1987) 'The fly on the wall of the inner sanctum: observing company directors at work', in G. Moyser and M. Wagstaffe (eds), *Research Methods for Elite Studies*. London: Allen and Unwin. pp. 129–46.

Wittgenstein, L. (1953) *Philosophical Investigations*. (edited by G. Anscombe.) Oxford: Blackwell.

Wolcott, H.F. (1990) *Writing up Qualitative Research*. Newbury Park, CA: Sage.

Wood, S. (n.d.) 'Redundancy Research', mimeo.
Wooffitt, R.C. (1992) *Telling Tales of the Unexpected: the Organisation of Factual Discourse*. London and New York: Harvester Wheatsheaf.
Yearley, S. (1984) *Science and Sociological Practice*. London: Open University Press.
Yin, R. (1984) *Case Study Research*. Beverly Hills, CA: Sage.

Index

Abbott, P., 17
abstracts, 35
  preparing, 335–7
academic data sources, 260–1
academic reports, writing, 48, 328–44
access
  bargaining political exchange model, 55
  closed
    covert studies in, 57–9
    negotiating, 53–9
    overt studies in, 55–7
  framework for factors in, 53
  gaining, xii, 37–8, 52–67, 158–61
    ethical issues in, 62–4
  open, 59–62
    covert studies in, 60–2
    overt studies in, 59–60
  physical and social, 53–4, 59
ad hoc surveys, 260
Ajzen, I., 125, 134
All England Law Reports, 190
analysis
  of accounts, 287–305
  of ethnographic data, 163–70
  multi-level, 265–7
  of other researchers' data, 255–69
  of quantitative survey data, 239–54
  secondary *see* secondary analysis
analytic induction, 74–5, 235
analytic themes, 180
  notebook, 168
Anderson, P., 253
Annual Abstract of Statistics, 190
anomie, 22
anonymity, 52–67, 110, 147, 258, 308
Antal, F., 194
anthropology, 9, 154–5
Arber, S., 32–50, 68–92, 270
archives, 256, 261–2
  catalogue, 261–2
Armstrong, D., 14–16
assumptions, 10, 259
  about language, 148–50
  in discourse analysis, 291, 303–4
  in interaction analysis, 323
Atkinson, J.M., 171, 290, 304, 305, 308, 310, 326

attitude measurement, xii, 41–2, 116–34
  example, 118–21
  salience in, 42
attitude scale construction
  expectancy-value scaling, 125–6
  magnitude estimation, 125
  techniques of, 121–6
'attitude-behaviour problem', 117–18
attitudes, 100–1
  change over time, 139
  defining, 117–18
  dimensions of *see* constructs
  monotonic, 123
  non-monotonic, 123
attributes, 99–100
audience research, 76
audio recording *see* tape-recording
audio-visual recording *see* video recording
audiotyping transcription services, 147
Austin, J.L., 288
authenticity of documents, 195–6

Baltzell, E.D., 207, 215
Barthes, R., 198
Bauman, Z., 5, 6–7, 16
Bazerman, C., 329, 330
Becker, H., 167, 174, 194–5, 200, 344
behaviour, 100
  compound, 120
behavioural indicators, 117–18
beliefs, 101
Bell, C., 33, 49, 50, 55, 67
Berger, J., 193–4
bibliographical citation, 340–1
  Harvard convention, 341
  numbered superscripts, 341
Blalock, H.M., 31
Blau, P.M., 113
Boden, D., 310, 326
bodily movement, transcription of, 316–19
Bradburn, N.M., 106–7, 113, 114
brainstorming, 98, 227
Brannen, J., 70
Brannen, P., 56
British Sociological Association, 62–3, 65, 332
  Statement of Ethical Practice, 63, 65

WARNER MEMORIAL LIBRARY
EASTERN UNIVERSITY
ST. DAVIDS, PA 19087-3696